Moral Grandeur

and Spiritual Audacity

MORAL GRANDEUR

AND SPIRITUAL

AUDACITY

ESSAYS

ABRAHAM JOSHUA

HESCHEL

EDITED BY SUSANNAH HESCHEL

FARRAR, STRAUS AND GIROUX

NEW YORK

Farrar, Straus and Giroux
19 Union Square West, New York 10003

The Library of Congress has catalogued the hardcover edition as follows:
Heschel, Abraham Joshua, 1907–1972.
    Moral grandeur & spiritual audacity : essays / edited by Susannah
Heschel. — 1st ed.
        p.   cm.
    Includes bibliographical references (p.   ).
    ISBN 0-374-19980-9 (hardcover)
    1. Judaism—Essence, genius, nature.   2. Spiritual life—Judaism.
3. Judaism and social problems.   I. Heschel, Susannah.   II. Title.
BM45.H4549   1906
296—dc20

                                                    95-41392
                                                    CIP

Contents

Introduction

BY SUSANNAH HESCHEL

TO PRESIDENT JOHN F. KENNEDY, THE WHITE HOUSE, JUNE 16, 1963
I LOOK FORWARD TO PRIVILEGE OF BEING PRESENT AT MEETING TO-
MORROW AT 4 P. M. LIKELIHOOD EXISTS THAT NEGRO PROBLEM WILL
BE LIKE THE WEATHER. EVERYBODY TALKS ABOUT IT BUT NOBODY DOES
ANYTHING ABOUT IT. PLEASE DEMAND OF RELIGIOUS LEADERS
PERSONAL INVOLVEMENT NOT JUST SOLEMN DECLARATION. WE FOR-
FEIT THE RIGHT TO WORSHIP GOD AS LONG AS WE CONTINUE TO HU-
MILIATE NEGROES. CHURCH SYNAGOGUES HAVE FAILED. THEY MUST
REPENT. ASK OF RELIGIOUS LEADERS TO CALL FOR NATIONAL REPEN-
TANCE AND PERSONAL SACRIFICE. LET RELIGIOUS LEADERS DONATE
ONE MONTH'S SALARY TOWARD FUND FOR NEGRO HOUSING AND EDU-
CATION. I PROPOSE THAT YOU MR. PRESIDENT DECLARE STATE OF
MORAL EMERGENCY. A MARSHALL PLAN FOR AID TO NEGROES IS BECOM-
ING A NECESSITY. THE HOUR CALLS FOR HIGH MORAL GRANDEUR AND
SPIRITUAL AUDACITY.

ABRAHAM JOSHUA HESCHEL

"MORAL GRANDEUR AND SPIRITUAL AUDACITY"—I can't
imagine a better phrase to describe my father's work. The essays in this
book are gathered from his many academic and popular articles and
lectures, and like the telegram above, which he sent to President Kennedy,
they show us a religious leader who held both God and human beings
together in his thoughts at all times. Political and social problems were
his major concern, and what gave his politics such strength was the
religious insight he brought to bear on them. For him, politics and theology were always intertwined. After the civil-rights march in Selma, he
said, "I felt my legs were praying." Even as social protest was for him a
religious experience, religion without indignation at political evils was

also impossible: "To speak about God and remain silent on Vietnam is blasphemous," he wrote.

My father was a unique combination of a Hasidic voice of compassion and mercy, always seeing the goodness in other people, and a prophetic voice of justice, denouncing hypocrisy, self-centeredness, and indifference. My father wasn't interested in assigning blame or claiming victimhood, but as the Bible does, he showed us a vision of who we might become. His was a voice of inspiration, not argumentation, rooted in Jewish religious thought. What he once wrote of East European Jews applies to him as well: "Jewishness was not in the fruit but in the sap that stirred through the tissues of the tree. Bred in the silence of the soil, it ascended to the leaves to become eloquent in the fruit."[1] So, too, Jewishness infused my father like the sap of a tree, and his eloquence was the fruit of his deep Jewish piety and learning.

Particularly extraordinary is the diversity of those who regarded him as their teacher: Catholics, Jews, Protestants, whites and blacks, liberals and conservatives, pious and secular, Americans, Europeans, Israelis. His life challenges our conventional expectations. Here is a rabbi whose books were praised by Pope Paul VI as helping to sustain the piety of Catholics; an Orthodox Jew with a white beard and yarmulke marching for civil rights and demonstrating against the war in Vietnam; an immigrant from Poland whose work is included in anthologies of exceptional English prose.

My father described himself as a "brand plucked from the fire of Europe," rescued from Poland by an American visa just six weeks before the Nazi invasion. His survival was a gift, because he became a unique religious voice in an era in which religion was in grave danger, according to his own analysis. The Hasidic Jewish world of Eastern Europe in which he was raised was far from the environment in which he wrote and taught in the United States. He came from a rebbe's family in Poland, from a Jewish civilization that was suddenly eradicated in the middle of his lifetime by the Germans, in whose universities he had studied and in whose language he had written about Jewish religious thought. Despite the horrors he experienced—the murder of his mother, sisters, friends, and relatives, the destruction of the world which had nourished him—his life continued to reflect the holy dimension he was able to evoke in his own original and unique words.

Words, he often wrote, are themselves sacred, God's tool for creating the universe, and our tools for bringing holiness—or evil—into the world. He used to remind us that the Holocaust did not begin with the building of crematoria, and Hitler did not come to power with tanks and guns; it all began with uttering evil words, with defamation, with language and propaganda. Words create worlds, he used to tell me when I was a child.

They must be used very carefully. Some words, once having been uttered, gain eternity and can never be withdrawn. The Book of Proverbs reminds us, he wrote, that death and life are in the power of the tongue.

MY FATHER was born in Warsaw on January 11, 1907, the youngest child of Moshe Mordechai and Reizel (Perlow) Heschel. His mother and father were each descended from distinguished Hasidic rebbes, a family of nobility in the Jewish world. Nearly all the great Hasidic leaders of Eastern Europe, those who inspired and led the pietistic revival that began in the eighteenth century, were among my father's ancestors. He cherished and revered them. I remember as a child how often he used to take small, fragile books from his shelf, Hasidic *seforim*, show them to me, read a little with me, and tell me with awe about the great-grandfathers who had written them. This is your inheritance, he would say. Far from feeling burdened by the greatness of his heritage, he felt gratitude, humbleness, and reverence for his ancestors. "I was very fortunate," he told an interviewer, "in having lived as a child and as a young boy in an environment where there were many people I could revere, people concerned with problems of inner life, of spirituality and integrity. People who have shown great compassion and understanding for other people."[2]

As a small child he was accorded the princely honors given the families of Hasidic rebbes: adults would rise when he entered the room, even when he was little, recognizing that he was a special person. He would be lifted onto a table to deliver *drushas*, learned discussions of Hebrew texts. He was considered an *illui*, a genius. His world was one of intense piety and religious observance, and he felt grateful, as he described much later, that he grew up surrounded by people of spiritual nobility. As the baby of the family, he was loved and fussed over by his older sisters, Sarah, Devorah Miriam, Esther Sima, and Gittel, and his brother, Jacob. He was teased and coddled the way youngest children of large families are. He was only three years old when his oldest sister, Sarah, married their first cousin, the Kapitshinitzer rebbe, and he remembered being at the wedding, running around excitedly among the adults. Even as a small child he took his religious obligations very seriously. He seemed amused and embarrassed when he told me that when he was sent as a five year old on an errand to a female neighbor, he would ask that the object he was borrowing be placed on a table—according to ultra-Orthodox custom, a man should not give or receive from a woman's hand.

His was a large extended family. His mother was the twin sister of the Novominsker rebbe, Alter Israel Simon Perlow, who lived in Warsaw, and there were many cousins, nieces, and nephews. The family's first tragedy came in 1916, when my father was nine years old and his father died during an influenza epidemic. It was devastating for the family. Shortly before I turned nine, I developed a fear that the same thing might happen to me. I asked him, over and over, how he could survive such a terrible thing. He used to say, in a way that was so sad for me to hear, that he just wished he could talk to his father again, just once more, even for one hour.

As a teenager my father began publishing his first articles, short studies, in Hebrew, of talmudic literature, which appeared in a Warsaw rabbinical publication, *Sha'are Torah*, in 1922 and 1923. When he grew older, he began to read secular books, in addition to his Talmud studies. He said his mother worried at not hearing him chant Gemara while he studied, knowing that he was reading what he should not. Finally, with the approval of his family, he decided to go to Vilna to study at a Gymnasium. There he completed his examinations on June 24, 1927, at the Mathematical–Natural Science Gymnasium. He also became involved with a Yiddish poetry group, Jung Vilna, and published, as his first book, a volume of Yiddish poems, *Der Shem Hamefoyrosh: Mentsch*, written during his years in Vilna and published in Warsaw in 1933, dedicated to his father's memory.[3] The poems were greeted warmly in the worlds of Yiddish and Hebrew *belles lettres*; they brought him to the attention of, among others, Chaim Nachman Bialik, who wrote to him from Israel with an enthusiastic letter of congratulations.

Among my father's childhood friends from Warsaw few survived. One who did was the Yiddish writer Yechiel Hoffer, who immigrated to Israel and wrote autobiographical novels in which my father appears as a young man. Another was Zalman Shazar, a Zionist and Hebrew writer who later became President of the state of Israel. They remained good friends throughout their lives; letters from Shazar to my father, written in Hebrew, address him, "To the friend of my soul, master of joy, son of holy people." In 1970, on the occasion of President Shazar's eightieth birthday, my father wrote a tribute to him in Yiddish: "He is a Jew who lives with visions. He carries in himself a song that calls and awakens sleeping souls."* My father also gave President Shazar a mezuzah that had once stood on the doorpost of the synagogue of the Baal Shem Tov, the founder of Hasidism, in the little East European town of Mezibizh.

After Vilna, in 1927, my father went to study in Berlin, to participate in what he felt was the great center of European intellectual and cultural life. He enrolled at the Hochschule für die Wissenschaft des Judentums

---

* "A *brokhe dem nosi*" (Greetings to President Shazar on his eightieth birthday) in *Die goldene Keyt*, Tel Aviv, No. 68 (1970), p. 26. Shazar sent a telegram to the Israel Bonds dinner honoring my father in December 1970: "To Abraham Joshua Heschel, my cherished friend . . . The descendant of so saintly a line now brings to American Jewry sparks of holiness and true radiance."

and at the Friedrich Wilhelm Universität, today's Humboldt University. On April 29, 1929, he passed examinations in German language and literature, Latin, mathematics, German history, and geography, given to foreign students by the University of Berlin, and became a matriculated student.* He studied philosophy as his main concentration at the university, with secondary work in art history and Semitic philology. At the Hochschule he trained in the modern scientific study of Jewish texts and history. His teachers there included some of the great names of German-Jewish scholarship: Chanoch Albeck, Ismar Elbogen, Julius Guttmann, and Leo Baeck. Down the street from the Hochschule was the Orthodox rabbinical seminary, founded by Esriel Hildesheimer. The theological differences between the two seminaries could not have been greater, and it is amusing that they were located at either end of "Artillerie" Street. While most of the students and faculty at the two seminaries did not interact, my father was one of the few able to move easily between the two institutions, sustaining friendships and respect at both.

In December 1929, my father passed examinations at the Hochschule in Hebrew language, Bible and Talmud, *Midrash*, liturgy, philosophy of religion, and Jewish history and literature; and in May 1930, he was awarded a prize by the Hochschule for a paper on "Visions in the Bible." He was also appointed an instructor, lecturing on talmudic exegesis to the more advanced students. On July 16, 1934, he passed his oral examinations and was granted a rabbinical degree by the Hochschule, with a graduating thesis on "Apocrypha, Pseudepigrapha and Halakha."

When I was growing up and asked my father for stories about his early life, he described the efforts of each of his professors in Berlin to convince him to write his doctoral dissertation under that professor's direction. They considered him highly gifted and each wanted him as a student. But the support he received from the university's faculty began to change after 1933.

Just three weeks after Hitler came to power, my father took his oral examinations for his doctorate at the University of Berlin, on February 23, 1933. His examiners included Max Dessoir (philosophy), Heinrich Maier (philosophy), Albert Erich Brinckmann (art history), and Eugen Mittwoch (Semitic philology). He was questioned about a remarkably broad range of topics. Dessoir and Maier asked him about Descartes, Leibniz, Kant, Husserl, materialism, and metaphysics. Brinckmann focused on Italian Renaissance art, and Mittwoch asked about the prophet Amos, especially Chapter 4, and the prophet Hosea. Dessoir noted that

---

* These tests were supplementary to those he passed in Vilna and granted him admission to study at a university.

my father seemed nervous and inhibited.[4] Not surprising, considering Hitler's accession to power.

My father's dissertation, entitled *Das prophetische Bewußtsein* (Prophetic Consciousness), was submitted in December 1932 and evaluated by his two main professors, Dessoir and Alfred Bertholet of the theology department, who held the chair in Old Testament, with an interest in Religionsgeschichte (phenomenology of religion).* Both Dessoir and Mittwoch lost their positions at the university in 1935 as a result of Nazi anti-Semitic purges of the faculty; Bertholet retired in 1937, replaced by Johannes Hempel, an active member of the pro-Nazi German Christian Movement.

My father's doctoral degree was expected† a few months later, but there were difficulties. His dissertation had to be published in order for him to receive his degree, but he had no money for publication costs. Worse, it became increasingly difficult after Hitler came to power for a Jew to publish an academic book in Germany. For the next few years, he submitted requests every few months to the dean of the faculty for extensions of the deadline for publication; the dean granted his requests, always saluting him in the language of the day: "Heil Hitler." Finally, in the spring of 1936, the book, *Die Prophetie*, was published by the Polish Academy of Sciences, of Cracow, with costs underwritten by the Erich Reiss Publishing House in Berlin.[5] My father, who was otherwise not well inclined toward Poland after the war, always expressed gratitude toward the academy for that publication. Without his official degree from the university, he would have had difficulties escaping Europe. Moreover, the academy had been willing to intervene with the Polish consulate to secure governmental permission from Germany to distribute the book of a Jewish author in German bookstores.[6] With special permission, the University of Berlin accepted a non-German publisher as legitimate, and my father was finally

---

* Max Dessoir, born in Berlin in 1867, was editor of the *Zeitschrift für Aesthetik und allgemeine Kunstwissenschaft*; he became a full professor of philosophy at the University of Berlin in 1920. Alfred Bertholet, born in Basel in 1868, became full professor of Old Testament theology at the University of Berlin in 1928.

† Dessoir's evaluation was enthusiastic, critical only of technical aspects, including organization, neologisms, and language. His comments are primarily a summary of the main argument, concerning divine pathos. He notes, for example, that divine pathos is not a predicate, a part of God's essence, but arises in response to human deeds. Pathos endows a personal God, he writes, with moral norms, gives God a chance for self-expression, and lies at the root of our own religious feeling.

By contrast, Bertholet was more restrained in his comments, criticizing the dissertation for failing to give greater emphasis to what Bertholet saw as the prophets' feeling of being threatened by God for noncompliance. The dissertation, Bertholet wrote, should have paid more attention to examples of prophecy outside the Old Testament, to what he called the predecessors of the pre-exilic prophets described in the study.

awarded his diploma on December 11, 1935, three years after completing his work.

When *Die Prophetie* finally appeared, the reviews were highly favorable. The book received notice in popular and academic journals, Christian and Jewish, in Germany and in other countries. The distinguished Old Testament scholar Otto Eissfeldt, writing in a German Protestant theology journal, praised the book, calling its understanding of the God of the Bible "correct and important," and saying that the book "deserves the attention of Old Testament scholars as well as theologians generally."[7] The evaluation in *The Philosophical Review*, published in the United States, was that the book "may well be regarded as one of the most important contributions to the general philosophy of religion that the last few years have produced."[8] The positive response is even more remarkable in light of the growing calls by many Protestants in the Third Reich for eradicating the Old Testament from the Christian canon. To prove their devotion to Nazism, some Christians had called for a purging of everything Jewish, and even declared Jesus an Aryan whose goal was the elimination of Judaism from the face of the earth. As a Jewish book, the Old Testament had no place in Christian Scriptures, they argued. If the Nazis wanted a *Judenrein* Germany, they would create a *Judenrein* Christianity, and they believed that being a true follower of Jesus meant being an anti-Semite.

While such attacks against the Old Testament and against the Jewishness of Jesus had already arisen in Germany during the nineteenth century, they grew in intensity during the late 1920s and '30s with the rise of the so-called German Christian movement, a pro-Nazi group of Protestants that included bishops, pastors, professors of theology, as well as laypeople. It quickly became a powerful force within the churches. Many years later, in his 1965 inaugural address at Union Theological Seminary, my father reminded his audience that the Nazis attacked Christianity as well as Judaism, and he called for both communities to unite against the threat:

Nazism has suffered a defeat, but the process of eliminating the Bible from the consciousness of the Western world goes on. It is on the issue of saving the radiance of the Hebrew Bible in the minds of man that Jews and Christians are called upon to work together. None of us can do it alone. Both of us must realize that in our age anti-Semitism is anti-Christianity and that anti-Christianity is anti-Semitism.[9]

After completing his university studies, my father continued to live in Berlin. He taught at the Hochschule, as well as at the Jüdisches Lehrhaus in Berlin, and he served as reader and editor of a series of books, "Judentum in Geschichte und Gegenwart," for the Erich Reiss publishing house. He witnessed Hitler's accession to power on January 30, 1933, followed by the burning of the Reichstag in March, as well as the book burning in April, in a large open square in the middle of the University of Berlin. His disgust at what he witnessed was expressed in an anonymously published Yiddish poem, "A Day of Hatred," which appeared in a Warsaw newspaper. My father told me the chilling story of the evening he attended a concert in Berlin and Hitler suddenly arrived. Everyone present had to rise. As soon as possible, my father left the hall. And he used to describe the abandonment he felt from Christian colleagues who did not speak up on behalf of the Jews. I can imagine how he must have felt, having completed a book on the prophets, to witness Protestant and Catholic professors of the Old Testament debating whether the Christian canon should consist only of the New Testament. Even some who spoke up on behalf of the Old Testament defended their position by arguing that the Old Testament was not really a Jewish book; Judaism, they said, was a degenerate, post-biblical phenomenon. Still, my father received help, as did many others, from the anti-Nazi Quaker community in Frankfurt am Main, whose leader, Rudolf Schlosser, became his friend. My father delivered a powerful lecture, "The Meaning of This Hour," to the Quakers of Frankfurt in February 1938 on the responsibility of religious leaders in Nazi Germany. Schlosser and his colleagues, in turn, were very helpful to my father, writing letters of character reference to the American consulate in support of his visa application.[10]

Most remarkable to me is how my father continued, during those years in Nazi Germany, to nurture his own religious life. For several months he rented a room from a Frankfurt Orthodox Jewish family named Simon, whose daughters recently told me that in 1937 my father never wavered in his piety, even continuing the custom of *nagel wasser* (rinsing the hands first thing upon awakening, in order to begin the day with a prayer).

Throughout the 1930s my father tried to secure a position outside Germany. He sent letters and copies of his publications to colleagues throughout Europe and the United States, seeking help. He had published several scholarly essays on aspects of medieval Jewish philosophy, as well as books on Maimonides (also published in French translation, in 1936) and Abravanel (published in Polish translation in 1937), and some shorter essays in the popular press, and they were all well received.

The offer to write a book on Maimonides came to him as a surprise. In 1935 he had visited Erich Reiss, owner of a publishing house in Berlin, to recommend the work of a friend. Reiss was so impressed by my father that he asked him to write a book on Maimonides, whose jubilee year was being celebrated, and within two weeks of feverish work, the manuscript was completed. My father was just twenty-eight years old.

The book was praised in German newspapers as "ideal," "rich," and a "work of art." The biography presents the historical and political context in which Maimonides lived, together with a remarkably clear summary of his thought, but it also tries to understand his personal conflicts and struggles and how they are reflected in his thought. What emerges is a complex, sensitive human being, in sharp contrast with the somewhat austere figure presented in other studies. For my father, the central issue was not how to reconcile Maimonides's philosophical and halachic writings, or solving the extent of his rationalist, Aristotelian interpretations of Judaism, but evoking his inner, spiritual life. He shows, for example, the devastating impact of his brother's sudden death on Maimonides's reconsideration of the problem of evil, and concludes: "Maimonides never lost his faith in the just and meaningful working of the universe. His experience did not turn him against God but, to all appearances, against himself."[11] The book also raises the question of Maimonides's own efforts to attain prophetic inspiration, a controversial topic he discusses in far greater detail in a Hebrew essay published in 1945.[12] Ultimately, the biography is a spiritual as well as an intellectual portrayal that broadens the image of Maimonides from a strictly rationalist philosopher to someone with profound spiritual concerns as well.

During the 1930s my father lectured frequently around Germany to Jewish groups and began to achieve recognition from scholars and intellectuals. He describes, in his personal correspondence, his enthusiasm when he met people whose work he admired. In March 1936 he spent several days in Frankfurt and began a friendship with Ludwig Feuchtwanger, Martin Buber, and Eduard Strauss, all of whom had read his book on the prophets.

In November 1936 Buber asked my father if he would be willing to become the director of the Mittelstelle für Jüdische Erwachsenen Bildung in Frankfurt, and after an exchange of letters, my father accepted the offer when the two men met in Berlin on January 22, 1937, just after my father's thirtieth birthday. On March 3, 1937, he left Berlin and moved to Frankfurt. A few days later he was invited to Buber's home, where a lively debate about *Die Prophetie* took place. In a letter dated March 26, 1937, my father wrote:

The last days in Frankfurt were lovely. Many people from throughout Germany took part in the conference of the Mittelstelle. Between Feuchtwanger—a very spiritual man—and me a friendship developed. We understood each other excellently and wished we could spend a few days together. Perhaps for that reason I will one day visit Munich. The most delightful was a discussion with Buber, to whom I gave my article in the *Rundschreiben* to read. He: "It's a level too high! The part on prayer [text] is good, the part on praying [what prayer is] does not belong in the *Rundschreiben*." I: "The assignment is not to learn to read the text but to learn how to pray. The second is more important." Friendly quarrel. Buber pushed Eduard Strauss into the discussion by saying, "Heschel is a lovely youngster, but so stubborn!" This discussion went on so that I long with joy for the next one . . . It went so well and I think about the next time with a happy heart.

In another letter my father described some of his differences with Buber: "In the decisive question I have to say no to him. An apotheosis of the Bible is not permissible. The holiness of the Bible is due to its origins. There is no autarky in it."

Soon after arriving in Frankfurt, my father completed his short biography of Abravanel,[13] the distinguished Jewish philosopher who lived during the period of the expulsions from Spain and Portugal at the end of the fifteenth century. The book was published as part of the celebration of the five hundredth anniversary of Abravanel's birth, in Lisbon in 1437. Aware of the parallels between those experiences and the situation of the Jews in Nazi Germany, my father conceived the work as a book of comfort for his fellow European Jews. He concluded by pointing out that the Jewish expulsion from Iberia was followed by the conquest of the New World, which took place without their participation. "Had the Jews remained in the Iberian peninsula, they would certainly have participated in the actions of the Conquistadors. When the Conquistadors arrived in Haiti, there were 1,100,000 inhabitants; twenty years later there were only 1,000 remaining."[14]

Just as he did in his books on Maimonides and on the prophets, my father sought to portray something of the personality and character of Abravanel. With all the tragedy he had experienced, he wrote, Abravanel identified not with Jeremiah and his lamentations over the destruction of Jerusalem but with Isaiah and Ezekiel and their optimistic promises of messianic redemption. "No Jew can read this sentence in these historic days without being moved," wrote one reviewer in 1937.[15]

His desire to comfort the German Jews was accompanied by some chastisement. In a brief but extraordinary article, "Die Marranen von Heute," published in the newspaper of the Berlin Jewish community in September 1936, my father described the German Jews as inverted Marranos.[16] Unlike the baptized Jews of Spain, who were Christian on the outside and Jewish on the inside, the German Jews today, he wrote, are Jewish on the outside but not on the inside. Persecuted for being Jewish, they are ignorant of Judaism and its spiritual riches, so that their inner lives are empty. Feuchtwanger wrote to him that the article "spoke to my soul" (*war mir aus der Seele gesprochen*),[17] and invited him to write for the Bavarian Jewish newspaper which he edited.

My father's contacts with the Christian communities of Germany were mixed. Many of his professors were Christian, and his books were generally well received by them. But he was also appalled by the lack of action on the part of Christian leaders on behalf of the Jews. He used to tell me about a Jesuit librarian who said he could not speak out against the Nazi treatment of the Jews for fear that the Nazis would close down the library. Given such attitudes, my father's later writings on the imperative for religious people to speak out against social injustice reveal a personal dimension. At first-hand he knew Christians who were anti-Semitic; later he wrote that religion cannot coexist with racism: "Racism is satanism, unmitigated evil . . . You cannot worship God and at the same time look at man as if he were a horse."[18]

Securing a position outside Germany was not easy. He was invited by the Society of Friends in England to teach at their school in Woodbrooke, but he was unable to obtain a visa for England. In February 1938 he received an invitation from the Jewish community of Prague to teach at a rabbinical school they were trying to establish, beginning in the academic year 1938–39.[19] The Jewish community in Czechoslovakia had secured a promise of support from President Edŭard Beneš in April 1936, and Charles University had agreed to house the seminary in its philosophy faculty. The budget had been established and the course of study was planned, but the political crisis at the end of September brought the project to an end.[20] In renewed contacts during the spring of 1938, however, my father remained interested; a second letter, dated March 17, 1938, thanked him for his "expression of willingness to enter into negotiations."

MY FATHER'S TIME in Germany ceased abruptly. At the end of October 1938, Jews living in Germany but holding Polish passports were suddenly arrested and deported. He had rented a room in the large home of a Jewish family named Adler in a tiny, quiet, residential section of Frankfurt. Suddenly, in the middle of the night, the Gestapo arrived and gave him one hour to pack two suitcases. He quickly gathered his manuscripts and books and then carried two very heavy suitcases through the streets of Frankfurt to police headquarters, where he was held overnight in a tiny cell. The next morning he was put on a train packed with deported Jews. He told me he had to stand for the duration of a three-day journey to Poland. Denied entry into Poland, the Jews were held at the border in miserable conditions, many remaining for months. The local Poles refused to give the Jews food. My father was fortunate: his family soon secured his release, and he joined them in Warsaw. For the next ten months he lectured on Jewish philosophy and Bible at Warsaw's Institute for Jewish

Studies, whose stately white marble building is one of the few in Europe associated with my father that remain standing today.

He used to describe how Poles underestimated the dangers of a German threat, confident that the famed Polish cavalry would be victorious. My father continued to struggle to find a way out of Europe, and at the last moment, just six weeks before the German invasion of Poland, he succeeded in leaving Warsaw for London.

My father escaped thanks to Julian Morgenstern, the president of Hebrew Union College in Cincinnati, who had been trying for several years to secure visas from the State Department to bring Jewish scholars out of Europe. Michael Meyer has described the terrible obstacles Morgenstern encountered at the State Department, as well as his perseverance.[21] He was finally given only five visas. My father's name had been recommended by several colleagues, on the basis of his publications and reputation in Germany. That he was unmarried helped; visas for spouses and children were more difficult to obtain, since the college had to take responsibility for the financial maintenance of the entire family. The formal letter from Dr. Morgenstern invited my father to serve as a Research Fellow in Bible and Jewish philosophy for two years, at an annual salary of $500, plus board and lodging in the college dormitory. My father was first told by the American consul in Warsaw that he would have to be placed on a quota visa and wait nine months before his case was even considered. Instead, he appealed to the American consul in Stuttgart. He finally received his American visa in January 1940, and reached New York in March.

My father's deportation from Germany in the midst of the efforts to secure the visa made the process more difficult. In April 1939 he had to return from Warsaw to Stuttgart to attend to paperwork at the American consulate there. Finally, in the summer of 1939, he was able to leave Poland for England, where his brother, Jacob, was serving as rabbi to an Orthodox congregation. My father remained in London for six months, and together with other refugee Jewish scholars and the help of the Theodor Herzl Society in London, he established an Institute for Jewish Learning in February 1940. The students were refugees, many en route to Palestine. During his months in London, my father also attempted to secure work for friends who were still in Germany. He was in close contact with Arthur Spanier, who had served as director of the Judaica division of the Prussian State Library until he was fired in 1935 because he was a non-Aryan, and who subsequently worked as an instructor and librarian at the Hochschule in Berlin. In 1938 Spanier fled to Holland, and through him my father was able to send money and food to his mother and one surviving sister in Warsaw. Although Spanier struggled for years to obtain a visa for the United States, he never succeeded. In 1942 he was arrested in Holland and he died in Bergen-Belsen.

When the Nazis invaded Poland, my father's sister Esther was killed in a bombing. His mother and sister Gittel had to abandon their apartment, and their circumstances became very difficult. They sent postcards in which they worried lovingly about his well-being and begged for news of his safety. "Each day that we receive a letter from you," Gittel wrote, "is a holiday for us." Both were ultimately murdered, his mother in Warsaw, Gittel most probably in Treblinka. Another sister, Devorah, who was married and living in Vienna, was eventually deported to Theresienstadt on October 2, 1942, and from there sent to Auschwitz, where she was murdered upon her arrival on May 16, 1944.

My father never returned to Germany, or to Austria, or to Poland. He once wrote: "If I should go to Poland or Germany, every stone, every tree would remind me of contempt, hatred, murder, of children killed, of mothers burned alive, of human beings asphyxiated."[22]

AFTER RECEIVING his American visa, my father arrived in New York in March 1940. He stayed at first with members of his family. His oldest sister, Sarah, and her husband and most of their children had already arrived from Vienna, and there were also other cousins from Warsaw. His position in Cincinnati was not professor but instructor. He was given a room in the student dormitory, where he also kept his own food, since the cafeteria was not kosher. The students were a disappointment to him as well, because their background in Jewish texts was much weaker than that of his students at the Berlin seminary.

The years in Cincinnati were lonely. My father struggled constantly to bring his mother and sister from Warsaw, and to save other friends, colleagues, and relatives who remained stranded in Europe. They wrote to him, begging for help. He was frustrated with the American Jewish community, which he felt did not recognize the emergency. The news from Europe became worse and worse. He continued to receive mail from his mother and sisters and tried unsuccessfully to secure visas; he learned of their murder while he was in Cincinnati. Within his immediate family, the only survivors were those who fled before the war began: his brother, Jacob, who left Vienna for London with his wife, Susie, and daughter, Thena, in 1939, and his sister, Sarah, and her husband, the Kapitshinitzer rebbe, and their children, who left Vienna in February, 1939, for New York.

Some of the rabbinical students at Hebrew Union College became his friends, helping him improve his English, and he also became friendly with members of the faculty. He particularly enjoyed Professor Abraham

Cronbach, famous for his biblical stories, with whom he visited a home for unwed mothers in Cincinnati. He wondered what the biblical message would be and was moved by Professor Cronbach's presentation of Hagar's story.

It was in Cincinnati that my father first met my mother, Sylvia Straus, at the home of Professor and Mrs. Jacob Marcus. My mother, a concert pianist, had come to Cincinnati from her hometown, Cleveland, to study with Severin Eisenberger. That evening she was asked to play the piano, and my father fell in love with her. Shortly thereafter he attended her concert at the Cincinnati music conservatory and took her out to celebrate. Within a few months, he was offered a position at the Jewish Theological Seminary in New York, the seat of the Conservative movement. After hearing her play, Arthur Rubinstein urged my mother to study with the pianist Eduard Steuermann, who also lived in New York. My parents were married in December 1946 in Los Angeles, where my mother's parents had moved.

It is striking that my father did not undertake major theological work until after he was married. During the early years of their marriage, he completed his most important books, masterpieces of religious thought that seemed to pour out of him: *Man Is Not Alone* (1951), *The Sabbath* (1951), *God in Search of Man* (1952), *Man's Quest for God* (1954). At the same time, he was able to give voice to his mourning for the destruction of his family and the world of East European Jews. He was asked to speak on East European Jewish life in 1946 at YIVO, the Institute for Jewish Scientific Research in New York, where he delivered an elegy in Yiddish so moving that the audience, composed mainly of secular Yiddish writers, spontaneously stood up at the end of the speech and said *kaddish*, the Jewish memorial prayer for the dead. That speech was later expanded and published in his book *The Earth Is the Lord's.*

In many ways my father's evocation of East European Jews was a description of his own personality. He writes of the sheer joy of being Jewish, the vitality, the love of learning, and also the tenderness, the gentleness, the sincerity and deep trust of other people that characterized East European Jews—and himself. His panegyric to Polish Jews is striking in comparison to the way they were usually portrayed in the work of modern historians, particularly those of Germany, who tended to view their Polish compatriots as an embarrassment for their lack of assimilation and for their mystical piety. By contrast, these German historians held up the cosmopolitan Sephardic Jews of Spain as models of Jews who were intellectually and culturally assimilated.[23] My father's purpose was to depict the spirituality of the East European Jews, their inner life, a precious religious civilization that was wiped out by the Nazis. He also wrote several important scholarly articles on early Hasidism, the pietist movement of Eastern Europe that began during the eighteenth century; and he received a Guggenheim Fellowship in 1954 to write a biography of the movement's founder, Rabbi Israel Baal Shem Tov.[24] At the end of his life, he wrote two books on Hasidism—a two-volume Yiddish study of Menachem Mendl of Kotzk, a famed nineteenth century Hasidic master, and *A Passion for Truth*, a comparison of the Kotzker and Søren Kierkegaard. For my father, Hasidism was an extraordinary moment in Jewish spiritual history: "Then came Rabbi Israel Baal Shem Tov and brought heaven down to earth . . . In the days of Moses, Israel had a revelation of God; in the days of the Baal Shem, God had a revelation of Israel. Suddenly, there was revealed a holiness in Jewish life that had accumulated in the course of many generations."[25]

How could the spirituality of Hasidism, the holiness of East European Jewish life, now utterly destroyed, be expressed in the language of postwar America? Just as his doctoral dissertation had challenged the interpretive categories of modern biblical scholarship, his first English articles were radical challenges to the conventional categories used by scholars of religion to interpret religious experience. His articles of the 1940s, reprinted in this volume, begin by contending that conventional categories used to understand piety, prayer, and holiness are reductionist and inappropriate. Instead of understanding piety on its own terms, for example, scholars too often reduce it to a psychological phenomenon, or criticize it as irrational and counterproductive. He used to say in his lectures, "Just as you cannot study philosophy through praying, you cannot study prayer through philosophizing."[26] In *Man Is Not Alone* he wrote: "Evaluating faith in terms of reason is like trying to understand love as a syllogism and beauty as an algebraic equation."[27] Instead, he argued that piety is a phenomenon that must be described on its own terms, as an attitude, a way of thinking in which the pious person feels God to be always close and present: "Awareness of God is as close to him as the throbbing of his own heart, often deep and calm, but at times overwhelming, intoxicating, setting the soul afire."[28] Piety gives rise to reverence, which sees the "dignity of every human being" and "the spiritual value which even inanimate things inalienably possess."[29] Exploitation and domination are utterly foreign to genuine piety, and possession of things leads only to loneliness. Instead, the pious person's "affinity with God is his persistent aspiration to go beyond himself," to be devoted to goals and tasks and ideals. For the pious person, destiny means not simply to accomplish, but to contribute.[30] "In aiding a creature, he is helping the Creator. In succoring the poor, he is taking care of something that concerns God. In admiring the good, he is revering the Spirit of God."[31]

My father also stressed the objective nature of religion, rejecting academic studies of religion which reduce it to a response to moments of social crisis or psychological stress. Millenarian movements, for example, are conventionally understood as responses to social crises; prayer for rain in periods of drought is conventionally interpreted in functionalist terms: praying holds the community together at a time when social cohesion is threatened. To my father such approaches merely described the social consequences of religion, not the meaning of religion itself, "as if instead of describing the inner value of a work of art we were to apprehend it by its effects on our mind or feelings."[32] Rather than a function of human nature, a response to an emotion or social situation, religion is an order of being, the holy dimension of existence that is present whether or not it is perceived by us.[33]

Ultimately religion is not based on our awareness of God but on God's interest in us. In prayer, for example, we seek not to make God visible but to make ourselves visible to God.[34] That gentle upheaval of the relationship is central to my father's theology. It is not we who seek to understand God; it is God who is in search of us. Even more, it is God who is in need of us: "To be is to stand for, and what human beings stand for is the great mystery of being God's partner. God is in need of human beings."

God's need of us, what my father calls "divine pathos," is the central pillar of his theology and what makes it distinctive among Jewish thinkers. Yet it is not idiosyncratic; my father bases his understanding of divine pathos on a long, deep tradition within Judaism, most prominent in kabbalistic and Hasidic writings, but also found in the heart of rabbinic Judaism. Indeed, his three-volume study of rabbinic theology—published in Hebrew as *Torah min Ha-Shamayim b'Espakloriah shel Ha-Dorot (Revelation in the Mirror of the Generations)*—demonstrates that concepts supposed to have originated with classical kabbalah in the Middle Ages began to be articulated in antiquity by the rabbis who shaped halachic Judaism. In his highly original reading of talmudic and midrashic texts, my father brings forth the theological concerns and controversies that animated rabbinic discussions. He shows, for example, that *agada* is the site of intricate theological discussion and debate by the rabbis, and he traces two distinct theological schools within rabbinic Judaism. Even within the Talmud he finds belief in God's need of human beings, and he traces conflicting rabbinic understandings of revelation, as experiential and propositional, which bear differing implications for halachic decisions.

One looks hard to find discussion of political activism in my father's scholarly and theological writings of the 1940s and '50s. As he later explained in an interview, it was revising his dissertation on the prophets for publication in English during the early 1960s that convinced him that he must be involved in human affairs, in human suffering.

MY FATHER first met Martin Luther King, Jr., in January 1963 and began his long involvement in the civil-rights movement. They met at a Chicago conference on religion and race sponsored by the National Conference of Christians and Jews and became good friends as well as colleagues. Writing, lecturing, and demonstrating on behalf of civil rights, my father was an effective figure. When the police blocked the entrance to FBI headquarters in Manhattan, it was he who gained entry to present a petition protesting police brutality against civil-rights demonstrators in Alabama.

When he joined the famous Selma march in 1965, he was welcomed as one of the leaders in the front row of marchers, with Dr. King, Ralph Bunche, and Ralph Abernathy. In an unpublished memoir he wrote upon returning from Selma, my father describes the extreme hostility he encountered from whites in Alabama, from the moment he arrived at the airport, and the kindness he was shown by Dr. King's assistants, particularly the Reverend Andrew Young, who watched over him during the march with great concern. Just before the march began, a service was held in a small chapel, where my father read Psalm 27, "The Lord is my light and my salvation; whom shall I fear?"* and Dr. King gave a sermon describing three typologies among the children of Israel in the wilderness. For my father, Dr. King's emphasis on the exodus, rather than on Jesus, as a model for the movement was important, and he invited Dr. King and his family to join us at our Passover Seder. Dr. King's assassination in April 1968 came just before Passover; we had expected him to spend the holiday with us.

For my father the march was a religious moment. He wrote in his memoir: "I thought of my having walked with Hasidic rabbis on various occasions. I felt a sense of the Holy in what I was doing. Dr. King expressed several times to me his appreciation. He said, 'I cannot tell you how much your presence means to us. You cannot imagine how often Reverend Vivian and I speak about you.' Dr. King said to me that this was the greatest day in his life and the most important civil-rights demonstration." With sadness, my father added, "I felt again what I have been thinking about for years—that Jewish religious institutions have again missed a great opportunity, namely, to interpret a civil-rights movement in terms

---

* He wrote in an unpublished memoir that he had originally intended to read Psalm 15, "O Lord, who shall sojourn in thy tent?," but changed his mind after he arrived in Selma.

of Judaism. The vast number of Jews participating actively in it are totally unaware of what the movement means in terms of the prophetic traditions."

About six months after the Selma march, my father, together with John Bennett and Richard Neuhaus, founded what became one of the strongest organizations opposed to the war in Vietnam, Clergy and Laymen Concerned about Vietnam.[35] Over and over, in speeches at universities, synagogues, and anti-war rallies, he denounced the murder of innocent people in Southeast Asia and proclaimed, "In a free society, some are guilty, but all are responsible." However difficult it may be to stop the war today, he said, it will be even more difficult tomorrow; the killing must end now.

Whether or not Dr. King should speak out publicly against the war in Vietnam was a topic discussed constantly in our home during the mid-1960s. Would his public opposition to the war hurt the civil-rights movement? Which was the better political course, and which was the greater moral good? Under the auspices of Clergy and Laymen Concerned, Dr. King first spoke out publicly against the war in Manhattan's Riverside Church in the spring of 1967. The atrocities committed by U.S. forces in Vietnam, and the obvious political futility of a war against guerrillas, were condemned by him and by my father, just as they and other war opponents were branded as anti-American subversives. But the real subversiveness, my father stated that evening, was the American government:

Our thoughts on Vietnam are sores, destroying our trust, ruining our most cherished commitments with burdens of shame. We are pierced to the core with pain, and it is our duty as citizens to say no to the subversiveness of our government, which is ruining the values we cherish . . . The blood we shed in Vietnam makes a mockery of all our proclamations, dedications, celebrations. Has our conscience become a fossil, is all mercy gone? If mercy, the mother of humility, is still alive as a demand, how can we say yes to our bringing agony to that tormented country? We are here because our own integrity as human beings is decaying in the agony and merciless killing done in our name. In a free society, some are guilty and all are responsible. We are here to call upon the governments of the United States as well as North Vietnam to stand still and to consider that no victory is worth the price of terror, which all parties commit in Vietnam, North and South. Remember the blood of the innocent cries forever. Should that blood stop to cry, humanity would cease to be.

The crimes committed in Vietnam were subversive to our values, and to our religious lives, he insisted. Someone may commit a crime now and teach mathematics an hour later. But when we pray, all we have done in our lives enters our prayers.[36] As he had articulated in his early essays in the 1940s, the purpose of prayer is not petitionary. We do not pray in order to be saved, my father used to stress, we pray so that we might be worthy of being saved. Prayer should not focus on our wishes, but is a moment in which God's intentions are reflected in us.[37] If we are created in the image of God, each human being should be a reminder of God's presence. If we engage in acts of violence and murder, we are desecrating the divine likeness.

The anguish my father felt over the war in Vietnam was relentless; I often found him in the middle of the night, unable to sleep. The tension grew worse in the spring of 1967, as hostile Arab countries threatened Israel with a military buildup and UN troops withdrew from their peace-keeping positions. Israel's extraordinary military success in the Six-Day War was a great relief, and my father flew there immediately. The trip inspired his magnificent evocation of the land of Israel's religious signif-icance to Judaism, *Israel: An Echo of Eternity*.

Contrary to the claims of some critics, my father's Zionist writings did not begin in 1967, nor was his commitment to Israel mitigated by his depiction of Judaism as a religion concerned with holiness in time. His Zionist writings began much earlier, as indicated by some of the essays included in this volume, and even in his writings on time, he warned that Judaism teaches "not to flee from the realm of space; to work with things of space, but to be in love with eternity . . . To disparage space and the blessings of things of space is to disparage the works of creation . . . Time and space are interrelated."[38]

Zionism for my father was not solely a political issue, and he was critical of much of Zionist theory for its single-minded political and secular emphases. Neither statehood nor cultural nationalism, he argued, could substitute for Judaism's religious teachings. He presented these views in the United States and in Israel, often at Zionist conventions, where he warned that simply living in the state of Israel was no panacea for resolving issues of Jewish identity.

My father and mother and I made our first trip to Israel in the summer of 1957. The establishment of the state seemed like a miracle, and my father used to speak about it to me with a tone of wonder. In the summer of 1965 we spent two months in Israel, when my father was the official guest of President Zalman Shazar. He was invited to lecture throughout the country. He returned frequently in subsequent years, to lecture and to visit friends. Of the few friends he had from Europe who had survived the war, several lived in Israel, including President Shazar and the pe-diatrician Aaron Brand, a friend from Berlin days.

Throughout the years of his social activism, my father maintained close and constructive relationships with Christian leaders. He was invited by President John Bennett of Union Theological Seminary to serve as the

Harry Emerson Fosdick Visiting Professor in 1965–66; he served on the board of directors of organizations as diverse as the United Greek Orthodox Charities; the Martin Luther King, Jr., Center for Nonviolent Social Change; the Committee for the Defense of William Stringfellow and Anthony Towne; Jesse Jackson's Operation Breadbasket; the Jewish Peace Fellowship; and Trees for Vietnam—among others.

His reputation as a theologian of significance within the Christian community began with a glowing review by Reinhold Niebuhr of *Man Is Not Alone* in 1951.[39] Abraham Heschel, Niebuhr wrote, was "one of the treasures of mind and spirit by which the persecutions, unloosed in Europe, inadvertently enriched our American culture . . . It is a safe guess that he will become a commanding and authoritative voice not only in the Jewish community but in the religious life of America."[40] What a contrast between the German Protestant theologians of the 1930s, debating whether the Old Testament should be eliminated from the Christian canon, and Niebuhr's positive view of Hebrew Scripture and of Judaism. This led to further contacts between them and ultimately into a close friendship. They were neighbors and often took walks together. Niebuhr's praise and the friendship that developed between them were profoundly important to my father; for him they were hopeful signs of a new kind of relationship between Jews and Christians. Niebuhr himself asked my father to deliver the eulogy at his funeral, which he did—the text appears in these pages. Niebuhr, he used to say, understood his work better than anyone else. With all the differences in their beliefs, both had similar understandings of the role of a theologian—not simply philosophical discussion, but political activism—and they shared a deep love of the Hebrew Bible.

My father's most important achievement in Christian–Jewish relations came with his involvement with the Second Vatican Council during the mid-1960s. At the invitation of the American Jewish Committee, my father traveled to Rome, where he formed a friendship with Cardinal Bea, who directed the composition of *Nostra Aetate*, the Vatican's pronouncement concerning relations with non-Catholic religions. My father met with Pope Paul VI on several occasions, as well as with Cardinal Willebrands of Holland, and he took a strong stand during the moments when it seemed the Council was weakening its declaration concerning the Jews.

In 1971 my father traveled through Italy on a lecture tour, accompanied by my mother. A private audience with Pope Paul VI was arranged for them in Rome, on March 17. Describing the visit afterward in a private memoir, my father said how pleased he was that the Pope had seen his writings as a help to Catholics to strengthen their faith:

When the Pope saw me he smiled joyously, with a radiant face, shook my hand cordially with both his hands—he did so several times during the audience. He opened the conversation by telling me that he is reading my books, that my books are very spiritual and very beautiful, and that Catholics should read my books. He expressed his blessing that I may continue to write more books. He then added that he knows of the great impact my books are having upon young people, which he particularly appreciates.

My father had close personal relationships with several distinguished Catholic theologians, monks, and nuns, including Gustav Weigl, Thomas Merton, Theodore Hesburgh, Corita Kent, and Leo Rudloff, abbot of the Benedictine monastery in Vermont, and in the anti-war movement he worked closely with Daniel and Philip Berrigan. He was often invited to speak at Catholic colleges, and his writings continue to be read by Catholics as texts for spiritual meditation. He felt an affinity with Catholics, in part based on the centrality of canon law and formal ritual within Catholicism, but also because of the deep and vibrant spiritual traditions within Catholicism. With Protestants, my father shared a training in critical biblical scholarship and a liberal theological tradition committed to social activism.

My father's closest friends did not necessarily share all of his commitments; some were Jews with differing political convictions, others were Christians involved with him in political work. Two of his best friends were his former student, the late Rabbi Wolfe Kelman, executive director of the Rabbinical Assembly, and the Reverend William Sloane Coffin, who served as chaplain at Yale University during the last years of my father's life. Both were exuberant personalities, friends who loved to tell stories, laugh, and celebrate. Wolfe and my father worked at the Jewish Theological Seminary and often walked home together; they would arrive at my father's apartment building, but in order to continue the conversation, my father would keep walking another half mile to Wolfe's building. Then Wolfe would turn around and walk my father home. Wolfe was a trusted friend, a confidant, and a source of support, and he showed his friendship by calling my mother several times a week in the years after my father died.

Bill Coffin's visits with us, often after anti-war rallies at which he and my father spoke, were moments of great celebration. There was a thrill in our household when he was about to arrive, and from the moment he walked in the door, with his big, booming laugh, the excitement began. He played the piano with my mother, traded stories with my father, and helped me with my homework. "Father Abraham" was the nickname with which he teased my father, and my father would respond by teaching him Hebrew prayers.

"ISN'T IT A BURDEN to have a famous father?" people often ask me. But just imagine what kind of a father Abraham Heschel would be. I was only vaguely aware of my father's fame when I was growing up; as a father, he was wonderful. Ever warm, loving, and affectionate, he was someone I could confide in and always receive a sensitive and understanding response. I was free to interrupt him at any moment; he was never annoyed, but always looked up from his writing with a big smile of delight and exclaimed, "Susie!" as though we hadn't seen each other in ages. He loved being a father, playing with me and my friends, even making up games for my birthday parties. American popular culture was utterly foreign to our home. My father had no idea of sports, popular music, movies, or TV. I remember as a child teasing him, saying that he should Americanize himself, become "the sporty type," wear brown sport jackets instead of gray or blue suits, and learn to play golf.

Walking with my father was not a matter of reaching a destination but of creating a private time for talk. He would stop every few feet and discuss a point, then go a little farther. He loved to take walks on Sabbath afternoons, in Riverside Park, across from our apartment building. When I was a little girl, he was always delighted to play games to keep me amused, and even corralled his colleagues to join us in Simon Says or Red Light, Green Light. And when I grew tired from the walk, he would put me on his shoulders and carry me.

From my youngest years I was aware of discrimination against women, particularly in religious circles, and complained about it to my father. He always agreed with me, supporting me when I wanted a Bat Mitzvah and an *aliyah* for my sixteenth birthday, and agreeing that aspects of Jewish observance that were unfair to women had to be changed. He even suggested that I apply to the rabbinical school at the Jewish Theological Seminary, confident that one day women would be accepted there as students.

Looking back, I find it most remarkable that my father was never moody or irritable. If he became upset or angry, the mood lasted a minute and disappeared. His warmth, hugs, and kisses were always ready; he exuded love toward me and my mother. It was extraordinary how well matched my parents were. That they loved and meshed with each other's quite different family was remarkable, but they had the same values and the same instincts about people. My parents rarely went out for entertainment, preferring to stay home. Each evening, before bed, they would drink tea and talk, sometimes playing Chinese checkers. Watching them sit together at the dining room table, talking and laughing, is a vivid memory. Another is my mother reading my father's lectures in the hours before they were to be given, and how she would advise him to emphasize a certain point or take out a controversial statement that seemed too strongly worded. He always listened to her, and told her afterward how right she had been. He joined her world, too. He loved her to play the piano for him and to go to concerts with her. When my mother had chamber music at home, often weekly when I was growing up, my father would listen while he worked in his study, then join the musicians for tea and the chocolate cake I would bake while they played.

My father's book on the *Sabbath*, one of the most popular of his writings, evokes the spirit he created with my mother in our home, in which the Sabbath was both peacefully quiet and filled with celebration. The book beautifully describes the rabbinic, kabbalistic, and Hasidic understandings of the Sabbath experience; together, my parents brought the text to life.

The Sabbath was the time my parents entertained, usually at Friday-night Sabbath dinner, or at a high tea at four o'clock on Saturday afternoons. Their guests were faculty members and students from the seminary, and conversations were lively. Nearly all my parents' friends were professors who had come to the United States from Europe, and they loved to tell stories about European Jewish life, or reminisce about professors and colleagues and rabbis they had known in Europe. There was some sadness that they were describing a world that no longer existed, but their stories had such vividness that they seemed to keep that world alive.

It was on a Sabbath that my father died. We were planning to go to the synagogue together on the morning of Saturday, December 23, 1972, but he never awakened. In Jewish tradition it is considered a sign of great piety to merit a peaceful death in one's sleep, even more so to die on the Sabbath. Such a death is called a kiss from God.

MOST OF THE WORLD that my father knew no longer exists. He was, as he wrote, "a brand plucked from the fire of Europe," and he became God's gift to us. The soil of Jewish piety in which he was bred was destroyed, but through him that world did not vanish. Like the Baal Shem Tov, he brought heaven down to earth, and in his writings we have a revelation of the holiness of Jewish life.

MY MOTHER, Sylvia Straus Heschel, and I are delighted to present this volume of my father's essays. Originally published in a wide range of academic and popular periodicals, they have not been easily accessible to readers. Both of us are moved by the ever-growing interest in my father's work, by the many letters we continue to receive from his readers, and by the attention to his theology throughout the world, from Europe to South America to China.

We are deeply grateful for the devotion of my father's publisher and close friend, Roger W. Straus, who has brought his books to print for the past half century. One of the world's great editors, Robert Giroux has given meticulous attention to my father's writings for many years, and his understanding of his style has enhanced this volume. In their hands, my father's books have always been treated with care and esteem.

In the course of preparing these essays for publication, several friends have offered generous assistance. I would like to thank Leonard Wolf and David Guralnik for translating the Yiddish poem "A Day of Hate." Professor Doris Bergen and Professor Dagmar Herzog graciously helped with translations from German to English. My father's magnificent Hebrew essay *"Pikuach Neshama"* cannot be rendered with full beauty and nuance in English, but I appreciate the help of the many friends and colleagues who lent great time and effort to the translation: Rabbi Moshe Adler, Dr. David Ariel, Professor Moshe Berger, Dr. Aryeh Cohen, Rabbi Samuel Dresner, and Rabbi Alan Lettofsky. Elisheva Urbas, managing editor at Farrar, Straus and Giroux, gave particularly careful consideration to the details of editing and publication. I would also like to thank Professor Marilyn Reizbaum for her very helpful advice concerning the book's introduction. We are grateful to each of them. A generous research grant from the Cleveland Foundation, shepherded by Carol Willen, allowed this project to proceed with added speed.

It is extraordinary that so many people told us they felt privileged to assist in the work of this project. Their love for my father is yet another sign that his influence continues, and that his memory is indeed a blessing.

I

EXISTENCE AND

CELEBRATION

To Be a Jew: What Is It?

THERE IS A HIGH COST of living to be paid by a Jew. He has to be exalted in order to be normal in a world that is neither propitious for nor sympathetic to his survival. Some of us, tired of sacrifice and exertion, often wonder: Is Jewish existence worth the price? Others are overcome with panic; they are perplexed and despair of recovery.

The meaning of Jewish existence, the foremost theme of any Jewish philosophy, is baffling. To fit it into the framework of personal intellectual predilections or current fashions of our time would be a distortion. The claim of Israel must be recognized *before* attempting an interpretation. As the ocean is more than what we know about it, so Judaism surpasses the content of all philosophies of it. We have not invented it. We may accept or reject, but should not distort it.

It is as an individual that I am moved by an anxiety for the meaning of my existence as a Jew. Yet when I begin to ponder about it, my theme is not the problem of one Jew but of all Jews. And the more deeply I probe, the more strongly I realize the scope of the problem. It embraces not only the Jews of the present but also those of the past and those of the future, the meaning of Jewish existence in all ages.

What is at stake in our lives is more than the fate of one generation. In this moment *we*, the living, are Israel. The tasks begun by the patriarchs and prophets, and carried out by countless Jews of the past, are now entrusted to us. No other group has superseded them. We are the only channel of Jewish tradition, those who must save Judaism from oblivion, those who must hand over the entire past to the generations to come. We are either the last, the dying, Jews or else we are those who will give new life to our tradition. Rarely in our history has so much been dependent upon one generation. We will either forfeit or enrich the legacy of the ages.

JUDAISM IS NOT a chapter in the history of philosophy. It does not lend itself to be a subject of reflection for armchair philosophers. Its understanding cannot be attained in the comfort of playing a chess game of theories. Only ideas that are meaningful to those who are steeped in misery may be accepted as principles by those who dwell in safety. In trying to understand Jewish existence a Jewish philosopher must look for agreement with the men of Sinai as well as with the people of Auschwitz.

We are the most challenged people under the sun. Our existence is either superfluous or indispensable to the world; it is either tragic or holy to be a Jew.

It is a matter of immense responsibility that we here and Jewish teachers everywhere have undertaken to instill in our youth the will to be Jews today, tomorrow, and forever and ever. Unless being a Jew is of absolute significance, how can we justify the ultimate price which our people was often forced to pay throughout its history? To assess Judaism soberly and farsightedly is to establish it as a good to be preferred, if necessary, to any alternative which we may ever face.

The task of Jewish philosophy today is not only to describe the essence but also to set forth the universal relevance of Judaism, the bearings of its demands upon the chance of man to remain human. Bringing to light the lonely splendor of Jewish thinking, conveying the taste of eternity in our daily living, is the greatest aid we can render to the man of our time who has fallen so low that he is not even capable of being ashamed of what happened in his days.

This surely I know—the source of creative Jewish thinking cannot be found in the desire to compare and to reconcile Judaism with a current doctrine. A noble person does not compare himself with anybody else. The intellectual passion of medieval Jewish philosophers was not bent on making Judaism compatible with Aristotelianism but, rather, having absorbed the philosophic ideas of their time, they were anxious to apply and adjust those ideas to the teachings of our fathers. Man is creative only when he is neither apologetic nor propagandistic. It is true, Judaism has no strategic boundaries, being exposed not only to cynicism and the denial of the divine but also to the powerful impact and even deliberate missionary efforts of other creeds. Yet the strength of truth lies not in refuting others but in understanding itself, in being consistent with itself.

Judaism is a source, not only an object of philosophy. Jewish philosophy is basically the self-understanding of Judaism, the self-understanding of the Jew, just as the paramount topic of philosophic reflection is man himself.

Jewish philosophy is an obligation to the Jewish people. What is going on in the studyrooms of Jewish thinkers has a fateful effect upon what will happen in the lives of the Jews. We have to comprehend in order to prepare for the future of a shattered people. We do not write for a future *Genizah*. We explore Jewish literature because we love and affirm Jewish living.

WE WERE NOT BORN by mere chance as a by-product of a migration of nations or in the obscurity of a primitive past. The idea of Israel came first, and only then did we come into the world. We were formed according to an intention and for the sake of an idea. Our souls tremble with the echo of unforgettable experiences and with the sublime expectation of our own response. To be a Jew is to be committed to the experience of great ideas, "to act and to hear." The task of Jewish philosophy is to formulate not only these ideas but also the depth of that commitment in vivid, consistent thinking. The task of Jewish philosophy is to make our thinking compatible with our destiny.

In trying to set forth that commitment and that destiny we feel a discrepancy between the depth of our experience and the short reach of our power of expression. What we have seen in the lives of our people is so much greater than what we will ever be able to say. We are all involved in the playing of a drama staged by Israel with God as the attentive audience. Philosophy of Judaism is the attempt to write a review of that performance, to formulate its principles, and to say why we take part in that drama.

Philosophy of Judaism has often been formulated as a set of dogmas, shed from nature like catkins from a tree. Yet the essence is not in the mature fruit; the essence is in the sap that stirs through the tissue. To understand Judaism we must penetrate to its core. The surface may seem to be gnarled and hard like the branches of an ancient tree, but our faith, suffering, striving cut the crust of dogma off the soft, growing cells. Our dogmas are allusions, intimations, our wisdom is an allegory, but our actions are definitions.

Trust in these beliefs is not found in self-detachment, in brooding, gazing, musing—but by striking at the amazing sources that are within ourselves and letting our hidden forces emanate in our thoughts, deeds, words. In exposing ourselves to God we discover the divine in ourselves and its correspondence to the divine beyond ourselves. That perception of correspondence, our discovering how acts of human goodness are allied with transcendent holiness, the sense of the sacred context of our candid compassion—is our most precious insight.

Just as humanity is more than a set of principles, so is Judaism more than a set of dogmas. Judaism is our genesis, not our wisdom; it is not grist for the mill of a mind. It is as real as a law that operates in history, preceding the vicissitudes of contemplation. Not an ideal, a desirable aim of the mind, an eye for the future, but a condition of existence, not choice but destiny. It is impossible for us to survive without the sense of life's earnestness: as if we had given a pledge in advance of our entrance into the concert of history.

Our failure in faith gives us no authority to reject or reduce the inner wealth that has come down to us from our ancestors. Only by applying a clear-sightedness, an urge and a craving comparable to those stored up in the forms of Israel's faith, only by a spiritual intensity equal to that of our teachers who expressed them, and in whose lives the experience of the spiritual has often been like breathing of the common wind, can we reach the depth of meaning hidden beneath the crust of beliefs. On the other hand, it is absurd to assume that we can heal our shattered souls by outlawing aggressive thinking, that we can revive our suppressed faith by substituting frantic nostalgia for sober conviction or worship of rituals for walking with God.

ONE OF THE MALADIES of our time is shattered confidence in human nature. We are inclined to believe that the world is a pandemonium, that there is no sense in virtue, no import to integrity; that we only graft goodness upon selfishness, and relish self-indulgence in all values; that we cannot but violate truth with evasion. Honesty is held to be wishful thinking, purity the squaring of the circle of human nature. The hysteria of suspicion has made us unreliable to ourselves, trusting neither our aspirations nor our convictions. Suspiciousness, not skepticism, is the beginning of our thinking.

This sneering doctrine holds many of us in its spell. It has profoundly affected the character and life of modern man. The man of today shrinks from the light. He is afraid to think as he feels, afraid to admit what he believes, afraid to love what he admires. Going astray he blames others for his failure and decides to be more evasive, smooth-tongued, and deceitful. Living in fear he thinks that the ambush is the normal dwelling place of all men. He has failed to pick up in his youth the clue of the unbroken thread of truthfulness that would guide him through the labyrinth.

Indeed, life appears dismal if not mirrored in what is more than life. Nothing can be regarded as valuable unless assessed by something higher in value than itself. Our survival depends upon the conviction that there is something that is worth the price of life. Our survival depends upon a sense of the supremacy of what is lasting. That sense or conviction may be asleep, but it awakens when challenged. In some people it lives as a sporadic wish; in others it is a permanent concern.

What I have learned from Jewish life is that if a man is not more than human, then he is less than human. Judaism is an attempt to prove that in order to be a man, you have to be more than a man; that in order to be a people, we have to be more than a people. Israel was made to be a "holy people." This is the essence of its dignity and the essence of its merit. Judaism is a link to eternity, kinship with ultimate reality.

What are the roots out of which we draw that consciousness, that contact with the sublime? A sense of contact with the ultimate dawns upon most people when their self-reliance is swept away by violent misery. Judaism is the attempt to instill in us that sense as an everyday awareness. It leads us to regard injustice as a metaphysical calamity, to sense the divine significance of human happiness, to keep slightly above the twilight of the self, ready to perceive the constant dawn in our souls.

We are endowed with the consciousness of being involved in a history that transcends time and its specious glories. We are taught to feel the knots of life in which the trivial is intertwined with the sublime. There is no end to our experience of the dangerous grandeur, of the divine earnestness of human life. Our blossoms may be crushed, but we are upheld by the faith that comes from the core of our roots. We are not deceived by the obvious, knowing that all delight is but a pretext for adding strength to that which is beyond joy and grief. We know that no hour is the last hour, that the world is more than the world.

WHY IS MY BELONGING to the Jewish people the most sacred relation to me, second only to my relation to God? Israel is a spiritual order in which the human and the ultimate, the natural and the holy enter a lasting covenant, in which kinship with God is not an aspiration but a reality of destiny. For us Jews there can be no fellowship with God without the fellowship with Israel. Abandoning Israel, we desert God.

Judaism is not only the adherence to particular doctrines and observances but primarily the living *in* the spiritual order of the Jewish people, the living *in* the Jews of the past and *with* the Jews of the present. Judaism is not only a certain quality in the souls of the individuals but primarily the existence of the community of Israel. Judaism is neither an experience nor a creed, neither the possession of psychic traits nor the acceptance of a theological doctrine, but the living in a holy dimension, in a spiritual sphere. Our share in holiness we acquire by living in the Jewish community. What we do as individuals is a trivial episode; what we attain as Israel causes us to grow into the infinite.

Israel is the tree, we are the leaves. It is the clinging to the stem that keeps us alive. Israel has not erred, even though some of its branches have fallen off. Its substance can be sustained only within its roots, within the depth and unutterableness of its being.

There is more madness than sanity in this world. Israel is one of the few healing herbs that have not withered away in the dust-laden winds of history. It is a unique source in the spiritual life of mankind, offering so much of what is valid and fit to guide the soul.

There has perhaps never been more need of Judaism than in our time, a time in which many cherished hopes of humanity lie crushed. We should be pioneers, as were our fathers three thousand years ago. The future of all men depends upon their realizing that the sense of holiness is as vital as health. By following the Jewish way of life we maintain that sense and preserve the light for mankind's future visions.

This is a time of simple alternatives. Mankind has arrived at the narrowest isthmus in its history, with no possibility of avoiding the dilemma of total peace or total calamity. As Jews, too, we have to face our existence in terms of sharp alternatives: we either surrender to the might and threat of evil or persist in the earnestness of our existence.

To be loyal to Judaism means to affirm it even at the price of suffering. We are attached to life, and still Judaism is dear to us. Our fate is often hard to bear. Yet we bear it for all men. There will be no humanity without Israel.

It is our destiny to live for what is more than ourselves. Our very existence is an unparalleled symbol of such aspiration. By being what we are, namely Jews, we mean more to mankind than by any particular service we may render.

I have faith in God and faith in Israel. Though some of its children have gone astray, Israel remains the mate of God. I cannot hate what God loves. Rabbi Aaron the Great used to say: "I wish I could love the greatest saint as the Lord loves the greatest rascal."

In the face of confusing enigmas we submit our incomprehension to the source of grace and meaning that undeniably fill the world. In communing with stillness we exchange thoughts for light and see the brotherhood of joy and pain, of grief and hope, of mountain and grave.

There is a holy order in the wilderness of history; there is consoling beauty in the fading of cherished hopes. For human hopes are merely the reflected rays of an incandescent promise that never expires. We may falter and fade away, but our sacred tears are like dew that falls on a soil that no treason can desecrate.

WE WHO CEASELESSLY TOIL and strive to rule the atoms and the stars fail to grasp what it means to be a man. Or have we ever understood what it means to be a Jew? Listening to the past, attuned to the striving of ancestors, we perceive that to be a Jew is to hold one's soul clean and open to the flow of that stream of striving, so that God may not be ashamed of His creation.

Judaism is a gift of God. It is not something that we inaugurate, not our attainment, but our inheritance, the accumulated experience of ages. It is to be acquired, not produced. We live not only on what we have created but also on what our ancestors have received.

The essence of conscious living is to act according to aspirations, to strive for ends which we set for ourselves. The human will is blind and can never by its own power envision the ends of our actions. Ideals grasped by the mind in history's rare hours of spiritual insight are like sparks of orientation, glittering before our will during the long seasons of obscurity. To Israel the ideals are more than means of orientation. The great events of the past were not visions of the mind but impregnations of the will. Our souls became fertile, waiting to give birth. We have no choice. To us, therefore, the conception of the past is the source of what is vital in the future.

Being a Jew is a part of a continued existence. Suddenness of conversion is alien to our mentality. We carry the past in our will.

Duration does not mean mere survival, mere enduring on this planet. It means that the great events of our history endure in us. We are a channel for the flow of Israel's memory. Words piercing our ears, we may ignore and even try to drive away; yet they do not cease to ring in our dreams. Our duration is our memory.

Without solidarity with our fathers, the solidarity with our brothers will remain feeble. The vertical unity of Israel is essential to the horizontal unity of *klal Israel*. Affiliation with what is undying in Israel, the acceptance of what was unanimous throughout the ages, the endeavor to integrate the teachings and aspirations of the past into our own thinking will enable us to be creative, to expand, not to imitate or to repeat. Survival of Israel means that we carry on our independent dialogue with the past. Our way of life must remain to some degree intelligible to Isaiah and Rabbi Yochanan ben Zakkai, to Maimonides and the Baal Shem.

We do not consider the past to be a model of perfection. We do not indulge in conserving antiquities. Yet whenever we are faced with the alternative of betraying the past and accepting the dogmas of intellectual fashion, we should recall that neither an individual man nor a single generation by its own power can erect the bridge that leads to Truth. By treating lightly that which has been created throughout the ages, we can easily forfeit what is spiritually reliable. "And ye shall not profane the holy things of the children of Israel, that ye die not" (Numbers 18: 32).

Harassed, pursued with enmity and wrong, our fathers continued to feel joy in being Jews. "Happy are we. How good is our destiny, how pleasant our lot, how beautiful our heritage." What is the source of that feeling?

The quest for immortality is common to all men. To most of them the vexing question points to the future. We Jews think not only of the end but also of the beginning. We have our immortality in the past.

As parts of Israel we are endowed with a very rare, a very precious consciousness, the consciousness that we do not live in a void. We never suffer as so many others do from a fear of roaming about in the emptiness of time. We own the past and are, hence, not afraid of what is to be. We remember where we came from. We were summoned and cannot forget it, as we wind the clock of eternal history. We remember the beginning and believe in an end. We live between two historic poles: Sinai and the Kingdom of God.

Israel exists not in order to be but in order to dream the dream of God. Our faith may be strained, but our destiny is anchored to the ultimate. Who can establish the outcome of our history? Out of the wonder we came and into the wonder we shall return.

BELONGING TO ISRAEL in the Diaspora is in itself a spiritual act. It is utterly inconvenient to be a Jew. The very survival of our people is a *kiddush Hashem*. We live in spite of peril. Our very existence is a refusal to surrender to normalcy, to security and comfort. Experts in assimilation, the Jews could have disappeared even before the names of modern nations were known. Still, we are patient and cherish the will to perpetuate our essence.

We are Jews as we are men and women. The alternative to our existence as Jews is spiritual suicide, disappearance. It is *not* a change into something else. Judaism has allies but no substitute. It is not an analogy of other peoples, creeds, or religions. "It is a people that shall dwell alone, and shall not be reckoned among the nations" (Numbers 23:9). We are the only example of a people who has become identified with a religion. The entire people, not just a select group, has grown to be a symbol.

The people of Israel groaned in distress. Out of Egypt, the land of plentiful food, they were driven into the wilderness. Their souls were dried away; there was nothing at all: no flesh to eat, no water to drink. All they had was a promise: to be led to the land of milk and honey. They were almost ready to stone Moses. "Wherefore hast Thou brought us up out of Egypt, to kill us and our children and our cattle with thirst?" they cried. But after they had worshipped the Golden Calf—when God had decided to detach Himself from His people, not to dwell anymore in their midst but to entrust an angel with the task of leading them out of the wilderness to the Promised Land—Moses exclaimed: "If Thou Thyself dost not go with us, take us not out of the wilderness" (Exodus 33:15). This, perhaps, is the secret of our history: *to choose to remain in the wilderness rather than to be abandoned by Him.*

Israel's experience of God has not evolved from search. Israel did not discover God. Israel was discovered by God. Judaism is *God's quest for man*. The Bible is a record of God's approach to His people. More statements are found in the Bible about God's love for Israel than about Israel's love for God.

We have not chosen God; He has chosen us. There is no concept of a chosen God but there is the idea of a chosen people. The idea of a chosen people does not suggest the preference for a people based upon a discrimination among a number of peoples. We do not say that we are a selected people. The "chosen people" means a people approached and chosen by God. The significance of this term is primarily in relation to God rather than in relation to other peoples. It signifies not a quality inherent in the people but a relationship between the people and God.

OUR LIFE IS BESET with difficulties, yet it is never devoid of meaning. The feeling of futility is absent from our souls. Our existence is not in vain. Its meaning may not be explicable to us, yet even when we do not know *what* it is, we know *that* it is. There is a divine earnestness about our life. This is our dignity. To be invested with dignity means to represent something more than oneself. The gravest sin for a Jew is to forget what he represents.

We are God's stake in human history. We are the dawn and the dusk, the challenge and the test. How strange to be a Jew and to go astray on God's perilous errands. We have been offered as a pattern of worship and as a prey for scorn, but there is more still in our destiny. We carry the gold of God in our souls to forge the gate of the kingdom. The time for the kingdom may be far off, but the task is plain: to retain our share in God in spite of peril and contempt. There is a war to wage against the vulgar, against the glorification of the absurd, a war that is incessant, universal. Loyal to the presence of the ultimate in the common, we may be able to make it clear that man is more than man, that in doing the finite he may perceive the infinite.

1951

The Moment at Sinai

LITTLE IS RECORDED or remembered either about the life and character of Euclid or about the way in which his *Elements* came into being. The laws of his geometry are timeless, and the moment in which they first dawned upon the human mind seems to have no bearing upon their meaning and validity. Time and thought, act and content, author and teaching are not related to each other. In contrast, the words of the Bible are not suspended; they do not dangle in an air of timelessness. Here time and thought, act and content, author and teaching are profoundly related to each other. The Bible reflects its divine as well as its human authorship; expressed in the language of a particular age, it addresses itself to all ages; disclosed in particular acts, its content is everlasting. The word of God is in time and in eternity. It preceded the creation of the world, the beginning of time, and is given to us in the setting of time. It is therefore continually in need of new understanding.

The Bible is not a system of abstract ideas but a record of happenings in history. Indeed, some of the biblical maxims and principles may be found or could have been conceived elsewhere. Without parallel in the world are the events it tells about and the fact of taking these events as the points where God and man meet. Events rather than abstractions of the mind are the basic categories by which the biblical man lives; they are to his existence what axioms are to measuring and weighing. Man does not steal because of a timeless imperative but because he was told by God not to steal; the Sabbath is kept not because it is of timeless value—because it is good to rest—but because God commanded us to rest.

The God of the philosopher is a concept derived from abstract ideas; the God of the prophets is derived from acts and events. The root of Jewish faith is, therefore, not a comprehension of abstract principles but an inner *attachment to those events*; to believe is to remember, not merely to accept the truth of a set of dogmas. Our attachment is expressed by our way of celebrating them, by the weekly reading of the Pentateuch rather than by the recital of a creed. To ignore these events and to pay attention only to what Israel was taught in these events is like tearing out a piece of flesh from a living body.

AN AESTHETIC experience leaves behind the memory of a perception and enjoyment; a prophetic experience leaves behind *the memory of a commitment*, not only of a perception. Revelation was not an act of enjoyment. God spoke and man not only perceived but also accepted the will of God. Revelation lasts a moment, acceptance continues.

This, then, is given to us in Jewish tradition: not an idea of, but a commitment to, revelation. Our task is to examine our attitude to that commitment. Is there any meaning to our being loyal to events that happened more than two thousand years ago?

Biblical revelation must be understood as an *event*, not as a *process*. What is the difference between process and event? A process happens regularly, following a relatively permanent pattern; an event is extraordinary, irregular. A process may be continuous, steady, uniform; events happen, intermittently, occasionally. The term "continuous revelation" is as logical as the term "a round square." Processes are typical; events are unique. A process follows a law; events create a precedent. Nature is made up of processes—organic life, for example, may be described as consisting of the processes of birth, growth, and decay; history consists primarily of events—what lends human, historical character to the life of Pericles or Aristotle are not the organic processes through which he went but the anomalous, surprising and unpredictable acts, achievements, or events which distinguished him from other human beings.

The term "event" is a pseudonym for "mystery." An event is a happening that cannot be reduced to a part of a process. It is something we can neither predict nor fully explain. To speak of events is to imply that there are happenings *in the world* that are beyond the reach of our explanations. What the consciousness of events implies, the belief in revelation claims explicit; namely, that there is a voice of God *in the world*—not in heaven or in any unknown sphere—that pleads with man to do His will.

What do we mean by "the world"? If we mean an ultimate, closed, fixed, and self-sufficient system of phenomena behaving in accord with the laws known to us, then such a concept would exclude the possibility of admitting any super-mundane intervention or penetration by a voice not accounted for by these laws. Indeed, if the world as described by natural science is regarded as the ultimate, then there is no sense in searching for the divine which is by definition the ultimate. How could there be one ultimate within the other?

The claim of the Bible is absurd, unless we are ready to comprehend that the world as scrutinized and depicted by science is but a thin surface of undisclosed depths. Order is only one of the aspects of nature; its reality is a mystery given but not known. Countless relations that determine our life in history are neither known nor predictable. What history does with the laws of nature cannot be expressed by a law of nature.

Among many difficulties is this: There would have to be a leak, a flaw in the perfect mechanism of mind and matter to let the spirit of God penetrate its structure. To assume that the world for all its immense grandeur is a tiny cymbal in the hand of God, on which at certain times only one soul vibrates though all are struck; in other words, to assume that the entire complex of natural laws is transcended by the freedom of God would presuppose the metaphysical understanding that the laws of nature are derived not from a blind necessity but from freedom, that the ultimate is not fate but God. Revelation is not an act of interfering with the normal course of natural events but the act of instilling a new creative moment into the course of natural events.

The chain of causality and of syllogistic reasoning, in which things and thoughts are fettered, is fixed in the space of endless possibilities like the tongue hanging in a silent bell. It is as if all the universe were fixed to a single point. In revelation the bell rings, and words vibrate through the world.

A process has no future. It becomes obsolete and is always replaced by its own effects. We do not ponder about last year's snow. An event, on the other hand, retains its significance even after it has passed; it remains important because and regardless of its effects. Great events, just like great works of art, are significant in themselves. Our interest in them endures long after they are gone.

It is, indeed, one of the peculiar features of human existence that the past does not altogether vanish, that some events of hoary antiquity may hold us in their spell to this very day. Events which are dead, things which are gone, can be neither sensed nor told. Of course, not all events of the past survive or are worthy of survival. Much of the past must be discarded. An act to which God is not a partner is like "chaff before the wind." To the ears of history there is no perfect past. History may be described as an attempt to overcome the dividing line between past and present, as an attempt *to see the past in the present tense.*

Such understanding of time is not peculiar to historians. It is shared unknowingly by all men and is essential to civilized living.

It is a supreme necessity for human beings to live in more or less durable and dependable relations to each other. There is a variety of such relations, as, for example, marriage, friendship, professional organizations, and international conventions. With some exceptions, such as those which grow out of parenthood, social relations are not given naturally; they do not originate in a process; they are initiated in an act or in an event *at a definite moment of time*. These relations can endure only if we remain loyal to the promise we have made or to the agreements into which we have entered. They collapse when our loyalty ceases.

The paradoxical nature of such loyalty is obvious. Why should a person be bound all his life by what he did or said at one single moment of it? And yet civilized men have never failed to admit that their promise had some force to affect their future acts. People believe in the mortality of time; they claim that the past is dead forever. Indeed, the moment in which a promise is made is quickly gone: gone from our calendar, gone from our clocks. And yet we are willing to regard it as if it were immortal. In other words, we accept events that happened at moments gone by as if those moments were still present, as if those events were happening now.

The decisive event in the spiritual history of our people was the act that occurred at Sinai. It had a twofold significance. One in opening up a new relationship of God to man, in engaging Him intimately to the people of Israel; and second in Israel's accepting that relationship, that engagement to God. It was an event in which both God and Israel were partners. God gave His word to the people, and the people gave its word of honor to God.

That word of honor was not given by one generation alone. All generations of Israel were present at Sinai. It was an event that happened at a particular time and also one that happened for all time. "Nor is it with you only that I make this sworn covenant, but with him who is not here with us this day as well as with him who stands here with us this day before the Lord our God" (Deuteronomy 29:13–14).

It was an act of transcending the present, *history in reverse*: thinking of the future in the present tense. It was a prophetic foresight, for to be a prophet is to be ahead of other people's time, is to speak of the future in the present tense.

The contemporaries of Moses succeeded in transcending the present and committed subsequent generations to follow the word of God, because of their ability to think of life in terms of time.

They had no space, they had no land; all they had was time and the promise of a land. Their future depended upon God's loyalty to His own promise, and their loyalty to the prophetic events was the essence of their future.

Some of us may think: How unwise of our ancestors to have committed all future generations to a covenant with God. Yet the life of a historic people is not unlike the life of an individual. As we have seen, there is no civilized living without acts of entering upon social relations, and such acts imply the acceptance of a commitment, the making of a promise, or the taking of a pledge. To enter into a relation with God the people had to accept a commitment.

Socrates taught us that a life without thinking is not worth living. Now, thinking is a noble effort, but the finest thinking may end in futility. In thinking man is left to himself; he may soar into astral space and proclaim the finest thoughts, yet what will be the echo and what its meaning for the soul?

The Bible teaches us that life without commitment is not worth living; that thinking without roots will bear flowers but no fruit. Our commitment is to God, and our roots are in the prophetic events of Israel.

In the light of the Bible, history, then, is not a mere succession of *faits accomplis*, things done and no longer worth arguing against. In the eyes of God nothing is ever lost; the past is always present. Though events do not run according to a predestined plan, and though the ultimate goal can never be expressed in one word or in words at all, we believe that history as a whole has a meaning that transcends that of its parts. We must remember that God is involved in our doings, that meaning is given not only in the timeless but primarily in the timely, in that task given here and now. Great are man's possibilities. For time is but a little lower than eternity, and history is a drama in which both man and God have a stake. In its happenings we hear the voice as well as the silence of God.

The spirit of philosophy has often been characterized as the quest of values, as a search for that which is of greatest value. What is the spirit of the Bible? Its concern is not with the abstract concept of disembodied values, detached from concrete existence. Its concern is with man and his relation to the will of God. The Bible is the quest for the righteous man, for a righteous people. "The Lord looks down from heaven upon the children of man, to see if there are any that act wisely, that seek after God. They have all gone astray, they are all alike corrupt; there is none that does good, no, not one" (Psalms 14:2–3).

To the discerning eye the incidents recorded in the Bible are episodes of one great drama: the quest of God for man, His search of man, and man's flight from Him.

Judaism is a *way of thinking*, not only a way of living. And this is one of its cardinal premises: The source of truth is found not in "a process forever unfolded in the heart of man" but in unique events that happened at a particular moment in history. There are no substitutes for revelation, for prophetic events. Jewish thought is not guided by abstract ideas, by a generalized morality. At Sinai we have learned that spiritual values are not only aspirations in us but a response to a transcendent appeal addressed to us. Greek philosophy is concerned with *values*; Jewish thought dwells on *mitzvot*.

The mere attachment to events does not fully express the essence of Jewish living. Event is a formal category, describing the fact of pure happening. To speak of a pure event, of an event in and of itself, is to speak of an anticipated abstraction that exists nowhere except in the minds of some theologians. The movement of revelation must not be separated from the content of revelation. Loyalty to what was uttered in the event is as essential as the belief in the reality of the event. The event must be fulfilled, not only believed in. Revelation is the beginning, our deeds must continue, our lives must fulfill it.

Yet we must not idolize the moment or the event. The will of God is eternal, transcending all moments, all events, including acts of revelation. The significance of time depends upon what is done in time in relation to His will. The moment at Sinai depends for its fulfillment upon this present moment, upon all moments. Had Israel been disloyal subsequent to Sinai, that great moment would have been deprived of all meaning. The tablets are broken whenever the Golden Calf is called into being. We believe that every hour is endowed with the power to lend meaning to or withhold meaning from all other hours. No moment is as a moment able to bestow ultimate meaning upon all other moments. No moment is the absolute center of history. Time is a circle whose center is everywhere and whose periphery is nowhere.

1953

Existence and Celebration

THIS OCCASION* is indeed an honor for me as well as a source of embarrassment. You all know, I am sure, the ancient Jewish belief that a person who carries out a *mitzvah* brings an angel into being. The angel joins him and escorts him wherever he goes. A person who has done numerous *mitzvot* is surrounded and escorted by a crowd of angels. You, ladies and gentlemen, who are involved in doing such a multitude of *mitzvot*, have brought together in this hall so many celestial beings that I am utterly overwhelmed. I have never spoken to such a vast assembly of angels. How does one deliver an address to such a host? In fact, I feel as if I were in heaven.

You know, Saturday night is the time to tell Hasidic stories. So I will tell you about Rabbi Moshe of Uhely, who had a dream: He was transported to heaven. There he was led to the chamber where the fabulous sages of the Talmud were spending their eternal life. His heart swelled with emotion. When he entered the chamber, he looked around. And what did he see? Long tables like those to be found in a house of learning, and the sages were sitting around the tables, engrossed in study. He felt keen disappointment: Is that all there is to heaven? Suddenly he heard a voice: "You are mistaken. The sages are not in heaven, heaven is in the sages."

The voice, I might say, broke a secret. Our tradition seen from the outside looks like an intricate structure of deeds, of rituals and acts of charity. But a structure may be massive, imposing but also dark. It is the light within those who inhabit the structure that radiates the splendor.

* The occasion was the annual Herbert R. Abeles memorial address given at the thirty-fourth General Assembly of the Council of Jewish Federations and Welfare Funds.

The beauty of the structure reflects the glory within the person. "Eternal life He planted within us." What is within our being here and now is seed and matrix. Heaven is the radiance of the divine, but our ability to share in heaven is the emanation of our own soul.

Having spoken about heaven, let me say a few words about hell. Hell, too, reflects the situation here on earth. And so it came about that relativism had become a major trend in the world above and as a result hell had become an existential experience rather than an independent self-subsistent abode.

Through the application of advanced methods of adjustment techniques and group therapy, the inmates of hell became perfect masochists; in this way torment became a most delightful experience, and the entire infernal establishment, the work of generations of devils and fiends, became a heavenly Las Vegas.

The administration became alarmed. The devil in chief down to the petty orderlies raged with indignation, but they were totally powerless. Because, as is well known, the devil's power extends only to management. The souls are beyond his reach. And so the inmates were having a delightful time.

One young devil, however, an impulsive fellow, could not contain his rage. He lost self-control and rashly detonated the fuse of nuclear explosives. The results were disastrous. Hell was burned down to the ground, and all its inmates became homeless.

A conference was called by the superintendents of hell to discuss a new building program. As you know, there is no scarcity of eminent architects in heaven. From the masters of the pyramids and the Acropolis to Christopher Wren, Frank Lloyd Wright, and Le Corbusier, they all came, including the leading contractors of all times, and were invited to submit bids and blueprints. However, after much research and deliberation, it became clear that the funds required for the construction of a new and modern hell would be exceedingly high and absorb the heavenly budget for many years, and who in heaven has a heart to spend so much money on hell?

So a different proposal was moved and adopted. Paradise or heaven had by that time become very old. Let the inmates of hell move into the old heaven and let us get involved in building a new heaven.

Looking at the past, I see, if I may oversimplify the picture, a mixture of failures and achievements. The failures were due to well-meaning but shortsighted thinking, to a pedestrian ideology; the achievements were due to a magnanimity of spirit, to the heaven in the heart.

There was a fire in our recent history, and much of our intellectual property burned down. Many theories lie in ashes, some of our cherished ideologies are mere apparitions. It is hard to lay the ghosts to rest. What shall we do? To remake society in order to adjust conditions to defunct opinions, to reconstruct an abode of obsolete thoughts, would be exceedingly expensive. Let us better concentrate on a new vision.

To be sure, this is not an easy task. Most people think only once in their lives, usually when they are at college. After that their minds are made up, and their decisions, utterances are endless repetitions of views that have in the meantime become obsolete, outworn, unsound. This applies to politics, scholarship, the arts as well as to social service. Views, just as leaves, are bound to wither, because the world is in flux. But so many of us would rather be faithful to outworn views than to undergo the strain of re-examination and revision. Indeed, intellectual senility sets in long before physical infirmity. A human being must be valued by how many times he was able to see the world from a new perspective.

Jewish charity in America, a golden chapter in our history, has for a long time been imaginative, dynamic, and creative. But human beings that we are, we tend to become unaltered in our habits and to move unnoticeably into a dead end.

A RADICAL CHANGE has taken place in the social structure of our community, in the order of needs, in its spiritual climate. There is a new anxiety, a new expectation in our community. For our communal work not to sink into a state of either irrelevance or obsolescence, let us examine the premises, requirements, and goals of our situation today.

Since the earliest day of Jewish settlement in the New World, a basic premise and motivation for Jewish welfare programs was to prevent our people from becoming dependent upon or a burden to the general Christian community. "It would have been unthinkable for the Jewish group to countenance that any Jew be forced to appeal to outsiders, and particularly to the state or to other church groups. This sentiment was to persist long after the separation of church and state and the availability of governmental assistance to all the population on a nonsectarian basis.

"Over the whole of the nineteenth and into the twentieth centuries, Jewish philanthropists were to express satisfaction and pride that there were few Jews to be found on the public charity rolls or in the public almshouses."[1]

Looking at the past, I see, if I may repeat what I said before, a medley of failures and achievements. The failures were due to those whose facility for reading the signs of our destiny was limited to Braille; the achievements were due to those who knew how to view the present in the future tense, who resisted obliteration of our script, demanding the use of sight, love, and uncommon sense.

However, with the development of the welfare state, social security, unemployment insurance, anti-poverty programs, Medicare, etc., and the complete integration of the Jew in American society, that old premise is becoming obsolescent. Some of the needs we served in the past are now cared for by federal and local agencies. What Jewish charities are offering now, impressive and important as it is in quality, is in substance auxiliary or secondary to what the state is doing.

Another aspect in need of revision is *isolationism of charity*. An old Jewish principle proclaims: The world stands on three pillars: on learning, on worship, and on charity.[2] We are not going to invite a friend to sit on a tripod, a stool designed to have three legs, when two legs are missing.

In the face of the economic misery of immigrants, when saving human lives was a crying emergency, concentration on material aid was an act of supreme wisdom. However, our situation today is a spiritual emergency crying for moral and intellectual relief.

Judaism does not live by charity alone, just as man does not live by bread alone. Generosity and care for human life as exemplified in the work of Jewish charity do not grow in the wilderness of soul; they thrive in a climate of rich understandings and ancient commitments. Deterioration in climate, fading of these understandings, vanishing of these commitments—and Jewish charity will wither. What happened to the Jewish labor unions may happen to our welfare organizations. They will be taken over by other minority groups.

A GENERATION AGO, the requirement was to integrate the immigrants into American society. Today the problem is not how to adjust our people to the manners and habits of society but how to keep them from vanishing in the abyss of drabness and vulgarity, how to resist being committed to the nationwide prisons of triviality, how to cultivate the Jewish art of sensing the glory through acts of daily celebration. Integration has been achieved; it is Jewish integrity we must strive for. We have succeeded in receptivity; we must prepare for the test of creativity.

The attitude of the Christian community in America has undergone a radical change. Instead of hostility there is respect and expectation, belief that Jews have a message to convey, significant insights which other people might share.

This expectation is a challenge to the Jewish community, demanding responsible attention. The primary issue is not defense but wisdom, self-understanding, communication.

OUR TRADITION has never assumed that the qualities of being a Jew are gained with ease and sustained without strain. Did not Moses experience how difficult it was to impart wisdom, to nurture faithfulness? We could have made a vital contribution to America by teaching how serious the business of living is, and how continuous, thorough, and unending the process of educating is. Instead, we surrendered our insights and adopted for our own selves the assumption that the good life is easygoing.

We all pay heavily for earlier disregard of the power of evil, of the essentially unredeemed nature of society, of the dangerous tensions of being human. I was unprepared for the shock of the sudden realization that progress is not automatic, that it may involve climbing a ladder of absurdities. Modern man's discovery of the fundamental aloneness and solitude in a universe indifferent to his fate is due to an expectation that it was in the universe where care for what is ultimately precious was to be found. He now suffers from the collapse of naïve self-deception and oversimplification.

Our era marks the end of simplification, the end of personal exclusiveness, the end of self-defense through aloofness, the end of a sense of security. We find ourselves in a situation in which the distinction between the affluent and the indigent, between the successful and the shlemiels, is becoming obsolete. In the realm of character, in the depth of the soul, in groping for a way out of a creeping sense of futility, in moments of being alone and taking account of our lives, we are all indigent and in need of assistance.

The community has changed, but our image of the community has not been sufficiently revised. The needs, the woes have been radically altered, but our conception of need is unfading. There is starvation in the hearts, but the mind lies fallow.

What is the image of the Jew we have been seeking to serve? It is a man with appendicitis who needs a hospital, who is nonsectarian and does not care for *kashruth*, or the graduate of a medical school who seeks a position as an internist. By now most of us can rely on health insurance for taking care of our own medical bills, and hospitals do not indulge in discrimination. However, there are deeply personal needs that call for help. It is on the level of intimate concern, in matters of conscience, where we all are disturbed, very much dependent on community agencies.

The crisis is deeper, the intellectual standards are higher. The average Jew is not an immigrant who has to spend his evenings in sweatshops and has no time to read a book. Ideologies which fall below the intellectual standards appropriate for our generation sound outlandish, if not grotesque. Let us discard the old weapons.

In September 1939, when Poland was attacked by German tanks, paratroopers, and Stukas, the Polish Army went forth to challenge the German enemy with horses, the splendid Polish cavalry.

The Jew may die of ignorance, of emptiness of heart. It is not a vision of a greater idea that plays havoc in our midst. The Jew may vanish not knowing why. A whale, the monster of absurdity, is swallowing up our people, consuming memory and conscience, all the pledges of our soul. We are docile, slaying ourselves in oblivion, having gone through anesthetization in our homes and country clubs.

OUR INSTITUTIONS maintain too many beauty parlors. Our people need a language and we offer them cosmetics. Our people need style, learning, conviction, exaltation, and we are concerned about not being admitted to certain country clubs.

To paraphrase the words of the prophet Isaiah: What to me is the multitude of your organizations? says the Lord. I have had enough of your vicarious loyalty. Bring no more vain offerings; generosity without wisdom is an evasion, an alibi for conscience.

We are ingenious in fund-raising, which is good; we are shipwrecked in raising our children, which is tragic. We give of our wealth to many good causes; we lose our substance in abandoning our children to fetishism. I wish we would give priority to teaching and inspiring our children to live as Jews.

We may claim to be a success,, but in the eyes of Jewish history we may be regarded as a failure.

THE PHILANTHROPIST ought to learn that by his efforts he may be continually helping to defeat the very aims which he has in mind. The social worker must not become a cog in a welfare machine inducing illusions.

The peculiar difficulty is the unique complexity and precariousness of Jewish existence. The will to live is no match against the adversity and pressure to disappear. Indeed, a considerable section of our community is dissolving slowly, mindlessly, casually. In addition there are those whose basic view of Jewish existence is a *theory of negativity* and who openly maintain that Judaism is not worth living; it is not a culture but a malaise. These people are actively engaged in smashing Jewish commitment.

"The American way of death" conceals the fact of death. Is it not possible that some of our institutions and manners operate in the style of Forest Lawn Cemetery in Los Angeles?

A CAMPAIGN of spiritual liquidation is going on in many places, smirching our souls, degrading our dignity, decimating our legacy, and there is no Anti-Defamation League to fight against Jewish prejudice and self-hatred.

We finance, support, and acclaim those who continue to denigrate the reverence and the waiting, adding fuel to the autos-da-fé in which treasures of the soul are consumed by the fires of self-hatred.

Prior to 1945 many of us thought that assimilation of the Jews would be a calm, quiet, peaceful process. We have since discovered that assimilation or alienation is a rage, a burst of anger, an inflammation of the mind. Wellsprings of defamation are found not alone among the Gentiles.

There is a type of Jew who feels apart from his people, and whose essential attitude is derision; to him strength means denigration of his own people.

It is easier to detest than to revere. There are in our community witty men without learning who continue to carry on an obsolete rebellion against the ghetto. The virus of contempt is very much alive in many hearts, powerful enough to obscure, even to arrest the development of a sense of wonder and appreciation. A perception of the grandeur of Judaism may be conceived and even sustained for a while, yet self-hatred, constantly at work, carries with it a power of contraception, frustrating and aborting any possible sense of openness to Judaism. The effect is immunity to the claim and vision of our tradition.

HOW DO I RELATE myself to the community of which I am a part? A relationship distorted breeds anxiety, resentment, hostility. A relationship restored comes about through understanding, shared meaning, love.

A person cannot honor that which does not affect his finer sensibilities, his conscience, his sense of meaning.

Every one of us gives birth to Judaism in the shape of his existence. Those of us who can no longer nourish, mother, or bear it, who feel not one with it, seek to wrest free from it. In such people's lives Judaism is a miscarriage, with all the anguish, labor, and pain that accompany such an experience.

Fortunately the present Jewish generation contains forces of both alienation and appreciation, both reverence and hostility, both escape and involvement. The pot is boiling over, much is spilled and lost. Yet much of it is still there.

A Jew cannot maintain a relationship of detachment to his situation. He either loves or hates his being a Jew. Judaism is either esteemed or despised, detested or revered, honored or dishonored.

Judaism is not a theory, a no-man's-land. It cannot be understood through a telescope. The only way to understand it is through involvement and intellectual engagement.

To disregard it is to discard it, to disclaim it. Is it not true that ignorance breeds contempt?

For us assembled here there can be neither escape nor neutrality where such responsibilities lie. We are in the front lines. We must all realize that prejudice and resentment come more easily to man than insight and appreciation. Love is health, and truth is the only serum; yet truth is a product of learning, and love is scarce.

In seeking to understand our situation in the light of our own history, the problem challenging us most deeply is: *What is our answer to Auschwitz?*

Hitler had all of us in mind: the Jews of St. Louis no less than the Jews of Salonika. Bergen-Belsen, Dachau, Treblinka—I could have been there, too. What is our answer?

The answer is not to be given in a phrase; the answer must fill our soul with a conviction: holy, holy is the word Jew. Our task is to seek how to think, how to live in a way compatible with such grandeur.

There are two Hebrew names for the Jew: *Yehudi*, the first three letters of which are the first three letters of the Ineffable Name, and *Israel*, the end of which, *el*, means God.

What is our answer?

Gratitude for the sublime calling of being a Jew, seeking to illumine the mysterious meaning of that calling. Such seeking cannot be done by each of us going alone.

We are still at the beginning of history. There is so much more in our souls than we have been able to utter. What providence holds in store for us surpasses the contributions made by our people in the ages bygone. Had the generation of the Maccabees surrendered to Hellenism, Judaism would have remained a footnote in history books, and how different the history of humanity would have been.

What is Jewish existence? The experience of a spiritual embrace, the sense of being included in the meaning of mystery, defiance of drabness, being a branch of a tree of life, moving, swaying, and staying on, a fragrance of eternity, saying and concealing, witnessing unawares.

There is a legacy to convey, an excellence of the mind, a sensitivity to the demand for sanctification of time, for quiet exaltation.

What is it that brings us together at this conference? What is it that we have in common?

IT IS A commitment to a high purpose that we have in common, a love, a realization however dim that we are partners, protagonists in a most noble and necessary enterprise, in which our receiving is so much greater than our giving.

The enterprise of our welfare organization is noble because we seek to keep our people strong, to enable our people to discover its powerful legacy, its sacred dignity; to enable our people not to throw away some of the world's most precious insights.

It is noble because the light we seek to maintain in our own existence is powerful enough to enrich and to radiate light to other peoples.

It is a necessary enterprise because the predicament of contemporary man is such that it is more than ever our duty to recover the intellectual relevance of our tradition.

My essential suggestion is that the greatest good we can effect for the greatest number of people today is *intellectual aid*.

FEW PEOPLE will fail in entertaining deep respect for the generosity of our community expressed through our welfare agencies. What I pray for is that we may prove worthy of respect for *wisdom* in applying our generosity.

False modesty, the assumption that all our community can do is offer physical relief, is an affront to our dignity.

Compassion is strong and alive, the sense of dignity murky and confused. Dignity is in the awareness of what I, as an individual, stand for, in the awareness that I represent a degree of greatness, a legacy, a reality much larger than my own being. The substance of such dignity is knowledge, involvement in sacred drama, reverence, the intuition of a high purpose.

Successful in many endeavors, we have been derelict in the most important area of Jewish responsibility: in education, in the task of conveying Torah to our children. We have abdicated our role as fathers. Every father's dream is to be a "regular guy" rather than the bearer of a tradition, a person to be held in esteem by his child—and home is becoming a place to run away from.

WE HAVE surrendered our responsibility to shape the inner life of our children to others. In a speech given at a students' homecoming service, a young lady said about her father: "He has given me a car, a trip to Europe, clothes and a bank account, but not what I craved most: *guidance*." "The fathers have eaten sour grapes, and the children's teeth are set on edge."

Our young people are bewildered, perplexed about the meaning of being human, about the meaning of being a Jew. There is a waiting for meaning, but meaning is kept a well-guarded secret. We have a wonderful generation of young people. They are alert, sensitive, eager for understanding, capable of appreciation. It is we who fail them. Instead of conveying the intellectual splendor and the deep humanity of our heritage, we offer them infantile conceptions, stereotypes, clichés.

Many of us are wise about many things, and ignorant about our own selves. To be sure, "It is splendid for the wise man to know everything, but the next best thing is not to be ignorant of himself" (Plato).

A Jewish nonsectarian is a non sequitur, a contradiction in terms. How can one expect a Jew devoid of his legacy to understand his identity?

The dynamics of our existence is not *perpetuum mobile* but continuous creation, continuous cultivation of an affinity for those inspired by the God of Abraham.

I KNOW THAT our social workers are involved in an eager search for new methods; what I plead for is a search for Jewish authenticity. The test of integrity is a sense of intellectual fascination with being a Jew. Our failure is in not being disturbed, hurt, upset over the decline of authenticity in depth, over the possibility that we may all become casualties of complacency and happiness.

Non-Jews seem to have a greater appreciation of Judaism than Jews. Numerous scholars on university faculties frequently express painful regret that Jewish students are devoid of knowledge about the oldest cultural and religious tradition in the world.

I grew up in an awareness that Jews are running away from Judaism. This was true in Poland, where I was born; in Germany, where I studied; and in America, where I found a home in 1940. In those years spiritual problems were considered irrelevant, but since 1945 I have been surprised by an extraordinary change. People do not run away anymore but, on the contrary, indicate sensitivity to concern for spiritual orientation.

This is therefore a great hour in Jewish history, and one that probably occurs only once in two hundred years. In this hour we, the living, are "the people of Israel." The tasks, begun by Abraham, Moses, Amos, and continued by their descendants, are now entrusted to us. We are either the last Jews or those who will hand over the entire past to generations to come. We will either forfeit or enrich the legacy of ages.

We all remember the days when being reminded of one's Jewish background would cause embarrassment, when a lecture in which Jewish thought emerged as relevant was resented, when quoting from the Bible was a sign of being obscurantist or reactionary.

What amazes me is to discover that together with a decline of affection for being a Jew on the part of our older people we witness a rise of appreciation on the part of many of our younger people.

OUR YOUNG people are disturbed at parents who are spiritually insolvent. They seek direction, affirmation; they reject complacency and empty generosity.

There is a waiting in many homes, in many hearts, for guidance, instruction, illumination, a waiting which is often intense, pressing, nationwide. So many are heartsick at the spiritual failure of our community.

Why is little aid given to the people in moral distress, in intellectual perplexity and agony? We are about to build a Mount Sinai School of Medicine; what about a Mount Sinai School of Judaism? One gets the impression that Mount Sinai never goes with Torah.

We care for the mentally retarded; what about the spiritually retarded? We extend relief to the financially poor; what about those who are intellectually confused? The revival of religious concern has caught our institutions by surprise, unprepared, and hardly able to convert concern into commitment, groping into study, vagueness into clarity.

It is our duty to do our utmost in restoring physical health, but it is sinful to ignore the most essential requirement of being a person: the sense of significant being. Our community's need of thought, understanding, intellectual expansion is profound and urgent. If not satisfied, we will all be bankrupt.

In Jewish social service, the largest task to the largest number is to save us from guilt in squandering the greatest heritage in the world, from failure to convey inner power, love, and understanding to children and youth.

JUDAISM DOES NOT always simplify itself in order to accommodate fashion or society. It must maintain immunity from stereotypes and oversimplification. It demands nonconformity with what prevails in the marketplace, the courage to be different, depth of insight in a world where inane and meretricious values are acclaimed through the loudspeakers. The atmosphere in which we live, far from being a vacuum, is filled with negation of what we stand for. The home is no longer a castle; its doors are open to commercialism, cynicism, and vulgarity. This is why home-made Judaism is not enough. Many of us are distressed. Parents' labor so often turns out to be a Sisyphean effort. Let us remember that the Jewish future is being shaped on the college campuses, not in old folks' homes or hospitals.

To maintain devotion to Judaism, to succeed in the effort to convey my appreciation to my child, I need a community, as we all do. In this emergency we call upon the Federation: Help us! Let us create an atmosphere of learning, a climate of reverence.

Such an atmosphere will come into being when the individual Jew ceases to be a spectator and becomes a partisan and partner. As spectators we are disdainful, sneering; as partisans we are responsible, sensitive to what the moment demands, and convinced that the sense of meaning grows not by spectacular acts but by quiet deeds, day by day.

Such an atmosphere will be created when ignorance and distortion of Jews are replaced by a return to reverence, by involvement in learning.

We must create a climate of elucidation, of pronouncing our people's waiting for meaning, by discovering and teaching the intellectual relevance of Judaism, by fostering *reverence for learning and the learning of reverence.*

We as a community are committed to the principle that learning is our daily bread, compassion the essential sign of being human. We are a community that maintains that a table in the home is an altar, that we must start every day with an act of celebration, that the conclusion of a day is in a moment of self-examination.

We need a revolution in Jewish life. Institutions seem to thrive in an anti-intellectual climate, to thrive on evasion of educational and spiritual issues of existence. Criticism of institution is taboo. The dogma of institutional infallibility seems to be tacitly accepted.

THERE ARE TWO WORDS I should like to strike from our vocabulary: "surveys" and "survival."

Our community is in spiritual distress, and some of our organizations are often too concerned with digits. Our disease is loss of character and commitment, and the cure of our plight cannot be derived from charts and diagrams.

When surveys become an obsession, a sacred cow that eats up vast energies, they may yield confirmation of little more than what we know in advance. It is in such a spirit that undertaking surveys is an evasion of creative action, a splendid illusion.

To ascertain facts one must employ a method appropriate to the facts. Some facts are subject to measurement, while others are immeasurable. The number of children receiving no Jewish education may be established by statistics, while the alarming inadequacy of most of Jewish education as well as the bankruptcy of understanding thus revealed—the two issues which ought to occupy us intensely—require a different perspective of thinking. The delusive clarity of detached facts has prevented us from engaging in seeking ways of dealing with the meaning of the facts.

Sociological descriptions are helpful in expanding awareness of the facts. They should not be expected to unlock resources of creative imagination by which to modify the facts.

In contrast to those who call for *amor fati*, we call for *ahavath Israel*, for joy in being what we are, love for those who share our commitments.

How did Mendele translate auto-emancipation into Yiddish? A *sgule tsu yidishe tsores*. How should we translate Jewish philanthropy into good Yiddish? Philanthropy comes from *phileo*, love, and *anthropos*, man. Jewish philanthropy is *ahavath Israel*.

Yet love must be fostered. It is the result of perceptions of beauty, of moments of appreciation. Our task is to make such perceptions, such moments possible.

Preoccupation with the notion of survival is the result of utilitarian philosophy according to which Judaism is a means to an end, a device or contrivance to preserve the Jewish people. Such a doctrine is built upon the myth that all creativity is the product of the biological will to live. However, a doctrine that regards Judaism as a contrivance is itself a contrivance and can therefore not entertain the claim to be true.

The significance of Judaism does not lie in its being conducive to the mere survival of a particular people but rather in its being a source of spiritual wealth, a source of meaning relevant to all peoples.

SURVIVAL, mere continuation of being, is a condition man has in common with animals. Characteristic of humanity is concern for what to do with survival. "To be or not to be" is not the question. Of course, we all are anxious to be. How to be and how not to be is the question. The true problem is *how* to survive, what sort of future to strive for. It is the power and vision of time to come that determine time present. What is important is attaining certainty of being worthy of survival.

Survival is not an impersonal process, it requires above all a subject that survives, a self worthy of survival. Historic continuity is a mental, not only a physical, condition and cannot be conceived apart from a self that is both involved in continuity as well as making it possible. Since the self of our community is becoming increasingly stagnant, dormant, it is more urgent to be concerned about *revival* than about *survival*.

It is more productive to be preoccupied with enhancing the present than to nurture fears about the future.

According to a medieval custom, called *ikkuv ha-keriah*, any individual who had just grievance against another one and failed to gain attention of the authorities had the right to interrupt the Sabbath morning service in the synagogue, to prevent and to delay the reading of the Torah, until the case was heard publicly and justice rendered.

I often feel as if the hour had come for a moratorium on testimonial dinners and building programs, for an *ikkuv ha-keriah*, for a suspension of some of our activities and campaigns in order to gain time for reflection and self-examination, to stand still and to reflect!

I do not believe that repression is America's major problem, as some writers maintain. America's problem number one is the *self-profanation of man*, the perversion of the eighteenth-century conception of the pursuit of happiness, the *loss of reverence*, the *liquidation of enthusiasm* for the attainment of transcendent goals.

Our conception of happiness is based on an oversimplification of man.

Happiness is not a synonym for *self-satisfaction*, complacency, or smugness. Self-satisfaction breeds futility and despair. All that is creative in man stems from a seed of *endless discontent*. New insight begins when satisfaction comes to an end, when all that has been seen, said, or done looks like a distortion.

The aim is the maintenance and fanning of a discontent with our aspirations and achievements, the maintenance and fanning of a craving that knows no satisfaction. Man's true fulfillment depends upon communion with that which transcends him.

The cure of the soul begins with a *sense of embarrassment*, embarrassment at our pettiness, prejudices, envy, and conceit; embarrassment at the profanation of life. A world that is full of grandeur has been converted into a carnival.

Man is too great to be fed upon uninspiring pedestrian ideals. We have adjusted ideals to our stature, instead of attempting to rise to the level of ideals. The ceiling of aspiration is too low: a car, color television, and life insurance. Modern man has royal power and plebeian ideals.

To the ear of a Jew who is attuned to the voice of the prophets, some of the celebrated theories of our age sound like intellectual slang. Over against all pedestrian conceptions, the Bible speaks of life in the *language of grandeur*, with a vision of sublime goals that surpasses the glamour of all empires, the summit of all theories.

Judaism is *spiritual effrontery*. The tragedy is that there is disease and starvation all over the world, and we are building more luxurious hotels in Las Vegas. Social dynamics is no substitute for moral responsibility.

The most urgent task is to destroy the myth that accumulation of wealth and the achievement of comfort are the chief vocations of man. How can adjustment to society be an inspiration to our youth if that society persists in squandering the material resources of the world on luxuries in a world where more than a billion people go to bed hungry every night? How can we speak of reverence for man and of the belief that all men are created equal without repenting the way we promote the vulgarization of existence?

WHAT THE world needs is a sense of ultimate embarrassment. Modern man has the power and the wealth to overcome poverty and disease, but he has no wisdom to overcome suspicion. We are guilty of misunderstanding the meaning of existence; we are guilty of distorting our goals and misrepresenting our souls. We are better than our assertions, more intricate, more profound than our theories maintain. *Our thinking is behind the times.* In our hands it became a platitude, adapted to the intellectual recession of the modern era. It has become an amenity of comfortable living, dividends without investment, with religious institutions—regarded as public kitchens—offering peace of mind free of charge. The demands are modest, and pretentious the rewards.

Nonchalantly we have gambled away the sublime insights of Jewish piety, the noble demands of Jewish law and observance.

This is the vocation of the few to be the witness *par excellence,* to insist that *man without God is a torso,* that life involves not only the satisfaction of selfish needs, but also the satisfaction of a divine need for human justice and nobility.

The Western world is a world committed to the God of Abraham. What is at stake in this grave hour of history is the right understanding of that commitment. It is no accident that, in a considerable part of the world, the Bible has been eliminated.

The tyranny of conformity tends to deprive man of his inner identity, of his ability to stand still in the midst of flux, to remain a person in the midst of a crowd. Thus the threat to modern man is loss of personhood, vanishing of identity, sinking into anonymity, not knowing who he is, whence he comes and where he goes.

Being a Jew makes anonymity impossible. A Jew represents, stands for, proclaims—even in spite of himself. The world never sees the Jew as an individual but rather as a representative of a whole tradition, of a whole people. A Jew is never alone.

Who is a Jew? A person whose integrity decays when unmoved by the knowledge of wrong done to other people.

Who is a Jew? A person in travail with God's dreams and designs; a person to whom God is a challenge, not an abstraction. He is called upon to know of God's stake in history; to be involved in the sanctification of time and in building of the Holy Land; to cultivate passion for justice and the ability to experience the arrival of Friday evening as an event.

Who is a Jew? A person who knows how to recall and to keep alive what is holy in our people's past and to cherish the promise and the vision of redemption in the days to come.

Who is a Jew? A witness to the transcendence and presence of God; a person in whose life Abraham would feel at home, a person for whom Rabbi Akiba would feel deep affinity, a person of whom the Jewish martyrs of all ages would not be ashamed.

Hasidism as a

New Approach to Torah

HASIDISM REPRESENTS a great enigma. It is first of all the enigma of the impact of one great man, the Besht. Of course many attempts have been made to explain this enigma. Here is one man who in a very short time, within twenty years, was able to capture the majority of the Jewish people and to keep them under his spell for generations. What was there about him that was not to be found in other great Jewish personalities like Maimonides or even Reb Isaac Luria or Rebbe Akiva? This one man in a little town brought into the world a new spirit, and that spirit captured without the use of modern media a major part of the Jewish people within twenty years. How do you explain that?

The answers given are partly sociological, partly historical; I believe there is also a Hasidic answer to this Hasidic riddle. That answer was given by Rebbe Hirsh of Zydathov, a very great personality in his own right, who told the following story: In Poland in those days, namely in the eighteenth century, a king was nominated, as a matter not of heritage but of election. Noblemen would get together from all over the country and they would elect a king. The king could also be a citizen of a foreign country, so naturally whenever a king died and there was a possibility of election, many princes and aristocrats from all over Europe would vie for that honor. And this is what happened. The king passed away and immediately various princes eager to become King of Poland would send their representatives to Poland, their public-relations men, if I may say so, each one trying to sing the praises of his candidate. He is the wisest of all men, one representative said. He's the wealthiest, said another; the kindest, said a third. This went on for days, and no decision was reached. Finally one representative decided he would take his candidate, the prince himself, bring him to the people, and say, Here he is, look at him, see how grand he is. And that man was elected.

Many Jews talked about God, but it was the Besht who brought God to the people. This in a way is an answer, perhaps the best answer to the question of how to explain the unbelievable impact in such a short time of this great man. What was his contribution?

This contribution was that he brought about renewal of man in Judaism. The Jewish people is not the same since the days of the Besht. It is a new people. Other personalities contributed great works, they left behind impressive achievements; the Besht left behind a new people. Other people produced new ideas, new doctrines; the Besht opened sources of creativity, which fortunately to some degree are still open today. He brought a new light into Jewish life.

Many aspects of Jewish existence which seemed petrified he suddenly made almost ethereal, or at least liquid; he liquefied them. To many Jews the mere fulfillment of regulations was as the essence of Jewish living. Along came the Besht and taught that Jewish life is an occasion for exaltation. Observance of the Law is the basis, but exaltation through observance is the goal.

In other words, the greatness of the Besht was that he was the beginning of a long series of events, a long series of moments of inspiration. And he holds us in his spell to this very day. He who really wants to be uplifted by communing with a great person whom he can love without reservation, who can enrich his thought and imagination without end, that person can meditate about the life and being of the Besht. There has been no one like him during the last thousand years.

But I must also say that it is a tragedy that this great movement is essentially an oral movement, one that cannot be preserved in written form. It is ultimately a living movement. It is not contained fully in any of its books. It is more than can enter books. There are shades of meaning in uttering a Hasidic idea, a certain accent, a spirit, even a manner of speaking which is vital to the substance of speaking in Hasidic law.

HASIDISM IS NOT given to be an object of lecturing. One can be a witness to it but one cannot lecture about it. In other words, Hasidism has a very personal dimension, it is a very personal experience, it cannot be made the theme of a report. What does it mean to be a Hasid? To be a Hasid is to be in love, to be in love with God and with what God has created. Once you are in love you are a different human being. Do you criticize a person you are in love with? The Hasidim are in love with God. Even, strangely enough, in love with the world. The history of Hasidism is a history of being in love with God's story. That is the history of Hasidism. Indeed, he who has never been in love will not understand and may consider it a madness. That is why there is so much opposition to Hasidism, more than we are willing to admit.

In the eyes of those who are Hasidim, those who oppose it deserve pity more than anything else. Let me give an example. Someone came to a rabbi to complain that certain people tell Hasidic tales, Hasidic stories, and in this way they take time away from the study of Torah, which is a *mitzvah*. "Is it not so that he who interrupts his study of Torah eventually goes to hell, according to the Talmud? How can you tolerate Hasidim, who do not study all the time?" So the rabbi answered this man. "You know, the Hasidim are not afraid of going to hell, because they are building a new *gan eden*, a new heaven." "What is wrong with the old *gan eden*?" "The old *gan eden* isn't enough for Hasidim. The Talmud asks, What is *gan eden*? *Gan eden* is the place where Jews sit in the halls of the glory and luster of the divine. But to the Hasidim the luster of the divine is not enough. They would like to be attached to God Himself, not just to His luster, so that all paradise and all *gan eden* are not enough." And that *gan eden* experience is very essential.

MOST THINGS that have been said about Hasidism, Hasidism is not. To an average superficial writer, Hasidism means to be gay, to drink a little vodka. Hasidism is not that. It is true that it is important to understand that the Hasidim would drink a *L'-chaim* from time to time. But how did they understand it? He who has never been present at the scene, at the moment that Hasidim drink vodka, cannot know what it means to be holding the essence of his world. Vodka in Hebrew is called *yayinsaraf;* *bruandt* wine in German. And there are two ways of purification, said a great rebbe. One is with water, the ancient Jewish act of purification, submerging in the water. But there is a finer way of purification, because the immersion in water does not last forever. There is a kind of purification that is more lasting—to be on fire. We can clean metal in fire. To Hasidim, to drink *yayinsaraf* is to be on fire, to remember that God is a consuming fire. It is not just gaiety, it is great discipline living in a number of extraordinary relations, commitments, entertaining a number of basic convictions. It is above all the cultivation of the inner life, a complex of sensibilities.

Hasidism must be understood in terms of great insights and teachings. It is equally important to remember that Hasidism is preserved not only in the form of teachings but also in the language of stories, tales. Third, Hasidism can be properly understood only if one realizes its leaning upon classics, on interpretations of biblical or rabbinic texts. The most important aspect of Hasidism is that it lives in personalities; without the charismatic person there is no teaching of Hasidism.

IN ADDITION, there are many phases of Hasidism. It was first an intellectual revolution. To understand the context of its origin we have to study the documents preserved at the beginning of the eighteenth century. There was a tremendous fascination in those days for what we call *pilpul*, with what may be called sharpness, intellectual wit in the study of the Torah and Talmud. It represented a desire to sublimate feelings into thoughts, to transpose dreams into syllogisms. The sages expressed their grief in formulating keen theoretical difficulties and their joy in finding solutions to a contradiction of a disagreement between Maimonides, who lived in the twelfth century, and Rabbi Shlomo Aderetz, who lived in the thirteenth century. They had to speak to one another, there was no division in time, they were all together. And there were sharp challenges all the time. That was how they sublimated their entire existence. It was sharp but dry as dust, with all other aspects of existence ignored. For example, there were many books published. I myself know of thirty or forty anthologies. What was their favorite topic in those days? *Pshetlach. Pshetl* is the opposite of *pschat*, although the word *pshetl* is derived from *pschat*. *Pschat* means the literal simple meaning. *Pshetl* says the opposite: there is no literal meaning, there is always something behind it. In other words, when I say, "Give me a piece of bread," I don't really mean a piece of bread. I mean to answer a difficult passage in a commentary written in the twelfth century, which is noted by an authority of the fifteenth century. *Pshetl* is always an attempt to find the dialectics in the most simple things, and this is what the talmudic scholars used to love.

And when a preacher came to deliver a sermon, would he speak about daily human problems? No, he spoke of the terrible excitement about the fact that Laban, Jacob's father-in-law, did not treat Jacob well. Why didn't he treat Jacob well? Because he had a serious disagreement with him about an obscure subtle issue in Jewish criminal law. Since Jewish criminal law is very complicated, there are fifty-five possibilities of explaining it, and this is what caused the disagreement. Actually, Laban and Jacob disagreed the same way as did Abbaye and Rava in the third century. But it was dry like dust. Anybody who has gone through such an education would know what it means. What is left is astuteness, acumen. It is always syllogisms on top of syllogisms, a pyramid on top of three other pyramids. You're always walking from one roof to another. You don't just walk straight, you're always jumping, leaping; there's no straight thinking. The Jews loved this Talmudic study, but the soul was not rested. There was very little for the heart. It was always so dry, so remote from existence, without the slightest awareness that there was also an inner life in human problems. There were no human problems, only legal problems.

CAME THE BAAL SHEM and changed the whole thing. He introduced a kind of thinking that is concerned with personal, intimate problems of religion and life. Some of these problems had smaller problems. Hasidism's major revolution was the opposition to what was generally accepted in Judaism—namely, that study is an answer to all problems. Study was considered more important than any other observance, certainly more important than prayer. Prayer was on the decline. It lost its vitality, it was deprived of spontaneity. One of the first tasks the Baal Shem faced was to bring about the resurrection of prayer. When he and his disciples went to a town, they would not just deliver a sermon about observance; they would stand and pray, thus setting an example of how to pray. To this day the Baal Shem remains one of the greatest masters of prayer in Jewish history.

Why was the study of Torah considered more important than prayer? Because, as mentioned in a beautiful book written in the Middle Ages, what is the difference between Torah and prayer? When you study Torah God speaks to you; when you pray you speak to God. Naturally, the study of Torah must be regarded as more important than prayer. Came the Baal Shem and exalted the role of prayer. The marvel of man's uttering words in the presence of God is tremendously important and vital. By stressing the mystery of uttering words, he projected new insights into the importance of speech, of words. The doctrine of prayer and the doctrine of study as developed by the Baal Shem are based upon the discovery of the meaning and the reality of a spoken word. Suddenly a word became greater than the person. And he who does not know that a word is greater than a person does not even know how to pray or how to read the Torah.

What is the meaning of studying Torah? the Baal Shem asks. You have to study it in a new way. Learning is a means to an end. To study Torah, he says, means to sense that which transcends Torah. When God created heaven and earth He created also a light, the infinite light, the marvelous light that is absolute, ever warming, penetrating, eternal. But because of the failure of creation and the decline of goodness in the world, God hid that eternal light. Where did He hide it? He hid it in the words of the Torah. When the Besht read the words of the Torah, he was able to sense that light. He was able through that light to see everything that goes on in the world and beyond this world. Study, he also insisted, is a means to an end, not an end itself.

What is the means, what is the end? The end is a person himself. There is a famous story of how a man came to a rebbe for the first time in his life. He was already advanced in years, he was almost thirty years old. "It's the first time I come to a rebbe," the man said. The rebbe asked him, "What did you do all your life?" He answered, "I have gone through the Talmud four times." "How much of the Talmud has gone through you?" asked the rebbe.

The Baal Shem made men very great, he saw men in a new light. He took men seriously, very seriously. And therefore he had an extraordinary appreciation of the nature of the Jew. He maintained that every Jew could be a sanctuary. The ancient Temple in Jerusalem could be rebuilt by every Jew within his own soul. And out of this inner sanctuary would grow the incense, the smoke of the incense, in the rich heaven. Every Jew could rebuild the Temple and establish its altars.

This is why so much is at stake in human existence. The Baal Shem took the tradition of Jewish learning, the Talmud and Kabbalah, mysticism, and gave it a new luster and a new meaning. He was very much influenced by and adopted quite a number of ideas from Jewish mysticism, kabbalah, but he gave them a new slant, a new accent. To use a Hasidic term, he tried to consolidate the abstractions and philosophic reflections of Jewish mysticism into what he called a way of worship, an existential way, an application to human terms rather than letting them stay in their naked abstraction.

What is exciting about Hasidism is that it faces existence as it is without camouflage. It is open to tragedy and suffering, it opens up sources of compassion and insight. My father used to tell me a story about our grandfather, the lover of Israel. He was asked by many other rebbes, "How come that your prayers are always accepted and our prayers are not?" He gave the following answer: "You see, whenever some Jew comes to me and pours out his heart and tells me of his misery and suffering, I have such compassion that a little hole is created in my heart. Since I have heard and listened to a great many Jews with their problems and anguish, there are a great many holes in my heart. I'm an old Jew, and when I start to pray I take my heart and place it before God. He sees this broken heart, so many holes, so many splits, so He has compassion for my heart and that's why He listens to me. He listens to my prayers."

Compassion, the love of life and the love of people—these are difficult things to comprehend and to attain. It takes a great deal of inner cultivation to attain real love and real compassion. It takes also a new conception about the relevance of beauty and the marvel and mystery of everything that exists. And this is given in Hasidism.

A relatively unknown statement of the Baal Shem Tov which I cherish is a comment on the famous verse in the Book of Ecclesiastes: "Vanity, oh vanity, everything is vanity." Said the Baal Shem: "This is the true meaning of the verse in the light of the last verse of the whole book. A man who says what God has created is vanity, vanity of vanities, anything he does, his studies, his goodness, his worship are vanity, what chutzpah, what blasphemy! How dare men say that life is vanity?" Life is a great experience and a great opportunity for exaltation for the greatest. In a period of such depression, such cynicism, to rediscover that what God has created has a meaning and to rediscover that God Himself is a meaning without all the mysteries is really something that speaks to modern men. Therefore, ultimately the great message that Hasidism can give to us is hope and exaltation.

Israel as Memory

WHY DID OUR HEARTS AND MINDS throughout the ages turn to Eretz Israel, to the Holy Land? Because of memory, because of hope, because of distress.

Because of memory. There is a slow and silent stream, a stream not of oblivion but of memory, from which we must constantly drink before entering the realm of faith. To believe is to remember. The substance of our very being is memory, our way of living is retaining the reminders, articulating memory.*

Jewish memory, far from turning into a collection of stale reminiscences, was kept alive by the power of hope and imagination, transcending the limits of believing. What seemed unbelievable became a foregone conclusion.

After the destruction of Jerusalem, the city did not simply become a vague memory of the distant past; it continued to live as an inspiration in the hearts and minds of the people.

Jerusalem became a central hope, a symbol of all hopes. It became the recurring theme of our liturgy. Thus even when the minds were not aware of it, the words reminded us, the words cried for restoration of Zion and intensified the link, the attachment.

Yehudah Halevi, the famed Jewish poet of the eleventh century, expresses this feeling in the following lines:

> Would that I have wings that I could wend my way to Thee, O Jerusalem, from afar!

---

* See Heschel, *Man Is Not Alone* (New York, 1951), pp. 161 ff. According to Jewish mysticism, forgetting comes from the realm of evil and the unclean. Had the tablets containing the Ten Commandments not been broken, there would have been no forgetting. See *Zohar* I, 193b.

I will make my own broken heart find its way amidst your broken ruins.
I will fall upon my face to the ground, for I take much delight in your stones
*   and show favor to your very dust.*
The air of your land is the very life of our soul.

When Jerusalem was destroyed, the sages decreed that each person make remembrance of Jerusalem every day in every place. Thus they said, "A person shall lime the walls of his home, but leave a corner untouched . . . A person shall traverse all the courses of a repast, and leave some morsel untouched . . . A woman shall make her jewelry and make some part incomplete, for it is said, 'If I forget you, O Jerusalem.' "

Numerous rituals are performed in remembrance of the destruction—*zecher lehurban.* Three weeks of sorrow, particularly nine days of mourning, are part of our liturgical year. The "three weeks" end on the ninth day of the Hebrew month of Av, which is a fast of twenty-four hours, observed year after year in recollecting the destruction of the land and the people. People assemble in the synagogues, take off their shoes; they sit on the floor with bowed heads, crying for the land, reciting the Book of Lamentations.

In joy and in grief Zion is never absent from our thoughts. The liturgical words of comfort which are said to people in mourning are: "May the Lord comfort you among all those that mourn for Zion and Jerusalem." Even to this day, at the conclusion of the joyous ritual of a wedding, a glass is broken in remembrance of the destruction of Jerusalem. In the benedictions that solemnize the wedding, a prayer is said for the joy of Jerusalem.

May Zion rejoice
as her children are restored to her in joy.
Praised be Thou, O Lord,
who causes Zion to rejoice at her children's return . . .
Praised be Thou, O Lord our God,
King of the Universe,
who created joy and gladness,
bride and groom,
mirth, song, delight, and rejoicing,
love, brotherhood, peace, and fellowship.
O Lord our God,
May there soon be heard
in the cities of Judah
and in the streets of Jerusalem,
the voice of joy and gladness,
the voice of bride and groom,
the jubilant voice of those

joined in marriage under their bridal canopy,
the voice of young people
feasting and singing . . .

When the newborn is received into the community, a blessing is pronounced that "he may become worthy to ascend in the holy pilgrimage of the three festivals," and when the dead is laid to rest, a small sack of earth from the Holy Land is placed under his head. In life and in death we have never parted from the Holy Land. At the conclusion of each meal, reciting grace, we say, "Take pity, O Lord our God, on Israel Thy people, on Jerusalem Thy city, on Mount Zion the habitation of Thy glory . . . Build Jerusalem, the Holy City, speedily, in our own days . . ." In the penitential liturgy we pray, "Remember Mount Zion, remember, O Lord, the affection of Jerusalem, never forget the love of Zion; Thou wilt arise and have pity on Zion; for it is time to favor her, for the appointed time has come."

For these many ages, in many lands, whether in Spain or in India, in Egypt or in Poland, no day, no evening passes without praying for Zion and Jerusalem. We pray for her recovery, we pray for her redemption, for her prosperity and for her peace.

Three times every day, wherever on earth he stood, whatever his anguish, every Jew entreated his Maker: "Have mercy, O Lord, and return to Jerusalem Thy city." And again: "May our eyes behold Thy return in mercy to Zion." At festivals, a few pray: "May it be Thy Will, O Lord our God and God of our fathers, that Thou again have mercy upon us . . . Bring us to Zion Thy city, with song, to Jerusalem, the site of Thy sanctuary, with everlasting joy . . ."

Attachment to the land of Israel so dominates our liturgy that the prayers for dew and for rain accord with the seasons of the Holy Land rather than with the climates of the lands in which the worshippers recite the prayers.

"At midnight I rise to praise Thee," said King David (Psalms 119:62). The evening is a time for study, midnight is a time for song and praise.

A harp was hung over David's bed, and at midnight the north wind would blow and it would play by itself. Then the king was constrained to rise from his bed, and till the dawn flushed the eastern skies, he would break out into song and praise.[1]

The music was not silenced with the disappearance of the harp of David. It kept awake many pious Jews even during the Middle Ages. Throughout ten centuries there were those who would rise at midnight every night, except Friday night, put on clothes of mourning, cover the head with ashes, sit on the floor, recite prayers expressing grief over the destruction of the Temple and the suffering of God's children in the dispersion. A whole liturgy developed for this service, part of which was a confession of sins that are the cause of deferring the manifestation of the glory of God and the establishing of the kingship of God on earth.[2]

This service, observed in many lands by mystics, by Hasidim as well as by simple people in the stillness of the night, in the privacy of their homes, ended on a note of certainty that God's glory will prevail.

Sermons were preached in the synagogues and houses of study about the sanctity of the land, and even sermons which did not deal with this theme would frequently conclude with the words "And a redeemer shall come into Zion. Amen."

HISTORY SEEMS to present to us the depressing spectacle of a bewildering variety of thoughts and beliefs and, above all, of the passing away of every thought and belief ever held by men, of vanishing loyalties, of unabashed betrayals. The loyalty of the Jewish people to the promise is itself an anchor of meaning.

Any attempt to impair the vital link between Israel the people and Israel the land is an affront to biblical faith. The horrendous sin of the children of Israel in the wilderness was the worship of the Golden Calf—yet that sin was forgiven. However, when, under the influence of those who were sent by Moses to scout out the land and who upon return spread calumnies about the land, the Israelites lost their faith in ever entering the land— that sin was not forgiven (Numbers 14:29ff.). For the spies who spread slander about the land were not forgiven. For the sin of the spies and the acceptance of the slander by the people, the entire generation which left Egypt died in the wilderness. The Blessed Holy One could forgo His own honor but could not forgive the transgression in slandering the Promised Land.

What we have witnessed in our own days is a reminder of the power of God's mysterious promise to Abraham and a testimony to the fact that the people kept its pledge: "If I forget you, O Jerusalem, let my right hand wither" (Psalms 137:5). The Jew in whose heart the love of Zion dies is doomed to lose his faith in the God of Abraham, who gave the land as an earnest of the redemption of all men.

We have never abandoned the land, and it is as if the land has never abandoned the Jewish people. Attempts to establish other civilizations in the land ended in failure. Numerous conquerors invaded the land: Romans, Byzantines, Arabs, Kurds, Mongols, Mamelukes, Tartars, and Turks. But what did these people make of the land? No one built the state or shaped a nation.

The land did not respond.

We Cannot Force People

to Believe

I FULLY UNDERSTAND the feeling of those who in good faith find themselves unable to proclaim themselves Jews in the religious sense and nevertheless are attached to the people, the state of Israel, and the Hebrew tongue. I weighed the problem and considered both the *halacha* and reality. In what respect do I mean reality? It is a fact that there were those in our nationalist movement who tried to base Jewish existence on nationality alone, and to make a distinction between people and religion. One does well to emphasize that "the people in Israel does not consider itself a separate nation from the Diaspora Jewry." I know how deeply some are concerned about the existence of our people in the Diaspora. Our existence as a people is like a mountain suspended from a hair; anxiety concerning this rests on us like a double-edged sword. Yet, in my opinion, the government's decision can only do harm. I am referring to the decision that "the religion and nationality of an adult will be recorded as 'Jew' if he declares in good faith that he is a Jew and not a member of any other religion."

It is an axiom of our life that the people of Israel and the Torah (I shall not use the word "religion") are a closely integrated reality. The government's decision splits this reality into two spheres: the people is one thing, Torah another. A theory which proposes that there is a Jewish people without a religion necessarily implies that there is a Jewish religion without a people. Such a distinction is likely to lead to a schism in Jewish life. It could also bring about a basic change in the essence of the people and the essence of the Torah. The people will be like all peoples, the Torah like all religions. The first change would bring about denial that the Jewish people exists, while the second would turn the Jewish religion into a church and a sect. Such a schism would also lead to the possibility that a Jew converting to Christianity would remain a Jew.

It is a fact that in the heart of many a Jew the faith of the God of Abraham and his Torah is no more. It is, however, also a fact that many no longer have faith in the existence of our people—just as in modern times the belief in the return of Zion evaporated. But just as there is an evil angel who rains down one drop which brings destruction, there is a good angel who rains down a drop of faith. This drop is what keeps us alive. The era of religion is not over yet. Our children are daily coming closer to us. I do not believe in the downfall of faith; rather, in its invigoration and reawakening.

Both logic and daily experience prove that it is impossible to base Jewish existence in the Diaspora on secular Jewish culture. All the hopes nourished by the Diaspora writers for the creation of a secular culture were trampled underfoot and dashed. All that remain to us is the Torah, and one's heart's desire to find a road to a life which would have an aspect of eternal life. You are of the opinion that in the state of Israel "there is no danger of Jews assimilating among non-Jews." I think that the danger of spiritual assimilation lurks everywhere; even the holiness of rebuilding of the land of Israel will not afford protection. I am well aware of the difficulties involved, and can feel the anguish of those who find the world of the *halacha* too narrow for them. The trouble is that some see all of Judaism reflected in its Law; in their concern for the letter of the Law they give up the Jewish spark. They make the fence more important than the tradition it is meant to protect. Such extremism and severity do us great harm; even the Creator of the world, finding that a world could not exist by justice alone, combined the quality of justice with the quality of mercy. Flexibility, not fanaticism, is needed.

We cannot force people to believe. Faith brought about by coercion is worse than heresy. But we can plant respect in the hearts of our generation. Like the wicks of the candle, many wait to hear the tidings that the spirit of God is hovering on the face of the deep, and to enjoy the light of that spirit. The trouble is that they do not know the light that is in Judaism. Many . . . who recoil from the shadows have never in their lives seen the light.

Some of the public heretics are secret believers, but we have not yet found a way to express ourselves to them who despise faith learned by rote. Struck by confusion they stray in worlds not ours.

Perhaps I may be permitted to note that now that Israel is firmly established, the time has come to reexamine some ideas of our national movement. We should question the validity of the theory that religion is only a means to an end—a device for preserving the people. This theory is based on the premises originating in mental obtuseness. This people is an eternal people. Its very purpose is basically a religious one. We can go even further and say: Israel's Torah has as its mission a search for an answer to the problem most basic in private and public life. Every definition perverts. The term "Jew" is a concept both religious and national. As a religious concept it has a fixed definition; as a national concept its meaning is obscure. For such a case we say that it is better not to define than to define and thereby destroy what has been built up.

A Time for Renewal

WHO IS A JEW? A witness to the transcendence and presence of God; a person in whose life Abraham would feel at home, a person for whom Rabbi Akiba would feel deep affinity, a person of whom the Jewish martyrs of all ages would not be ashamed.

Who is a Jew? A person whose integrity decays when unmoved by the knowledge of wrong done to other people.

Who is a Jew? A person in travail with God's dreams and designs; a person to whom God is a challenge, not an abstraction. He is called upon to know of God's stake in history; to be involved in the sanctification of time and in building of the Holy Land; to cultivate passion for justice and the ability to experience the arrival of Friday evening as an event.

Who is a Jew? A person who knows how to recall and to keep alive what is holy in our people's past and to cherish the promise and the vision of redemption in the days to come.

How to assure the survival of the Jews? The best prophet of the future is our past. How did we meet the assaults and challenges of change and decay, of persecution and contempt, and survive as a people down through centuries? We had no might, no allies, no friends, no territory, no visible establishment to keep us intact, loyal, whole. The answer often given that we were held together by the strength of the concept or idea of one God, and that allegiance to it overcame the power of kings and tyrants as well as the contempt and hatred of neighbors, is a fume of fancy. The Jews were often attacked in the name of other attractive and powerful myths and ideas, and still resisted the temptations of conversion and assimilation. Moreover, man is made of flesh and blood, he has a heart as well as a mind. Could man live by abstraction alone?

What kept our integrity alive was a commitment of heart and soul, love that goes with character and conviction.

The wisest answer to the enigma of our survival may be found in the famous saying that God, Israel, and Torah are one. The three realities are inseparable, interdependent, and the commitment to these realities is appreciation and love.

A life in which one of these commitments is missing becomes a tripod with two legs. And yet the three are not of equal standing and must be seen in the proper order of importance. Confusion in the order—a malady that often occurs in history—results in distorting fundamental perspectives, vital values.

Classical Reform Judaism concentrated on ethical monotheism as the essence of Judaism, disregarding Torah and Israel. Secular nationalism has made the people of Israel its central concern, disregarding God and Torah. While modern ultra-Orthodoxy, in its eagerness to defend observance, tends to stress the supremacy of the Torah, equating Torah with the *Shulhan Aruch*, in disregard of God and Israel, frequently leading to religious behaviorism.

Implicit in my opening statements about Abraham and Rabbi Akiba is the necessity of living in accord with our tradition; of living as much as possible—and perhaps a little more than possible—according to the discipline of faith and *halacha*.

THE ZIONIST IDEA embraces not only the land but also the people, and by people we mean both the biological reality as well as the essential thoughts and commitments it stands for. "*Der Zionismus ist die Heimkehr zum Judentum noch vor der Ruckkehr ins Judenland,*" "Zionism is the return to Judaism even before returning to the land of the Jews," said Herzl, in his opening address at the first congress. Indeed, Judaism without *halacha* is like a tree cut off at its roots. In fact, the disparagement of faith and *halacha* threatens the very existence of our people. There is danger which calls for most urgent attention. For more than 1,800 years we were a people without a land. Now we face the possibility of a land without a people.

Today all we have are either individuals rummaging for leftovers of the heritage of a people perished, of communities extinguished, or individuals untroubled by agony over a thousand years vanished, over countless souls cut off from us, thinking that the present moment is the whole, that the self can live without a past.

And yet what we know about Abraham and of Rabbi Akiba is not only law. In fact, most of what is contained in the *Chumash* or *Tenach* is nonlegal ideas or tales. Similarly rabbinic literature contains both *halacha* and *agada*, and the thinking of Judaism can only be adequately understood as striving for a synthesis between receptivity and spontaneity, a harmony of *halacha* and *agada*.

There is a general assumption that the rabbis were naïve, simpleminded, and unreflective people. How such an assumption can be generalized in regard to such a galaxy of men whose subtle and profound judgments in *halacha* have remained an intellectual challenge to all future students is difficult to see. It is refuted by any unbiased analysis of their *agadic* sayings, which clearly indicate that their inner life was neither simple nor idyllic.

Halacha represents the strength to shape one's life according to a fixed pattern; it is a form-giving force. *Agada* is the expression of man's ceaseless striving, which often defies all limitations. *Halacha* is the rationalization and schematization of living; it defines, specifies, sets measure and limit, placing life into an exact system. *Agada* deals with man's ineffable relations to God, to other men, and to the world. *Halacha* deals with details, with each commandment separately; *agada* with the whole of life, with the totality of religious life. *Halacha* deals with the law; *agada* with the meaning of the law. *Halacha* deals with subjects that can be expressed literally; *agada* introduces us to a realm which lies beyond the range of expression. *Halacha* teaches us how to perform common acts; *agada* tells us how to participate in the eternal drama. *Halacha* gives us knowledge; *agada* exaltation.

Halacha gives us norms for action; *agada* vision of the ends of living. *Halacha* prescribes, *agada* suggests; *halacha* decrees, *agada* inspires; *halacha* is definite, *agada* is allusive.

The terminology of *halacha* is exact, the spirit of *agada* is poetic, indefinable. *Halacha* is immersed in tradition, *agada* is the creation of the heart.

Halacha, by necessity, deals with the laws in the abstract, regardless of the totality of the person. It is *agada* that keeps on reminding us that the purpose of performance is to transform the performer, that the purpose of observance is to train us in achieving spiritual ends. "It is well known that the purpose of all *mitzvot* is to purify the heart, for the heart is the essence." The chief aim and purpose of the *mitzvot* performed with our body is to arouse our attention to the *mitzvot* that are fulfilled with the mind and heart, for these are the pillars on which the service of God rests.

The *halachot* refine man's character, *agadot* "sanctify the name of the Holy One, blessed be He among us."

To maintain that the essence of Judaism consists exclusively of *halacha* is as erroneous as to maintain that the essence of Judaism consists exclusively of *agada*. The interrelationship of *halacha* and *agada* is the very heart of Judaism. *Halacha* without *agada* is dead, *agada* without *halacha* is wild. Pan-*agadic* Judaism is doomed to extinction.

Halacha is the body of the Torah, and the Torah of Israel was preserved only by the power of *halacha*, by the power of the forms of *mitzvot* and good deeds: and all of the poetry and mysticism, thoughts and beliefs, survived only by its merit. *Agada* cleaves, is linked to *halacha*, and has no existence without *halacha*. *Agada* is as a flame which depends upon the hot coal of the *halacha*, and he who separates the two extinguishes the light of Judaism which burns in the flame. To sum up: He who says I cherish only *agada* will eventually forfeit what he cherishes.

"If it is your will to know Him who spoke and the world came into being, learn *agada*. For by so doing you will perceive Him who spoke and the world came into being and cleave to His ways." The voice of *halacha* is powerful, its voice breaks the cedars; *agada* is a still, small voice. *Halacha* is like a flow of mighty waters; *agada* is the spirit of God hovering over the face of the waters.

And so, *halachic* authorities, due to historical and sociological factors, not only gained the upper hand but even frequently fostered disparagement of *agada*. In many periods of history acumen stood higher than intuition, *pilpul* suppressed poetry. While *halacha* triumphed, *agada* declined.

THE LAND WHERE *halachic* acumen reached its climax was Babylonia, while the most exquisite and profound *agada* came into full bloom in the land of Israel.

With the renewal of Jewish life in the Holy Land there was hope for a renewal of the creative power of both *halacha* and *agada*. Indeed, was it not in Safed where a renaissance of spiritual insight came to pass? Was it not in modern history that we were blessed with the marvelous flowering of *agada* in the form of Hasidism?

Yet many leaders today, whose learning and zeal evoke respect, remain unaware that some of their decisions contain an element of a pan-*halachic* heresy.

This land was rebuilt by those who lived continuous renunciation of luxuries and careers for the sake of the people—*mesirat nefesh* as a way of living, not an occasional episode; renunciation not because of a negation and contempt for life, but because of love and enthusiasm for a goal.

The Zionist idea did not originate in law, in *halacha*; it originated in the soul, in love of Israel, in *agada*. Most of those who were guided exclusively and rigorously by *halacha* raised serious objections to the Zionist movement.

Modern Zionism came into being as an outburst of insight, first as a dream, then as a poetic vision, and finally as action. For two thousand years the Jewish soul was filled with longing, with waiting, until it responded to a call and translated two thousand years of prayer into deeds of heroic quality.

Were the men of *halacha* the only people engaged in rebuilding the land? Indeed, it was the mysterious will of God that non-observant Jews should have been the leaders endowed with foresight and the charisma to awaken our people. Saving so many lives, they led our people to the land of our fathers.

This historic fact is of far-reaching importance in understanding the nature of Jewish existence.

From the day of the prophet Malachi, who says of Elijah that God will send him before "the great and dreadful day," Elijah was regarded as the precursor of the Messiah. The helper in distress, he also appears in our legends to sages and saints, assisting them in solving spiritual problems.

One such problem was faced by one of our great men of the past.

"Two things I love wholeheartedly: Torah and Israel. However, I am not sure which one I love more."

The response of Elijah was:

"The accepted opinion seems to suggest that the Torah is most important, as the verse reads, with regard to the Torah, 'The Lord made me as the beginning of his way' (Proverbs 8:22). However, I think that not the Torah but Israel is most important. For the prophet has said: 'Israel is holy to the Lord: the first fruits of his harvest' (Jeremiah 2:3)."

Those who bless the Lord for the miraculous achievement of the Zionist goal should seriously ponder the response of Elijah: "I think that not the Torah but Israel is most important."

One of the greatest authorities of rabbinic tradition, Rabbi Simeon ben Yohai, of the second century, said, "It is written, 'For as the days of a tree shall be the days of my people' (Isaiah 65:22). A 'tree' signifies the Torah, as it is stated. 'It (the Torah) is a tree of life to them that lay hold upon it' (Proverbs 3:18). Now, which was created for the sake of which? Was the Torah created for the sake of Israel or vice versa? Surely the Torah was created for the sake of Israel."

One of the marvels of Jewish history is the development in our people of a quality rarely paralleled in the world: love of Torah. Yet in many of today's scholars love of Torah, a passionate intoxication, is leading to a replacement of the love of God, even suppressing love of Israel.

One gains the impression that ultra-Orthodoxy sometimes falls into the trap of placing the Torah above God, of placing *mitzvot* higher than reverence for God.

Yet what does our tradition teach us? It is a duty to study Torah. While it is also a duty to love God, one often gets the impression that love of Torah has replaced love of God. And love of God involves love for his children, even children who went astray, rather than hatred of Israel, which we witness in many places.

The spirit of the Rabbi of Satmar hovers over our rabbinic authorities, while the spirit of Rabbi Levi Izhak of Berditshev is taboo.

THE TIME CALLS for renewal, self-purification, rejuvenation. Yet ultra-Orthodox establishment remains like a medieval castle, with most of its leaders engaged in building fences and walls instead of homes. As a result, the spirit of Judaism is felt by vast multitudes of young people to be a jail, not a joy. When they are forced to visit the establishment, they feel like inmates waiting to be released. The walls have many guards, but there are too few windows.

The beginning of piety is compassion; the death of piety is in public demonstrations. The only way to create an atmosphere of faith is to grow spiritually in privacy.

Much of religious Judaism consists of boxes of makeup. Prayer comes from the heart, not from politics. Before our eyes conduct and soul grow coarse. "Is there no balm in Gilead? Is there no physician there? Why, then, is not the health of the daughter of my people recovered?" (Jeremiah 8:22).

There is a rather substantial step to take: the question of the exclusive ultimacy of *halacha*. But take the step we must, not only to prevent its alienation from our people, but primarily because it is an act of seeing the truth of our traditions.

It is a time to act for God, set aside the Torah (or the uncompromising rigidity of some of our laws).

There was a time when we could assume the absoluteness of rigid *halachism*, a time when such a stance was constructive and holy. But we live today in a world filled with unprecedented demands on our conscience, cruel challenges to human dignity and compassion; to hide exclusively behind the walls and fences of rigorism is to suppress our love of Israel and understanding of God.

Many wonderful minds continue to spend their time on evolving sophisticated *pilpulistic* solutions to illusory legal problems while the burning issues are: what to do with leisure time; how to abstain from labor on the Sabbath and not be bored; how to stop the exemption of girls from volunteering for service in the hospitals, where people often die because there is no nurse to offer help? I am grateful to God that in the official establishments and hotels *kashruth* is observed. But what hurts is the question why it is only required for butcher shops to be under religious supervision? Why not insist that banks, factories, and those who deal in real estate should require a *hechsher* and be operated according to religious law? When a drop of blood is found in an egg, we abhor the idea of eating the egg. But often there is more than one drop of blood in a dollar or a lira and we fail to remind the people constantly of the teachings of our tradition.

In the classical rabbinic decision-making the flexible human condition not infrequently served as a factor in reaching a *halachic* decision. *Agadic* considerations served as a basis for legal judgment.

THERE MAY BE a modicum of truth that the secret of our survival is a will to live. But the will to live persists only if there is a meaning to live by.

There is a passion that animates the Jewish soul: a craving for ultimate meaning. Sacred and precious as it is to fight for our people living in dignity and security, the questions that vex young people are: What is the ultimate meaning of living in security and dignity? What direction should determine our way of living? What values to cherish? What qualities to cultivate?

I believe that the ultimate meaning of existence is to be a *religious witness*.

Why a witness? Because the reestablishment of the state of Israel is an unprecedented incredible event in man's spiritual history. Its sheer existence is an exclamation of the power of the Jewish spirit over the chaos of history. Those who are present at the unfolding of such a marvel must bear witness to the world, to generations to come.

What do I mean by a religious witness? Compassion for God and reverence for man, celebration of holiness in time, sensitivity to the mystery of being a Jew, sensitivity to the presence of God in the Bible.

The most radical change that occurred in our century is the elimination of the Hebrew Bible from the greater part of the world. It is no accident that Russia, China, and India are opposed to us.

Whether the people of America, England, and France retain authentic friendship for the state of Israel will depend upon whether the vision of the prophets and the voice of the God of Israel will not completely vanish from their minds.

For the sake of God, for the sake of Israel and the world, the people Israel and the state of Israel must emerge as religious witnesses, to keep the consciousness of the God of Abraham and the reverence for the Bible alive in the world. Yes, this is our task. We Jews are messengers who forgot the message. How to recall the message? How to proclaim it? How to live it?

This is a golden hour in Jewish history. Young people are waiting, craving, searching for spiritual meaning. And our leadership is unable to respond, to guide, to illumine. With Zion as evidence and inspiration, as witness and example, a renewal of our people could come about.

Pikuach Neshama:

To Save a Soul

THE HUMAN BEING IS UNIQUELY GRACED with the ability to search the soul and reflect, For what purpose am I alive? Does my life have a meaning, a reason? Is there a need for my existence? Will anything on earth be impaired by my disappearance? Would my absence create a vacuum in the world? And if we say that there would be a void and an impairment in the world, and that this means that my life has value beyond its simple existence, is it incumbent upon me to fulfill a purpose in this life? Do I exist that I might build or restore?

EVERY PERSON moves in two domains: in the domain of nature and in the domain of the spirit. Half slave, half king, he is bound by the laws of nature, but at the same time able to subdue and dominate them. As a creature of nature, he is born perforce and has no need for the same legitimacy or self-justification. As the Talmud remarks, "One does not examine applicants for food." As a creature of spirit, however, he takes stock of himself and of his world. He yearns to find a reward from all his toils, and he searches for that which is special in his life. Does existence simply mean to seize and eat, to seize and drink, or does it have a double meaning: to exist and to serve a purpose?

The purpose of human existence is an age-old problem. Kohelet was not the only one to agonize over it. The debate over this problem is an ancient one and many have debated it at great length. We are not free to ignore it today. One may not appoint a proxy to engage in spiritual struggles. And just as the generations are not equal, so, too, the efforts extended in finding a solution are not equal. The question of the purpose

Translated by Aryeh Cohen and Samuel Dresner; edited by Susannah Heschel.

of our lives as Jews is doubly serious and constitutes a double-edged sword over the Jewish scholar. Our continued existence highlights the question to which we cannot close our eyes: Is it worthwhile to live as a Jew? It is a question that stirs in the heart of each one of us.

Our historical experience has taught us that our existence as Jews is not in the category of things which neither help nor hurt. The opposite is true: to be a Jew is either superfluous or essential. Anyone who adds Judaism to humanity is either diminishing or improving it. Being a Jew is either tyranny or holiness. Moreover, the life of a Jew requires focus and direction, and cannot be carried out offhandedly. One who thinks that one can live as a Jew in a lackadaisical manner has never tasted Judaism.

The very existence of a Jew is a spiritual act. The fact that we have survived, despite the suffering and persecution, is itself a sanctification of God's name. We continue to exist, in spite of the scorn of the complacent, the torrents of hatred, and the dangers that constantly lie in wait for us. We always have had the option to solve the "Jewish Question" through conversion, and had we stopped being Jews, we would not have continued as thorns in everyone's flesh, and we would not have remained an object of scorn. As individuals we would have tasted a life of serenity and security. After all, the Jew is an expert at adaptation and assimilation, and it would not be too much for him to mix with the nations, without their taking note of his joining them. Nevertheless, generation upon generation have withstood the test of their faith. Many blows could not douse the flame. With dedication we guard the fire, the truth, and the wonder.

It is out of neither laziness nor habit that we cleave to the root of our soul. We know that even in normal times we have been required to pay a high price for our existence. We know that we are obliged to bear a double burden of responsibility. Yes, Jewish existence comes at a high price; yet Jewish life is dear to us. It is spiced with a unique charm, radiating a light that delights the soul, a light that graces all our actions. Even simple things, like eating and drinking, rise through it toward the Supreme and acquire a spiritual aspect.

TO LIVE AS A JEW means to feel the soul in everything, in others and in our own existence. And this soul requires spiritual elevation. Everything that has within it the spirit of life longs for repair. Like candlewicks waiting to be lit, so we wait for the action that has a slight bit of pure intention, a grain of refinement. The soul in us will not find satisfaction merely in physical fulfillment. In each of us flickers the longing for Shabbatness, for beauty, for serenity. Anyone who chains and represses these longings and allows the powers of the soul to disperse to no good end not only contaminates his self, but also contributes to the world's destruction. For the soul which degenerates is the mother of all sins and the source of all evil. And all the evil afflictions such as hate, haughtiness, and jealousy stem from the spirit of human beings.

AND PEOPLE, what do they do? The major part of our energy we invest in "fixing (*tikkun*) our clothing," i.e., improving the outer skin while ignoring the inner essence. The soul goes mad and degenerates while the world continues with business as usual, as if waiting for the Destroyer to arrive and return it to a formless void (*tohu va-vohu*). The purpose of Judaism is to destroy the instinct toward madness which lurks at the gate of the human soul, to cause something of the world of divine nobility to dwell in this world, and to prepare the soul to delight in some of the radiance of Eden while in this world.

What is the meaning of nobility? A person possessing nobility is one whose hidden wealth surpasses his outward wealth, whose hidden treasures exceed his obvious treasures, whose inner depth surpasses by far that which he reveals. Refinement is found only where inwardness is greater than outward appearance. The hidden is greater than the obvious, depth greater than breadth. Nobility is the redeemed quality which rises within the soul when it exchanges the transient for the permanent, the useful for the valuable.

THE SATAN of publicity dances at the crossroads, moving with full strength. Who is the wise man who has not gone out after him, following his drums and dances? We tend to lick the dust of his feet in order to gain fame. In truth, the soul has only that which is hidden in its world, that which is sealed in its treasure houses. The quality of a person is internal. He does not live by what his mouth says but by the secret. The honor of a person is a secret.

The whole honor of Judaism is internal, in the depths, in the small containers that are hidden from sight. Even the stone tablets that were given with loud voices were broken. Blessing is not in noise; beauty is not in the top of trees but rather in the roots which are open to the Ancient Fountain.

A PERSON cannot see the beauty of life unless he remembers that the Finite (*Sof*) and the Infinite (*Ein Sof*) kiss each other; that the One who is enthroned on high is concerned with all below. We live always at one with eternity. Eternal life has been planted in our midst. A family table is an altar in our house. Each and every one of us can determine for ourselves and for the whole world whether we become innocent or guilty. And the most common acts that a person does are compared in their importance to things which are eternal. Judaism teaches us to view any injustice—robbery or violence—or human oppression as a major tragedy and to feel divine joy at bringing happiness to a mortal. One who curses a human is insulting his Maker and one who loves others gives pleasure to God.

Every human being is a kind of reminder of God (*Shiviti*), and all things are like traces of God's footprints in a barren desert. Through all the things in the world it is possible to come close to the Source. It is incumbent upon us, as Jews, to imitate the footprints, and remove the veil from God, who is masked in the costume of the world.

M A N Y E R A S have passed since our visionaries and prophets began shaking the human conscience with the anguished cry that all flesh had corrupted its ways on earth, that the earth was filled with violence, in religion as in politics, with individuals as with communal affairs. However, along with this, the prophets sparked in us the vision and the desire to repair and improve the world. We clearly are heretics if we believe that human affairs are predetermined in an inviolable manner. Each day and each era have the potential to be Friday, and it is incumbent upon us to learn how to prepare on a weekday for the Sabbath. We lack the power to prematurely force the advent of the end of days, but we are able to add to the sacred from the profane. And it is possible to accomplish such additions every hour. Preparation is necessary even in commonplace matters, for you cannot reach the significant without beginning with the insignificant. The same heavens that are stretched out over the ocean also cover the dust on an abandoned path. And though the destruction of evil and the eradication of malice are not easy tasks, laving one's hands before eating bread and reciting the blessing over the bread are not to be trampled upon and made light of.

W E A R E F A I T H F U L to the purpose of the world, not by paying it lip service or by philosophical inquiry. We cling to the secret of life with a cleaving born of fate, whether we are aware of it or not, and therefore we do not stumble in the dark, nor are we frightened by spirits and phantoms. Judaism is as a candle to the soul. It teaches us to hold on to the melody in the cacophony of life, how to burn off the thorns of the fleeting and the vulgar from the midst of the vineyard of our existence. It teaches us to listen for the miraculous pulse of life, which beats demonstratively through the veins of the universe. For the believing Jew, the dreadful feeling that one's life is empty, that one's efforts have been in vain, is foreign. A Jew knows the secret of a blessing—a blessing over all things which benefit us; the joy of a Jew is not in vain.

THE LIFE OF A JEW is comparable to one who walks through fire: either he will be burned and the flame will immolate him or he will emerge purified and the light will shine above him. Objectively, one could say to every person: If you want to live a spiritual life which is complete and righteous, then live as a Jew. Our fate is a sign and a mission. That which happened to Israel will happen to the whole world. Mt. Sinai is now suspended above all the nations. If they accept the Torah, good; if not, they will be buried amid the finest elements of their culture.

THESE DAYS even an infant can see that humanity stands at the edge of an abyss. We have learned that one can be a villain even though very cultured and expert in science. The possibility of saving the world from destruction depends on the recognition that there is a supreme criterion by which we must evaluate all human values and that there is something that rises above all the achievements of the arts and sciences, above all the accomplishments of an individual or a people.

What is this criterion? How does one measure dominion, beauty, wealth, power? The soul of every human being possesses within it the tendency to value those things that it likes, and to bow down to that which appears to be valuable. This is a test that everyone passes. How easy it is to be attracted by outward beauty, and how hard it is to remove the mask and penetrate to that which is inside. If a Greek poet, for example, had arrived at Samaria, the capital of the Kingdom of Israel, he would have been surprised and overcome with emotion; he would have praised and lauded in verse the idols, the beautiful temples and palaces which the kings of Israel and their ministers had built. But the prophet Amos, after visiting Samaria, did not sing, nor did he bow to the glory of the ivory buildings. When he looked at the buildings of carved stone, at the ivory temples and the beautiful orchards, he saw in them the oppression of the poor, robbery and plunder. External magnificence neither entranced him nor led him astray. His whole being cried out in the name of the Lord: "I loathe the pride of Jacob, and I detest his palaces." Could it be that the prophet Amos's heart—the purest of that generation—was not captivated and did not tremble before beauty? Was the prophet Amos lacking all feeling and appreciation for beauty?

WHEN THE ANNUAL congress of the Nazi Party convened in Nuremberg in 1937, journalists from all over the world, such as *The Times* of

London, described with enthusiasm the demonstrations of the various Nazi organizations. They could not find enough adjectives to praise the physical beauty, the order, the discipline, and the athletic perfection of the tens of thousands of young Nazis who marched ceremoniously and festively before the leader of the "movement." These writers who were so excited by the exterior splendor lacked the ability to see the snakes in the form of humans—the poison that coursed through their veins, which not long after would bring death to millions of people.

JUDAISM TEACHES us that beauty which is acquired at the cost of justice is an abomination and should be rejected for its loathsomeness.

All values are esteemed only to the extent that they are worthy in the sight of God, for only through the Divine Light is their light seen. Treasures of the world, though they be marked by beauty and charm, when they diminish the image of the divine will not endure. Fortunate is the person who sees with eyes and heart together. Fortunate is the person who is not entranced by the grand façade or repulsed by the appearance of misery. This is the mark of the spiritual personality; chic clothes, smiling faces, and artistic wonders which are filled with evil and injustice do not entrance him. Architectural wonders and monumental temples, which seem to testify to glory and honor, power and strength, are loathsome to him if they were built with the sweat of slaves and the tears of the oppressed, if they were raised with wrongdoing and deceit. Hypocrisy which parades under the veil of righteousness is worse to him then obvious wrongdoing. In his heart any religious rite for which the truth must be sacrificed is revolting. Deeds which Jews are commanded to perform are for the purpose of coupling the beautiful and the good, for the sake of the unification of grace and splendor. The criterion by which we judge beauty is integrity, the criterion by which we judge integrity is truth, and truth is the correspondence of the finite to the infinite, the specific to the general, the cosmos to God.

It is possible that the future of civilization is dependent on this spiritual power, on the ability to achieve this correspondence. It is of the essence of spirituality to perceive the hidden transcendence which is in the habitual, to hear the afflicted voice even in the heralding of victory, to hear the sound of the stone which cries out from the wall.

Those who think that Judaism stands only on the internal virtues, on psychological attributes alone, are mistaken. To be a Jew means to have both a Jewish soul and a Jewish spirit. The soul is created together with the body, but it is incumbent upon the person to acquire the spirit upon which the soul is dependent, and the Jewish soul is dependent upon the Jewish spirit.

What are the roots from which we draw the ability to cleave to the spirit of Judaism? What is the well from which we draw the unique ability to taste its essence and the strength to stay in contact with the endless reality? There are many among us from whom this essence has been taken, but even they tremble with reverence when the storms of suffering pass over them. At that time their confidence in their spirit and power melts away. It is the aim of the Torah of Israel to breathe into us the trembling of holiness and reverence, so that it fills our hearts at all times.

The historical experience of our day teaches us that the person who is only a human being is actually less than human. Judaism teaches us that to remain a people we must be more than a people. Israel is destined to be a holy people. This is the essence of our mission, the essence of our yearnings. From this essence emerges the divine seriousness which hovers above our being, as well as our reverence for our own existence.

What is this reverence? What is the characteristic which determines the honor of a person? This is not an obvious characteristic. We do not honor a person for his countenance, his physical stature, or his natural talents. Our honor as human beings is of an importance that does not stem from within ourselves. A person's honor represents an importance which is greater than his own importance. The glory of a nation rests upon its king, the glory of knowledge rests upon the scholar, and the glory of the Creator rests upon the created.

This sort of importance hovers above every Jew. A Jew represents a value greater than his own value as an individual. A Jew who forgets his nobility—there is no greater transgression than that.

We are partners with God, partners in everyday actions. We do not walk alone. We are not solitary in our toils or forsaken in our efforts. The smallest one is a microcosm of the Greatest One. A reciprocal relationship binds each lowly one with the One on High.

THE FATE OF our people is not fully in our control. From ancient times the children of Israel made a covenant with God. All subsequent generations preserved this relationship, in which they invested the best of energies, thereby transforming Israel's destiny into a holy entity. Holiness is that aspect of something that does not belong to us but, rather, belongs to God. Holiness lies in the apparent trivialities that God receives from us while we are on this earth. The Torah has repeated to us often: Human beings are the source of holiness, and human will—not dreams and visions—is the anvil upon which holiness is formed. A person enters his silo and, referring to a section of the grain, declares: "This portion is *Terumah.*" Immediately his *Terumah* is sanctified and may be eaten only by priests. A Jew writes a verse containing the name of God on a piece of parchment, and the parchment becomes holy. The head of the High Court in Jerusalem, when determining the day upon which the new month should begin, declares: "It is holy," and behold, that day is holy. And when Israel declared at Sinai, "We will act and we will understand," it became a holy nation.

For generation after generation, the children of Israel have repeated: "We will act and we will understand." In the academies and in the synagogues, in the flames of the Inquisition and in the concentration camps, in the marketplaces of the far-flung reaches of the Exile, and in the kibbutzim of the land of Israel. And this people became a holy nation.

MANY OF US detest the idea of holiness and consider it to be a waste of time, a meaningless concept, the invention of primitive man, notwithstanding the fact that this concept is rooted in the heart of every cultured person. Everyone knows the power of the spoken word. What really happens when a person opens his mouth and promises something? Superficially, only sounds emanate from vocal cords, and the lips are merely moving. So what of it? Why do we assume that loyalty to one's word is the basis of all human relationships? The promise that was given, the contract that is made—is sacred, and one who desecrates it destroys the foundation upon which all of communal life is established. Until the moment I speak, the choice is mine, but once the words have left my mouth, I may not rescind or desecrate them. Willingly or unwillingly, the word spoken by me controls me. It becomes a sacred power which has dominion over me, lurking at my door and compelling my compliance.

WE JEWS fully recognize that we are in the grip of a history which cannot be forced into the boundaries of a single civilization. Even at a time when we are imprisoned in a Tower of Babel, in the midst of a cacophony of self-aggrandizers for whom "nothing they may propose to do will be out of their reach," we discern echoes from another world. How is it possible for a mere mortal to perceive an echo emanating from a world which is beyond history and civilization?

The nations of the world have produced many thinkers who have striven to reach God by intellectual inquiry alone. They have, in fact, dived deep into the stormy waters, but have come up with naught. God cannot be grasped by the intellect. The Jews have a different way: "We will act and we shall understand." Reaching God—the understanding—arrives together with the act, emanates from within the act (the Kotzker rebbe). When we fulfill a *mitzvah* and perform a desirable action, we achieve the cleaving of humanity with God. It is as if in our actions, in the depths of our existence, "we see the thunder."

THE LIFE of Israel teaches us of the correspondence between the spiritual power within us and God, who is above all the worlds. He "who chose to dwell in a thick cloud abides with them in the midst of their uncleanness." There exists a harmony between the good deeds of a human and the Infinite Holiness, between the compassion of a human being and the mercy of the Eternal. The spirituality that flows from our actions is not fleeting, transient, or solitary in a silent cosmos. The music of refined actions, the melody of a noble soul, is woven into the tapestry of eternal music which God Himself composed.

We believe in the possibility of unifying the divine within us with the Infinite Divine, which exists outside of us; we believe that a small bit of lovingkindness in a mortal's heart joins with Eternity; and that ordinary actions are no less significant than the most exalted of projects.

IN OUR VOCABULARY, whether in Hebrew or in Yiddish, one of the most common words is the word *mitzvah*. This word cannot be translated into any other language. The Christians did not accept the idea of the *mitzvah*, only the idea of "sin," and they even transformed the meaning of this term. For them, sin possesses a positive force, an essence. For us, the word "sin" has mainly a negative connotation. To sin means to fail, to take an inappropriate step ("He who moves hurriedly blunders," Proverbs 19:2); or it connotes the failure to find a thing in its appropriate place ("You will know that all is well in your tent; when you visit your home you will not fail," Job 5:24); or in *hiph'il*, it means to miss the target ("Every one of them could sling a stone at a hairbreadth and not miss," Judges 20:25).

The primary connotation of the word *averah* (transgression) is also negative. *Averah* means: not to do, to disregard, or to cross the fixed boundary. ("Then the king's courtiers who were in the palace gate said to Mordecai, Why do you disobey [*'over*] the king's order?" Esther 3:3). "One might think that if one's father or mother orders him to transgress [*la'avor*] any one of the commandments written in the Torah . . ." (Sifra, Kedoshim, 1). The same word also means forgiveness ("Who is a God like you, forgiving iniquity and remitting [*'over*] transgression," Micah 7:18).

In Yiddish—from whose expressions one can gain great insight into the soul of the Jewish people—*averah* means to spoil something, or to do something for naught. For example, a Yiddish adage states: "If you speak to a deaf person, such speech is a sin, an *averah* (i.e., for naught).

Mitzvah in Yiddish means to do what is good, in a positive, concrete sense. "Do me a *mitzvah*, give me a glass of water." In Hebrew we say: "The wise in heart takes *mitzvot*" (Proverbs 10:8). "Beautify yourself in His presence through the performance of *Mitzvot*" (Talmud bShabbat 133). Consider also the expressions: "To perform a *mitzvah*"; "To involve oneself in mitzvot"; "to seize a mitzvah"; "To acquire a *mitzvah* (in the synagogue)." The real import of this term is revealed through many such expressions. Is it at all possible to do justice in any other language to Resh Lakish's dictum: "Even the empty ones among your people are as filled with *mitzvot* as a pomegranate (is filled with fruit seeds)"?!

Indeed, internal radiance is not quantifiable and routinized actions do not illuminate. We are even taught that the sins of the pure at heart are more desirable than are the good deeds of the arrogant. However, what will become of the artist who lacks tools, or the craftsman who is bereft of materials? Likewise the musician, whose inner world is permeated with overwhelming and inspired musical images: what is such a person able to accomplish or contribute if he or she lacks instruments with which to articulate these images?

EVERY MORNING, when the Jew recites the prayer "Fortunate are we, how good is our lot!" his mouth and heart are in sync. What is the nature of this joy? I believe it emanates from the fact that we do not subsist in a hollow, vacuous universe. We do not feel that we are wandering through chaos, that we are building on nothingness, that our lives are just an accidental shrub, and that our culture is the aftergrowth of much ado about nothing. The feeling—which exists among the other nations—that time is a great abyss does not oppress us. The life of Israel is stretched between two historical poles: the Exodus from Egypt and the messianic kingdom.

THERE IS NO forgetting among the community of Israel. We have not abandoned our past nor have we denigrated our heritage. We know where we stand in time and we number our days in accordance with the calendar of eternity. One of the important characteristics of the spirit of Israel is its phenomenal capacity for remembering. Throughout the generations we have remained loyal to our past. A candle, once lit in the temple of our history, is never extinguished. This historical memory was not sustained through Jews filling themselves with knowledge about antiquity. The preservation of the past to which we refer is not a gathering of facts in the mind but, rather, rises out of love; it is the remembering which occurs in the heart.

In this manner our past is preserved in our souls and in our way of life. This preservation takes the form of an inner service, the renewal or remnant of first things, the grasping of the temporary and transient by the eternal. The present is sanctified by the memory of the past.

Belief likewise depends on memory. "I believe" means: "I remember." For what is belief? Every one of us, at least once in our lifetime, has been able to perceive the existence of the Creator. Every one of us, at least once, has merited a glimpse of the beauty, the serenity, and the strength which flow from the souls of those who have walked with God. However, such feelings and inspirations are not common occurrences. In the lives of most people they are as meteors which flare up for a moment and then disappear from sight. There are, however, people for whom these flashes ignite with them a light which will never be extinguished. Faith means: If you ever once merit that the Hidden One appears to you, be faithful to Him all the days of your life. Faith means: To guard forever the echo which once burst upon the deep recesses of our soul.

Just as an individual's memory determines the nature of his personality, so the collective memory determines the destiny of nations. How bitter are the lives of those who do not know who their ancestors were, who their childhood friends were, or who their sisters and brothers were? We see whole nations that have lost the power of memory and therefore who do not know their origins and their destinies. At times they are gripped by horror, feeling as if they were blinded, and they wander aimlessly in deep darkness upon a volcano. Their inner sight is dimmed, and the volcano is within them.

The power of collective memory is one of the characteristics of Israel. Even in the rush of time, we sat on the sturdy rock of memory, and our past has been preserved in our souls and our way of life. It is incumbent upon us to remember those events that occurred to our ancestors, events through which the spirit of God established residence in the history of our people. This ancient echo still rings in our ears, and even if we ignore it or attempt to silence it, our visions never cease to give it voice.

THE DAYS OF the past and the present are inextricably tied together. The love of the people Israel is inconceivable if we don't walk with the generations that produced us, and vice versa: without love for the Jews of our time—including even the frivolous and vacuous among them—we will not succeed in connecting with the Israel of the past. The unity of all generations and the unity of all those in our generation are dependent on each other. We must walk with the prophet Isaiah, Rabbi Yochanan ben Zakkai, Maimonides, and the Baal Shem Tov, just as we must interact with those who live among us today.

We are not of the opinion that everything that has the stamp of antiquity on it is of the finest. Many garments have been worn out, and many areas have been destroyed. Most people, moreover, tend to look upon everything in the past as useless, and they are willing to exchange the glory of ancient days for the shiny newness of today. They forget that it is not within the power of one individual or within the power of a single generation to construct the bridge which leads to Truth. Let us not discriminate against the structure which many generations have nourished and built up. "The sacred entities of the children of Israel—do not profane them!" (Numbers 18:32).

N O T O N L Y the children of Israel in a single generation but all the children of Israel in all generations comprise the nation. We share a single status and destiny. Even a Jew who stands at a distance wraps himself within his soul and prays: "May it be your will that my portion be bound up with the congregation of Israel."

The Jewish National Fund collection box is on a table in many Jewish houses today. Years ago young men, yeshiva students, would go around to houses and exchange empty boxes for the full ones. Once, a young boy went to empty the boxes in the town of Sanuk in Galicia, and as he entered the doorway of a shoemaker he said, "I've come to empty the Jewish National Fund box." At first the shoemaker was silent, then he asked the visitor to sit down. He removed his shoes and began to put new soles on them. The young man was dumbfounded. "What are you doing?" he asked. The shoemaker replied, "I am a poor person and I cannot afford to make contributions to the Jewish National Fund, so I want to put new soles on your shoes. You go around from house to house and your shoes get torn. I also wish to have a portion in this *mitzvah*."

Like this shoemaker, we all must strive to have a portion in the Temple on high and in the glory of the world. This is what our ancestors struggled for in all times and all lands.

J U D A I S M E X I S T S only in community. The primary concern of the Jew is not to merit an honorable seat in the Garden of Eden but, rather, that he assure the continued existence of the people Israel. "One who causes a deed to be performed is greater than one who performs it." The teacher is greater than the student. What is the one who looks out only for himself and his own perfection compared to? "To a Zaddik in a fur coat" (*Zaddik in pelz*). What is a "Zaddik in a fur coat"? If there is a chill in the house and we wish to warm our bodies, we have two choices: to light a fire in the stove or to put on a fur coat. What is the difference between lighting a fire and putting on the fur? When the fire is lit, I am warm and others are warm as well; when I wrap myself in fur, it is only I who am warm (the Kotzker rebbe).

AFTER THE FLOOD of evil swept over the world, that which remained of refinement wandered about as a forlorn dove between heaven and earth, searching for a resting place in the human conscience. This refinement is the Divine Presence (*Shekhinah*). Who will take pity upon this bereft dove if not we, the children of Israel?

The echoes of the terrible cries that came from the gas chambers, screams the like of which had never been heard in the course of human history, are too horrible to bear. Woe unto the generation in whose days human beings have become a dreadful disgrace. And yet never before has the superhuman power of our existence been as clearly manifest as it is in our time.

The millions of Jews who were destroyed bear witness to the fact that as long as people do not accept the commandment "Remember the Sabbath to keep it holy," the commandment "Thou shalt not kill" will likewise fail to be operative in life. Today we, few in number, are the generation upon whom devolves the obligation to preserve, to purify, and to transmit. We are a generation burdened with a weighty responsibility and with a mighty destiny. The future of Judaism is in the hands of the few. Will we be the last Jews?

From the day on which humans have been on this earth no temple has been so pure and sanctified with so much blood as has the existence of the Jewish nation. Every Jew who survived constitutes a remnant of a candle kindled by divine light, an ember snatched from the fire of evil. Unknowingly, every Jew is crowned with a crown of holiness. Every Jew must feel the glory hovering above the face of our existence. Great is our tragedy and great is our mission. And our major task is to save the heart of humanity, the heart that extends "to the heart of heaven" (Deuteronomy 4:11).

JUST AS IT IS incumbent upon us to be human beings, so is it our obligation to be Jews. Anyone who separates himself from Judaism commits spiritual suicide. Just as it is impossible to exchange one's body, so is it impossible to divest oneself of the divine image. Every people has a religion which it received from others; but we are the only people which are unified with our Torah. All parts of the nation, not only an elite few, have come to symbolize this unity. By persisting in our Judaism—by continuing as Jews—we contribute more toward the general welfare than we do through all our significant scientific contributions to the general culture.

When we attempt to explain the exalted status of Israel's destiny, we realize the inadequacy of our words. Even what our own eyes have seen is beyond our power of expression. Our life is like a play with many acts, which God, as it were, watches and hears. Who dares evaluate and judge our role in this drama?

IT IS SAID in the Talmud: "A person must ask, When will my deeds approach the deeds of the patriarchs?" The "patriarchs" are Abraham, Isaac, and Jacob. In the Torah, nothing is said about books they wrote or ideas they innovated. Instead, we are told tales of their adventures, their deeds, how they wandered from place to place to find food for their households, how they searched for brides, and so on and their actions became Torah. Hence we learn the purpose of Jewish existence: we are obligated to live lives that will become Torah, lives that are Torah.

Perhaps human beings have never been as much in need of Judaism as they are in our generation. The human species is on its deathbed. In order to seek a cure, we should not desecrate the Sabbath; rather, it is incumbent upon us to sanctify the weekdays. Like our ancestors three thousand years ago, we are called upon to be pioneers for the Torah of Israel and for the land of Israel, and bring their power to all the regions of the Diaspora. We must not forget that the hidden secret of our existence is to be found in the admonition: "Be ye holy." Only in holiness will we *be*. In keeping faith with our Judaism, we guard the hidden divine light and the noblest of visions, which have been saved for humanity's future.

The Meaning of Repentance

[*Published on the eve of Yom Kippur
in the* Gemeindeblatt der jüdischen Gemeinde zu Berlin,
16 September 1936]

THE MYSTERY OF PRAYER on the days of Rosh Hashanah presents itself with characteristic familiarity: it reveals itself to those who want to fulfill it, and eludes those who want only to know it.

Prayer on these days is a priestly service. When we pray we fulfill a sacred function. At stake is the sovereignty and the judgment of God.

The world has fallen away from God. The decision of each individual person and of the many stands in opposition to God. Through our dullness and obstinacy we, too, are antagonists. But still, sometimes we ache when we see God betrayed and abandoned.

Godliness is an absolute reality which exists through itself. It existed prior to the creation of the world and will survive the world in eternity. Sovereignty can exist only in a relationship. Without subordinates this honor is abstract. God desired kingship and from that will creation emerged. But now the kingly dignity of God depends on us.

At issue is not an eschatological vision, a utopia at the end of time, or a kingdom in the beyond. Rather, we are talking about the present, the world that has been bequeathed to us, a kingdom of everyday life. We have to choose God as king; we have "to take the yoke of the kingdom of God upon ourselves."

Does this demand—the essence of Jewish law—signify an esoteric symbol, a mystical act? It signifies a close, this-worldly and everyday act. The establishment or destruction of the kingly dignity of God occurs now and in the present, through and in us. In all that happens in the world, in thought, conversation, actions, the kingdom of God is at stake. Do we think of Him when we are anxious about ourselves or when, driven by apparent zeal for general concerns, we engage in life, whether deliberately or in a carefree way?

These days are dedicated to establishing God as king within us. The whole year long we call him "Holy God!"; on this day "Holy King!"

"God took on kingship over the peoples. God placed himself on the throne of his sacredness. The princes of the peoples are assembled. For the shields of the earth are God's."

The deepest human longing is to be a thought in God's mind, to be the object of His attention. He may punish and discipline me, only let Him not forget me, not abandon me. This single desire which links our life and our death will be fulfilled on the Days of Awe. The "Holy King" is a "King of Judgment." The season of Rosh Hashanah is the "Day of Memory," the "Day of Judgment."

Before the judgment and memory of God we stand. How can we prove ourselves? How can we persist? How can we be steadfast?

Through repentance.

The most unnoticed of all miracles is the miracle of repentance. It is not the same thing as rebirth; it is transformation, creation. In the dimension of time there is no going back. But the power of repentance causes time to be created backward and allows re-creation of the past to take place. Through the forgiving hand of God, harm and blemish which we have committed against the world and against ourselves will be extinguished, transformed into salvation.

God brings about this creation for the sake of humanity when a human being repents for the sake of God.

FOR MANY YEARS we have experienced history as a judgment. What is the state of our repentance, of our "return to Judaism"?

Repentance is an absolute, spiritual decision made in truthfulness. Its motivations are remorse for the past and responsibility for the future. Only in this manner is it possible and valid.

Some people, in moments of enlightenment, believed they saw in the year 1933 an awakening to God and of the community, and hoped Jews would be heralds of repentance. Yet we have failed, those who stayed here just as much as those who emigrated. The enforced Jewishness still sits so uneasily in many of us that a new wave of desertions could occur at any moment. The apostasy of the past is matched by the superficiality of today. Is this disappointment surprising? Repentance is a decision made in truthfulness, remorse, and responsibility. If, to be sure—as is often the case among us—instead of deliberate decision we have a coerced conversion; instead of a conscious truthfulness, a self-conscious conformity; instead of remorse over the lost past, a longing for it; then this so-called return is but a retreat, a phase.

Decay through return!—that is the apocalyptic *menetekel* inscription on the walls of our houses.

Marranos of a new metamorphosis: Jewish on the outside, Marranos of different degrees multiply within our ranks. Such victims of insincerity—as historical experience teaches—can become tragic.

It is also deplorable when a spiritual movement deteriorates into bustling and pretense. It is unclean when a holy desire is misused by the selfishness of the clever. When one wants to become a Jew because of the "situation," not out of honesty, the result is conflict and misery. Jewishness cannot be feigned!

There is no return to Judaism without repentance before God. Faithfulness to Him and to the community to the point of utmost readiness remains the fundamental idea of Jewish education.

We must recognize that repentance has yet to begin! Each person must examine whether one is part of a movement forced upon us by the environment or whether one is personally motivated, whether one is responding to pressure from outside or to an internal sense of urgency. At stake is not the sincerity of the motivation but the earnestness and honesty of its expression. This considered reflection has to become a permanent part of our conscience.

Not everyone is capable of maintaining self-examination. It is up to the teachers among us to explain the meaning and content of repentance. Enlightenment about repentance is the central task of our time.

It is a great good fortune that God thinks of us. We stand before the judgment and the memory of God. We know the reality of human judgment and we pray: God, you judge us! We must stand firm before the judgment. The possibility to do so is given to us. Woe to us if we cease; woe to us if God should forget us.

1936

On the Day of Hate

*[Written on the occasion of the Nazi book burning
at the University of Berlin in the spring of 1933]*

On the Sabbath day
At the middle hour, on shoulders, signboards, thresholds
There was a thump—a mass of filthy brown coats.
Watchmen, like a sudden growth of dreadful silent poison snakes
In deep, deep pleasure stood at every entrance
Throttling in a weakened nation every throat and door.
Whoever goes in—you'll be spat on by the laughter of the mob.

Householders, whether of palaces or storefront huts,
Stand like lepers behind hate-poisoned guardian steel bars.
Bandaged windowpanes foam and fester with bloody placards,
A patch on every wall,
A hated face besmeared on every signboard.

Race-pure Germans, happy holiday to you.
On this, your blasphemous holy day, hatred is your sanctity.
A people is a drum on which to beat money-greedy sounds,
Threshing out a harvest of years of envy and desire.
A shrieking finger points out all.
I give you gifts; and wish you luck.
In the mob's heart there's noise and robbery.
Every desire gets stolen ten thousand times.

The hunger for long knives becomes a yell.
The street is a volcano of hate.

Translated by Leonard Wolf

In each mouth a coil of eyeless curses.
And fiercer than those glares are haughty gestures.
The mob whinnies around the longed-for gallows.
The Jew is the world's plague.
A dog's fury is too mild for them.
Jewish justices betray with dark relationships.
In their cures, Jewish pharmacists pour poison and infection.
They are usurers, bloodsuckers, every one.
Drive their children from the schools,
Their orphans from their orphan homes,
And their sick out of the hospitals.

Israel's shame is holy.
Hand, drunk with the shame of human blood,
Paints blows, paints red, paints rage.
The mob stands watch at every window.
Howling, it stamps a mark of shame on every face.
The Jewish house is a humiliated ruin
An open, public toilet.

On every windowpane, the hand spits a burning Star of David,
The façades of Jewish houses gleam
Like holy curtains over outraged Torah-arks.
The Ineffable Name—a brilliant darkness—
The K I K E on every windowpane in flames.

II

NO TIME FOR

NEUTRALITY

No Time for Neutrality

ONE OF THE LESSONS we have derived from the events of our time is that we cannot dwell at ease under the sun of our civilization, that man is the least harmless of all beings. We feel how every minute in our civilization is packed with tension like the interlude between lightning and thunder. Man has not advanced very far from the coast of chaos. It took only one storm to throw him back into the sinister. If culture is to survive, it is in need of defenses all along the shore. A frantic call to chaos shrieks in our blood. Many of us are too susceptible to it to ignore it forever. Where is the power that could offset the effect of that alluring call? How are we going to keep the demonic forces under control?

This is the decision which we have to make: whether our life is to be a pursuit of pleasure or an engagement for service. The world cannot remain a vacuum. Unless we make it an altar to God, it is invaded by demons. This is no time for neutrality. We Jews cannot remain aloof or indifferent. We, too, are either ministers of the sacred or slaves of evil. The only safeguard against constant danger is constant vigilance, constant guidance. Such guidance is given to him who lives in the reality of Israel. It is a system in which human relations rest upon two basic ideas: the idea of human rights and the idea of human obligations. In the present crisis we have learned that consciousness of our rights fades away when our sense of obligation subsides; that our duties become chains when we surrender that to which we have a just claim. There is a boundless realm of living that, if it is not to be stultified, cannot be placed under the control of either ethics or jurisprudence. How to become a master in that realm, not to curb but to shape, is a supreme challenge to intelligence.

LIVING CANNOT be treated piecemeal; it must be treated as a whole. Living is circulation; the elements of spirit absorbed by it are digested and burned. Injecting good manners or rules of conduct will not solve the problem. Life is in need of an all-embracing significant form, which should have bearing directly or indirectly on every aspect of it. Weak men rebel at such an idea, denouncing it as tyranny. But the thoughtful will not be intimidated by seeming inconvenience.

Judaism has tried to place human living in a general system of significance, to integrate our scattered actions into a whole. Through a system of rituals, observances, benedictions, man is to eliminate the chance, to drive out the nonsense from his life.

It is the small in which the great becomes real. It is the weekday in which the Sabbath is reflected.

The Torah has not imposed upon Israel a tyranny of the spirit. It does not violate human nature. On the contrary, the road to the sacred leads through the secular. The spiritual rests upon the carnal, like "the Spirit that hovers over the face of the water." Jewish living means living according to a system of checks and balances. We are not asked anything that cannot be responded to. We are not told: Love thy enemy, but: Do not hate him, and positively: "If thou meet thine enemy's ox or his ass going astray, thou shalt surely bring it back to him again" (*Exodus* 23:4).

Although there is no celebration of our animal nature, recognition of its right and role is never missing. Judaism does not despise the carnal, teaching, on the contrary: "Hide not yourself from your own flesh."

Our Fathers knew how to care for the most distant in the most immediate. They knew that the passing is a reflection of the lasting, that tables in our humble homes may become consecrated altars, that a single deed of an individual man may decide the fate of all mankind. They disliked the rough, the coarse, the haphazard, and tried to lend a metaphysical dignity to their deeds. Not only the extraordinary days, not only the Sabbath, even their weekdays had a form. Everything was keyed to a certain style. Every detail of life had its own physiognomy, its individual stamp.

One can serve God with the body, even with one's passions; one must only be able to distinguish between the dross and the gold. This world acquires flavor only when a little of the other world is mingled with it. Without nobility of the spirit, the flesh is full of darkness.

WHY SHOULD Jews observe the particular forms of living prescribed by Torah and tradition? To those who search for the original reasons, lost and forgotten in the routine of ages, the commandments become significant when explained and prove to be related to a rational purpose, to something known. Others leave all explanations behind, never stumbling where understanding fails. To them the commandments are precious, because they are related to the unknown.

Indeed, any reason we may advance for submitting to a commandment merely points to one of its aspects, omitting more than describing. To say that the precepts have meaning is less accurate than to say that they are sources of emergent meaning.

Justifying the commandments by the aid they render to diet, hygiene, or the enjoyment of beauty, we catch only a glimpse of a light's reflections. Given out as unrefracted rays are unique values, not obtained from other sources. The *mitzvot* are full of hidden brilliance of the holy. What is out of sight is suddenly blazing in our thoughts.

To outsiders the *mitzvot* may appear like hieroglyphic signs—obscure, absurd, chains of lifeless legalism. To those who do not strive to share in the unexampled and surpassing, observance may become dreary, irksome routine. While to those who want to tie their lives to the lasting, the *mitzvot* are an art, pleasing, expressive, full of condensed significance. "Thy statutes have been my songs," said the psalmist (119:54). No particular reasons can describe the exclusive flavor of the *mitzvot*. What is wretched and in appalling need becomes gentle and enchanting as if we own a bit of the Beyond.

JUDAISM IS both an assurance and an urge. It is the assurance that man can realize the good in his life, that man's relation to the transcendent can be both immediate and constant. It tells us that righteousness can be achieved, that the way to integrity is open. "For this charge which I am enjoining on you today is not beyond your power, nor is it out of reach . . . The matter is very near you, on your mouth and in your mind, for you to observe" (Deuteronomy 30:11–14). "You have been told, O man, what is good" (Micah 6:8).

Judaism urges the Jew to become attentive to the presence of the infinite. It opens his eyes to the abundant possibilities of creating the good, to the redemptive powers inherent in the *mitzvot*.

The idea of *mitzvah* occupies the focus of the Jew's attention. An analysis of the usage of the term *mitzvah* in both Hebrew and Yiddish and the phrases in which it occurs would disclose a universality and complexity of meaning. To the mind of the Jew the idea of *mitzvah* bears more reality than the idea of *averah*. The term *mitzvah* is one of the most frequently used terms in his vocabulary, much more indeed than the idea of *averah*. Stronger than the belief in original sin is our belief in original innocence. In Christian languages the relation of frequency and importance of the two terms is just the reverse. In fact, there seems to be no precise equivalent for *mitzvah* in Western languages. Moreover, there the term "sin" assumed the connotation of something substantial, a meaning that is alien to the term *averah*, which often meant expending to no purpose.

Out of sheer punctiliousness in observing the Law, one may come to be oblivious of the living Presence. What is the objective of observance if not to be sensitive to the spirit, to the spirit in oneself and in all things? Man is no mere reflection of the Above; he is a source of light. Divesting himself of the husks, his inner splendor may illuminate the world. God has instilled in him something of Himself, hence the momentous importance of what he does with his life.

Most vividly the Jews feel that the world is not redeemed, that the present order of things is appalling. There is no anxiety in Judaism about personal salvation. What matters is universal salvation. The task is important, not who does it. If there should be a situation in which either you or I could do a *mitzvah*, I should let you do it. If there should be a situation in which either you or I should be compelled to do an *averah*, I should do it myself.

When the *maggid* of Meserich heard a voice from the beyond saying that because he had dared to challenge a heavenly decision he was deprived of his share in the future life, he was overjoyed, because from now on he would be certain to serve "for the sake of heaven." "Better is one hour of return and good deeds in this world than the whole life in the world to come."

Israel was not only the hearer of the voice, Israel became the voice. A unique relation with the divine was inaugurated. Instead of a religious experience in which there is separation between the perceiving man and the perceived Supreme Being, between the subject and the object, the divine—human integration was discovered. The pious Jew knew that in doing *mitzvot* he was like God. He felt that his faith *was* God. For what is faith if not the seed of the divine sown in our souls? A seed which must mature in order to yield. The Jew realized that his giving was obtaining, his prayer—inspiration, his demand—a grant; his talking to God was God talking to Himself.

JUDAISM IS averse to generalities. Its tendency is to make ideas convertible into reality, to interpret metaphysical insights as patterns for action, to endow the most remote principles with bearing upon our everyday conduct. In its tradition the vague became definite, the abstract concrete, the absolute historic.

What are the events that endow us with awareness of God? We do not gain that awareness by the mind's assault upon the riddles of the universe, or in the mind's surrender and waiting for guidance. The Jewish form of religious experience is always in acts, in carrying out a command, in our instilling a spiritual quality into the things we are doing.

There are those who attempt to grasp God by speculation alone. We

Jews have a unique way of religious experience. Israel's reply to Moses —"We will do and we will hear"—was interpreted to mean: *In doing* we perceive. By enacting the spiritual on the stage of life, we perceive our kinship with the divine. Our acts, then, are waves that flow toward the shore of God. In the Jewish mind the action sings and regularity of fulfillment is the rhythm by which we utter our tunes. Our dogmas are allusions, intimations; our creed is an allegory, yet our actions are definitions.

We do not imitate; we respond. To our souls the fulfillment of a *mitzvah* is a way of entering into fellowship with the ultimate will. In giving ourselves to the goal we feel how He is a partner to our acts.

Jewish Law is a sacred prosody, for the divine sings in our deeds, the divine is disclosed in our deeds. Our effort is but the counterpoint to the music of His will. Judaism is living shared with God.

Resorting to the divine invested in us, we do not have to bewail the fact of His shore being so far away. In our sincere compliance with His commands, the distance disappears. It is not in our power to force the Beyond to become Here; but we can transport the Here into the Beyond.

Symbolism and Jewish Faith

FROM TIME IMMEMORIAL man has been concerned with the question of how to create a symbol of the Deity, a visible object in which its presence would be enshrined, wherein it could be met and wherein its power would be felt at all times.

That religious eagerness found an ally in one of man's finest skills: the skill to design, to fashion, and to paint in material form what mind and imagination conceive. They became wedded to each other. *Art* became the helpmate of *religion*, and rich was the offspring of that intimate union. It is only through religion and cult that the consciousness of higher laws could mature and be imposed "upon the individual artist, who would otherwise have given free rein to his imagination, *style.*" "There, in the sanctuary, they took their first steps toward the sublime. They learned to eliminate the contingent from form. Types came into being; ultimately the first ideals."[1] Religion and cult inspired the artist to bring forth images of majesty, magnificent temples and awe-inspiring altars, which in turn stirred the heart of the worshipper to greater devotion. What would art have been without the religious sense of mystery and sovereignty, and how dreary would religion have been without the incessant venture of the artist to embody the invisible in visible forms, to bring his vision out of the darkness of the heart, and to fill the immense absence of the Deity with the light of human genius? The right hand of the artist withers when he forgets the sovereignty of God, and the heart of the religious man has often become dreary without the daring skill of the artist. Art seemed to be the only revelation in the face of the Deity's vast silence.

One is overwhelmed by the sight of the great works of art. They represent in a deep sense man's attempt to celebrate the works of God. God created heaven and earth, and man creates symbols of heaven and symbols of earth. Yet man is not satisfied with the attempt to praise the work of God; he even dares to express the essence of God. God created man, and man creates images of God.

A distinction ought to be made here between *real* and *conventional* symbols. A *real symbol* is a visible object that represents something invisible; something present representing something absent. A real symbol represents, e.g., the divine, because it is assumed that the divine resides in it or that the symbol partakes to some degree of the reality of the divine. A *conventional symbol* represents to the mind an entity which is not shown, not because its substance is endowed with something of that entity, but because it suggests that entity, by reason of relationship, association, or convention, e.g., a flag.

An image is a real symbol. The god and his image are almost identified. They are cherished as the representatives of the gods; he who has the image has the god. It is believed that the god resides in the image or that the image partakes to some degree of the power and reality of the god. A victor nation would carry off the god-image of the conquered nation, in order to deprive it of the presence and aid of its god. In the fifteenth century, before the common era, a statue of the goddess Ishtar of Nineveh was carried with great pomp and ceremony from Mesopotamia to Egypt, obviously for the purpose of letting Egypt enjoy the blessings which the goddess by her presence would bestow upon the land.[2] As Durkheim remarked, the images of a totem creature are more sacred than the totem creature itself. The image may replace the Deity.

What was the attitude of the prophets toward that grand alliance of religion and art? What is the attitude of the Bible toward the happy union of priest and artist? Did Israel contribute toward cementing that matrimony? Did it use its talents to create worthy symbols of the one God it proclaimed by inspiring its artists to embody in stone the Creator of heaven and earth? Indeed, if a religion is to be judged by the degree to which it contributes to the human need for symbolism, the Decalogue should have contained a commandment saying: Thou shalt make unto thee a symbol, a graven image or some manner of likeness . . . Instead, the making and worshipping of images was considered an abomination, vehemently condemned in the Bible.[3] If symbolism is the standard, then Moses will have to be accused of having had a retarding influence on the development of man. It is not with a sense of pride that we recall the making of the Golden Calf, nor do we condemn as an act of vandalism the role of Moses in beating it into pieces and grinding it very small, "until it was as fine as dust," and casting "the dust thereof into the brook that descended out of the mount."

It is perhaps significant that the Hebrew word that came to denote symbol, *semel*, occurs in the Bible five times, but always in a derogatory sense, denoting an idolatrous object.[4]

Nothing is more alien to the spirit of Judaism than the veneration of images. According to an ancient belief, the prophet Elijah, "the angel of the covenant," is present whenever the act of circumcision is performed. To concretize that belief, a vacant chair, called "Elijah's chair," is placed near the seat of the *sandek* (godfather).[5] This is the limit of representation: a vacant chair. To place a picture or statue of the prophet on it would have been considered absurd as well as blasphemous. To Jewish faith there are no physical embodiments of the supreme mysteries. All we have are signs, reminders.

THE SECOND COMMANDMENT implies more than the prohibition of images; it implies the rejection of all visible symbols for God; not only of images fashioned by man, but also of "any manner of likeness, of any thing that is in heaven above, or that is in the earth beneath, or that is in the water under the earth." The significance of that attitude will become apparent when contrasted with its opposite view.

It would be alien to the spirit of the Bible to assert that the world is a symbol of God. In contrast, the symbolists exhort us: "Neither say that thou hast now no Symbol of the Godlike. Is not God's Universe a Symbol of the Godlike; is not Immensity a Temple . . . ?"[6]

What is the reason for that sharp divergence? To the symbolists, "All visible things are emblems . . . Matter exists only spiritually, and to represent some Idea and *body* it forth."[7] The universe is "a mechanism of self-expression for the infinite." The symbol is but the bodying forth of the infinite, and it is the very life of the infinite to be bodied forth.[8]

Now, the Bible does not regard the universe as a mechanism of the self-expression of God, for the world did not come into being in an act of self-expression but in an act of creation. The world is not of the essence of God, and its expression is not His. The world speaks to God, but that speech is not God speaking to Himself. It would be alien to the spirit of the Bible to say that it is the very life of God to be bodied forth. The world is neither His continuation nor His emanation but His creation and possession.

The fundamental insight that God is not and cannot be localized in a thing[9] was emphatically expressed at the very moment in which it could have been most easily forgotten, at the inauguration of the Temple in Jerusalem. At that moment Solomon exclaims:

But will God in very truth dwell on earth? Behold, heaven and the heaven of
heavens cannot contain Thee; how much less this house that I have built!

—I Kings 8:27

God manifests Himself in *events* rather than in *things*, and these events
can never be captured or localized in things.

How significant is the fact that Mt. Sinai, the place on which the
supreme revelation occurred, did not retain any degree of holiness! It did
not become a shrine, a place of pilgrimage.

The realization that the world and God are not of the same essence is
responsible for one of the great revolutions in the spiritual history of man.
Things may be *instruments*, never *objects of worship*. *Matzo*, the *shofar*,
the *lulav* are not things to be looked at, to be saluted, to be paid homage
to, but things to be used. Being instruments they have symbolic meaning,
but they are not primarily regarded as symbols in themselves. A symbol
—because of its inherent symbolic quality—is an object of contemplation
and adoration.

To a reverent Catholic the cross is a sacred symbol. Gazing at its shape,
his mind is drawn into contemplation of the very essence of the Christian
faith.

Thomas Aquinas taught that the cross was to be adored with *Latria*,
i.e., supreme worship, and argued that one might regard a cross or an
image in two ways: (1) in itself, as a piece of wood or the like, and so no
reverence should be given to a cross or to an image of Jesus; (2) as
representing something else, and in this way one might give to the cross
relatively, i.e., to the cross as carrying one's mind to Jesus—the same
honor given to Jesus *absolutely*, i.e., in Himself. Adoration is also given
to the Sacred Heart, as well as to images and relics of the saints.[10] In
contrast, the image and shape of the scrolls, of a *shofar* or a *lulav* do not
convey to us any inspiration beyond reminding us of its function and our
obligation.

The spirit of Christian symbolism has shaped the character of church
architecture: "A noble church structure may be 'a sermon in stone.' "
According to Germanos, the Patriarch of Constantinople (715–30), the
church is heaven on earth, the symbol of the Crucifixion, the Entomb-
ment, and the Resurrection. From the fifth century, symbolism permeated
the architecture of the Byzantine church building in all its details. "The
sanctuary, the nave and aisles were the sensible world, the upper parts of
the church the intelligible cosmos, the vaults the mystical heaven."[11] A
similar spirit is to be found in Western Christianity, where, for example,
the shape of church buildings is that of a cross, embodying the basic
symbol of Christianity. The altar is often raised three or seven steps,
signifying the Trinity or the seven gifts of the Holy Spirit.

In Jewish Law, which prescribes countless rules for daily living, no directions are given for the shape of a synagogue building.[12]

Any form of architecture is legally admissible. The synagogue is not an abode of the Deity but a house of prayer, a gathering place for the people. Entering a synagogue, we encounter no objects designed to impart any particular idea to us. Judaism has rejected the picture as a means of representing ideas; it is opposed to pictographic symbols. The only indispensable object is a Scroll to be read, not to be gazed at.

There is no *inherent* sanctity in Jewish ritual objects. The candelabrum in the synagogue does not represent another candelabrum either in Jerusalem or in heaven. It is not more than you see. It has no symbolic content. According to Jewish Law, it is prohibited to imitate the seven-branched candelabrum as well as other features of the Temple in Jerusalem for ritual purposes. "A man may not make a house in the form of the Temple, or an exedra in the form of the Temple hall, or a court corresponding to the Temple court, or a table corresponding to the table [in the Temple] or a candlestick corresponding to the candlestick [in the Temple], but he may make one with five or six or eight lamps, but with seven he should not make, even of other metals [than gold] . . . or even of wood."[13] The anointing oil must not be produced in the same composition to be used outside the Sanctuary. "It is holy and shall be holy unto you" (Exodus 30:32).

The purpose of ritual art objects in Judaism is not to inspire love of God but to enhance our love of doing a *mitzvah*, to add pleasure to obedience, delight to fulfillment. Thus the purpose is achieved not in direct contemplation but in combining it with a ritual act; the art objects have a religious function but no religious substance.

Jewish artists often embellished manuscripts and title pages with pictures of Moses and Aaron. Yet such decorations were regarded as ornaments rather than symbols.

And yet there is something in the world that the Bible does regard as a symbol of God. It is not a temple or a tree, it is not a statue or a star. The one symbol of God is *man, every man*. God Himself created man in His image, or, to use the biblical terms, in His *tselem* and *demuth*. How significant is the fact that the term *tselem*, which is frequently used in a damnatory sense for a man-made image of God, as well as the term *demuth*—of which Isaiah claims (40:18) no *demuth* can be applied to God—are employed in denoting man as an image and likeness of God!

Human life is holy, holier even than the Scrolls of the Torah. Its holiness is not man's achievement; it is a gift of God rather than something attained through merit. Man must therefore be treated with the honor due to a likeness representing the King of Kings.

Not that the Bible was unaware of man's frailty and wickedness. The divine in man is not by virtue of what he does but by virtue of what he is. With supreme frankness the failures and shortcomings of kings and prophets, of men such as Moses or David, are recorded. And yet Jewish tradition insisted that not only man's soul but also his body are symbolic of God. This is why even the body of a criminal condemned to death must be treated with reverence, according to the Book of Deuteronomy (21:23). He who sheds the blood of a human being, "it is accounted to him as though he diminished [or destroyed] the divine image."[14] And in this sense Hillel characterized the body as an "icon" of God,[15] as it were, and considered keeping one's own body clean an act of reverence for its Creator.[16]

As not one man or one particular nation but all men and all nations are endowed with the likeness of God, there is no danger of ever worshipping man, because only that which is extraordinary and different may become an object of worship. But the divine likeness is something all men share.

This is a conception of far-reaching importance to biblical piety. What it implies can hardly be summarized. Reverence for God is shown in our reverence for man. The fear you must feel of offending or hurting a human being must be as ultimate as your fear of God. An act of violence is an act of desecration. To be arrogant toward man is to be blasphemous toward God.

> He who oppresses the poor blasphemes his Maker,
> He who is gracious to the needy honors Him.
>
> —*Proverbs* 14:31

"You must not say, since I have been put to shame, let my neighbor be put to shame . . . If you do so, know whom you put to shame, for in the likeness of God made He him."[17] Rabbi Joshua ben Levi said: "A procession of angels pass before man wherever he goes, proclaiming: *Make way for the image (eikonion) of God.*"*

---

* *Deuteronomy Rabba* 4, 4; see *Midrash Tehillim*, Chapter 17. That one lives in the company of angels, "ministers of the Supreme," was something one is expected by *Jewish Law* to be always conscious of. This is evidenced by the prayer *hithhabdu, Berachoth* 60b and *Mishne Torah, Tefillah* 7, 4. The general belief, based on Psalms 91:11, is clearly stated in *Tacanith* 11a. According to *Exodus Rabba* 32, 6, and *Tanhuma, Mishpatim*, end, angels are assigned to a person according to the good deeds he performs; *Seder Eliahu Rabba*, Chapter XVIII, edition Friedmann, p. 100. Compare also the statement of the two "ministering angels" that accompany a person on Sabbath eve on his way from the synagogue to his home, *Shabbath* 119b. "Rabbi Simeon said: When a man rises at midnight and gets up and studies the Torah till daylight, and when the daylight comes he puts the phylacteries with the holy impress on his head and his arm, and covers himself with his fringed robe, and as he issues from the door of his house he passes the *mezuzah* containing the imprint of the Holy Name on the post of his door, then four holy angels join him and issue with him from the door of his house and accompany him to the synagogue and proclaim before him: Give honor to the image of the Holy King, give honor to the son of the King, to the precious countenance of the King." *Zohar* III, p. 265a.

And what is more, biblical piety may be expressed in the form of a supreme imperative: *Treat yourself as a symbol of God.* In the light of this imperative we can understand the meaning of that astounding commandment: "You shall be holy, for I the Lord your God am holy" (Leviticus 19:2).

It is often claimed that "Hebrew monotheism has ended by raising the Deity too far above the earth and placing Him too far above man."* This is a half-truth. God is indeed very much above man, but at the same time man is very much a reflection of God. The craving to keep that reflection pure, to guard God's likeness on earth, is indeed the motivating force of Jewish piety.

The *tselem*, or God's image, is what distinguishes man from the animal, and it is only because of it that he is entitled to exercise power in the world of nature. If he retains his likeness, he has dominion over the beast; if he forfeits his likeness, he descends, losing his position of eminence in nature.[18]

The idea of man's divine likeness is, according to one opinion in the Talmud, the reason for the prohibition to produce the human figure. The statement in Exodus 20:20, "You shall not make with Me (*itti*) gods of silver, or gods of gold," should be rendered as if it were written, "You shall not make my symbol [*otti*; *ot* means symbol], namely, man, gods of silver, or gods of gold."[19]

What is necessary is not *to have a symbol* but *to be a symbol.* In this spirit, all objects and all actions are not symbols in themselves but ways and means of enhancing the living symbolism of man.

The divine symbolism of man is not in what he *has*—such as reason or the power of speech—but in what he *is* potentially: he is able to be holy as God is holy. To imitate God, to act as He acts in mercy and love, is the way of enhancing our likeness. Man becomes what he worships. "Says the Holy One, blessed be He: He who acts like me shall be like me."[20] Says Rabbi Levi ben Hama: "Idolators resemble their idols (Psalms 115:8); now how much more must the servants of the Lord resemble Him."[21]

And yet that likeness may be defiled, distorted, and forfeited. It is from the context of this problem that the entire issue of Jewish symbolism must be considered. The goal of man is to recognize and preserve His likeness, or at least to prevent its distortion.

But man has failed. And what is the consequence? "I have placed the

* "It was left for the Christian religion to call down its god from the heights of heaven to earth, and to represent this god by means of art." (A. D. Seta, *Religion and Art*, New York, 1914, p. 148.) Indeed, this was not the way of Judaism which insisted upon its worship being independent of art. It is life itself that must represent the God of Israel.

likeness of my image on them and through their sins I have upset it" is the dictum of God.[22]

The likeness is all but gone. Today, nothing is more remote and less plausible than the idea: man is a symbol of God. Man forgot whom he represents or *that* he represents.

There is one hope. The Midrash interprets the verse Deuteronomy 1:10 as if it were written: "Lo, today you are like the stars in heaven, but in the future you will resemble the Master."[23]

II CONCEPTUAL SYMBOLS

LET US NOW TURN to the problem of conceptual symbols. In the past several decades, the interest in symbolism has become a decisive trend in contemporary thinking. This is no accident. As long as man believes in his ability to comprehend the world directly, as long as he is impressed by that which *is* rather than concerned to express what he *thinks*, symbolism is one of the techniques of human understanding. When man becomes the measure of good and evil, when truth is regarded as that which the mind creates, symbolism becomes the sole technique of human understanding.

Kant has demonstrated that it is utterly impossible to attain knowledge of the world, because knowledge is always in the form of categories and these, in the last analysis, are only representational constructions for the purpose of apperceiving what is given. Objects possessing attributes, causes that work, are all mythical. We can say only that objective phenomena are regarded *as if* they behaved in such and such a way, and there is absolutely no justification for assuming any dogmatic attitude and changing the "as if" into a "that." Salomon Maimon was probably the first to sum up Kantian philosophy by saying that only *symbolic knowledge* is possible.[24]

To the contemporary physicist the world of sense—perception—is of no relevance whatsoever. The familiar world is abandoned for abstracts, graphs, and equations. His elements are not the familiar phenomena but electrons, quanta, potentials, Hamiltonian functions, and the like. Science is purely operational, concerned merely with the manipulation of symbols.

In the light of such a theory, what is the status of religious knowledge? We must, of course, give up the hope ever to attain a valid concept of the supernatural in an objective sense, yet because for practical reasons it is useful to cherish the idea of God, let us retain that idea and claim that while our knowledge of God is not objectively true, it is still *symbolically* true.

Thus, symbolism became the supreme category in understanding religious truth. It has become a truism that religion is largely an affair of
symbols. Translated into simpler terms, this view regards religion as a
fiction, useful to society or to man's personal well-being. Religion is then
no longer a relationship of man to God but a relationship of man to the
symbol of his highest ideals: there is no God, but we must go on worshipping His symbol.

The idea of symbolism is, of course, not a modern invention. New
only is the role it has now assumed. In earlier times, symbolism was
regarded as a form of *religious thinking*; in modern times, religion is
regarded as a form of *symbolic thinking*.

Is religion the sum of mind plus symbol? Is the mind-symbol relationship the only ultimate form of relationship in which man stands to God?
Is symbolic understanding of God all that religion has to offer? If God is
a symbol, then religion is child's play. What is the value of searching for
a goal that will forever remain unknown? Moreover, if God has no mercy
and offers no light to those who grope for Him, does He deserve man's
desperate efforts to reach Him?

To religion, however, the immediate certainty of faith is more important
than all metaphysical reflection, and the pious man must regard religious
symbolism as a form of *solipsism*, and just as he who loves a person does
not love a symbol or one's own idea of the person but the person himself,
so he who loves and fears God is not satisfied with worshipping a symbol
or worshipping symbolically.

Symbols are substitutes, cherished whenever the object we are interested
in is momentarily or permanently beyond our reach. Unable to find a
direct approach to its object (or a direct way of expressing itself), the mind
accepts a symbol in place of the original object of its interest. The premise
of religious symbolism is the assumption that God lies beyond the ken of
our minds and will therefore never be apprehended or expressed directly
but only through the symbol. Now, the second part of that premise is not
logically necessitated by the first. If the knowledge of God is beyond the
reach of man, what gives us certainty to assume that there is a symbol
that may serve as His representative?

Symbols can be taken seriously only if we are convinced of man's ability
to create legitimate symbols, namely, of his ability to capture the invisible
in the visible, the absolute in the relative. Their validity will, furthermore,
depend upon our being in possession of criteria by means of which we
could decide which symbols represent and which misrepresent the object
we are interested in; which to accept and which to reject. Yet in order to
prove the validity of symbols in general and in order to judge the adequacy
of particular symbols, we must be in possession of a knowledge of the

symbolized object that is independent of all symbols. To justify and to judge symbols we are in need of *non-symbolic* knowledge.

Symbols are means of communication. They communicate or convey to us what they represent. Consequently, in order to understand or to appreciate a symbol, we must be in possession of a knowledge of what the symbol stands for. Does not this prove that symbols are secondary to religious knowledge?

And is it conceivable that a religious person would, once he has realized the fictional nature of symbolism, be willing to accept a substitute for God? He will reject not only substitutes for the religious reality but also substitutes for spontaneous expression. Such substitutes distort our vision, stifle our inner life. Giving to symbolic objects what is due to God and directing the soul to express itself by proxy, symbolism degenerates into a *vicarious religion*.

Of a violinist who is moving his bow over the strings of his violin we do not say, he is performing a symbolic act. Why? Because the meaning of his act is in what he is doing, regardless of what else the act may represent. In rendering a service to a friend, I am not primarily conscious of carrying out an act which should symbolize my friendship; the act *is* friendship. Symbolism is not something that characterizes all aspects of human life. Why are there no symbols in morality? Because a moral deed is endowed with intrinsic meaning; its value is in itself, not in what it stands for.

No one eats figuratively, no one sleeps symbolically; so why should the pious man be content to worship God symbolically?

Those who are in the dark in their lonely search for God; those to whom God is a problem, or a Being that is eternally absent and silent; those who ask, "How does one know Him? Where can one find Him? How does one express Him?" will be forced to accept symbols as an answer.

But Judaism is not a religion of an unknown God. It is built upon a rock of certainty that God has made known His will to His people. To us, the will of God *is neither a metaphor nor a symbol nor a euphemism* but more powerful and more real than our own existence.

III SYMBOLISM AND JEWISH LIVING

IS, PERHAPS, the content of the Bible, the manner in which the will of God was made known to man, symbolic?

Reading carefully the words of the Bible, we realize that the essence of biblical piety is not to be found in the employment of symbols but in something quite different. When the Book of Deuteronomy exclaims:

"What does the Lord thy God ask of thee?" the answer given is "To fear the Lord thy God, to walk in all His ways, and to serve the Lord thy God with all they heart and all they soul, to keep for thy good the command-ments of thy Lord and His statutes, which I command you this day" (10:12 ff.).

He who loves with all his heart, with all his soul, with all his might, does not love symbolically. Nor does the term "to serve God" refer to a symbolic attitude. The term "service" may be used in two ways: symbol-ically and literally. When a person is appointed honorary president or honorary secretary of an organization, he is serving symbolically and is not required to carry out any functions. Yet there are others who actually serve an organization or a cause.

What was it that the prophets sought to achieve? To purge the mind of the notion that God desired symbols. The service of God is an extremely concrete, an extremely real, literal, and factual affair. We do not have to employ symbols to make Him understand what we mean. We worship Him not by employing figures of speech but by shaping our actual lives according to His pattern.

The symbolists claim that the literal meaning of Scripture is not the important matter, only the spiritual truths hidden beneath it; while Jewish tradition insists that the biblical verse must never be divested of *peshat*, of its naked meaning; without the reality of the naked word the spirit is a ghost. Even the mystics who cherished the allegorical meaning of Scrip-ture, and regarded the hidden significance as superior to the plain, naked meaning, always insisted that the secret rests upon the plain.

The power of the Bible is in its not being absolutely dependent upon man's symbolic interpretations. The prophets do not live by the grace of preachers. Their words are significant even when taken literally. They do not speak in oracles but in terms of specific actions. Love thy neighbor as thyself has strictly literal meaning, and so has the commandment to observe the seventh day. Judaism has tried to teach that holiness is vital, that the things of the spirit are real. The Torah is not in heaven. The voice of God is unambiguous; it is the confusion of man, of the best of us, that creates the ambiguity. It tells us precisely how God wants us to act. Performing a sacred deed we are not aware of symbolizing religion; a sacred act *is* religion.

Religious observance has more than two dimensions; it is more than an act that happens between man and an idea. The unique feature of religious living is in its being *three-dimensional*. In a religious act man stands before God. He feels addressed or commanded to act. "Greater is he who acts because he is commanded by God than he who acts without being commanded by Him."[25] The symbolic meaning of an act expresses only what the act means to man in relation to an idea; it does not convey what the act means in relation to God.

Does man stand in a symbolic relation to God? To the outsider, religion may appear as a symbol, just as to those who see a man weep, weeping is a symbol of grief, pain, or fear. Yet to the afflicted man weeping is not a symbol. God was not a symbol to him who exclaimed, "Though He slay me, yet will I trust in Him."[26] Do we pray symbolically? Do we implore Him for symbolic aid?

Symbols have their place in the outer court of religion. What is found in the inner sanctuary is neither speculative nor artistic pageantry but the simplicity and immediacy of insight, faith, and dedication. There are many symbols in Judaism, but they have auxiliary importance; their status is that of *minhag.** Jewish observance comprises both *mitzvot* [commandments] and *minhaggim* [customs]. The rabbis were careful to distinguish between Law and custom.[27] Customs are symbols born of the mind of man; *mitzvot* are expressions and interpretations of the will of God.

Moses was not concerned with initiating a new cult but with creating a new people. In the center of Jewish living is not a cult but observance; the former is a realm of its own, the latter comprises all of life. Since the destruction of the Temple in Jerusalem, Judaism has had a minimum of cult and a maximum of observance. The prophetic fight against the mendacity of spurious ceremonies has left its trace in our lives. There is a minimum of show, of ceremonialism in Jewish religion, even in public worship. Ceremonies are for the eye, but Judaism is an appeal to the spirit. The only ceremony still observed in the synagogue is the blessing of the priests—but then the congregation is required to close its eyes.

We rarely object to ceremonialism in the observance of state affairs or in courtroom proceedings or to the elaborate ritualism of academic celebrations at American universities. Should we not say that the private and domestic acts must likewise have something that would stamp them as out of the ordinary, and that *mitzvot* are essentially ceremonies?

Ceremonialism has the pedagogical value of emphasizing the extraordinary character of an occasion. In becoming a daily habit it loses its value. A ceremony is an emphasis on a deed. Yet adding an aesthetic veneer, decorum, and solemnity, it remains very much on the surface.

A *mitzvah* is performed when a deed is outdone by a sigh, when divine reference is given to a human fact. In a *mitzvah* we give the source of

---

* "Said Abaye: Now that it has been said that symbols are of significance, a man should make a regular habit of eating, at the beginning of the year, pumpkin, fenugreek, leek, beet and dates (these grow in profusion and are symbolic of prosperity)," *Horayoth* 12a.

an act, rather than the underlining of a word. Ceremonies are performed for the sake of onlookers; *mitzvot* are done for the sake of God. Ceremonies must be visible, *spectacular*, a *mitzvah* is spurious when turning impressive.

Mitzvot are sanctifications rather than ceremonies. Without faith, the festivities turn dull and artificial. The aesthetic satisfaction they offer is meager compared with that obtained from listening to a symphony, for example.

Symbols are human forms of expression. Yet is eloquence the essence of piety? Is religion a function of man's power of expression? Is it one of the many dialects of man's language, comparable to art, poetry, and philosophy? The theory that religion is a form of expression is a theory that thinks too much about what man says and ignores the fact that in the face of the ultimate problems he has nothing or very little to say.

The goal of religion is not primarily to help us to express ourselves but to bring us closer to God. *Empathy* rather than expression is the way of piety. The function of *mitzvot* is not to express ourselves but to express the will of God. The most important fact is that God speaks. And he who knows that God speaks cannot regard his own need for speaking and self-expression as being of supreme concern. The supreme concern is how to understand God's speech, God's expression. The *mitzvot* are words of God which we try to understand, to articulate. The whole world was created by His word, and, figuratively speaking, all things are signs of His alphabet, which we must learn to decipher.

Granted that the need for symbolization is a basic human need, the task of religion would not be to satisfy that need but rather to supply the norms for the right satisfaction of that need. Thus, the essential role of religion would be, if necessary, to prevent certain forms of symbolization. Symbolism may be characteristic of human nature, but religion is more than an aid in the development of the merely human; its goal is to raise the human to the level of the holy.

The primary function of symbols is to express *what we think*; the primary function of the *mitzvot* is to express *what God thinks*. Religious symbolism is a *quest for God*, Jewish observance is a *response to God*. In fulfilling the *mitzvot* our major concern is not to express our feelings but to comply, to be in agreement with the will of God.

Jewish piety is an answer to God, expressed in the language of *mitzvot* rather than in the language of *symbols*. The *mitzvah* rather than the symbol is our fundamental category. What is the difference between the two categories?

The use of symbols whether in the form of things or in the form of actions is required by custom and convention; the fulfillment of *mitzvot* is required by the Torah. Symbols are relevant to man; *mitzvot* are relevant to God. Symbols are folkways; *mitzvot* are God's ways. Symbols are expressions of the human mind; what they express and their power to express depend on a mental act of man; their significance is gone when man ceases to be responsive to them. Symbols are like the moon, they have no light of their own.

Mitzvot, on the other hand, are expressions or interpretations of the will of God; they are divine commandments. While they are meaningful to man, the source of their meaning is not in the understanding of man but in the love of God. The essence of a *mitzvah* is in its being relevant to God, *regardless* of what it may mean to man; its meaning often transcends the understanding of man. Unintelligible symbols we discard; *mitzvot* we cherish regardless of our understanding. It is the *mitzvah* that lends more meaning to us than the meaning we ascribe to it.

A symbol is *man's reference to God*; a *mitzvah* is *God's reference to man*. As a symbol, the act of blowing the *shofar* on New Year's Day would have no meaning to God. In carrying out a *mitzvah* we acknowledge the fact of God having addressed man and His being concerned with our fulfillment of His will.

Symbols serve a cognitive function; they try to make the unknown intelligible, to make the distant present. In contrast, the *mitzvot* do not interpret the essence of God to us or instruct man about the mysteries.

Symbols are created for the sake of *signifying*; *mitzvot* were given for the sake of *sanctifying*. This is their function: to refine, to ennoble, to sanctify man. They confer holiness upon us, whether or not we know exactly what they signify.

A symbol is a thing, a *mitzvah* is a task. A symbol *is*, a *mitzvah* is an act that *ought to be*, done. Symbols have a psychological, not an ontological status; they do not affect any reality, except the psyche of man. *Mitzvot* affect God. Symbols evade, *mitzvot* transcend reality. Symbols are less, *mitzvot* are more than real.

Jewish festivals do not contain any attempt to re-create symbolically the events they commemorate. We do not enact the Exodus from Egypt or the crossing of the Red Sea. Decisive as the revelation of Sinai is, there is no ritual to re-create or to dramatize it. We neither repeat nor imitate sacred events. Whatever is done in religious observance is an original act. The Seder ritual, for example, recalls; it does not rehearse the past.

There was never any doubt that all ritual acts have an ultimate meaning, yet their immediate relevance to us does not lie in their symbolic meaning but in their being commandments of God. Jewish piety demands their fulfillment regardless of whether we comprehend their symbolic meaning. We may not comprehend the wisdom of God, but we are certain of understanding the will of God.

Does the absence of symbolic understanding imply that Jewish observance is nothing but a physical performance? Jewish tradition insists that no performance is complete without the participation of the heart. It asks for the *kavanah*, for inner participation, not only for external action. Yet there is a difference between symbolic understanding and what tradition means by *kavanah*.

Kavanah is awareness of the will of God, rather than awareness of the reason of a *mitzvah*. Awareness of symbolic meaning is awareness of a specific idea; *kavanah* is awareness of an ineffable situation. It does not try to appropriate what is part of the divine mystery. It is *kavanah* rather than symbolic understanding that evokes in us ultimate joy at the moment of doing a *mitzvah*.

It is, for example, possible to justify the ritual washing of the hands before a meal as a reminder of a similar priestly ceremony at the Temple in Jerusalem. Yet what is characteristic of Jewish piety is not to be mindful of that reason but to forget all reasons and to make a place in the mind for the awareness of God.

Indeed, the certainty of being able to do the will of God lends to the *mitzvot* a meaning compared with which all particular explanations seem platitudes. What reason could compete with the claim "This is the will of God"?

Moreover, who would be willing to sacrifice his dearest interests for observing the Sabbath just because it symbolizes creation or the redemption from Egypt? If the Jews were ever ready for such a sacrifice, it was not because of a symbolic idea but because of God. The ideal of Judaism is to serve for the sake of God, not for the sake of symbols.

The validity of a symbol depends upon its intelligibility. An object loses its symbolic character when people forget what it stands for. Yet in Judaism the knowledge of what the commandments symbolize was not considered essential. *Halacha* has never regarded the understanding of symbolic meaning as a requirement for the proper fulfillment of a *mitzvah*.

The striking fact is that the symbolic meaning of the *mitzvot* was neither canonized nor recorded. Had such understanding ever been considered essential, how did it happen that the meaning of so many rituals has remained obscure? Had it been known and had its knowledge been regarded as essential, it would not have fallen into oblivion but would have been transmitted to posterity by a people that so faithfully preserved its heritage.

Let us take an example. On the Feast of Booths we are commanded to carry four kinds of plants. The significance of that ritual is not given in the Bible. So the rabbis offered a symbolic interpretation: The stem of the palm tree corresponds to the human spine, the leaf of the myrtle to the eye, the willow leaf to the mouth, and the *etrog* to the heart.[28] What is the status of that interpretation? It was not claimed to be the authentic original meaning of the ritual. Nor was its awareness considered essential to the fulfillment of the ritual. The symbolic interpretation is one of several offered. It has devotional meaning.

We must distinguish between that which is *only a symbol* and that which is *also a symbol*. A flag serves only one function, namely, to serve as a symbol; beyond its symbolic function it is a meaningless object. A temple, on the other hand, has a very definite meaning as a building, regardless of its symbolic function. In the same sense, religious observance, such as the ritual of the four plants, may assume symbolic meaning; it is *also* a symbol, yet its essence is in its being a *mitzvah*.

A system of symbolism implies if not established or canonized meaning, then at least some unanimity of its understanding. The teeming multiplicity of symbolic interpretations of Jewish rituals advanced in the course of the past two thousand years testifies to the fact that symbolic meaning is merely an *afterthought*. No one has succeeded in discovering a system of symbolic meaning by which all *mitzvot* could be explained with some degree of consistency. The numerous attempts to explore the semantics of the *mitzvot* have been futile. If Judaism is a system of symbolism, then it must be regarded as a forgotten system.

The essence of Judaism is a demand rather than a creed. It emphasizes the centrality of the act. The act of studying is more important than the possession of knowledge. There is more reflection about the deed than contemplation about the dogma.

Just as an image becomes an idol, a deed may become a habit. Its truthfulness is surrendered when it assumes independence and becomes self-perpetuating and more sacred than God who commanded it.

What is the purpose and the justification of symbolism? It is to serve as a *meeting place* of the spiritual and the material, of the invisible and the visible. Judaism, too, had such a meeting place—in a qualified sense—in the Sanctuary. Yet in its history the point of gravity was shifted from space to time, and instead of a place of meeting came a *moment of meeting*; the meeting is not in a thing but in a deed.

Ritual acts are moments which man shares with God, moments in which man identifies himself with the will of God. Symbols are detached from one's being; they are apart from the soul. Yet God asks for the heart, not for the symbol; he asks for deeds, not for ceremonies.

IV SYMBOLISM AND IMMEDIACY

ESSENTIAL TO human thought is not only the technique of symbolization but also the *awareness of the ineffable*.[29] In every mind there is an enormous store of not-knowing, of being puzzled, of wonder, of radical amazement. While the mind manufactures ideas, translating insights into symbols, the deeper knowledge remains: what *is* we cannot say.

Thus, what characterizes man is not only his ability to develop words and symbols but also his being compelled to draw a distinction between the utterable and the unutterable, to be stunned by that which is and cannot be put into words. It is the *sense of the ineffable* that we have to regard as the root of man's creative activities in art, thought, and noble living. The attempt to convey what we see and cannot say is the everlasting theme of mankind's unfinished symphony, a venture in which adequacy is never achieved. There is an eternal disparity between the ultimate and man's power of expression.

Science does not know the world as it is; it knows the world in human terms. Scientific knowledge is symbolic knowledge. Trying to hold an interview with reality face to face, without the aid of human terms or symbols, we realize that what is intelligible to our mind is but a thin surface of the profoundly undisclosed.

The awareness of the unknown is earlier than the awareness of the known. Next to our mind are not names, words, symbols but the nameless, the inexpressible, being. It is otherness, remoteness upon which we come within all our experience.

Just as the simpleminded equates appearance with reality, so does the overwise equate the expressible with the ineffable, the symbolic with the metasymbolic.

The awareness of the ineffable, of the metasymbolic, is that with which our search must begin. Philosophy, enticed by the promise of the known, has often surrendered the treasures of higher incomprehension to poets and mystics, although without the sense of the ineffable there are no metaphysical problems, no awareness of being as being, of value as value.

A recent publication which undertook to analyze the concept of value concludes with the following statement:

Our essay has ended with the unsayable. We cannot in a correct language formulate an answer to our question: What is value? . . . Should we not give up the whole undertaking as unnecessarily self-frustrating? I think not. I need not and I shall not conceal the fact that I have my own moments of despondency when I am tempted to throw aside the whole philosophical endeavour to find an answer to such questions as, What is value? What is fact? What is truth? What is entailment? What is designation? And I suspect that this despondency is not peculiar to me and my individual inadequacies as a philosopher; I suspect that everyone who has seriously wrestled with these issues must have at some time experienced it . . .

It is not then to be wondered at that we end with the unsayable: This we should expect. The objective should be to postpone this inevitable result as long as possible, to push the unsayable as far back as we can, to let the object speak for itself only after we have said as much as can be said to bring out what is not obvious.

If the present essay has been successful in postponing ultimate taciturnity for a few thousand words, this is the only sort of success its author could realistically have aimed at, always providing that this postponement has not destroyed or signally lessened the final vision . . . Nothing can be done, save to return constantly to the task of pushing the obvious further back . . .

This whole appeal to the obvious, to the revelation of what cannot be said, as the ultimate arbiter of philosophic disputes may be disconcerting to some prosaic minds. It smacks too much of mysticism, but it is mysticism in its most plebeian and I hope unobjectionable garb. There is meant no escape to some ecstatic experience, some high, emotional plane achieved only by the few on rare occasions. The vision appealed to is that which is obvious in all experience, and which is revealed in the sense of our everyday language, a sense that is felt by everyone using that language in everyday situations.

It is hoped that this essay has met this test, that it has not only postponed by some two-hundred-odd pages the appeal to the obvious (in this sense), but, resting finally on this appeal, really has retained the obvious, that it has remained true to our feelings for everyday language in pushing back into the unsayable but seen an answer to the question, What is value?[30]

This is the difference between religion and philosophy. Religion *begins* with the sense of the ineffable; philosophy *ends* with the sense of the ineffable. Religion begins where philosophy ends.

A symbol is by definition not the ultimate; it is the representative of something else. What is ultimate is not translated into symbols; the ultimate is an antonym of the symbolic.

We must distinguish between *symbolic knowledge*—which we obtain through logical operations, such as analysis and syllogism—and *immediate understanding*, which enables us to acquire insights which are not derived from symbols but from an intimate engagement with what is real. Insights such as the meaning of joy or the difference between beauty and ugliness or the awareness of temporality, of the transitoriness of existence, we do not acquire through the mediation of symbols but through direct acquaintance.

The soul of the religious man lives in the depth of certainty: This is what God wants me to do. Where that certainty is dead, the most powerful symbolism will be futile.

The whole history of religion is filled with the struggle between the pursuit of idols and the worship of Him whose name is ineffable; *between symbolic knowledge and metasymbolic understanding*; between employing symbols as *means* and accepting them as *ends*. In the past symbols have often served as substitutes for insight, for immediate perception; as an alibi for faith. The need for symbolism does not always arise when the power to pray increases. When in medieval Christianity symbolism threatened to smother the immediacy of faith, the Reformation raised its voice against it. Today there is a clamor for symbolism perceptible in both Jewish and Christian circles.

Is the present-day cry for symbols a cry for God? Is the craving for ceremonies an expression of a more profound care for the will of God? These are the questions our critical sense must ask.

Symbolism is so alluring because it promises to rehabilitate beliefs and rituals that have become meaningless to the mind. Yet what it accomplishes is to reduce beliefs to make-believes, observance to ceremony, prophecy to literature, theology to aesthetics.

Symbols are aesthetic objects: either things to be looked at that please the senses and demand nothing in return or ideas that offer enjoyment without involving us in ultimate commitments. A symbol is often like a plaything, an imitation of reality, cherished for the emotional satisfaction it affords. Symbolism, indeed, is an aesthetic category.

The quest for symbols is a *trap* for those who seek the truth. Symbols may either distort what is literally true or profane what is ineffably real. They may, if employed in the inner chamber of the mind, distort our longing for God into mere aesthetics.

When their meaning becomes stale, symbols die. But what is worse, the heart of faith dies of an overdose of symbolism. It is better that symbols die and faith should live.

Symbolism undermines the certainty of history, implying that even God did not succeed in conveying His will to us, and that we did not succeed in understanding His will. Man speaks in symbols; God speaks in events and commands.

Realizing all this, one begins to wonder whether symbolism is an authentic category of prophetic religion—whether it is not a device of higher apologetics, a method of rationalization?

The uniqueness of the Bible is not in its symbolism. The religions of Egypt, Rome, India were rich in symbolism; what they lacked was not the symbol but the knowledge of the *living God*. The uniqueness of the Bible is in disclosing the will of God in plain words, in telling us of the presence of God in history rather than in symbolic signs or mythic events. The mysterious ladder which Jacob saw was a dream; the redemption of Israel from Egypt was an iron fact. The ladder was in the air, while Jacob's head was on a stone.

"You do not believe, said Coleridge; you only believe that you believe. It is the final scene in all kinds of worship and symbolism."[31]

Let us never forget: *If God is a symbol, He is a fiction*. But if *God is real*, then He is able to express His will unambiguously. Symbols are makeshifts, necessary to those who cannot express themselves unambiguously.

There is darkness in the world and horror in the soul. What is it that the world needs most? Will man-made symbols redeem humanity? In the past, wars have been waged over differences in symbols rather than over differences in the love of God. Symbols, ceremonies are by their very nature particularistic. Symbols separate us, insights unite us. They unite us regardless of the different ways in which they are expressed. What we need is honesty, stillness, humility, obedience to the word of God. What we need is a *new insight* rather than new symbols.

Symbols without faith are unnecessary baggage. Our task is to overcome the callousness of soul, to be led to a plane where no one can remain both callous and calm; where His presence may be defied but not denied, and where, at the end, faith in Him is the only way.

What we ought to strive for is to find out whether we have a common concern, whether, e.g., we are interested in atonement at all. Then the question of what symbols express atonement is secondary. What we need is immediacy. The ultimate human need is the need for a meaning of existence. This will not be found through introducing a set of symbols.

Harsh and bitter are the problems which religion comes to solve: ignorance, evil, malice, power, agony, and despair. These problems cannot be solved through generalities, through philosophical symbols. Our problem is: Do we believe what we confess? Do we mean what we say?

We do not suffer symbolically; we suffer literally, truly, deeply; symbolic remedies are quackery. The will of God is either real or a delusion.

This is our problem: "We have eyes to see but see not; we have ears to hear but hear not." There is God, and we do not understand Him; there is His word and we ignore it. This is the problem for us. Any other issue is relevant insofar as it helps us to meet that challenge.

The Spirit of Jewish Prayer

IT IS WITH A SENSE of great responsibility that I undertake to discuss with you such a sacred topic, a topic which is called one of the most sublime things in the world, matters that stand on the heights of the universe, that are of supreme importance.

I am going to discuss not only the spirit of Jewish prayer but also the state of prayer in the present day synagogue. The time has come for a self-examination. Let us search and try our ways and return to the Lord. To find a cure we must have the courage to study the ills.

In advancing some critical remarks I do not mean, God forbid, to take a superior attitude. In all honesty, my criticism will be to a considerable degree self-criticism. I am conscious of the great work which members of this assembly are doing, and it is with respect and affection that I address my remarks to this audience. Moreover numerous conversations with some of my own former students assembled here tonight give me the right to feel that I am not going to speak to you but for you. I am going to be in a sense your emissary.

"Poor in worthy deeds, I am horribly frightened in Thy presence, who are enthroned and receiving praise from Israel." I speak to you on prayer, "though I am not deserving nor qualified for the task." "Open my mouth, O Lord, and my lips will proclaim your praise."

I

OUR SERVICES are conducted with pomp and precision. The rendition of the liturgy is smooth. Everything is present: decorum, voice, ceremony. But one thing is missing: *life.* One knows in advance what will ensue. There will be no surprise, no adventure of the soul; there will be no sudden burst of devotion. Nothing is going to happen to the soul. Nothing unpredictable must happen to the person who prays. He will attain no insight into the words he reads; he will attain no new perspective for the life he lives. Our motto is monotony. What was will be, and there is nothing new in the synagogue. The fire has gone out of our worship. It is cold, stiff, and dead. Inorganic Judaism. True, things are happening; of course, not within prayer, but within the administration of the synagogues. Do we not establish new edifices all over the country?

Yes, the edifices are growing. Yet worship is decaying.

Has the synagogue become the graveyard where prayer is buried? Are we, the spiritual leaders of American Jewry, members of a burial society? There are many who labor in the vineyard of oratory; but who knows how to pray, or how to inspire others to pray? There are many who can execute and display magnificent fireworks; but who knows how to kindle a spark in the darkness of a soul?

Some of you may say, I am going too far! Of course, people still attend "services"—but what does this attendance mean to them? Outpouring of the soul? Worship? Prayer, synagogue attendance, has become a benefaction to the synagogue, a service of the community rather than service of God, worship of the congregation rather than worship of God. People give some of their money to UJA, and some of their time to the synagogue.

The modern synagogue suffers from a *severe cold*. Our congregants preserve a respectful distance between the prayerbook and themselves. They say the words "Forgive us for we have sinned," but of course they are not meant. They say, "Thou shalt love the Lord thy God with all thy heart . . ." in lofty detachment, in complete anonymity, as if giving an impartial opinion about an irrelevant question.

An air of tranquillity, complacency prevails in our synagogues. What can come out of such an atmosphere? The services are prim, the voice is dry, the synagogue is clean and tidy, and the soul of prayer lies in agony. You know no one will scream, no one will cry, the words will be still-born.

People expect the rabbi to conduct a service: an efficient, expert service. But efficiency and rapidity are no remedy against devotional sterility. Orthodox rabbis worry about the *bimah* being in the right place. What about the heart being in the right place? What about prayer?

We have developed the habit of *praying by proxy*. Many congregants seem to have adopted the principle of vicarious prayer. The rabbi or the cantor does the praying for the congregation. In particular, it is the organ that does the singing for the whole community. Too often the organ has become the prayer leader. Indeed, when the organ begins to thunder, who can compete with its songs? Men and women are not allowed to raise their voices, unless the rabbi issues the signal. They have come to regard the rabbi as a master of ceremonies.

Is not their mood, in part, a reflection of our own uncertainties? Prayer has become an empty gesture, a figure of speech. Either because of lack of faith or because of *religious bashfulness*. We would not admit that we take prayer seriously. It would sound sanctimonious, if not hypocritical. We are too sophisticated. But if prayer is as important as study, if prayer is as precious a deed as an act of charity, we must stop being embarrassed at our saying a prayer with devotion.

Ours is a great responsibility. We demand that people come to the synagogue instead of playing golf, or making money, or going on a picnic. Why? Don't we mislead them? People take their precious time off to attend services. Some even arrive with profound expectations. But what do they get? What do they receive? Sometimes the rabbi even sits in his chair, wondering: Why did all these people flock together? Spiritually helpless, the rabbi sits in his chair taking attendance.

There is another privation: the loss of grace. Our prayers have so little charm, so little grace, so little grace. What is grace? The presence of the soul. A person has grace when the throbbing of his heart is audible in his voice; when the longings of his soul animate his face. Now, how do our people pray? They recite the prayerbook as if it were last week's newspaper. They ensconce in anonymity—as if prayer were an impersonal exercise—as if worship were an act that came automatically. The words are there, but the souls who are to feel their meaning, to absorb their significance, are absent. They utter shells of syllables, but put nothing of themselves into the shells. In our daily speech, in uttering a sentence, our words have a tonal quality. There is no communication without intonation. It is the intonation that indicates what we mean by what we say, so that we can discern whether we hear a question or an assertion.

It is the *intonation* that lends grace to what we say. But when we pray, the words are faint on our lips. Our words have no tone, no strength, no personal dimension, as if we did not mean what we said; as if we were reading paragraphs in Roget's Thesaurus. It is prayer without grace. Of course, we offer them plenty of responsive reading, but there is little responsiveness to what they read. No one knows how to shed a tear. No one is ready to invest a sigh. Is there no tear in their souls?

> *Is there no balm in Gilead?*
> *Is there no physician there?*
> *Why then is not the health*
> *Of the daughter of my people recovered?*

Assembled in the synagogue everything is there—the body, the benches, the books. But one thing is absent: soul. It is as if they all suffered from *spiritual absenteeism.* In good prayer, words become one with the soul. Yet in our synagogues, people who are otherwise sensitive, vibrant, arresting, sit there aloof, listless, lazy. The dead do not praise God. Those who are spiritually dull cannot praise the Lord.

That we sensed that this is a problem is evidenced by the many valiant but futile attempts to deal with it. The problem, namely, of how to increase synagogue attendance. A variety of suggestions have been made, e.g., to bring the prayerbook up-to-date by composing shorter and better prayers; to invite distinguished speakers, radio commentators, and columnists, to arrange congregational forums, panels, and symposia; to celebrate annual projects such as "Jewish Culture Sabbath," "Jewish War Veterans Sabbath," "Boy Scouts Sabbath," "Interfaith Sabbath" (why not a "*Sabbath* Sabbath"?); to install stained-glass windows; to place gold, silver, or blue pledge cards on the seats; to remind people of their birthday dates. Well intentioned as these suggestions may be, they do not deal with the core of the issue. *Spiritual problems* cannot be solved by *administrative techniques.*

The problem is not how to fill the buildings but how to inspire the hearts. And this is a problem to which techniques of child psychology can hardly be applied. The problem is not one of synagogue attendance but one of spiritual attendance. The problem is not how to attract bodies to enter the space of a temple but how to inspire souls to enter an hour of spiritual concentration in the presence of God. The problem is time, not space.

II

PRAYER IS an extremely embarrassing phenomenon. Numerous attempts have been made to define and to explain it. I will briefly mention four of the prevalent doctrines.

The doctrine of Agnosticism claims that prayer is rooted in superstition. It is "one of humanity's greatest mistakes," "a desperate effort of bewildered creatures to come to terms with surrounding mystery." Thus, prayer is a fraud. To the worshipping man we must say: "Fool, why do you in vain beseech with childish prayers, things which no day ever did bring, will bring, or could bring?"[1] Since it is dangerous fraud, the synagogue must be abolished. A vast number of people have, indeed, eliminated prayer from their lives. They made an end to that illusion.

There are some people who believe that the only way to revitalize the synagogue is to minimize the importance of prayer and to convert the synagogue into a center. It is something which the Talmud characterizes as sin: "To call a holy ark a chest and to call a synagogue a community center."[2]

Let us face the situation. This is the law of life. Just as man cannot live without a soul, Judaism cannot survive without God. Our soul withers without prayer. A synagogue in which men no longer aspire to prayer is not a compromise but a defeat; a perversion, not a concession. To pray with devotion may be difficult; to pray without it is ludicrous.

There are people who seem to believe that religious deeds can be performed in a spiritual wasteland, in the absence of the soul, with a heart hermetically sealed; that external action is the essential mode of worship, pedantry the same as piety; as if all that mattered is how men behaved in physical terms; as if religion were not concerned with the inner life.

Such a conception, which we would like to call *religious behaviorism*, unwittingly reduces Judaism to a sort of sacred physics, with no sense for the imponderable, the introspective, the metaphysical.

As a personal attitude religious behaviorism usually reflects a widely held theology in which the supreme article of faith is *respect for tradition*. People are urged to observe the rituals or to attend services out of deference to what has come down to us from our ancestors. The *theology of respect* pleads for the maintenance of the inherited and transmitted customs and institutions and is characterized by a spirit of conformity, excessive moderation, and disrespect of spontaneity. The outlook of religious behaviorists comes close to the view embodied in Seneca's saying *Tamquam legibus iussa non tamquam dis grata* (Observe religious customs because they are commanded by law, not because they are desired by the gods).

Wise, important, essential, and pedagogically useful as the principle "respect for tradition" is, it is grotesque and self-defeating to make of it the supreme article of faith.

Religious behaviorism is a doctrine that dominates many minds, and is to a large measure responsible for the crisis of prayer.

There is another definition which is being perpetuated all over the country in sermons, synagogue bulletins, and books: *Prayer is the identification of the worshipper with the people of Israel*, or the occasion for immersing ourselves in the living reality of our people. It is built on a theology which regards God as a symbol of social action, as an epitome of the ideals of the group, as "the spirit of the beloved community";[2] as "the spirit of a people, and insofar as there is a world of humanity . . . the Spirit of the World";[3] as the "Creative Good Will" which makes cooperation in our moral endeavor possible.[4]

"An act of identification with the people" is, phenomenologically speaking, the definition of a political act. But is a political phenomenon the same as worship? Moreover, is the act of identification with the Jewish people necessarily an act of serving God? Who is our model: Elijah, who disassociated himself from the congregations of his people, or the prophets of the Baal, who led and identified themselves with their people? The prophets of Israel were not eager to be in agreement with popular sentiments. Spiritually important, essential, and sacred as the identification with the people Israel is, we must not forget that what lends spiritual importance and sanctity to that identification is Israel's unique association with the will of God. It is this association that raises our attachment to the people Israel above the level of mere nationalism.

The doctrine of prayer as a social act is the product of what may be called the "sociological fallacy," according to which the individual has no reality except as a carrier of ideas and attitudes that are derived from group existence. Applied to Jewish faith, it is a total misunderstanding of the nature of Jewish faith to overemphasize the social or communal aspect. It is true that a Jew never worships as an isolated individual but as a part of the people Israel. Yet it is within the heart of every individual that prayer takes place. It is a personal duty, and an intimate act which cannot be delegated to either the cantor or to the whole community. We pray with all of Israel, and every one of us by himself. Contrary to sociological theories, individual prayer came first, while collective prayer is a late phenomenon which is not even mentioned in the Bible. *

Such sociological perspectives forfeit the unique aspects of Judaism. Do we, in the moment of prayer, concentrate on the group? We read in the Psalms: "Give ear to my words, O Lord, understand my meditation." According to the Midrash, David said, "Lord of the World, at the time when I have strength to stand before Thee in prayer and to bring forth words—give ear! At a time when I have no strength to bring forth words—understand what is in my heart, understand my faltering."[5] Can the sociological definition of prayer as an act of identification with the group be applied to this Midrash?

The doctrine maintains that the individual self of the worshipper is the whole sphere of prayer life. The assumption is that God is an idea, a process, a source, a fountain, a spring, a power. But one cannot pray to an idea, one cannot address his prayers to a fountain of values. To whom, then, do we direct our prayers? Yes, there is an answer. As a recent writer put it: We address "prayers to the good within ourselves."[6]

I do not wish to minimize the fact that we all suffer from an egocentric

---

* From the time of Moses, our teacher, of blessed memory, until the Great Assembly . . . the people Israel, wherever they lived, were not accustomed to gathering—morning, afternoon, and night—in one particular place for the purpose of communal prayer. Rather, everyone would pray by himself wherever he happened to be. For we have not found in the prophets and the writings that communal prayer was established until after the destruction [of the First Temple in 586 BCE], when the members of the Great Assembly established the Eighteen Benedictions and the recitation of the *Kedushah*, which requires a prayer quorum of ten. Rabbi Moshe Mi-Trani, Bet Elohim, Venice, 1576.

predicament. Our soul tends to confine itself to its own ideas, interests, and emotions. But why should we raise the egocentric affliction to the status of a virtue? It is precisely the function of prayer to overcome that predicament, to see the world in a different setting. The self is not the hub but the spoke of the revolving wheel. It is precisely the function of prayer to shift the center of living from self-consciousness to self-surrender.[7]

Religious solipsism claims that we must continue to recite our prayers, for prayer is a useful activity. The ideas may be false; it is absurd to believe that God "hearkens to prayers and supplications", but we should say all this because it is good for one's health. It is a useful fiction, therapeutics by a lie. There is no God who hears our prayers but we pray as if . . .

Is it really good for one's health? I think it is old-fashioned and short-sighted psychology to assume that duplicity, "the mouth says one thing, the heart another," could be good for one's health.

We are descendants of those who taught the world what true worship is. Our fathers created the only universal language there is: the language of prayer. All men in the Western world speak to God in the language of our prayers, of our Psalms. Is it not proper to ask our fathers: What is the spirit of Jewish prayer? But are we ready to ask the question? Are we qualified to understand the answer? The difficulty of our situation lies in the fact that we have inherited physical features of our fathers but failed to acquire some of their spiritual qualities. Biologically we are Jews, theologically we are pagan to a considerable degree. Our hands are the hands of Jacob, but our voice is often the voice of Esau.

There are bitter problems which religion has to solve: agony, sin, despair. There is darkness in the world. There is horror in the soul. What has the community of Israel to say to the world?

Gentlemen, we worry a great deal about the problem of church and state, synagogue and state. Now what about the synagogue and God? In fact, sometimes there is a greater separation between the synagogue and God than between the synagogue and state.

Now what qualifies a person to be a rabbi? What gives him the right, the privilege to represent the word of God to the people of God? I have been in the United States of America for thirteen years. I have not discovered America, but I have discovered something in America. It is possible to be a rabbi and not to believe in the God of Abraham, Isaac, and Jacob.*

* "It would appear that the God-concept of the preponderant majority of the rabbis is free from anthropomorphism and the notion of the first cause. Only two rabbis in the entire group of 218 define God as a first cause, and only one out of every seven, as literal creator of the

It has become a habit with modern Jews and Jewish movements to behead, to decapitate biblical verses. Some such decapitated verses have become famous slogans. The name of the BILU movement is an abbreviation of "House of Jacob, come and let us walk . . ." (Isaiah 2:5); the essence of the verse, "in the light of God," was omitted. Disciples of Ahad H'am proclaimed, "Not by might, nor by power, but by spirit . . ." (Zechariah 4:6). Yet the prophet said "my spirit." The Jewish National Fund has as its official motto "And the land shall not be sold in perpetuity" (Leviticus 25:23); the end, "for the land is Mine," was omitted. During the last war the popular slogan among Russian Jews was "I shall not die, but live" (Psalm 118:17); the continuation, "and declare the works of the Lord," was dropped.

Prayer is the microcosm of the soul. It is the whole soul in one moment; the quintessence of all our acts; the climax of all our thoughts. It rises as high as our thoughts. Now, if Torah is nothing but national literature of Jewish people, if the mystery of revelation is discarded as superstition, then prayer is hardly more than a soliloquy. If God does not have power to speak to us, how should we possess the power to speak to Him? Thus, prayer is a part of a greater issue. It depends upon the total spiritual situation of man and upon a mind within which God is at home. Of course, if our lives are too barren to bring forth the spirit of worship, if all our thoughts and anxieties do not contain enough spiritual substance to be distilled into prayer, an inner transformation is a matter of emergency. And such an emergency we face today. *The issue of prayer is not prayer; the issue of prayer is God.* One cannot pray unless he has faith in his own ability to accost the infinite, merciful, eternal God.

Moreover, we must not overlook one of the profound principles of Judaism. There is something which is far greater than my desire to pray, namely, God's desire that I pray. There is something which is far greater than my will to believe, namely, God's will that I believe. How insignificant is the outpouring of my soul in the midst of this great universe! Unless it is the will of God that I pray, unless God desires our prayer,[8] how ludicrous is all my praying.

---

universe—the two supernaturalistic responses. The remainder believe that the nature of God is best expressed as: (a) "the sum total of forces which make for greater intelligence, beauty, goodness; (b) the unitary creative impulse which expresses itself in organic evolution and human progress; (c) the symbol of all that we consider good and true." The first of these three views of God is by far the dominant one.

"With respect to the God-idea, no appreciable difference can be seen between Conservative and Reform wings. These two groups differ, however, from the Orthodox group, a majority of whom think of God primarily as a creator. In both the Conservative and the Reform wings this concept of God which best expresses the views of the rabbis is held by only about 8 percent of the respondents."—J. Zeitlin, *Disciples of the Wise* (New York, 1945), p. 76.

We cannot reach heaven by building a Tower of Babel. The Jewish way *to* God is a way *of* God. God's waiting for our prayers is that which lends meaning to them.

III

HOW SHOULD we define prayer? Since it is, first of all, a phenomenon of the human consciousness, we must ask: What is it that a person is conscious of in a moment of prayer? There is a classical statement in rabbinic literature that expresses the spiritual minimum of prayer as an act of the consciousness of man: *Know before Whom you stand.* * Three ideas are contained in this definition. †

1. *Know* (or understand). A certain understanding or awareness, a definite attitude of the mind is the condition *sine qua non* of Jewish prayer. Prayer cannot live in a theological vacuum. *It comes out of insight.*

Prayer must not be treated as if it were the result of an intellectual oversight, as if it thrived best in the climate of thoughtlessness. One needs understanding, wisdom of the spirit to know what it means to worship God. Or at least one must endeavor to become free of the folly of worshipping the specious glory of mind-made deities, free of unconditional attachment to the false dogmas that populate our minds.

To live without prayer is to live without God, to live without a soul. No one is able to think of Him unless he has learned how to pray to Him. For this is the way man learns to think of the true God—of the God of Israel. He first is aware of His presence long before he thinks of His essence. And to pray is to sense His presence.

There are people who maintain that prayer is a matter of *emotion*. In their desire to "revitalize" prayer, they would proclaim: Let there be emotion! This is, of course, based on a fallacy. Emotion is an important *component*; it is not the *source* of prayer. The power to pray does not depend on whether a person is of a choleric or phlegmatic temperament. One may be extremely emotional and be unable to generate that power. This is decisive: worship comes out of insight. It is not the result of an intellectual oversight.

---

* When Rabbi Eleazar took ill, his students arrived to visit with him. They said to him, "Teach us etiquette." He said to them, "When you pray, know before whom you stand" (Berachot 28b; Avot de-Rabbi Natan (Version A, Chapter 19). See Orchot Chayyim of Rabbi Eleazar Ha-Gadol, Chapter 18: "My son, when you come before your Creator, you must enter in fear and awe, and when you pray, know before whom you stand."

† The sentence consists of three parts: The main verb in the imperative "know." Dependent on this main verb is the clause "before whom you stand," which can be broken up into two segments, the adverbial phrase "before whom," which contains the interrogative pronoun, and "you stand," which is the subject and verb of the subordinate clause.

What is more, prayer has the power to generate insight; it often endows us with an understanding not attainable by speculation. Some of our deepest insights, decisions, and attitudes are born in moments of prayer. Often where reflection fails, prayer succeeds. What thinking is to philosophy, prayer is to religion. And prayer can go beyond speculation. The truth of holiness is not a truth of speculation—it is the truth of worship.

"The Rabbi said: I am amazed that the prayer for understanding was not included in the Sabbath liturgy! For if there is no understanding, how is it possible to pray?"[9]

Know before whom you stand. Such knowledge, such understanding is not easily won. It "is neither a gift we receive undeservedly nor a treasure to be found inadvertently." The art of awareness of God, the art of sensing His presence in our daily lives cannot be learned offhand. "God's grace resounds in our lives like a staccato. Only by retaining the seemingly disconnected notes comes the ability to grasp the theme."[10]

That understanding we no longer try to acquire. In the modern seminaries for the training of rabbis and teachers the art of understanding what prayer implies is not a part of the curriculum. And so it is not the Psalmist, Rabbi Jehudah Halevi, Rabbi Isaiah Horovitz, or Rabbi Nahman of Bratslav; it is Hegel, Freud, or Dewey who has become our guide in matters of Jewish prayer and God.

2. *Before whom.* To have said before *what* would have contradicted the spirit of Jewish prayer. *What* is the most indefinite pronoun. In asking *what*, one is totally uncommitted, uninitiated, bare of any anticipation of an answer; any answer may be acceptable. But he who is totally uncommitted, who does not even have an inkling of the answer, has not learned the meaning of the ultimate question, and is not ready to engage in prayer.[11] If God is a *what*, a power, the sum total of values, how could we pray to it? An "I" does not pray to an "it." Unless, therefore, God is at least as real as my own self; unless I am sure that God has at least as much life as I do, how could I pray?

3. *You stand.* The act of prayer is more than a process of the mind and a movement of the lips. It is an act that happens between man and God—in the presence of God.

Reading or studying the text of a prayer is not the same as praying. What marks the act of prayer is the decision to enter and face the presence of God. To pray means to expose oneself to Him, to His judgment.

If "prayer is the expression of the sense of being at home in the universe,"[12] then the Psalmist who exclaimed, "I am a stranger on earth, hide not Thy commandments from me" (119:19), was a person who grievously misunderstood the nature of prayer. Throughout many centuries of Jewish history the true motivation for prayer was not "the sense of being at home in the universe" but the sense of *not* being at home in the universe. We could not but experience anxiety and spiritual home-lessness in the sight of so much suffering and evil, in the countless ex-amples of failure to live up to the will of God. That experience gained in intensity by the soul-stirring awareness that God Himself was not at home in a universe where His will is defied, where His kingship is denied. *The Shekinah is in exile*, the world is corrupt, *the universe itself is not at home* . . .

To pray, then, means to bring God back into the world, to establish His kingship, to let His glory prevail. This is why in the greatest moments of our lives, on the Days of Awe, we cry out of the depth of our disconcerted souls, a prayer for redemption:

And so, Lord our God, grant Thy awe to all Thy works, and your dread to all Thou hast created, that all Thy works may fear Thee, and all who have been created prostrate themselves before Thee, and all form one union to do Thy will with a whole heart.

Great is the power of prayer. For to worship is to *expand the presence of God* in the world. God is transcendent, but our worship makes Him immanent. This is implied in the idea that God is in need of man: His being immanent depends upon us.[13] When we say, Blessed be He, we extend His glory, we bestow His spirit upon this world. "Magnified and sanctified . . . " May there be more of God in this world.

Decisive is not the mystic experience of our being close to Him; decisive is not our *feeling* but our *certainty* of His being close to us—although even His presence is veiled and beyond the scope of our emotion. Decisive is not our emotion but our *conviction*. If such conviction is lacking, if the presence of God is a myth, then prayer to God is a delusion. If God is unable to listen to us, then we are insane in talking to Him.

The true source of prayer, we said above, is not an emotion but an insight. It is the insight into the mystery of reality, *the sense of the ineffable*, that enables us to pray. As long as we refuse to take notice of what is beyond our sight, beyond our reason; as long as we are blind to the mystery of being, the way to prayer is closed to us. If the rise of the sun is but a daily routine of nature, there is no reason to say, *In mercy Thou givest light to the earth and to those who dwell on it . . . every day constantly.* If bread is nothing but flour moistened, kneaded, baked, and then brought forth from the oven, it is meaningless to say, *Blessed art Thou . . . who bringest forth bread from the earth.*

The way to prayer leads through *acts of wonder* and *radical amazement*. The illusion of total intelligibility, the indifference to the mystery that is everywhere, the foolishness of ultimate self-reliance are serious obstacles on the way. It is in moments of our being faced with the mystery of living and dying, of knowing and not-knowing, of love and the inability to love—that we pray, that *we address ourselves to Him who is beyond the mystery*.

Praise is our first response. Aflame with inability to say what His presence means, we can only sing, we can only utter words of adoration.

This is why in Jewish liturgy *praise* rather than *petition* ranks foremost. It is the more profound form, for it involves not so much the sense of one's own dependence and privation as the sense of God's majesty and glory. *

IV

THERE IS a specific difficulty of Jewish prayer. There are laws: how to pray, when to pray, what to pray. There are fixed times, fixed ways, fixed texts. † On the other hand, prayer is worship of the heart, the outpouring of the soul, a matter of devotion. Thus, Jewish prayer is guided by two opposite principles: order and outburst, regularity and spontaneity, uniformity and individuality, law and freedom. ‡ These principles are the two poles about which Jewish prayer revolves. Since each of the two moves in the opposite direction, equilibrium can be maintained only if both are of equal force. However, the pole of regularity usually proves to be stronger than the pole of spontaneity, and as a result, there is a perpetual danger of prayer becoming a mere habit, a mechanical performance, an exercise in repetitiousness. The fixed pattern and regularity of our services tends to stifle the spontaneity of devotion. Our great problem, therefore, is how not to let the principle of regularity impair the power of devotion. It is a problem that concerns not only prayer but the whole sphere of Jewish observance. He who is not aware of this central difficulty is a simpleton; he who offers a simple solution is a quack.

It is a problem of universal significance. Polarity is an essential trait of

---

* Significantly, prayers written in our time are essentially petitional. Prayers of praise often sound like self-praise.

† According to Rabbi Yose, "He who alters the form of benedictions fixed by the wise has failed to fulfill his obligations" (*Berachoth* 40b; *Yerushalmi Berachoth* VI, 2, 10b). Rabbi Meir declares it to be the duty of everyone to say one hundred benedictions daily (*Menahoth* 43a, see *Numbers Rabba* XVIII).

‡ The contrast between order and outburst is made clear through the term *keva*. Shammai said: "Make your Torah (in the sense of legal decisions made by the scholar) *keva* (a fixed thing)." Do not be lenient to yourself and severe to others, nor lenient to others and severe to yourself. See Avot 1:15 and the explication in Avot de-Rabbi Natan, p. 47, Chapter 23, section 2, Schechter edition. In contrast Rabbi Shimeon said, When you pray, do not make your prayer a fixed thing (*keva*) (Avot 2:18). Rabbi Eliezer said: He who makes his prayer a fixed thing (*keva*), his prayer is not an act of grace (Mishnah Berachot 4:4).

all things in reality, and in Jewish faith the relationship between *halacha* and *agada* is one of *polarity*. Taken abstractly they seem to be mutually exclusive, yet in actual living they involve each other. Jewish tradition maintains that there is no *halacha* without *agada* and no *agada* without *halacha*; that we must neither disparage the body nor sacrifice the spirit. The body is the discipline, the pattern, the law; the spirit is the inner devotion, spontaneity, freedom. The body without the spirit is a corpse; the spirit without the body is a ghost.

And yet the polarity exists and is a source of constant anxiety and occasional tension. How to maintain the reciprocity of tradition and freedom; how to retain both *keva* and *kavanah*, regularity and spontaneity, without upsetting the one or stifling the other?

At first sight, the relationship between *halacha* and *agada* in prayer appears to be simple. Tradition gives us the text, we create the *kavanah*. The text is given once and for all, the inner devotion comes into being every time anew. The text is the property of all ages, *kavanah* is the creation of a single moment. The text belongs to all Jews, *kavanah* is the private concern of every individual. And yet the problem is far from being simple. The text comes out of a book, it is given; *kavanah* must come out of the heart. But is the heart always ready—three times a day—to bring forth devotion? And if it is, is its devotion in tune with what the text proclaims?

In regard to most aspects of observance, Jewish tradition has for pedagogic reasons given primacy to the principle of *keva*; there are many rituals concerning which the law maintains that if a person has performed them without proper *kavanah*, he is to be regarded *ex post facto* as having fulfilled his duty. In prayer, however, *halacha* insists upon the supremacy of *kavanah* over the external performance, at least, theoretically.* Thus, Maimonides declares: "Prayer without *kavanah* is no prayer at all. He who has prayed without *kavanah* ought to pray once more. He whose thoughts are wandering or occupied with other things need not pray until

---

* The polarity of prayer and the decision in favor of the element of *kavanah* is implied in the following discussion. The rabbis inquired: What is the Law if one has inadvertently failed to recite the Afternoon Service [i.e., its *Amidah* prayer]? Should he recite the Evening Service [i.e., its *Amidah* prayer] twice? Do we reason that, since the obligatory daily services substitute for the sacrifices [originally required at those times of day], we are to apply the principle "When its time has passed, a sacrifice can no longer be validly offered"? Or perhaps [we reason that] since prayer is a plea for mercy, one may pray whenever one wishes [and this would include the *Amidah* of the obligatory daily services]?

Come and hear [the following proof-dictum]: Rabbi Huna said in the name of Rabbi Isaac, who said it in the name of Rabbi Yochanan: One who has inadvertently failed to recite the Afternoon Service should recite the Evening Service twice, and the principle "When its time has passed, a sacrifice can no longer be validly offered" is inapplicable here (Berachot 26a).

he has recovered his mental composure. Hence, on returning from a journey, or if one is weary or distressed, it is forbidden to pray until his mind is composed. The sages said that upon returning from a journey, one should wait three days until he is rested and his mind is calm, then he prays."[14]

Significantly, Nahmanides insists that "prayer is not a duty," and he who prays does not perform a requirement of the law. It is not the law of God that commands us to pray; it is the love and "grace of the Creator, blessed be He, to hear and to answer whenever we call upon Him."*

In reality, however, the element of *keva*, of regularity, has often gained the upper hand over the element of *kavanah*. Prayer has become *zogenish*, lip service, an obligation to be discharged, something to get over with: "With their mouths and their lips they honor me while their hearts are far from me, and their awe of me is a human commandment they have earned by rote" (Isaiah 29:13).[15]

Typical is the common use of the term "service" for prayer. *Avodah* means both work, service, and worship. Yet "and to serve him with your whole heart" does not mean to work with your heart.† Service is an external act; worship is inwardness.

Prayer becomes trivial when ceasing to be an act in the soul. The essence of prayer is *agada*. Yet it would be a tragic failure not to appreciate what the spirit of *halacha*, Jewish law, does for it, raising it from the level of an individual act to that of an eternal intercourse between the people Israel and God; from the level of an occasional experience to that of a permanent covenant. It is through *halacha* that we belong to God not occasionally, intermittently, but essentially, continually. Regularity of prayer is an expression of my belonging to an order, to the covenant between God and Israel, which remains valid regardless of whether I am conscious of it or not.

How grateful I am to God that there is a duty to worship, a law to remind my distraught mind that it is time to think of God, time to disregard my ego for at least a moment! It is such happiness to belong to an order of the divine will. I am not always in a mood to pray. I do not always have the vision and the strength to say a word in the presence of God. But when I am weak, it is the law that gives me strength; when my vision is dim, it is duty that gives me insight.

---

* "It is certain that the entire matter of prayer is not at all a legal obligation. Rather, it proceeds from the steadfast love which the Creator, may He be blessed, bestows on us, in that He hears and answers us whenever we call to Him." Nahmanides's critical glosses on Maimonides's *Sefer HaMitzvot*, Mitzvah 5.

† Compare the expressions "strange worship" and "worship of the stars," i.e., idolatry.

We must not think, that *kavanah* is a small matter. It requires constant effort, and we may fail more often than we succeed. But the battle for *kavanah* must go on, if we are not to die of spiritual paralysis.

The rabbis insisted: In order to prevent the practice of repeating a prayer for superstitious or magical purposes, the Talmud ordains that a person who says the word "Hear" (O Israel) or the words "We thank Thee" twice, is to be silenced. Rab Pappa asked Abaye: But perhaps the person repeated his prayer because when he said the words the first time he did not have *kavanah*. So he repeated the prayer in order to say it with *kavanah*. Thus, there was no ground for suspecting him of indulging in superstition or magical practices. Why should we silence him? Answered Abaye: "Has anyone intimacy with heaven?" Has anyone the right to address God thoughtlessly as one talks to a familiar friend? "If he did not at first direct his mind to prayer, we smite him with a smith's hammer until he does direct his mind."*

Prayer is not for the sake of something else. *We pray in order to pray.* It is the queen of all *mitzvot*. No religious act is performed in which prayer is not present. No other *mitzvah* enters our lives as frequently, as steadily as the majesty of prayer.

In Jewish law the first tractate of the Mishnah is Berachot, the section on prayer. In Maimonides's *Mishneh Torah*, in Caro's *Shulhan Aruch*, the first section . . . deals with prayer. In *agada*, rabbinic theology, we are told that "prayer is greater than good deeds," "more precious than . . . sacrifices."[16] To Rabbenu Bahya ben Asher, the spiritual sphere that prayer can reach is higher than the sphere out of which inspiration of the prophets flows.[17]

The philosophy of Jewish living is essentially a philosophy of worship. For what is observance if not a form of worshipping God?

What is a *mitzvah*? A prayer in the form of a deed.

This is the way of finding out whether we serve God, or an idea of God—through prayer. It is the test of all we are doing. What is the difference between Torah and *Wissenschaft des Judentums*? If an idea we have clarified, a concept we have evolved can be turned into a prayer, it is Torah. If it proves to be an aid to praying with greater *kavanah*, it is Torah; otherwise it is *Wissenschaft*. Prayer is of no importance unless it is of supreme importance. "When baseness is exalted among men" (Psalms 12:9). These are the things which are of supreme importance, but which men treat with contempt.[18]

---

* One who says, We give thanks, we give thanks, he is silenced . . . Said Rabbi Pappa to Abaye: But perhaps [this is because] the person is not concentrating at first on what he is praying, but is concentrating the second time? He replied, Can one behave familiarly with heaven? If he did not pray with concentration from the outset, we hit him with a smith's hammer until he does (Berachot 33b–34a).

V

MY INTENTION is not to offer blueprints, to prescribe new rules—
except one: Prayer must have life. It must not be a drudgery, something
done in a rut, something to get over with. It must not be fiction, it must
not be flattened to a ceremony, to an act of mere respect for tradition.

If the main purpose of being a rabbi is to bring men closer to their
Father in heaven, then one of his supreme tasks is to pray and to teach
others how to pray. Torah, worship, and charity are the three pillars upon
which the world rests. To be a Jew implies the acceptance of the *preeminence of prayer.*

To be able to inspire people to pray one must love his people, understand
their predicaments and be sensitive to the power of exaltation, purification,
and sanctification hidden in our Prayer Book. To attain such sensitivity
he must commune with the great masters of the past, and learn how to
pour his own dreams and anxieties into the well of prayer.

We must learn to acquire the basic virtues of inwardness which alone
qualify a rabbi to be a *mentor of prayer.*

One of such virtues is a sense of *spiritual delicacy. Vulgarity* is deadness
to delicacy; the sin of incongruity; the state of being insensitive to the
hierarchy of living, to the separation of private and public, of intimate
and social, of sacred and profane, of farce and reverence.

In itself no act is vulgar; it is the incongruity of the circumstances, the
mixing up of the spheres, the right thing in the wrong context, the out-
of-placeness that generates vulgarity. The use of devices proper in mer-
chandising for influencing opinion about the quality of a work of music;
bringing to public notice a matter that belongs to the sphere of intimate
life,* having a marriage canopy at a bar mitzvah with parents and grand-
parents . . . marching with candles in their hands in a darkened auditorium
and a page boy marching behind the bar mitzvah boy, carrying a prayer
shawl, is vulgar; the marriage canopy belongs elsewhere.

For us, it is of vital importance to beware of *intellectual vulgarity.*
Many categories, conceptions, or words that are properly employed in the
realm of our political, economic, or even scientific activities are, when
applied to issues such as God or prayer, an affront to the spirit. Let us
never put the shoes in the Ark; let us try to regain a sense of separation,
of spiritual delicacy. Let us recapture the meaning of distinguishing.

The problem is not how to revitalize prayer; the problem is how to
revitalize ourselves. Let us begin to cultivate those thoughts and virtues

---

* A good illustration is the rabbinical dictum, All know for what purpose a bride is brought
into the bridal chamber, but whoever disgraces his mouth and utters an obscenity, even if he
had been granted a divine decree of seventy years of happiness, it will be turned for him into
evil (Ketubot 8b).

without which our worship becomes, of necessity, a prayer for the dead
—for ideas which are dead to our hearts.

We must not surrender to the power of platitudes. If our rational methods are deficient and too weak to plumb the depth of faith, let us go into
stillness and wait for the age in which reason will learn to appreciate the
spirit rather than accept standardized notions that stifle the mind and
stultify the soul. We must not take too seriously phrases or ideas which
the history of human thought must have meant in jest, as, for example,
that prayer is "a symbol of ideas and values," "a tendency to idealize the
world," "an act of the appreciation of the self." There was a time when
God became so distant that we were almost ready to deny Him, had
psychologists or sociologists not been willing to permit us to believe in
Him. And how grateful some of us were when told *ex cathedra* that prayer
is not totally irrelevant because it does satisfy an emotional need.

To Judaism the purpose of prayer is not to satisfy an emotional need.
Prayer is not a need but an *ontological necessity*, an act that expresses the
very essence of man. Prayer is for human beings, by virtue of our being
human.[19] He who has never prayed is not fully human. Ontology, not
psychology or sociology, explains prayer.

The dignity of man consists not in his ability to make tools, machines,
guns, but primarily in his being endowed with the gift of addressing God.
It is this gift which should be a part of the definition of man.*

We must learn now to study the inner life of the words that fill the
world of our prayerbook. Without intense study of their meaning, we feel,
indeed, bewildered when we encounter the multitude of those strange,
lofty beings that populate the inner cosmos of the Jewish spirit. It is not
enough to know how to translate Hebrew into English; it is not enough
to have met a word in the dictionary and to have experienced unpleasant
adventures with it in the study of grammar. A word has a soul, and we
must learn how to attain insight into its life.

This is our affliction—we do not know how to look across a word to
its meaning. We forgot how to find the way to the word, how to be on
intimate terms with a few passages in the prayerbook. Familiar with all
words, we are intimate with none.

---

* Exodus 22:22–23: You shall not abuse any widow or orphan. If you do abuse them, when
they cry out to me, I will surely heed their cry. Thus said David: Master of the Universe, even
a wicked person in Israel, when he comes to cry before you, you answer him right away. The
Holy One, Blessed be He, answered him: By your life, even if he would not cry out to me, I
would answer him, as it is said, "Call upon Me in times of trouble; I will rescue you and you
shall honor Me" (Psalms 50:15), and it further says, "When he calls on Me, I will answer him"
(Psalms 91:15). And say, "Before they will call, I will answer" (Isaiah 65:24). And therefore it
is essential that his call should be honest, as it is said: "God is close to all those who call upon
Him, who call upon Him in truth" (Psalms 145:18). Is it possible that he is close to all? We
are taught, "To all who call upon Him in truth" (Midrash Tehillim, 4:5).

As a result, we say words but make no decisions, forgetting that in prayer words are commitments, not the subject matter for aesthetic reflection, that prayer is meaningless unless we stand for what we utter, unless we feel what we accept. *A word of prayer is a word of honor given to God.* However, we have lost our sense for the earnestness of speech, for the dignity of utterance. Spiritual life demands the sanctification of speech. Without an attitude of piety toward words, we will remain at a loss how to pray.

Moreover, words must not be said for the sake of stiffening the mind, of tightening the heart. They must open the mind and untie the heart. A word may be either a blessing or a misfortune. As a blessing it is the insight of a people in the form of a sound, a store of meaning accumulated throughout the ages. As a misfortune it is a substitute for insight, a pretext or a cliché. To those who remember, many of the words in the prayerbook are still warm with the glow of our fathers' devotion. Such Jews we must aspire to recall. While those who have no such memory we must teach how to sense the spiritual life that pulsates through the throbbing words.

In the light of such a decision about the preeminence of prayer, the role as well as the nature of the sermon will have to be reexamined. The prominence given to the sermon, as if the sermon were the core and prayer the shell, is not only a drain on the intellectual resources of the rabbis but also a serious deviation from the spirit of our tradition. The sermon unlike prayer has never been considered as one of the supreme things in this world, matters that stand on the heights of the universe, that are of supreme importance. If the vast amount of time and energy invested in the search of ideas and devices for preaching, if the fire spent on the altar of oratory were dedicated to the realm of prayer, we would not find it too difficult to convey to others what it means to utter a word in the presence of God.

Preaching is either an organic part of the act of prayer or *hullin ba-azarah*, profanity in the domain of the sacred. Sermons indistinguishable in spirit from editorials in *The New York Times*, urging us to have faith in the New Deal, the Big Three, or the United Nations, or attempting to instruct us in the latest theories of psychoanalysis, will hardly inspire us to go on to the *musaf*, the final prayers, and to pray.

> *Through all generations*
> *we will declare Thy greatness;*
> *To all eternity*
> *we will proclaim Thy holiness;*
> *Thy praise, our God,*
> *shall never depart from our mouth.*

Preach in order to pray. Preach in order to inspire others to pray. The test of a true sermon is that it can be converted to prayer.

To the average worshipper many texts of perennial significance have become vapid and seem to be an assembly line of syllables. It is, therefore, a praiseworthy custom for the rabbi to bring forth the meaning of the prayers to the congregation. Unfortunately, some rabbis seem to think that their task is to teach popular *Wissenschaft,* and as a result some services are conducted as if they were *adult-education* programs. Dwelling on the historical aspects, they discuss, for example, the date of composition of the prayers, the peculiarities of their literary form or the supposedly primitive origin of some of our laws and customs.

What about the spirit of prayer? What about relating the people to the truth of its ideas? Too often, so-called explanation kills inspiration.* The suggestion that the Day of Atonement grew out of a pagan festival is, regardless of its scientific merit, hardly consonant with the spirit of the moment of *kol nidre,* the prayer recited at the beginning of the Day of Atonement.

Nor must prayer be treated as an ancestral institution. In explaining sections of the prayerbook our task is not to give a discourse about quaint customs or about "the way our fathers used to think." The prayerbook is not a museum of intellectual antiquities and the synagogue is not a house of lectureship but a house of worship. The purpose of such comments is to inspire "outpouring of the heart" rather than to satisfy historical curiosity; to set forth the hidden relevance of ideas rather than hypotheses of forgotten origins.

There is a book which everyone talks about, but few people have really read. A book which has the distinction of being one of the least known books in our literature. It is the Siddur, the prayerbook. Have we ever pondered the meaning of its words? Let us consider an example:

> Sing unto the Lord, a new song;
> Sing unto the Lord, all the earth.
>
> Psalm 96:1

> Praise Him, sun and moon,
> Praise Him, all you shining stars.
>
> Psalm 148:3

The Egyptian priest could not call upon the stars to praise the gods. He believed that the soul of Isis sparkled in Sirius, the soul of Horus in

---

* I am informed that a congregation listening to comments delivered before the *havdalah,* the prayer at the conclusion of the Sabbath, was told the following: "At the conclusion of the Sabbath, when the additional soul departs, one must be refreshed by smelling aromatic herbs, for at that moment, according to the Zohar, 'the soul and spirit are separated and sad until the smell comes and unites them and makes them glad.' However, this is, of course, not the true reason. The authentic origin of the ceremony is that in ancient times people ate a great deal on the Sabbath and a bad odor came out of their mouth. In order to drive out the odor, they used spices."

Orion, and the soul of Typhon in the Great Bear; it was beyond his scope to conceive that all beings stand in awe and worship God. In our liturgy we go beyond a mere hope; every seventh day we proclaim as a fact: The soul of everything that lives blesses Thy name. *

> They all thank,
> They all praise,
> They all say,
> There is none holy like the Lord.

Whose ear has ever heard how all trees sing to God? Has our reason ever thought of calling upon the sun to praise the Lord? And yet what the ear fails to perceive, what reason fails to conceive, our prayer makes clear to our souls. It is a higher truth, to be grasped by the spirit.

> All Thy works praise Thee

—*Psalms* 145:10

The trouble with the prayerbook is: it is too great for us, it is too lofty. Since we have failed to introduce our minds to its greatness, our souls are often lost in its sublime wilderness.

The prayerbook has become a foreign language even to those of us who know Hebrew. It is not enough to know the vocabulary; what is necessary is to understand the categories, the way of thinking of the prayerbook. It is not enough to read the words; what is necessary is to answer them.

Our prayerbook is going to remain obscure unless Jewish teachers will realize that one of their foremost tasks is to discover, to explain, and to interpret the words of the prayerbook. What we need is a *sympathetic* prayerbook *exegesis.*

Religious movements in our history have often revolved around the problem of liturgy. In the modern movements, too, liturgy was a central issue.

But there was a difference. To kabbalah and Hasidism the primary problem was *how to pray;* to the modern movements, the primary problem was *what to say.* What has Hasidism accomplished? It has inspired worship in a vast number of Jews. What have the moderns accomplished? They have inspired the publication of a vast number of prayerbooks. It is important for the Assembly to clarify its goal. Is it to make a contribution to bibliography or to endow our people with a sense of *kavanah?* There has been for many years a *Prayerbook* Commission. Why is there no *Prayer* Commission?

---

* The usual translation "shall bless" totally misses the meaning of the passage.

Modern Jews suffer from a neurosis which I should like to call the *prayerbook complex.*

True, the text of the prayerbook presents difficulties to many people. But the crisis of prayer is not a problem of the text. It is a problem of the soul. The prayerbook must not be used as a scapegoat. A revision of the prayerbook will not solve the crisis of prayer. What we need is a revision of the soul, a new heart rather than a new text. Did the Jews begin to pray with more *kavanah* since the reference to sacrifices was emended? Textual emendations will not save the spirit of prayer. Nothing less than a spiritual revolution will save prayer from oblivion.

Kavanah is more than attentiveness, more than the state of being aware of what we are saying. If *kavanah* were only presence of the mind, it would be easily achieved by a mere turn of the mind. Yet, according to the Mishnah, the pious men of old felt that they had to meditate an hour in order to attain the state of *kavanah*. In the words of the Mishnah, *kavanah* means "to direct the heart to the Father in heaven." It is not phrased, to direct the heart to the text or the content of the prayer. *Kavanah*, then, is more than paying attention to the literal meaning of a text. It is *attentiveness to God, an act of appreciation of being able to stand in the presence of God.*

Appreciation is not the same as reflection. It is one's being drawn to the preciousness of something he is faced with. To sense the preciousness of being able to pray, to be perceptive of the supreme significance of worshipping of God is the beginning of higher *kavanah*.

"Prayer without *kavanah* is like a body without a soul." "A word uttered without the fear and love of God does not rise to heaven." Once Rabbi Levi Izhak of Berditshev while visiting a city went to a synagogue. Arriving at the gate he refused to enter. When his disciples inquired what was wrong with the synagogue, they received the reply: "The synagogue is full of words of Torah and prayer." This seemed the highest praise to his disciples, and even more reason to enter the synagogue. When they questioned him further, Rabbi Levi Izhak explained: "Words uttered without fear, uttered without love, do not rise to heaven. I sense that the synagogue is full of Torah and full of prayer."

Judaism is not a *religion of space.* * To put it sharply, it is *better* to have

---

* "Rabbi Hama ben Hanina and Rabbi Oshaya were strolling near the synagogue of Lud. Rabbi Hama boasted: "How much money have my ancestors invested in these buildings!" Rabbi Oshaya replied: "How many souls have they wasted here! Were there no students of Torah to support instead?"

Rabbi Abin donated a gate to the Great Synagogue. When Rabbi Mana came to him, he boasted: "Do you see what I have done?" Said Rabbi Mana: " 'When Israel forgets its Creator, they build temples.' (Hosea 8:14) Were there no students of Torah to support instead?" (TJ Shekalim 5, end).

prayer without a synagogue than a synagogue without prayer.* And yet we always speak of *synagogue attendance* rather than of prayer. It is the right word for the wrong spirit. By being in the space of a synagogue while a service is being conducted one has not fulfilled his religious duty. Many of those attending Sabbath services arrive during the reading of the weekly Torah portion and leave without having read the Shema, Hear O Israel, or prayed the Amidah, the central liturgy, of the morning service—the two most important parts of the prayer.

Nor is it the primary purpose of prayer "to promote Jewish unity." As we said above, prayer is a personal duty, and an intimate act which cannot be delegated to either the cantor or the whole community. We pray with the whole community, and every one of us by himself. We must make clear to every Jew that his duty is to pray rather than to be a part of an audience.

The rabbi's role in the sacred hour of worship goes far beyond that of maintaining order and decorum. His unique task is to be a power for arousal, to endow others with a sense of *kavanah*. And as we have said, *kavanah* is more than a touch of emotion. *Kavanah* is insight, appreciation. To acquire such insight, to deepen such appreciation, is something *we must learn* all the days of our lives. It is something *we must live* all the days of our lives. Such insight, such appreciation, we must convey to others. It may be difficult to convey to others *what we think*, but it is not difficult to convey to others *what we live*. Our task is to echo and to reflect the light and spirit of prayer.

It was in the interest of bringing about order and decorum that in some synagogues the rabbi and cantor decided to occupy a position facing the congregation. It is quite possible that a reexamination of the whole problem of worship would lead to the conclusion that the innovation was an error. The essence of prayer is not decorum but rather an event in the inner life of men. One who prays should cast his eyes downward and raise his heart above. † "He who prays must turn his eyes down and his heart up." What goes on in the heart is reflected in one's face. It is

---

* "The Holy One, blessed be He, said to Israel, I said to you that, when you pray, you should pray in the synagogue that is in your town. And if you are not able to pray in the synagogue, pray in your fields. And if you are not able to pray in your fields, pray in your home. And if you are not able to pray in your home, pray on your bed. And if you are not able to pray on your bed, be aroused in your heart." This is what is meant by what is written, "Ponder it on your bed and be silent" (Psalms 4:5), Midrash Tehillim 4:9.

† Yebamot 105b; see also Rosh Hashana 26b: "On Rosh HaShannah, the more a person bends [is humble], the more effective is his prayer," and Rashi's comment: "When a person bends in his prayer, his face pressed to the ground, it is better, because of what is written, "My eyes and My heart shall be there . . ." (I Kings 9:3).

embarrassing to be exposed to the sight of the whole congregation in moments when one wishes to be alone with his God.

A cantor who faces the holiness in the Ark rather than the curiosity of man will realize that his audience is God. He will learn to realize that his task is not to entertain but to represent the people Israel. He will be carried away into moments in which he will forget the world, ignore the congregation and be overcome by the awareness of Him in whose presence he stands. The congregation then will hear and sense that the cantor is not giving a recital but worshipping God, that to pray does not mean to listen to a singer but to identify oneself with what is being proclaimed in their name.*

Kavanah requires preparation. Miracles may happen, but one must not rely on miracles. The spirit of prayer is frequently decided during the hour which precedes the time of prayer. Negatively, one is not ready to engage in certain activities, or even in light talk before he prays. And positively one must learn to perform a degree of inner purification before venturing to address the King of Kings. According to Maimonides, "One must free his heart from all other thoughts and regard himself as standing in the presence of the *Shekinah*. Therefore, before engaging in prayer, the worshipper ought to go aside a little in order to bring himself into a devotional frame of mind, and then he must pray quietly and with feeling, not like one who carries a weight and throws it away and goes farther."†

Let us pray the way we talk. Let us not just utter consonants and vowels. Let us learn how to chant our prayers. It is one of our tragedies that we did not know how to appreciate the very soul of our ancient speech, the style, and instead, have adopted a pompous monotonous manner. Let us try to recapture the last traces of our ancient style. Let us learn *to express* what we say.

We are the most challenged people under the sun. Our existence is either superfluous or indispensable to the world; it is either tragic or holy to be a Jew.

It is a matter of immense responsibility that we here and Jewish teachers everywhere have undertaken to instill in our youth the will to be Jews today, tomorrow, and forever and ever. Unless being a Jew is of absolute significance, how can we justify the ultimate price which our people was often forced to pay throughout its history? To assess Judaism soberly and farsightedly is to establish it as a good to be preferred, if necessary, to any alternative which we may ever face. This is often the only adequate perspective of evaluating Judaism, a perspective into which the world

---

* And for the prayer of the Shaliah Zibbur,
† Mishneh Torah, Laws of Prayer, Chapter 4:16.

currents do not tire to force us, whether in the name of Hellenistic culture, of Almohadic Islam, of medieval crusaders, of modern assimilation, or of contemporary Fascism. The truth is, we have more faith than we are willing to admit. Yet it is stifled, suppressed, and distorted by an irreligious way of thinking.

At this hour, O Lord, we open our thoughts to thee, in tears and contrition. We, teachers in Israel, stand at this present moment between all of the past and all of the future of the people of Israel. It is upon us to hand over the Torah, the holiness, the spirit of prophets, sages, and saints, to all the generations to come. If we should fail, much of Judaism will be lost, gone and forgotten. O Lord! we confess our failure. Day after day we have betrayed Thee. Steeped in vanity, envy, ambition, we have often labored to magnify our own names, although we said "Magnified and sanctified be His great name." Dazzled by the splendor of intellectual fads, we have accepted platitudes as dogmas, prejudices as solutions, although we repeated "And eternal life He has planted in our midst."

RETURN US, OUR FATHER, TO YOUR TORAH

Professor Heschel: Friends: *Mitzvot* were not given for enjoyment. Listening to the discussion this evening was no pleasure, so it must have been a very great *mitzvah*. I sensed a strange combination in the minds of most participants, a combination of peace of mind and despair.

What impressed me in this discussion was the fact that none of those who objected to my remarks about the state of prayer has claimed that his services are satisfactory, that prayer is alive.

My friends, through watching my own life I detected how serious my failures are. It is unlikely that I should have the monopoly on failure and that no one else should be suffering from similar inadequacies and ills. I am profoundly embarrassed by the inadequacy of my praying. I have no peace of mind, nor do I submit to despair.

Words have come to be very cheap, particularly in our circles. They ceased to be commitments. Gone is the sensitivity to their power. Yet bitter is the fate of those who forfeit completely the sense for their weight, for words when abused take vengeance on the abusers.

Of course, decorum is important. If we insist upon cultivating form and decorum in our homes, it would be wrong not to cultivate form and decorum in the synagogue. Yet is decorum the most vital, the most creative aspect of existence? One cannot live by decorum alone. As I did not question the importance of decorum, I did not object to the fine custom of interpreting passages of our liturgy. What I did object to was the kind of interpretation that is usually offered, namely historic information rather than commitment, rather than inner identification. You recall the examples. I have listened to such comments myself and was not moved to pray. Was it because my heart is made of stone?

When entering a synagogue, I said, "One knows in advance what will ensue. There will be no surprise, no adventure of the soul; there will be no sudden outburst of devotion. Nothing is going to happen to the person who prays." By that remark I did not mean that there has to be a new program or a new ceremony every week. I meant that something new, something fresh should happen in the heart of the rabbi whenever he prays, whether it be a sense of contrition, whether it be a new realization or a discovery in that *terra incognita*—the Jewish prayerbook. I do not refer to any supernatural events or to any scholarly discoveries. I refer to countless moments of insight which can be gained from communing with the individual words. I refer to the mystery that the same word may evoke ever new understandings when read with an open heart. I refer to the mysterious fact that what happens in the heart of one person conveys itself to all others present. One single individual may transform a whole congregation.

Gentlemen, what I plead for is the creation of a prayer atmosphere. Such an atmosphere is not created by ceremonies, gimmicks, or speeches, but by the example of prayer, by a person who prays. You create that atmosphere not around you but within you. I am a congregant and I know from personal experience how different the situation is when the rabbi is concerned with prayer instead of with how many people attend the service; the difference between a service in which the rabbi comes prepared to respond to thirty centuries of Jewish experience and one in which he comes to review the book of the month or the news of the day.

Now the organ. My criticism was from a psychological point of view. I am not deaf to music. I happen to appreciate what the organ is capable of conveying. But I must admit that I cannot compete with its immense power. I cannot speak while the organ sings. It is just too great for me. Jewish prayer is personal, not vicarious. It is something that must happen *within*, and not *for*, a person.

As to "responsive reading," I only stressed that we ought to worry more about responsiveness to reading.

The unresponsiveness to what we read is what appalls me. There is light in the words, but we ignore it. Almost any word, any passage has untold resources of meaning, paradoxical beauty, and depth. How many of us have ever pondered over the very first word of Ashrei, Psalm 145. What superhuman boldness to say I exalt you, my God, the king, and yet we say it three times each day. What a paradox for me to promise to lift up Him who is the Most High . . .

One of the discussants has said that there is no surprise in music, that when you come to hear a concert you know exactly what you are going to get. This, indeed, would come as a surprise to every lover of music. Why should one go to a concert twice? Every recital even by the same artist and even of the same work is a different performance, otherwise the artist would be guilty of the sin of boredom.

Now, about the relation of prayer to God. It was said, "None of us, *no matter how we conceive our philosophy of Judaism*, would ever dream of uttering that thought, that there could be prayer without God." Now, it matters very much how we conceive our philosophy of Judaism. What is God? An empty generality? An alibi? Some kind of an idea that we develop? I have been wrestling with the problem all my life as to whether I really mean God when I pray to Him, whether I have even succeeded in knowing what I am talking about and whom I am talking to. I still don't know whether I serve God or I serve something else. Unfortunately, many of us pick up any term developed by any philosopher, long after that philosophy itself has already died in the history of philosophy, and give it the name of God.

The question was asked what is my attitude toward the prayer of those who do not accept the conception of God that I discussed. Now, *I have not spoken of a concept* or demanded the acceptance of a definition. We Jews have no concepts; all we have is faith, faith in His willingness to listen to us. We have no information, but we sense and believe in His being near to us. Israel is not a people of definers of religion but a *people of witnesses* to His concern for man.

We have committed ourselves to Jewish experience, let us not distort it. We are not ready to emend the text and begin the Amidah, the central prayer of the Jewish liturgy, by saying, "Blessed be It, the Supreme Concept, the God of Spinoza, Dewey, and Alexander." Indeed, the term "God of Abraham, Isaac, and Jacob" is semantically different from a term such as "the God of truth, goodness, and beauty." Abraham, Isaac, and Jacob do not signify ideas, principles, or abstract values. Nor do they stand for teachers or thinkers, and the term is not to be understood like that of "the God of Spinoza, Dewey, and Alexander." The categories of the Bible are not principles to be comprehended but events to be continued. The life of him who joins the covenant of Abraham continues the life of Abraham. Abraham endures forever. We *are* Abraham, Isaac, Jacob.

There are no concepts which we could appoint to designate the greatness of God or represent Him to our minds. He is not a being whose existence can be proved by our syllogisms. He is a reality, in the face of which, when becoming alive to it, all concepts become clichés.

Genuine prayer does not flow out of concepts. It comes out of the awareness of the mystery of God rather than out of information about Him.

There is no one who has no theology. It is the false theologies silencing God that block and hamper us in our response to Him. It is our misdirected certainty and unfounded dogma that have stifled the heart of Jewish prayer. Everyone today will grant that there is a supreme deity that has ultimate power in the realm of being and values. But why is not God also granted the power to penetrate human lives? The power to reach the people of Israel? Is He omnipotent only in general but not in fact? It is just as wrong to place Him beyond all the beyonds as it once was to see Him inside every stone. He who claims to know that God is trapped in a closed system of silent unrelatedness, that He is behind the bars of infinity, that He cannot address us, is more dogmatic than I. With this kind of dogmatism we have to take issue.

As I said last night, unless God is at least as real as my own self, unless I am sure that God has at least as much life as I do, how could I pray? If God does not have the power to speak to us, how should we possess the power to speak to Him? If God is unable to listen to me, then I am insane in talking to Him.

The strange thing about many of our contemporaries is that their life is nobler than their ideology, that their faith is deep and their views are shallow, that their souls are suppressed and their slogans proclaimed. We must not continue to cherish a theory just because we embraced it forty years ago. Faith is not something that we acquire once and for all. Faith is an insight that must be acquired at every single moment.

Those who honestly search, those who yearn and fail, we did not presume to judge. Let them pray to be able to pray, and if they do not succeed, if they have no tears to shed, let them yearn for tears, let them try to discover their heart and let them take strength from the certainty that this too is a high form of prayer.

Toward an Understanding

of Halacha

IT IS A GREAT HONOR and a great responsibility to address the convention of the Central Conference of American Rabbis. I had the privilege of teaching for five years at the Hebrew Union College. In fact it was Dr. Julian Morgenstern who extended an invitation to me to come to the college while I was still in Warsaw, and it was through the Hebrew Union College that I was able to arrive in the United States in March 1940. It gives me great joy to be able to express my gratitude to him on this occasion.

I feel in a sense qualified to address this convention because I have, even after my leaving the college, maintained a deep concern for the spiritual problems that occupy many members of this conference.

The time available to me this evening is too limited to enable me to present a systematic view of Jewish theology. I have, therefore, decided not to offer a digest of a theological system but to make an attempt to contribute to the clarification of some of the problems that are being discussed by the members of this distinguished conference.

Your problems are not alien to me. I too have wrestled with the difficulties inherent in our faith as Jews. Whatever I am going to say tonight will, of course, be in need of further elaboration.

I

I CAME WITH great hunger to the University of Berlin to study philosophy. I looked for a system of thought, for the depth of the spirit, for the meaning of existence. Erudite and profound scholars gave courses in logic, epistemology, aesthetics, ethics, and metaphysics. They opened the gates of the history of philosophy. I was exposed to the austere discipline of unremitting inquiry and self-criticism. I communed with the thinkers of the past who knew how to meet intellectual adversity with fortitude, and learned to dedicate myself to the examination of basic premises at the risk of failure.

What were the trends of thought to which I was exposed at the university?

Kant, who held dominion over many minds, had demonstrated that it is utterly impossible to attain knowledge of the world . . . because knowledge is always in the form of categories, and these, in the last analysis, are only representational constructions for the purpose of apperceiving what is given. Objects possessing attributes, causes that work, are all mythical. We can only say that objective phenomena are regarded *as if* they behaved in such and such a way, and there is absolutely no justification for assuming any dogmatic attitude and changing the "as if" into a "that." Salomon Maimon was probably the first to sum up Kantian philosophy by saying that only *symbolic knowledge* is possible.

In the light of such a theory, what is the status of religious knowledge? We must, of course, give up hope of ever attaining a valid concept of the supernatural in an objective sense, yet since for practical reasons it is useful to cherish the idea of God, let us retain that idea and claim that while our knowledge of God is not objectively true, it is still *symbolically* true.

Thus, symbolism became the supreme category in understanding religious truth. It has become a truism that religion is largely an affair of symbols. Translated into simpler terms, this view regards religion as a *fiction*, useful to society or to man's personal well-being. Religion is not a relationship of man to God but a relationship of man to the symbol of his highest ideals. There is no God, but we must go on worshipping his symbol.

The idea of symbolism is, of course, not a modern invention. New is the role it has now assumed. In earlier times, symbolism was regarded as a form of *religious thinking*; in modern times religion is regarded as a form of *symbolic thinking*.

II

IT WAS AT an early phase of my studies at the university that I came to realize: *If God is a symbol, He is a fiction*. But if God is *real*, then He is able to express His will unambiguously. Symbols are makeshifts, necessary to those who cannot express themselves unambiguously.

There is darkness in the world and horror in the soul. What is it that the world needs most? Harsh and bitter are the problems which religion comes to solve: ignorance, evil, malice, power, agony, despair. These problems cannot be solved through generalities, through philosophical symbols. Our problem is: Do we believe what we confess? Do we mean what we say?

We do not suffer symbolically. We suffer literally, truly, deeply. Symbolic remedies are quackery. The will of God is either real or a delusion.

This was the most important challenge to me: "We have eyes to see but see not; we have ears to hear but hear not." Any other issue was relevant only insofar as it helped me to answer that challenge.

I became increasingly aware of the gulf that separated my views from those held at the university. I had come with a sense of anxiety: How can I rationally find a way where ultimate meaning lies, a way of living where one would never miss a reference to supreme significance? Why am I here at all, and what is my purpose? I did not even know how to phrase my concern. But to my teachers that was a question unworthy of philosophical analysis.

I realized that my teachers were prisoners of a Greek-German way of thinking. They were fettered in categories which presupposed certain metaphysical assumptions which could never be proved. The questions I was moved by could not even be adequately phrased in categories of their thinking.

My assumption was: Man's dignity consists in his having been created in the likeness of God. My question was: How must man, a being who is in essence the image of God, think, feel, and act? To them, religion was a feeling. To me, religion included the insights of the Torah, which is a vision of man from the point of view of God. They spoke of God from the point of view of man. To them God was an idea, a postulate of reason. They granted Him the status of being a logical possibility. But to assume that He had existence would have been a crime against epistemology.

The problem to my professors was how to be good. In my ears the question rang: How to be holy. At the time I realized that there is much that philosophy could learn from Jewish life. To the philosophers the idea of the good was the most exalted idea, the ultimate idea. To Judaism the idea of the good is penultimate. It cannot exist without the holy. The good is the base, the holy is the summit. Man cannot be good unless he strives to be holy.

To have an idea of the good is not the same as living by the insight, Blessed is the man who does not forget Thee.

I did not come to the university because I did not know the idea of the good but to learn why the idea of the good is valid, why and whether values had meaning. Yet I discovered that values sweet to taste proved sour in analysis; the prototypes were firm, the models flabby. Must speculation and existence remain like two infinite parallel lines that never meet? Or perhaps this impossibility of juncture is the result of the fact that our speculation suffers from what is called in astronomy a parallax, from the apparent displacement of the object, caused by the actual change of our point of observation?

III

IN THOSE MONTHS in Berlin I went through moments of profound bitterness. I felt very much alone with my own problems and anxieties. I walked alone in the evenings through the magnificent streets of Berlin. I admired the solidity of its architecture, the overwhelming drive and power of a dynamic civilization. There were concerts, theaters, and lectures by famous scholars about the latest theories and inventions, and I was pondering whether to go to the new Max Reinhardt play or to a lecture about the theory of relativity.

Suddenly I noticed the sun had gone down, evening had arrived.

From what hour is the Shema recited in the evening?

I had forgotten God—I had forgotten Sinai—I had forgotten that sunset is my business—that my task is "to repair the world under God's dominion."

So I began to utter the words "who with His word brings down the evening."

And Goethe's famous poem rang in my ear:

Ueber allen Gipfeln ist Ruh

O'er all the hilltops is quiet now.

No, that was pagan thinking. To the pagan eye the mystery of life is *Ruh'*, death, oblivion.

To us Jews, there is meaning beyond the mystery. We would say

O'er all the hilltops is the word of God

Ueber allen Gipfeln ist Gottes Wort.

The meaning of life is to do His will . . .

who with His word brings down the evening.

And His love is manifested in His teaching us Torah, precepts, laws

Ueber allen Gipfeln is God's love for man—

You have loved your people the House of Israel with eternal love
Torah and mitzvot, *laws and statutes you have taught us.*

How much guidance, how many ultimate insights are found in the Siddur.

How grateful I am to God that there is a duty to worship, a law to remind my distraught mind that it is time to think of God, time to disregard my ego for at least a moment! It is such happiness to belong to an order of the divine will.

I am not always in a mood to pray. I do not always have the vision and the strength to say a word in the presence of God. But when I am weak, it is the law that gives me strength; when my vision is dim, it is duty that gives me insight.

Indeed, there is something which is far greater than my desire to pray. Namely, God's desire that I pray. There is something which is far greater than my will to believe. Namely, God's will that I believe. How insignificant is my praying in the midst of a cosmic process! Unless it is the will of God that I pray, how ludicrous is it to pray.

On that evening, in the streets of Berlin, I was not in a mood to pray. My heart was heavy, my soul was sad. It was difficult for the lofty words of prayer to break through the dark clouds of my inner life.

But how would I dare not to *davn*? How would I dare to miss a *ma'ariv*? From what hour, *me'eimatai*, do we recite the Shema? Say rather, "Out of *eima*, out of fear of God do we read the *Shema*."

IV

THE FOLLOWING morning I awoke in my student garret. Now, the magnificent achievements in the field of physiology and psychology have, of course, not diminished but rather increased my sense of wonder for the human body and soul. And so I prayed

"Who created human beings with wisdom" and
"My God, the soul you have given me is pure."

Yet how am I going to keep my soul clean?

The most important problem which a human being must face daily is how to maintain one's integrity in a world where power, success, and money are valued above all else? How to remain clean amid the mud of falsehood and malice that soil our society?

The soul is clean, but within it resides a power for evil, "a strange god,"* that "seeks constantly to get the upper hand over man and to kill him; and if God did not help him, he could not resist it, as it is said, 'The wicked watches the righteous, and seeks to slay him.' "[1]

Every morning I take a piece of cloth—neither elegant nor solemn, of no particular aesthetic beauty, a *talit*, wrap myself in it, and say:

"How precious is Thy kindness, O God! The children of man take refuge in the shadow of Thy wings. They have their fill of the choice food of Thy house, and Thou givest them drink of Thy stream of delights. For with Thee is the fountain of life; by Thy light do we see light. Continue Thy kindness to those who know Thee, and Thy righteousness to the upright in heart."

But then I ask myself: Have I got a right to take my refuge in Him? to drink of the stream of His delights? to expect Him to continue His kindness? But God wants me to be close to Him, even to bind every morning His word as a sign on my hand, and between my eyes, winding the strap three times round the middle finger. I would remind myself of the word that God spoke to *me* through His prophet Hosea:

"I will betroth you to myself forever; I will betroth you to myself in righteousness and in justice, in kindness and in mercy. I will betroth you to myself in faithfulness; and you shall know the Lord." It is an act of betrothal, a promise to marry . . . It is an act of God, falling in love with His people. But the engagement depends on righteousness, justice, kindness, mercy.

v

WHY DID I decide to take *halacha* seriously in spite of the numerous perplexities in which I became enmeshed?

Why did I pray, although I was not in a mood to pray? And why was I able to pray in spite of being unprepared to pray? What was my situation after the reminder to pray *ma'ariv* struck my mind? The duty to worship stood as a thought of ineffable meaning; doubt, the voice of disbelief, was ready to challenge it. But where should the engagement take place? In an act of reflection the duty to worship is a mere thought, timid, frail, a mere shadow of reality, while the voice of disbelief is a power, well armed with the weight of inertia and the preference for abstention. In such an engagement prayer would be fought *in absentia*, and the issue would be

---

* Shabbath 105b. *"Begufo"* does not mean the body but the self or the essence of man; it is used by R. Abin as a paraphrase of "in thee," Psalms 81:10. Compare the expression *"gufei Torah,"* Mishnah Hagigah 1, 8, which means "the essentials of Torah"; see also Aboth 3, 18, *"gufei halacha."*

decided without actually joining the battle. It was fair, therefore, to give the weaker rival a chance: to pray first, to fight later.

I realized that just as you cannot study philosophy through praying, you cannot study prayer through philosophizing. And what applies to prayer is true in regard to the essentials of Jewish observance.

What I wanted to avoid was not only the failure to pray to God during a whole evening of my life but *the loss of the whole,* the loss of belonging to the spiritual order of Jewish living. It is true that some people are so busy with collecting shreds and patches of the law that they hardly think of weaving the pattern of the whole. But there is also the danger of being so enchanted by the whole as to lose sight of the detail. It became increasingly clear to me that the order of Jewish living is meant to be, not a set of rituals, but an order of all of man's existence, shaping all his traits, interests, and dispositions; "not so much the performance of single acts, the taking of a step now and then, as the pursuit of a way, being on the way; not so much the act of fulfilling as the state of being committed to the task, the belonging to an order in which single deeds, aggregates of religious feeling, sporadic sentiments, moral episodes become a part of a complete pattern" (270).*

The ineffable Name—we have forgotten how to pronounce it. We have almost forgotten how to spell it. We may totally forget how to recognize it.

VI

THERE ARE a number of ideas concerning Jewish Law which have proved most inimical to its survival, and I would like to refer to two. First is the assumption that either you observe all or nothing; all of its rules are of equal importance; and if one brick is removed, the whole edifice must collapse. Such intransigence, laudable as it may be as an expression of devoutness, is neither historically nor theologically justified. There were ages in Jewish history when some aspects of Jewish ritual observance were not adhered to by people who had otherwise lived according to the Law. And where is the man who could claim that he has been able to fulfill literally the *mitzvah* of "Love your neighbor as yourself"?

Where is the worry about the spiritual inadequacy of that which admittedly should not be abandoned? Where is our anxiety about the barrenness of our praying, the conventionality of our ceremonialism?

The problem, then, that cries for a solution is not everything or nothing, total or partial obedience to the law; the problem is authentic or forged,

---

* Numbers in parentheses in this essay refer to pages of the author's *Man Is Not Alone.*

genuine or artificial observance. The problem is not *how much* but *how to* observe. The problem is whether we *obey* or whether we merely *play* with the word of God.

Second is the assumption that every iota of the law was revealed to Moses at Sinai. This is an unwarranted extension of the rabbinic concept of revelation. "Could Moses have learned the whole Torah? Of the Torah it says, *The measure thereof is longer than the earth, and broader than the sea* (Job 11:9); could then Moses have learned it in forty days? No, it was only the principles thereof which God taught Moses."*

The role of the sages in interpreting the word of the Bible and their power to issue new ordinances is a basic element of Jewish belief and something for which our sages found sanction in Deuteronomy 17:11. The awareness of the expanding nature of Jewish Law was expressed by such a great saint and authority as Rabbi Isaiah Horovitz in his *Two Tablets of the Covenant*.

"And now I will explain the phenomenon that in every generation the number of restrictions [in the *halacha*] is increased. In the time of Moses, only what he had explicitly received at Sinai (the written law) was binding, plus several ordinances which he added for whatever reasons he saw fit. [However] the prophets, the Tannaim, and the rabbis of every generation [have continued to multiply these restrictions]. The reason is that as the venom of the serpent spreads, greater protection is needed. The Holy One provided for us three hundred and sixty-five prohibitions in order to prevent the venom from becoming too active. Therefore, whenever the venom of a generation grows virulent, more restrictions must be imposed. Had this [the spread of venom] been the situation at the time of the giving of the Torah, [those interdictions] would have been specifically included in it. However, instead, the later ordinances derive their authority from God's command—'make a protection for the law'—which means 'make nec-

---

* "Since the oral Torah, which Moses transmitted to Joshua and Joshua to the elders and so forth, even though it was a complete explanation of the Torah and the *mitzvot*, is not of any one time and generation, it would fail to be renewed, necessarily, and to be wonderful in judgment. And do not reply to me out of what is written in the second chapter of Megillah (19:2): 'What do we mean by "And everything that is about them, etc."'? This teaches us that the Holy One, Blessed be He, showed Moses the rulings of Torah and the rulings of sages and everything that the sages were in the future to devise.' Because I would reply that Moses never transmitted these things to anyone else at all. And the language specifically is as follows: They said, 'It teaches us that He *showed him*,' *not that he transmitted to him or taught him*. And if it had used either of those words, we would be obliged to understand that he had transmitted them and given them to Joshua. Because, after all, he was not stingy; for example, we read that he laid both hands on Joshua to ordain him although he was only commanded to use one hand. But instead it says: 'He showed him,' *visually only*, not in a way that would transmit it, just as a person shows something to a friend without giving it to him. And this is a fitting explanation and a true understanding" (Rabbi Yom Tov Lippmann Heller, *Tosaphot Yom Tov*, Introduction).

essary ordinances according to the state of each generation' and these have the same authority as the Torah itself."

There are times in Jewish history when the main issue is not what parts of the *halacha* cannot be fulfilled but what parts of the *halacha* can be and ought to be fulfilled, fulfilled as *halacha*, as an expression and interpretation of the will of God.

There are many problems which we encounter in our reflections on the issue of Jewish observance. Tonight I wish to discuss briefly several of these problems, namely: the relation of observance to our understanding of the will of God; the meaning of observance to man; the regularity of worship; inwardness and the essence of religion; the relevance of the external deeds.

VII

FROM a rationalist's point of view, it does not seem plausible to assume that the infinite, ultimate Supreme Being is concerned with my putting on *tefillin* every day. It is, indeed, strange to believe that God should care whether a particular individual will eat leavened or unleavened bread during a particular season of the year. However, it is that paradox— namely, that the infinite God is intimately concerned with finite man and his finite deeds; that nothing is trite or irrelevant in the eyes of God—which is the very essence of the prophetic faith.

There are people who are hesitant to take seriously the possibility of our knowing what the will of God demands of us. Yet we all whole-heartedly accept Micah's words: "He has showed you, O man, what is good, and what does the Lord require of you, but to do justice, and to love kindness and to walk humbly with your God." If we believe that there is something which God requires of man, then what is our belief if not *faith in the will of God, certainty of knowing what His will demands of us?* If we are ready to believe that God requires of us "to do justice," is it more difficult for us to believe that God requires of us to be holy? If we are ready to believe that it is God who requires us "to love kindness," is it more difficult to believe that God requires us to hallow the Sabbath and not to violate its sanctity?

If it is the word of Micah uttering the will of God that we believe in, and not a peg on which to hang views we derived from rationalist philosophies, then "to love justice" is just as much *halacha* as the prohibition of making a fire on the Seventh Day. If, however, all we can hear in these words are echoes of Western philosophy rather than the voice of Micah, does that not mean that the prophet has nothing to say to any of us?

VIII

A SERIOUS difficulty is the problem of the *meaning of Jewish observance*. The modern Jew cannot accept the way of static obedience as a shortcut to the mystery of the divine will. His religious situation is not conducive to an attitude of intellectual or spiritual surrender. He is not ready to sacrifice his liberty on the altar of loyalty to the spirit of his ancestors. He will only respond to a demonstration that there is meaning to be found in what we expect him to do. His primary difficulty is not in his inability to comprehend the *divine origin* of the law; his essential difficulty is in his inability to sense the *presence of divine meaning* in the fulfillment of the law.

Let us never forget that some of the basic theological presuppositions of Judaism cannot be justified in terms of human reason. Its conception of the nature of man as having been created in the likeness of God, its conception of God and history, of prayer, and even of morality, defy some of the realizations at which we have honestly arrived at the end of our analysis and scrutiny. The demands of piety are a mystery before which man is reduced to reverence and silence. In a technological society, when religion becomes a function, piety too is an instrument to satisfy his needs. We must therefore be particularly careful not to fall into the habit of looking at religion as if it were a machine which can be worked, an organization which can be run according to one's calculations.

The problem of how to live as a Jew cannot be solved in terms of common sense and common experience. The order of Jewish living is a spiritual one; it has a spiritual logic of its own which cannot be apprehended unless its basic terms are lived and appreciated.

It is in regard to this problem that we must keep in mind three things: (a) divine meaning is *spiritual* meaning; (b) the apprehension of divine meaning is contingent upon *spiritual preparedness*; (c) it is experienced *in acts* rather than in speculation.

a. The problem of ethics is: What is the ideal or principle of conduct that is *rationally* justifiable? While to religion the problem of living is: What is the ideal or principle of living that is *spiritually* justifiable? The legitimate question concerning the forms of Jewish observance is, therefore, the question: Are they spiritually meaningful?

We should, consequently, not evaluate the *mitzvot* by the amount of rational meaning we may discover at their basis. Religion is not within but beyond the limits of mere reason. Its task is not to compete with reason, to be a source of speculative ideas, but to aid us where reason gives us only partial aid. Its meaning must be understood in terms *compatible with the sense of the ineffable*. Frequently where concepts fail, where rational understanding ends, the meaning of observance begins. Its purpose is not essentially to serve hygiene, happiness, or the vitality of man; its purpose is to add holiness to hygiene, grandeur to happiness, spirit to vitality.

Spiritual meaning is not always limpid; transparency is the quality of glass, while diamonds are distinguished by refractive power and the play of prismatic colors.

Indeed, any reason we may advance for our loyalty to the Jewish order of living merely points to one of its many facets. To say that the *mitzvot* have meaning is less accurate than saying that they lead us to wells of emergent meaning, to experiences which are full of hidden brilliance of the holy, suddenly blazing in our thoughts.

Those who, out of their commendable desire to save the Jewish way of life, bring its meaning under the hammer tend to sell it at the end to the lowest bidder. The highest values are not in demand and are not salable in the marketplace. In spiritual life some experiences are like a *camera obscura*, through which light has to enter in order to form an image upon the mind, the image of ineffable intelligibility. Insistence upon explaining and relating the holy to the relative and functional is like lighting a candle in the camera.

Works of piety are like works of art. They are functional, they serve a purpose, but their essence is intrinsic, their value is in what they are in themselves.

b. Sensitivity to spiritual meaning is not easily won; it is the fruit of hard, constant devotion, of insistence upon remaining true to a vision. It is "an endless pilgrimage . . . a drive towards serving Him who rings our hearts like a bell, as if He were waiting to enter our lives . . . Its essence is not revealed in the way we utter it, but in the soul's being in accord with what is relevant to God; in the extension of our love to what God may approve, our being carried away by the tide of His thoughts, rising beyond the desolate ken of man's despair" (174).

"God's grace resounds in our lives like a staccato. Only by retaining the seemingly disconnected notes comes the ability to grasp the theme" (88).

c. What is the Jewish way to God? It is not a way of ascending the ladder of speculation. Our understanding of God is not the triumphant outcome of an assault upon the riddles of the universe or a donation we receive in return for intellectual surrender. Our understanding comes by the way of *mitzvah*. By living as Jews we attain our faith as Jews. We do not have faith in deeds; we attain faith through deeds.

When Moses recounted to the people the laws of the covenant with God, the people responded: "We will do and we will hear." This statement was interpreted to mean: *In doing we perceive.*

A Jew is asked to take a *leap of action* rather than a *leap of thought*: to surpass his needs, to do more than he understands in order to understand more than he does. In carrying out the word of the Torah he is ushered into the presence of spiritual meaning. Through the ecstasy of deeds he learns to be certain of the presence of God.

Jewish Law is a sacred prosody. The divine sings in our deeds, the divine is disclosed in our deeds. Our effort is but a counterpoint in the music of His will. In exposing our lives to God, we discover the divine within ourselves and its accord with the divine beyond ourselves.

If at the moment of doing a *mitzvah* once perceived to be thus sublime, thus divine, you are in it with all your heart and with all your soul, there is no great distance between you and God. For acts of holiness uttered by the soul disclose the holiness of God hidden in every moment of time. And His holiness and He are one.

I X

WHY SHOULD worship be bound to regular occasions? Why impose a calendar on the soul? Is not regularity of observance a menace to the freedom of the heart?

Strict observance of a way of life at fixed times and in identical forms tends to become a matter of routine, of outward compliance. How to prevent observance from becoming stereotyped, mechanical, was, indeed, a perennial worry in the history of Judaism. The cry of the prophet—"Their heart is far from me"—was a signal of alarm.

Should I reject the regularity of prayer and rely on the inspiration of the heart and worship only when I am touched by the spirit? Should I resolve: Unless the spirit comes, I shall abstain from praying? The deeper truth is that routine breeds attention, calling forth a response where the soul would otherwise remain dormant. One is committed to being affected by the holy, if he abides at the threshold of its realm. Should it be left to every individual to find his own forms of worship whenever the spirit moves him? Yet who is able to extemporize a prayer without falling into the trap of clichés? Moreover, spiritual substance grows in clinging to a source of spirit richer than one's own.

Inspirations are brief, sporadic, and rare. In the long interims the mind is often dull, bare, and vapid. There is hardly a soul that can radiate more light than it receives. To perform a *mitzvah* is to meet the spirit. But the spirit is not something we can acquire once and for all, but something we must constantly live with and pray for. For this reason the Jewish way of life is to reiterate the ritual, to meet the spirit again and again, the spirit in oneself and the spirit that hovers over all beings.

X

AT THE ROOT of our difficulties in appreciating the role of *halacha* in religious living is, I believe, our conception of the very essence of religion. "We are often inclined to define the essence of religion as a state of the soul, as inwardness, as an absolute feeling, and expect a person who is religious to be endowed with a kind of sentiment too deep to rise to the surface of common deeds, as if religion were a plant that can thrive only at the bottom of the ocean. Now, to Judaism religion is not a feeling for something that is but an *answer* to Him who is asking us to live in a certain way. *It is in its very origin a consciousness of duty, of being committed to higher ends*; a realization that life is not only man's but also God's sphere of interest" (175).

"God asks for the heart." Yet does he ask for the heart only? Is the right intention enough? Some doctrines insist that love is the sole condition for salvation (the Sufis, Bhakti-mārga), stressing the importance of inwardness, of love or faith, to the exclusion of good works.

Paul waged a passionate battle against the power of law and proclaimed instead the religion of grace. Law, he claimed, cannot conquer sin, nor can righteousness be attained through works of law. A man is justified "by faith without the deeds of the law."*

That salvation is attained by faith alone was Luther's central thesis. The antinomian tendency resulted in the overemphasis on love and faith to the exclusion of good works.

The Formula of Concord of 1580 condemns the statement that good works are necessary to salvation and rejects the doctrine that they are harmful to salvation. According to Ritschl, the doctrine of the merit of good deeds is an intruder in the domain of Christian theology; the only way of salvation is justification by faith. Barth, following Kierkegaard, voices Lutheran thoughts when he claims that man's deeds are too sinful to be good. There are fundamentally no human deeds which, because of their significance in this world, find favor in God's eyes. God can be approached through God alone.

XI

PARAPHRASING the Paulinian doctrine that man is saved by faith alone, Kant and his disciples taught that the essence of religion or morality would consist in an absolute quality of the soul or the will, regardless of the

---

* Romans 3:28. "By the deeds of the law there shall no flesh be justified in his sight; for by the law is knowledge of sin."

actions that may come out of it or the ends that may be attained. Accordingly, the value of a religious act would be determined wholly by the intensity of one's faith or by the rectitude of one's inner disposition. The intention, not the deed, the *how*, not the *what* of one's conduct, would be essential, and no motive other than the sense of duty would be of any moral value. Thus acts of kindness, when not dictated by the sense of duty, would not be better than cruelty; while compassion or regard for human happiness as such is looked upon as an ulterior motive. "I would not break my word even to save mankind," exclaimed Fichte. As if his own salvation and righteousness were more important to him than the fate of all men. Does not such an attitude illustrate the truth of the proverb: "The road to hell is paved with good intentions"? Should we not say that a concern with one's own salvation and righteousness that outweighs the regard for the welfare of one other human being cannot be qualified as a good intention?

The crisis of ethics has its root in formalism, in the view that the essence of the good is in the good intention. Seeing how difficult it is to attain it, modern man despaired. In the name of good intentions, evil was fostered.

To us this doctrine is the essential heresy. Judaism stands and falls with the idea of the absolute relevance of human deeds. Even to God we ascribe the deed. *Imitatio dei* is in deeds. The deed is the source of holiness.

"Faith does not come to an end with attaining certainty of God's existence. Faith is the beginning of intense craving to enter an active relationship with Him who is beyond the mystery, to bring together all the might that is within us with all that is spiritual beyond us. At the root of our yearning for integrity is a stir of the inexpressible within us to commune with the ineffable beyond us. But what is the language of that communion, without which our impulse remains inarticulate?

"We are taught that what God asks of man is more than an inner attitude, that He gives man not only *life* but also a *law*, that His will is to be served not only adored, *obeyed* not only *worshipped*. Faith comes over us like a force urging to action. We respond by pledging ourselves to constancy of devotion, committing us to the presence of God. This remains a life allegiance involving restraint, submission, self-control and courage.

"Judaism insists upon establishing a unity of *faith* and *creed*, of *piety* and *halacha*, of *devotion* and *deed*. Faith is but a seed, while the deed is its growth or decay. Faith disembodied, faith that tries to grow in splendid isolation, is but a ghost, for which there is no place in our psychophysical world.

"What *creed* is in relation to *faith*, the *halacha* is in relation to *piety*. As faith cannot exist without a creed, piety cannot subsist without a pattern of deeds; as intelligence cannot be separated from training, religion cannot be divorced from conduct. Judaism is lived in deeds, not only in thoughts.

"A pattern for living—the object of our most urgent quest—which would correspond to man's ultimate dignity, must take into consideration not only his ability to exploit the forces of nature and to appreciate the loveliness of its forms, but also his unique sense of the ineffable. It must be a design, not only for the satisfaction of needs, but also for the attainment of an end," the end of being a *holy people* (175–76).

XII

THE INTEGRITY of life is not exclusively a thing of the heart, and Jewish piety is therefore more than consciousness of the moral law. The innermost chamber must be guarded at the uttermost outposts. Religion is not the same as spiritualism; what man does in his concrete physical existence is directly relevant to the divine. Spirituality is the goal, not the way of man. In this world music is played on physical instruments, and to the Jew the *mitzvot* are the instruments by which the holy is performed. If man were only mind, worship in thought would be the form in which to commune with God. But man is body and soul, and his goal is to live so that both "his heart and his flesh should sing to the living God."

Moreover, worship is not one thing and living, another. Does Judaism consist of sporadic landmarks in the realm of living, of temples in splendid isolation, of festive celebrations on extraordinary days? The synagogue is not a retreat, and that which is decisive is not the performance of rituals at distinguished occasions but how they affect the climate of the entire life.

The highest peak of spiritual living is not necessarily reached in rare moments of ecstasy; the highest peak lies wherever we are and may be ascended in a common deed. There can be as sublime a holiness in fulfilling friendship, in observing dietary laws, day by day, as in uttering a prayer on the Day of Atonement.

Jewish tradition maintains that there is no extraterritoriality in the realm of the spirit. Economics, politics, dietetics are just as much as ethics within its sphere. It is in man's intimate rather than public life, in the way he fulfills his physiological functions, that character is formed. It is immensely significant that, according to the Book of Genesis, the first prohibition given to man concerned the enjoyment of the forbidden fruit.

"The fate of a people . . . is decided according to whether they begin culture at the right place—not at the soul. The right place is the body, demeanor, diet, physiology; the rest follows . . . contempt of the body is the greatest mishap." Judaism begins at the bottom, taking very seriously the forms of one's behavior in relation to the external, even conventional functions, and amenities of life, teaching us how to eat, how to rest, how to act. The discipline of feelings and thoughts comes second. The body must be persuaded first. "Thou shalt not covet" is the last of the Ten Commandments, even though it may be the first in the case history of the aforementioned transgressions. While not prescribing a diet—vegetarian or otherwise—or demanding abstinence from narcotics or stimulants, Judaism is very much concerned with what and how a person ought to eat. A sacred discipline for the body is as important as bodily strength.

XIII

IN ORDER TO attain an adequate appreciation of the preciousness that the Jewish way of living is capable of bestowing upon us, we should initiate a thorough cleaning of the minds. Every one of us should be asked to make one major sacrifice: to sacrifice his prejudice against our heritage. We should strive to cultivate an atmosphere in which the values of Jewish faith and piety could be cherished, an atmosphere in which the Jewish form of living is the heartily approved or at least respected pattern, in which sensitivity to *kashruth* is not regarded as treason against the American Constitution and reverence for the Sabbath is not considered conspiracy against progress.

Without solidarity with our forebears, the solidarity with our brothers will remain feeble. The vertical unity of Israel is essential to the horizontal unity of the Community of Israel. Identification with what is undying in Israel, the appreciation of what was supremely significant throughout the ages, the endeavor to integrate the abiding teachings and aspirations of the past into our own thinking will enable us to be creative, to expand, not to imitate or to repeat. Survival of Israel means that we carry on our independent dialogue with the past. Our way of life must remain such as would be, to some degree, intelligible to Isaiah and Rabbi Yochanan ben Zakkai, to Maimonides and the Baal Shem.

Let us be under no illusion. The task is hard. However, if it is true that the good cannot exist without the holy, what are we doing for the purpose of securing holiness in the world? Can we afford to be indifferent, to forget the responsibility which the position of leadership bestows upon us?

A wide stream of human callousness separates us from the realm of holiness. Neither an individual man nor a single generation can by its own power erect a bridge that would reach that realm. For ages our fathers have labored in building a sacred bridge. *We who have not crossed the stream must beware lest we burn the bridge.*

XIV

PROMPTED BY an intuition that we cannot live by a disembodied faith, many people today speak of the advisability of introducing "rituals, customs, and ceremonies." The Survey of Current Reform Practice conducted by the National Federation of Temple Brotherhoods confirmed an earlier observation that "Reform Judaism is determinedly engaged in helping to meet a fundamental need of every human being for *symbolism* and *ceremonialism*" and "for the poetry and beauty, for the mysticism and drama" which these provide for the satisfaction of man's emotional hunger.[2]

Gentlemen, is this approach in the spirit of prophetic Judaism? Is it symbolism that God desires? Is it ceremonialism that the prophets called for? Are "customs" and "ceremonies" the central issue of Jewish observance? "Customs" and "ceremonies" are an external affair, an aesthetic delight; something cherished in academic fraternities or at graduation exercises at American universities.

But since when has aesthetics become supreme authority in matters of religion? Customs, ceremonies are fine, enchanting, playful. But is Judaism a religion of play? What is the authentic origin of these terms— "customs" and "ceremonies"? I must confess that I have difficulty translating "ceremonies" into Hebrew. Customs—*minhagim*—have given us a lot of trouble in the past. *Minhagim* have often stultified Jewish life. According to Rabbenu Tam, the word *minhag* consists of the same four letters as the word *gehinom*.*

Let us beware lest we reduce the Bible to literature, Jewish observance to good manners, the Talmud to Emily Post.

There are spiritual reasons which compel me to feel alarmed when hearing the terms "customs" and "ceremonies." What is the worth of celebrating the Seder on Passover eve if it is nothing but a ceremony? An annual re-enactment of quaint antiquities? Ceremonies end in routine, and routine is the great enemy of the spirit.

A religious act is something in which the soul must be able to participate; out of which inner devotion, *kavanah*, must evolve. But what *kavanah* should I entertain if entering the *sukkah* is a mere ceremony?

---

* The word *minhag* (custom) can also imply *gehinom* (hell) when the letters are rearranged according to mystical word juxtapositioning.

Let us be frank. Too often a ceremony is the homage which disbelief pays to faith. Do we want such homage?

Judaism does not stand on ceremonies . . . Jewish piety is an answer to God, expressed in the language of *mitzvot* rather than in the language of "ceremonies." The *mitzvah* rather than the ceremony is our fundamental category. What is the difference between the two categories?

Ceremonies whether in the form of things or in the form of actions are required by custom and convention; *mitzvot* are required by Torah. Ceremonies are relevant to man; *mitzvot* are relevant to God. Ceremonies are folkways; *mitzvot* are ways to God. Ceremonies are expressions of the human mind; what they express and their power to express depend on a mental act of man; their significance is gone when man ceases to be responsive to them. Ceremonies are like the moon, they have no light of their own. *Mitzvot*, on the other hand, are expressions or interpretations of the will of God. While they are meaningful to man, the source of their meaning is not in the understanding of man but in the love of God. Ceremonies are created for the purpose of *signifying*: *mitzvot* were given for the purpose of *sanctifying*. This is their function: to refine, to ennoble, to sanctify man. They confer holiness upon us, whether or not we know exactly what they signify.

A *mitzvah* is more than *man's reference to God*; it is also *God's reference to man*. In carrying out a *mitzvah* we acknowledge the fact of God being concerned with our fulfillment of His will.

XV

AT THE RECENT convention of the Union of American Hebrew Congregations, the report of the Committee on Reform Practice, among other things, stated:

"It is *not the will of God* that dictates what the Reform Jew shall practice, as Orthodoxy holds that God's will does for its adherents, but what the Reform Jew feels *his will* to serve God justifies him in doing . . . Reform is a *religion of choice*, predicated on what its adherents feel God may require of them and often shaped by the influences of history and their associations with the total life of their people. Orthodoxy (sic!) is a *religion of divine command*, the acceptance of a law and a tradition which for its adherents have their roots in the Written and Oral Law which they believe came from God" (italics mine).

Is this religion of human will prophetic Judaism? Is this the spirit of "we will do and we will hear?"

Remember the words of Deuteronomy: "Beware, lest there be among you a man or woman, or family, or tribe, whose heart turns away this day from the Lord, our God . . . one who, when he hears the words of this sworn covenant, blesses himself in his heart, saying: I shall be safe (I shall have peace of mind), though I walk according to the dictates of my heart" (29:18 f.).

"Do not follow your own hearts" (Numbers 15:39). How can one pray, "Help us, O God, to banish from our hearts . . . self-sufficient leaning upon our own reason" (Union Prayer Book, p. 101), and proclaim at the same time that Judaism is basically a religion of man's will and choice?

Is it not our duty to insist that man is not the measure of all things? To deny that man is all and there is none else beside him? Don't we believe that God, too, has a voice in human life? Is it not the essence of prophetic Judaism to say: It is God who spoke to me, therefore I want to fulfill His will?

We read the words in the Union Prayer Book: "Enlighten our eyes in Thy law that we may cling to Thy commandments" (Union Prayer Book, p. 118). "May Thy law rule in the hearts of all Thy children" (Union Prayer Book, p. 122).

Which law? Is it the law of the Torah or the law of an ethical culture?

It is an important development that 25 percent of laymen and 28 percent of rabbis indicate a willingness to *"accept a code of practices required by every Reform Jew."* For many years rabbis have in speeches delivered at conventions of the Central Conference of American Rabbis voiced their sense of shock and grief at the state of religious chaos prevalent in modern congregations, and have urged the members of this conference to return to Jewish observance. May it be a *return* to a *halachic* way of life, not to customs and ceremonies.

Yom Kippur

THE IMPACT OF *erev* Yom Kippur was more powerful in my life than that of Yom Kippur itself. I don't know whether I can state this adequately; I find it almost impossible to convey. What really changed my life, and shaped my character, were the few hours before Yom Kippur. I am not going to give you a description. I can only say that they were moments in my life when I felt somehow more than human. These were very difficult hours. It was a great challenge for us to discover whether it was still possible for us in our civilization to go through such great experiences. It was great fear and trembling, great *pahad*, great awareness that you are now to be confronted. There was no fear of punishment, not even a fear of death, but the expectation of standing in the presence of God. This was the decisive moment. Get ready, purify yourself. Terribly lacking in explicitness, but tremendously powerful. And behind it a full sense of one's own unworthiness and a sense of contrition . . .

Let's talk about the "business" of Yom Kippur. What is it? It is the day in which God Himself purifies us. And we will either succeed or fail with our congregations to the degree that we are able to convey precisely such a basic concept . . . There is no *pahad* today, correct? We have no *pahad*. Everything is fine. Soon we will have helicopters in every courtyard . . . To make the mistake we are making is to forget how much anguish there is in every human being. Scratch the skin of any person and you come upon sorrow, frustration, unhappiness. People are pretentious. Everybody looks proud; inside he is heartbroken. We have not understood how to channel this depth of human suffering into religious experience. Forgive me for saying so, but we have developed Jewish sermons as if there were no personal problems. And when we do speak about the inner problems of men we borrow from psychoanalysis, *aleha hashalom* . . .

We are all failures. At least one day a year we should recognize it. I have failed so often; I am sure those present here have also failed. We have much to be contrite about; we have missed opportunities. The sense of inadequacy ought to be at the very center of the day.

But confessing our sins is not the only aspect of that day which we must emphasize. It is a day of great solemnity, because the day itself atones. This is the grandeur of the day, the mystery of the day. The real contrition was *erev* Yom Kippur; Yom Kippur is "good *Yontiv*."

If you don't mind, I'll tell you something my grandfather the *Oheiv Yisroel* said. We fast on both Yom Kippur and *Tisha B'av*. What is the difference between the two days? On *Tisha B'av*, he said, *ver ken essen* (who can eat)? On Yom Kippur, he said, since a Jew is like an angel, *ver darf essen* (who needs to eat)? I think that these few words offer an insight into the nature of Yom Kippur. To be angelic. It is not an empty phrase; it is a matter to be experienced and studied. One day a year we can transcend the human to enter the state of *ver darf essen*.

I would strongly advise you to stress and develop this aspect, along with the aspect of contrition. To put contrition another way, develop a sense of embarrassment. The root of any religious faith is a sense of embarrassment, of inadequacy. I would cultivate a sense of embarrassment. It would be a great calamity for humanity if the sense of embarrassment disappeared, if everybody was an all-rightnik, with an answer to every problem. We have no answer to ultimate problems. We really don't know. In this not knowing, in this sense of embarrassment, lies the key to opening the wells of creativity. Those who have no embarrassment remain sterile. We must develop this contrition or sense of embarrassment. Tell your congregation that the Book of Psalms is full of expressions of embarrassment. Teach them the meaning of sin, a word which has disappeared from the Jewish consciousness in America. We have no sin. We only have customs and ceremonies. The even more difficult, and more noble, task is transmitting the solemnity of the day. Yom Kippur is a day, *ver darf essen*.

These two ideas belong to the essence of the day.

Teaching Religion to

American Jews

I GREW UP in an awareness that Jews are running away from Judaism and religion. This was true in Poland, where I was born; in Germany, where I studied; and in America, where I found refuge in 1940. In those years spiritual problems were considered irrelevant, but during the last seven or eight years I have been surprised by an extraordinary change. People are not running away anymore, but on the contrary, they indicate concern for spiritual orientation.

This is, therefore, a great hour in Jewish history, and one that probably occurs only once in two hundred years. In this hour we, the living, are "the people of Israel." The tasks begun by the patriarchs and prophets and continued by their descendants are now entrusted to us. We are either the last Jews or those who will hand over the entire past to generations to come. We will either forfeit or enrich the legacy of ages.

But the depressing aspect of the situation is that we have thus far not succeeded in meeting the longing of our people for spiritual nourishment. The younger generation, which often seems way ahead of us, is dissatisfied with what we are offering. We are using stereotypes in our interpretation of Judaism. Most of our lives we continue to be slaves to our first experiences with it.

In consequence, the spirit of Judaism is often kept a well-guarded secret. We are often more concerned with sociology than we are with religion. Whenever two Jews get together and a third joins them, the question usually discussed is: "What are we—a nation, a people, or a religious group?" As though the only important question concerning Judaism and Jewish life were the sociological category to which it belongs!

The significance of Judaism does not lie in its being conducive to mere survival of a particular people but rather in its being a source of spiritual wealth, a source of meaning relevant to all peoples. Sociology, as a result, is not competent to bring out the full significance of Jewish thought and life. It can at best explain the origin of certain phenomena—why they are the way they are—not their meaning and value.

Our concern ought, therefore, to be less about technique and more about content. Judaism is not merely a matter of external forms—it is also a matter of inner living. Is Judaism still aware of inner living? We have a synagogue, certainly, but we have very little prayer. There are important institutions but no crucial commitments, many facts but no appreciation; indeed, the impulse to popularize has drained Judaism of a sense of the complexity, the subtlety, the reality of its teachings and *mitzvot*. What remains is a lifeless devotion to external actions, to a pattern of religious behaviorism that rests on a conviction of the utter irrelevance of theology and belief.

One of the most popular courses in Jewish educational curricula is "customs and ceremonies." It is true that customs and ceremonies have aesthetic value, but since when has aesthetics been the supreme authority in human life? What we actually have in Judaism is not "customs and ceremonies" but *mitzvot*. We cannot express the name of God in words, but we can express it in deeds. Let us teach *mitzvot*, therefore, instead of customs and ceremonies.

Our task, then, must be to teach Judaism as a subject of the deepest personal significance. One of the supreme things we need to worry about is what a Jew stands for in terms of ideas as well as in terms of inner experience. Judaism is an answer to man's ultimate questions, and unless we understand those questions, we cannot even recognize the answers.

In a sense, adult education ought to be a quest for forgotten questions and an endeavor to relate our tradition to those questions. Our effort must be to interpret Judaism in terms of human existence as well as in terms of the Jewish situation. It is important that each of us concern himself about the group, but it is equally important that we concern ourselves about what we are as individuals, as human beings. We must ask ourselves: What am I, a mass of protoplasm, a complicated robot, a tool-making animal? What is the meaning of my individual existence? Am I anything more than just a physical being? What does it mean to be a Jew? What does it mean to be responsible for three thousand years of living experience? How can we mediate between all of the past and all of the future?

I should like to suggest as a goal of adult Jewish education that every Jew become a representative of the Jewish spirit, that every Jew become aware that Judaism can be an answer to the ultimate problems of human existence and not merely a way of "handling observances." A philosophy of adult Jewish education ought to formulate what insights to set forth from and about our tradition. It should also show us how to adjust and express these insights so that they may become a part of the Jewish personality.

The Hebrew term for education means not only to train but also to dedicate, to consecrate. And to consecrate the adult must be our goal, difficult as it may be. We must enable him to participate and share in the spiritual experience of Jewish living; to explain to him what it means to live as a likeness of God. What is involved in being a Jew? Duties of the heart, not only external performance; the ability to experience the suffering of others, compassion and acts of kindness; sanctification of time, not the mere observance of customs and ceremonies; the joy of discipline, not the pleasures of conceit; sacrifice, not casual celebrations; contrition rather than national pride.

The key word is *Talmud Torah*, study. What we glorify is not knowledge, erudition, but study and the dedication to learning. According to Rabba, "when man is led in for judgment, he is asked . . . 'Did you fix time for learning?' "

Man is not asked how much he knows but how much he learns. The unique attitude of the Jew is not the love of knowledge but the love of studying. A learned rabbi in Poland, the story goes, was dismissed by his community because no light was seen in his house after midnight—a sign that he was not studying enough. It is not the book, it is the dedication that counts. Study is an act analogous to worship.

In our quest for forgotten questions, what should we study in our adult education programs? First, the Bible must become the central core of all our studies. Second, we need to devote ourselves to an intense, word-by-word study of the prayerbook. And third, we should attempt to recapture an appreciation of the religious spirit of East European Jewry.

THE BIBLE

IT IS TRUE, of course, that most synagogues offer adults the chance to study the Bible. But most of these classes are ineffectual. Instead of trying to bring forth the relevance of certain biblical passages and their lasting significance to us, we sometimes discuss their historic importance or their textual difficulties. Instead of standing face to face, soul to soul with the biblical word, we often try to stand above it by trying to show our own superiority to it. The fact that the prophets knew less about physics than we do does not imply that we know more than the prophets about the meaning of existence and the nature of man.

Nor is the "literary appreciation" approach more satisfactory. When I was a student in Germany, I often heard discussion about what a great collection of books the Bible is. What a great achievement, it was said, that Goethe's *Faust* begins with a scene from Job. We praise the Bible because it has had such a great impact on the English language and the development of English literature. But perhaps it is the other way around. Perhaps this is the greatness of English literature—that it was influenced by the Bible.

More than an epic about the life of heroes, the Bible is the story of every man in all climates and all ages. Its topic is the world, the whole of history, containing the pattern of a constitution of a united mankind as well as guidance toward establishing such a union. It shows the way to nations as well as to individuals. It continues to scatter seeds of justice and compassion, to echo God's cry to the world, and to pierce man's armor of callousness.

If we wish to learn, we must read carefully the words of the Bible in order to understand how the will of God is made known to man. The Bible tries to teach that holiness is vital, that the things of the spirit are real. Torah is not in heaven. The voice of God is unambiguous; it is the confusion of man, of the best of us, that creates the ambiguity. The Bible tells us how God wants us to act. *Love thy neighbor as thyself* has a strictly literal meaning, and so has the commandment to observe the seventh day. In performing a sacred deed, we are not aware of symbolizing religion; a sacred act *is* religion.

RABBINIC LITERATURE

SECOND IN importance is the study of rabbinic sources. These sources contain more than aphorisms, laws, or stories. They are the living response of our people to God's claim on man and examples of our people's effort to live in a way which is compatible with man's dignity as a being created in the image of God. Rabbinic literature is where the people Israel lived for ages, and to its pages all must turn who want to meet that people.

THE PRAYERBOOK

THE JEWISH prayerbook is a book which everyone talks about but few people have really read—a book which has the distinction of being one of the least known in our literature. Countless moments of insight can be gained by communing with its individual words. Since prayer is the essence of spiritual living, adult Jewish education must be concerned with communicating the insights and attitudes of mind which are indispensable to all prayer. The prayerbook will remain obscure unless Jewish teachers realize that one of their foremost tasks is to discover, to explain, and to interpret its words. What we need is a sympathetic prayerbook exegesis.

We must learn how to study the inner life of the words that fill the world of our prayerbook. Without intense study of their meaning, we feel indeed bewildered when we encounter the multitude of those strange lofty beings that populate the inner cosmos of the Jewish spirit. It is not enough to know how to translate Hebrew into English; each word has a soul.

This is our affliction—we do not know how to look across a word to its meaning. We forget how to find the way to the word, how to be on intimate terms with a few passages in the prayerbook.

As a result, we say words but make no decisions, forgetting that in prayer words are commitments, not the subject matter for aesthetic reflection, and that prayer is meaningless unless we stand for what we utter, unless we feel what we accept.

In this effort we can be helped by the example of the religious fervor which animated East European Jewry. In that period our people attained the highest degree of inwardness. In many ways that was the golden period in Jewish history. We must understand the sense of values that characterized the East European Jews in order to appraise the fact that their best intellects were devoted to the study, interpretation, and development of Torah.

Poor Jews, whose children knew only the taste of "potatoes on Sunday, potatoes on Monday, potatoes on Tuesday," sat like intellectual magnates. Their learning was essentially non-utilitarian, almost free of direct pragmatic designs, a spiritual experience. Carried away by the mellow, melting chant of Talmud reading, they would soar high in pure realm of thought, away from the boundaries of here and now, to a region where the *Shekinah* listens to what the children of men create in the study of His word. They were able to feel heaven in a passage of Talmud.

Central in the success of this reverential approach to adult education, which teaches the living spirit of Judaism, is the teacher. In Judaism there is no higher distinction than that of being a teacher. This has been so throughout our history. We do not celebrate kings and heroes, we celebrate teachers—Moses and Rabbi Akiba. The teacher is the central pillar of Jewish living, past, present, and future. According to Jewish tradition, God Himself teaches.

This implies that the teacher has a very great responsibility. He must mobilize all his personal power, love, insight, and understanding. The most clever gimmicks will not achieve anything of lasting value. Unless there is an inner engagement, an attachment, a personal appreciation of the subject matter, the finest instructor will become ineffective.

Most important of all, the teacher, in order to guide other adults into the promised land of the Jewish heritage, must have been there himself.

When asking himself: Do I stand for what I teach? do I believe what I say?, he must be able to answer in the affirmative. The modern teacher is a link in the chain of the tradition. He is the intermediary between the past and the present as well. In a sense, he is also the creator of the future of our people.

In that future, if the Jewish religion is to be taught to American Jews, each one of us bears a genuine personal responsibility. For the Jewish people is represented by every individual Jew. We need to remember where we came from, and the way to do this is by study of our great books. We are God's stake in human history. We must reawaken our consciousness of being involved in a history that transcends the interests and glories of particular dynasties and empires. The gravest sin for a Jew is to forget—or not to know—what he represents.

1956

Jewish Theology

WE MODERN JEWS operate in an anti-intellectual climate: for years there has been neglect of the study of theology. Since I do not come from an assimilated background, the atmosphere in which I grew up was full of theology. Day and night we spoke only about "prayer" and *kavanah* (undivided concentration, particularly in prayer) and about *Hakodosh Boruch Hu* (the Holy One, blessed be He), and about *mesirat nefesh* (extreme devotion; literally, "giving over one's soul"). What is this? It is Jewish theology. Of course, we believed in all the *dinim* and *minhagim* (laws and customs). In order to *Shlugen Kaporos* (ritual of atonement the day before Yom Kippur),* I had to get up at three o'clock in the morning. We used to have a *shochet* (ritual slaughterer) come to our home. But it wasn't the *Kaporos*, it was the atmosphere. *Erev* Yom Kippur was my great day of training in Jewish theology, because we knew what the problem was: "Do I have the right to survive the year without *tshuvah* (repentence; literally, 'return')?" It was actually living theology. *Vehayu hayecha tluim lecha miniged* (And your life shall hang in doubt before you—Deuteronomy 28:66). This was not merely performance (as I have often seen and observed) or what I call "religious behaviorism."

Many years ago, while working on my book *Man Is Not Alone*, I used to visit a distinguished scholar, a fine and learned man. "What are you working on now?" he asked me. I knew I couldn't say "On a sense of the ineffable," so I told him I was working on something about *elohus* (divinity,

A talk given to the Solomon Schechter School principals in New York at their May 1968 conference. It was transcribed and edited by Pesach Schindler. The question period which followed has been omitted.

* This ritual, especially among Hasidim, utilized a fowl which serves as the "scapegoat" (a Yiddish term).

theology). He said, "*Chas Vesholom!*" [God forbid!] That you must not touch; a Jew must not touch that!" Now, this is very typical. Historically it goes back to Spinoza.

Spinoza was the man who attempted to destroy Jewish theology. He found many admirers and they followed him (I discuss this in the early part of *God in Search of Man*). He claimed that the Bible, as such, has nothing relevant to say regarding philosophy and ideas. To him the Bible was not theology but only law. This concept was, paradoxically, taken over by Moses Mendelssohn. He must have grasped the situation existing in the Western world, that throughout the seventeenth and the eighteenth centuries there was only one book written about Judaism, and that was the *Tractatus*, by Spinoza. Since it was the only book available on Judaism in the Western language, it had the most profound impact on Christians and Jews alike. It is evident when studying Kant or Hegel that whatever they have to say concerning Judaism was derived from the *Tractatus*. Paradoxically, Moses Mendelssohn was profoundly influenced by this book and by its approach. Moses Mendelssohn's influence upon Jews, in turn, was enormous. Thus, a system was developed whereby Judaism was *halacha*, Law—nothing else.

This tremendous importance placed on *halacha* I heard not in Warsaw, where I grew up, but suddenly, in Berlin. Here was a kind of system based only on *halacha*, as if *halacha* could exist by itself—without *agada*, without Jewish theology. (I use the term *agada* as the Hebrew term for Jewish theology, since it is its source.) I suggest, therefore, that there is such a thing in Judaism as a *halachic* heresy: all one has to do is teach *dinim* and *minhagim*. I am opposed to the teaching of *dinim* and *minhagim* in isolation.

There is a text very common in Jewish schools called "Customs and Ceremonies." Many years ago I delivered a lecture to the Central Conference of American Rabbis on *halacha*, and there I suggested (as Rabbenu Tam* had already indicated) that customs—*minhagim*—are Otiot Gehinom.† "Ceremonies" is not a Jewish phrase at all. It was created by Gentiles and not by Jews. Judaism does not stand on "ceremonies." I can tell you that my approach to customs and ceremonies was highly resented at the lecture.

There is another danger, another block to Jewish theology. This danger is a more insidious one. I refer to the Hellenization of Jewish theology. The Hellenization of Jewish theology actually goes back to Philo. As Dr.

---

* A leading Talmud scholar of the Tosafist school in France and Germany during the twelfth century.

† The word *minhag* (custom) can also imply *gehinom* (hell) when the letters are rearranged according to mystical word juxtapositioning.

Wolfson has successfully proved, the impact of Philo on theology was radical. To oversimplify the matter: this approach would have Plato and Moses, for example, say the same thing. Only, Plato would say it in Greek and Moses in Hebrew. Consequently, you can say that Moses was a sort of Hebrew Plato. This view has had a great impact on much of Jewish medieval philosophy. They talk about God in the language of the Greeks.

Now, we live in a very strange situation today. Let me again point to the difficulties. We are essentially trained in a non-Jewish world. This is where we obtain our general training. We are inclined to think in non-Jewish terms. I am not discouraging exposure to the non-Jewish world. I am merely indicating that it is not biblical thinking. It is not rabbinic thinking. It is not Hasidic thinking. It is non-Jewish thinking. A non-Jewish philosophy is fine. But we would also like to have in our thinking a Jewish view of things. We would like to apply the Bible and *Hazal*,* and they are often incongruent. If you take biblical passages or biblical documents or rabbinic statements, and submit them to a Greek mind, they often are absurd. They make no sense. But we do want to educate Jews. We wish to maintain Judaism. What can we do about it? May I say to you personally that this has been my major challenge, ever since I began working on my dissertation; that is: How to maintain a Jewish way of thinking? This was the major concern and the major thesis of my dissertation *Die Prophetie*. Since that day I consider this to be my major effort. It is not an easy enterprise.

Now, I don't want to discourage anyone or attack anyone. That is too simple. It is also dangerous. I can well understand that, at a time when Aristotelianism claimed to be the *great philosophy*, which provided the answers to all of the world's problems, at a time when Neo-Platonism became almost a religion, the Jews had to find a way to come to terms with it. But we live in a different situation. We live in a situation where the so-called academic philosophers are helpless. Analytic philosophy and symbolic philosophy proved helpless in the face of the tremendous emergencies in which we are involved day and night. In a sense, we are in a better situation trying to build Jewish theology.

I would like to report to you on a strange and highly interesting meeting that I attended about a week ago. A very important and distinguished thinker in America, a humanist, had an extraordinary idea to do something about the situation. He prepared a memorandum which, in its negative analysis, was excellent. The intention was to save American society and American civilization, in the name of humanism. This was fine from his point of view. But whom did he invite? The sensitive people present were

* Abbreviation of "Our Sages of blessed memory."

religious people, people from churches and synagogues. When he looked for people who were profoundly concerned in their heart and soul about the human situation, he involved people from the university's religious leadership and he brought a Jew. I cite this as an indication that we are confronted with a different situation intellectually today. We do not have to defend ourselves in the name of a philosophy that has a powerful answer to the truth. My task is, then, to try to make some suggestions to you as to how we should teach theological ideas, theological principles, in the spirit of our tradition, or in the Jewish way of thinking.

I suggest that we should primarily engage in dialogue. I shall speak to you for a while, and then I would like to hear your response. Let us see what we can do together. You must also understand that it is impossible for me to be comprehensive, or to deal with all problems. This is a preliminary discussion. I would like to advance a few principles.

If you were to ask me what I should teach first to young people about Jewish theology, I would say teach the *concept of man*. I have often suggested that the Bible is a book about man. It is not a book about God. It depicts God's anthropology rather than man's theology. The central issue in the Bible is man. Unless we understand the essential biblical claims concerning man, we cannot teach Jewish theology. What is the essential claim? To put it in a very minimal form, it is the infinite importance of man; what man can do and how man shall act.

The Bible has always been a paradox. Why? First (if you will forgive me, if I may be a little flippant), if I had to write the Bible, I would do a much better job. Why? The Bible is a terribly anti-religious book if you look at it with vulgar eyes. Look what happens in the Bible. Look at what the Ribono Shel Olam has done to the Jewish people. He took them out of Egypt, He showed *nisim v'niflous* (miracles and wonders), the ten plagues, the great revelation at Sinai, and a few days later, what do they do?

If I had to write a Bible, I would say that once they left Sinai, they become great Tzadikim and great Hasidim and the only thing that they did henceforth was to praise God. They would not murmur against Moshe Rabbenu. Instead, we have frequent rebellion. It was worse than at Columbia! Does this make sense in the light of all the great things that happened to them? And so the question I ask myself is: "Ribono Shel Olam, why do you bother with us?" That the Ribono Shel Olam should bother with us who are so rebellious and so ungrateful, so callous, so hard-necked, so stiff-necked is the great paradox. The only way to understand the paradox is that God takes man very seriously. When I speak to a young man I try to emphasize that his life is very great; it is a very serious thing; it has infinite possibilities, and there are infinite possibilities to do the holy and the good. This is how I would begin as a Jew. This is how I would begin with Jewish theology. The young man must be provided with a tremendous sense of importance with regard to his life, his existence, and the earnestness of being alive.

I have published a book on the nature of man, which deals with only a small part of this issue, entitled *Who Is Man?* Those who are interested may find a lengthy discussion concerning man in the chapter "Sacred Image of Man" in *Insecurity of Freedom*. In addition, in a book published in England, *The Concept of Man in Jewish Thought*, I attempted to portray the rabbinic and biblical concepts of man.

What are the theological principles behind the phenomenon of man? If I were to give you one principle with which I would begin now, over and above the idea of man and man's importance, I would have to establish this principle on the basis of insight derived from the Bible. It would have to be an insight in accord with all rabbinic thinking. It could not just appear as a doctrine. What is there that has to be said about God, from the point of view of Jewish theology? It should be a principle that should illuminate life. It should help us to understand the experience of religion, the religious experience of our people, and the religious experience of an individual.

If I had to make a statement about God, one that is fundamental in Judaism, it would be that *God is in search of man*. It is *the* fundamental statement about God in Judaism. It is the fundamental statement in the inner life of a human being in relation to God in the world. If I were to summarize all of human history as seen in the Bible, it would be a simple formula: *God in search of man*. It is a paradoxical formula, to be sure. It is not a Hellenistic formula. It is a biblical formula. It is a rabbinic formula.

Let me try to show you some of the implications. Allow me once again to be a little flippant. When the Ribono Shel Olam created the first man, he provided for all his needs. The first man had two very fine boys. They probably received a fine education, and still you know what Kayin did to Hevel. If the Ribono Shel Olam had consulted with me this morning, I would have said to him, "Leave the whole human species alone." No— He did not leave them alone. He began once again with the experiment. Two generations later, you realize what happened: Noah, the Flood. He attempted to save one family from the entire human species in the hope that out of this family will come forth a righteous generation. This hope never materialized. Came *Dor Hahaflagah* (the Tower of Babel) and another failure. Again I ask you, Ribono Shel Olam, why do you bother? No! He bothers.

Let us take Abraham now. What, for instance, will Avraham Avinu be when "Venivrechu vecha kol mishpechot haadamah"? And through

you shall all families of the earth be blessed (Genesis 12:3). But you see
what happened. Yitzchak was a very fine person. What about Yishmael?
No, He didn't get tired. He starts again with Yaakov Avinu. And so you
go down through the ages, through the history of the Jewish people. Look
at the time of the kings and look at the failures. Look how He has to send
prophets time and again, expressing anger and disgust. Ribono Shel Olam,
why do you bother? Why are you in search of man? Why are you still
searching and waiting? Searching for whoever it is that may come? To
create a better world; to create better species? God in search of man? Why?
And my answer to this would be: Because God is *in need* of man. The
idea of God being in need of man is central to Judaism and pervades all
the pages of the Bible, of *Chazal*, of talmudic literature, and it is understandable in our own time. In the light of this idea, of God being in
need of man, you have to entirely revise all the clichés that are used in
religious language.

For example, one of the issues which we have failed to teach in our
schools is the issue of *geulah*—redemption. This is central in Judaism.
But how will redemption, as it is understood later in Jewish literature,
come about? God is not going to redeem Israel while Israel remains passive.
God waits for Israel either to do *tshuvah* or to help bring about the
redemptive act of *geulah*. This was beautifully reflected in Jewish mysticism. It is significantly relevant to ourselves. God is not going to do it
alone. He needs us.

The whole conception of God's omnipotence, I suspect, was taken over
from Islam. God is almighty, and powerful. Man has nothing to say and
nothing to do except to keep quiet and to accept. But, actually, God needs
man's cooperation. There will be no redemption without the cooperation
of man. Omnipotence as such will not work. God cannot function in the
world without the help of man. And this is where *halacha, agada,** and
mitzvot begin to assume their crucial role. But all this has to be seen in
relation to God. In a very deep and strong sense God cannot be conceived
by us in complete detachment from man. God and man have to be thought
of together. I once suggested the definition of a prophet. A prophet is a
man who holds God and man in one thought and at one time. He does
not think of God without man and he does not think of man without
God. In a Hellenized theology we witness a complete split. God is there,
and man is here.

Now, there are many profound implications in the concept of God in
search of man, which I attempt to analyze and describe in great detail in
a variety of books. I do not know whether you are acquainted with my

---

* *Agada* is the extra-legal body in talmudic literature.

book *The Prophets*. One idea is that of *pathos*. This idea really is an explication of the idea of God in search of man. (An example may be found on page 231; also on page 484 following.) What interests me at this moment, in particular, however, is another idea which is central to Jewish literature and rabbinic literature, and missing in discussions on Jewish thought. Let me perhaps tell you bluntly that, while I have great respect for the system of dogmas developed by Maimonides, I have many serious reservations about them.*

Let me mention another idea that is missing, because it is so terribly Hellenized. This is the idea of the *Shekinah*.† Now, some of you may know my book *Torah Min Hashomayim*. In Volume I there is an entire section dealing with the *Torat Hashekinah*. Without the principle of God in search of man, the whole idea of *Shekinah* is not even intelligible. We have no right to eliminate this concept. It permeates rabbinic literature, post-rabbinic thought in Judaism, and it is missing in our discussions and in Maimonides's list of dogmas. Actually the idea of *pathos*, which I consider to be *the* central idea in prophetic theology, contains the doctrine of the *Shekinah*. Again, since the material is collected in *Torah Min Hashomayim*, particularly in attempting to show the resistance to the doctrine of *Shekinah* that was found in the school of Rabbi Yishmael, there is no need to discuss it with you. May I say, however, that without an understanding of the idea of *Shekinah* we fail completely to understand the field of Jewish theology or the theme of God in search of man which I consider to be the summary of Jewish theology.

Now, a number of revisions are needed. I already suggested to you that the idea of absolute omnipotence is somewhat missing in classical Jewish theology. This is really the impact of Islam. In Islam they went very far. Maimonides had to deal with it in a very beautiful way. Thus if you stress the idea of omnipotence, it means that God can do anything. For example, do you think that five and five are ten? But cannot God make five and five twelve? Says Maimonides: No. God Himself is bound by His own creations and by the reason that permeates these creations. So in a sense he fought the exaggerated conceptions of omnipotence. But he did not go far enough. I tell you that the idea of divine omnipotence, meaning, holding God responsible for everything, expecting Him to do the impossible, to defy human freedom, is a non-Jewish idea.

My friends, theology is a delicate subject. One must be aware of generalizations and clichés. Allow me to go into another aspect of Jewish

---

* For an elaboration of this view, see *Torah Min Hashomayim*, Vols. I, II, and III.

† The Divine Presence. In Jewish theology and mystical thought, the unique manifestation of the presence of God in the physical world.

theology, namely, the peculiar relationship between the *mystery and the meaning*. It is a central issue in understanding Jewish philosophy. In my own work I always try to wrestle with this relationship. I shall briefly indicate the significance of this relationship to understanding the Torah. Again, if I had had to write the Bible, do you know what I would have done? I would have described God saying to Abraham, "Your descendants will be a great people. Your descendants will enter Eretz Israel. They will be a successful people." Instead, He meets Abraham in a vision, and what does He tell him? They will be slaves *"B'eretz lo lahem, vavadum v'inu otam arba meot shanah."* * Then I will take them out! What kind of *tovah* has He done for us? He tortures our people for 400 years (actually it came out to be only 210 years) and then He gives them the assignment to conquer a very difficult land. Can you tell me that this is so terribly rational? Terribly civil? I tell you that I would have done it differently. I see Abraham, who is a great man, a great promise. I want him to be the father of a great people. "Here, go into the land and have it!" No, he has to go through pain and struggle. Why? This is the aspect of *mystery* in biblical understanding. We cannot ignore the aspect of mystery if we want to be true to Jewish thinking. So let us not always simplify issues. You cannot (and this is another principle that I would like to advance) reduce any aspect of Jewish theology into one principle. There are always two principles. There is always a polarity of two principles. To put it in a general way, there is a *mystery* and there is a *meaning*. There is a great deal that we can understand and there is a great deal that God holds in store for Himself, perhaps *l'atid lavo*. †

LET ME RELATE a little story which I believe belongs to this discussion. I hope that it will not sound too strange, because I already have said some things here which deviate from conventional Hellenized Jewish theology. About a year ago I received a letter from Toronto, from the Pontifical Institute. It is a very important institute in medieval philosophy and philosophy in general. They were convening an international congress of Catholic theologians and asked me to speak about the God of Israel and Christian renewal. I receive many invitations, but this invitation I took seriously. That such a body should invite me to speak and give judgment, so to speak, on the Ecumenical Movement, and for me to speak on the point of view of the God of Israel and Christian renewal, this I considered to be serious. I felt this to be a very difficult assignment. The theme was

---

* "[Thy seed shall be a stranger] in a land which is not theirs, and they will make them serve, and afflict them four hundred years" (Genesis 15:13).

† "In days to come."

boldly formulated. Yet if a congress of Christian theologians invited me, a Jew, to judge Christian renewal from the point of view of the God of Israel—from the point of view of Elohei Avraham, Elohei Yisrael, this is *important*. So I accepted the invitation. On the way to the printer, the title in the program was emasculated. I received the catalogue and it read: "The Jewish Notion of God and Christian Renewal." What happened? It is a typical story. Realism was replaced by "notionalism." The reality was turned into a notion. The notion of God. What else happened? Biblical words *Elohei Yisrael* were replaced by the jargon of scholastic manuals, "the notion of God." I do not approve of the term "the notion of God." The God of Israel is a name, not a notion. There is a difference between a "name" and a "notion." I am suggesting to you: don't teach notions of God, teach the name of God. A notion applies to all objects of similar properties. A name applies to an individual. The name "God of Israel" applies to the one and only God of all men. A notion describes, defines; a name evokes. A notion is derived from a generalization; a name is learned through acquaintance. A notion you can conceive; a name you call. I even suggested that notions and the name of God of Israel are profoundly incompatible. All notions crumble when applied to Him. A more appropriate title might have been: "The Jewish Experience of the Collapse of all Notions in Relation to God."

You asked me for a major principle in Jewish theology, so I shall give you a principle. I could have given you the principle of "the omnipotence"—"the highest being"; I could have given you the principle of "coalescence"—God and the principle of coalescence. No, my friends—this is not Jewish. This is not the true relationship of the Jew to the God of Israel. In other words, God is not the object of generalization. In a sense I would say that a notion is definitive, finished, final. But what we must strive for is an understanding.

Understanding is an act. It is a slow process. The intention of it is to receive, register, record, reflect, and reiterate. It is an act that may go on forever. Having a notion of friendship is not the same as having a friend, or living with a friend. The story of friendship cannot be fully told by what one friend thinks of the being and the attributes of the other friend. The process of forming an idea is one of generalization and abstraction. Such a process implies a distinction between a situation and an idea. Disregard of the fullness of what transpires leads to the danger of regarding the part as the whole. An idea of a theory of God can easily become a substitute for God. This is why I have always been careful not to define God in terms of one idea. God in search of man is an *ongoing process*. It is not a notion, it is a process. The prophets had no *idea* of God. What they had was an understanding.

Finally, what I suggested to them was a statement by Rabbi Simon ben Yohai found in the *Sifre*.

When I quoted this for the first time, I received letters from all parts of the country: "Such a Midrash does not exist." This is the *Sifre: Atem eydai n'um hashem, v'ani el.*[1] "You are my witnesses (says God) and I am God. Says Rabbi Simon ben Yohai, the disciple of Rabbi Akiba: "If you are my witnesses, I am God; if you are not my witnesses, I am not God."[2] Now, this is perhaps one of the most powerful statements found in rabbinic literature. It is paradoxical, to be sure, in that it indicates what I mentioned to you before—the necessity of cooperation. In this world God is not God unless we are His witnesses.

The supreme issue is not whether in the infinite darkness there is a being of grandeur that is the object of man's ultimate concern, but whether the reality of God confronts us as a *pathos*—God's ultimate concern with good and evil—or whether God is mysteriously present in the event of history. Whether being is contingent upon creation, whether creation is contingent upon care, whether my life is dependent upon His care, whether in the course of my life I come upon His guidance. I, therefore, suggest that God is either of no importance or of supreme importance.

God is He whose regard for me is more precious than life. Otherwise He is not God. *God is the meaning beyond the mystery.*

Perhaps I should read to you a story found in *Shevet Yehudah* which I read to the Catholic congress. "In 1492 the Jews of Spain were given the choice to be converted or to be expelled. The overwhelming majority left their homeland. Ships overcrowded with fugitives found difficulty landing, owing to the disease breaking out among them while on board ship. One of the boats was infested with the plague. The captain of the boat put the passengers ashore at some uninhabited place. There most of them died. Some of them set out on foot and gathered strength in order to search for settlement. There was one Jew among them who struggled on foot together with his wife and two sons. The wife grew faint and died, not being accustomed to such difficult walking. The husband picked up his children and carried them in his arms until he and they fainted from hunger. When he regained consciousness, he found that the sons had died also. In great grief he rose to his feet and raised his eyes to heaven and cried out: "Lord of the Universe, much have you done to make me deserve my fate, but this is a certainty, that a Jew I am, and a Jew I shall remain. Nothing that you have brought upon me is likely to be of any avail."

If you analyze the theology of this occurrence, you will find a kind of audacity that defies the usual definitions of faith.

The Mystical Element

in Judaism

THERE ARE PEOPLE who take great care to keep away from the mists produced by fads and phrases. They refuse to convert realities into opinions, mysteries into dogmas, and ideas into a multitude of words, for they realize that all concepts are but glittering motes in a sunbeam. They want to see the sun itself. When we are confined to our studyrooms, our knowledge seems to us a pillar of light, but when we stand at the door that opens out to the Infinite, we see how insubstantial is our knowledge. Even when we shut the door to the Infinite and retire to the narrow limits of notions, our minds cannot remain confined. Again, to some people explanations and opinions are a token of wonder's departure, like a curfew after which they may not come abroad. In the kabbalists, the drive and the fire and the light are never put out.

Like the vital power in ourselves that gives us the ability to fight and to endure, to dare and to conquer, which drives us to experience the bitter and the perilous, there is an urge in wistful souls to starve rather than be fed on sham and distortion. To the kabbalists God is as real as life, and as nobody would be satisfied with mere knowing or reading about life, so they are not content to suppose or to prove logically that there is a God; they want to feel and to enjoy Him; not only to obey, but to approach Him. They want to taste the whole wheat of spirit before it is ground by the millstones of reason. They would rather be overwhelmed by the symbols of the inconceivable than wield the definitions of the superficial.

Stirred by a yearning after the unattainable, they want to make the distant near, the abstract concrete, to transform the soul into a vessel for the transcendent, to grasp with the senses what is hidden from the mind, to express in symbols what the tongue cannot speak, what the reason cannot conceive, to experience as a reality what vaguely dawns in intuitions. "Wise is he who by the power of his own contemplation attains to the perception of the profound mysteries which cannot be expressed in words."[1]

The kabbalist is not content with being confined to what he is. His desire is not only to *know* more than what ordinary reason has to offer but to *be* more than what he is; not only to comprehend the Beyond but to concur with it. He aims at the elevation and expansion of existence. Such expansion goes hand in hand with the exaltation of all being.

The universe, exposed to the violence of our analytical mind, is being broken apart. It is split into the known and unknown, into the seen and unseen. In mystic contemplation all things are seen as one.[2] The mystic mind tends to hold the world together: to behold the seen in conjunction with the unseen, to keep the fellowship with the unknown through the revolving door of the known, "to learn the higher supernal wisdom from all" that the Lord has created and to regain the knowledge that once was in the possession of men and "that has perished from them."[3] What our senses perceive is but the jutting edge of what is deeply hidden. Extending over into the invisible, the things of this world stand in a secret contact with that which no eye has ever perceived. Everything certifies to the sublime, the unapparent working jointly with the apparent. There is always a reverberation in the Beyond to every action here: "The Lord made this world corresponding to the world above, and everything which is above has its counterpart below . . . and yet they all constitute a unity"[4]; "there being no object, however small, in this world, but what is subordinate to its counterpart above which has charge over it; and so whenever the thing below bestirs itself, there is a simultaneous stimulation of its counterpart above, as the two realms form one interconnected whole."[5]

Opposed to the idea that the world of perception is the bottom of reality, the mystics plunge into what is beneath the perceptible. What they attain in their quest is more than a vague impression or a spotty knowledge of the imperceptible. "Penetrating to the real essence of wisdom . . . they are resplendent with the radiance of supernal wisdom."[6] Their eyes perceive things of this world, while their hearts reverberate to the throbbing of the hidden. To them the secret is the core of the apparent; the known is but an aspect of the unknown. "All things below are symbols of that which is above."[7] They are sustained by the forces that flow from hidden worlds. There is no particular that is detached from universal meaning. What appears to be a center to the eye is but a point on the periphery around another center. Nothing here is final. The worldly is subservient to the otherworldly. You grasp the essence of the here by conceiving its beyond. For this world is the reality of the spirit in a state of trance. The manifestation of the mystery is partly suspended, with ourselves living in lethargy. Our normal consciousness is a state of stupor, in which our sensibility to the wholly real and our responsiveness to the stimuli of the spirit are reduced. The mystics, knowing that we are involved in a hidden history of the cosmos, endeavor to awake from the drowsiness and apathy and to regain the state of wakefulness for our enchanted souls.

It is a bold attitude of the soul, a steadfast quality of consciousness, that lends mystic character to a human being. A man who feels that he is closely enfolded by a power that is both lasting and holy will come to know that the spiritual is not an idea to which one can relate his will but a realm which can even be affected by our deeds. What distinguishes the kabbalist is the attachment of his entire personality to a hidden spiritual realm. Intensifying this attachment by means of active devotion to it, by meditation upon its secrets, or even by perception of its reality, he becomes allied with the dynamics of hidden worlds. Sensitive to the imperceptible, he is stirred by its secret happenings.

Attachment to hidden worlds holds the kabbalist in the spell of things more basic than the things that dominate the interest of the common mind. The mystery is not beyond and away from us. It is our destiny. "The fate of the world depends upon the mystery."[8] Our task is to adjust the details to the whole, the apparent to the hidden, the near to the distant. The passionate concern of the kabbalist for final goals endows him with the experience of surpassing all human limitations and powers. With all he is doing he is crossing the borders, breaking the surfaces, approaching the lasting sources of all things. Yet his living with the infinite does not make him alien to the finite.

THE EXALTATION OF MAN

IN THIS EXALTED world man's position is unique. God has instilled in him something of Himself. Likeness to God is the essence of man. The Hebrew word for man, *adam*, usually associated with the word for earth, *adamah*,[9] was homiletically related by some kabbalists to the expression "I will ascend above the heights of the clouds; I will be like (*eddamme*) the Most High" (Isaiah 14:14). Man's privilege is, as it were, to augment the divine in the world; as it is said, "Ascribe ye strength unto God" (Psalms 68:35).

Jewish mystics are inspired by a bold and dangerously paradoxical idea that not only is God necessary to man but man is also necessary to God, to the unfolding of His plans in this world. Thoughts of this kind are indicated and even expressed in various rabbinic sources. "When Israel performs the will of the Omnipresent, they add strength to the heavenly power; as it is said, 'To God we render strength!' " When, however, Israel does not perform the will of the Omnipresent, they weaken—if it is possible to say so—the great power of Him who is above; as it is written: "Thou didst weaken the Rock that begot thee"[10] (Deuteronomy 32:18). In the *Zohar* this idea is formulated in a more specific way. Commenting on the passage in Exodus 17:8, "Then came Amalek and fought with Israel in Rephidim," Rabbi Simeon said: "There is a deep allusion in the name 'Rephidim.' This war emanated from the attribute of Severe Judgment and it was a war above and a war below . . . The Holy One, as it were, said: 'When Israel is worthy below, my power prevails in the universe; but when Israel is found to be unworthy, she weakens my power above, and the power of severe judgment predominates in the world.' So here, 'Amalek came and fought with Israel in Rephidim,' because the Israelites were 'weak' [in Hebrew: *raphe,* which the *Zohar* finds in the name 'Rephidim'] in the study of the Torah, as we have explained on another occasion."[11] Thus man's relationship to God should not be that of passive reliance upon His Omnipotence but that of active assistance. "The impious rely on their gods . . . the righteous are the support of God."[12] The patriarchs are therefore called "the chariot of the Lord."[13] The belief in the greatness of man, in the metaphysical effectiveness of his physical acts, is an ancient motif of Jewish thinking.

Man himself is a mystery. He is the symbol of all that exists. His life is the image of universal life. Everything was created in the spiritual image of the mystical man. "When the Holy One created man, He set in him all the images of the supernal mysteries of the world above, and all the images of the lower mysteries of the world below, and all are designed in man, who stands in the image of God."[14] Even the human body is full of symbolic significance. The skin, flesh, bones, and sinews are but an outward covering, mere garments,[15] even though "the substances composing man's body belong to two worlds, namely, the world below and the world above."[16] The 248 limbs and 365 sinews are symbols of the 613 parts of the universe as well as of the 248 positive and 365 negative precepts of the Torah. Man's soul emanates from an upper region where it has a spiritual father and a spiritual mother, just as the body has a father and mother in this world.[17] The soul that abides in our body is a weak reflection of our upper soul, the seat of which is in heaven. Yet, though detached from that soul, we are capable of being in contact with it. When we pray, we turn toward the upper soul as though we were to abandon the body and join our source.

Man is not detached from the realm of the unseen. He is wholly involved in it. Whether he is conscious of it or not, his actions are vital to all worlds and affect the course of transcendent events. In a sense, by means of the Torah, man is the constant architect of the hidden universe. "This world was formed in the pattern of the world above, and whatever takes place in this earthly realm occurs also in the realm above."[18] One of the principles of the *Zohar* is that every move below calls forth a corresponding movement above."[19] Not only things, even periods of time are conceived as concrete entities. "Thus over every day below is appointed a day above, and a man should take heed not to impair that day. Now the act below stimulates a corresponding activity above. Thus if a man does kindness on earth, he awakens loving-kindness above, and it rests upon that day which is crowned therewith through him. Similarly, if he performs a deed of mercy, he crowns that day with mercy and it becomes his protector in the hour of need. So, too, if he performs a cruel action, he has a corresponding effect on that day and impairs it, so that subsequently it becomes cruel to him and tries to destroy him, giving him measure for measure."[20] Even what we consider potential is regarded as real and we may be held accountable for it: "Just as a man is punished for uttering an evil word, so is he punished for not uttering a good word when he had the opportunity, because he harms that speaking spirit which was prepared to speak above and below in holiness."[21]

The significance of great works done on earth is valued by their cosmic effects. Thus, e.g., "When the first Temple was completed another Temple was erected at the same time, which was a center for all the worlds, shedding radiance upon all things and giving light to all the spheres. Then the worlds were firmly established, and all the supernal casements were opened to pour forth light, and all the worlds experienced such joys as had never been known to them before, and celestial and terrestrial beings alike broke forth in song. And the song which they sang is the Song of Songs."[22]

Endowed with metaphysical powers, man's life is a most serious affair: "If a man's lips and tongue speak evil words, those words mount aloft and all proclaim, 'Keep away from the evil word of So-and-so, leave the path clear for the mighty serpent.' Then the holy soul leaves him and is not able to speak: it is in shame and distress, and is not given a place as before . . . Then many spirits bestir themselves, and one spirit comes down from that side and finds the man who uttered the evil word, and lights upon him and defiles him, and he becomes leprous."[23]

Man's life is full of peril. It can easily upset the balance and order of the universe. "A voice goes forth and proclaims: 'O ye people of the world, take heed unto yourselves, close the gates of sin, keep away from the perilous net before your feet are caught in it!' A certain wheel is ever whirling continuously round and round. Woe to those whose feet lose

their hold on the wheel, for then they fall into the Deep which is predestined for the evildoers of the world! Woe to those who fall, never to
rise and enjoy the light that is stored up for the righteous in the world to
come!"[24]

THE *EN SOF* AND HIS MANIFESTATIONS

MYSTIC INTUITION occurs at an outpost of the mind, dangerously
detached from the main substance of the intellect. Operating, as it were,
in no-mind's-land, its place is hard to name, its communications with
critical thinking often difficult and uncertain, and the accounts of its
discoveries not easy to decode. In its main representatives, the kabbalah
teaches that man's life can be a rallying point of the forces that tend toward
God, that this world is charged with His presence and every object is a
cue to His qualities. To the kabbalist, God is not a concept, a generalization, but a most specific reality; his thinking about Him full of forceful
directness. But He who is "the Soul of all souls"[25] is "the mystery of all
mysteries." While the kabbalists speak of God as if they commanded a
view of the Beyond and were in possession of knowledge about the inner
life of God, they also assure us that all notions fail when applied to Him,
that He is beyond the grasp of the human mind and inaccessible to
meditation.[26] He is the *En Sof*, the Infinite, "the most Hidden of all
Hidden."[27] While there is an abysmal distance between Him and the
world, He is also called All. "For all things are in Him and He is in all
things . . . He is both manifest and concealed. Manifest in order to uphold
the all and concealed, for He is found nowhere. When He becomes
manifest, He projects nine brilliant lights that throw light in all directions.
So, too, does a lamp throw brilliance in all directions, but when we
approach the brilliance we find there is nothing outside the lamp. So is
the Holy ancient One, the Light of all Lights, the most Hidden of all
Hidden. We can only find the light which He spreads and which appears
and disappears. This light is called the Holy Name, and therefore All is
One."[28]

Thus, the "Most Recondite One who is beyond cognition does reveal
of Himself a tenuous and veiled brightness shining only along a narrow
path which extends from Him. This is the brightness that irradiates all."[29]
The *En Sof* has granted us manifestations of His hidden life: He had
descended to become the universe; He has revealed Himself to become
the Lord of Israel. The ways in which the Infinite assumes the form of
finite existence are called *Sefirot*.[30] These are various aspects or forms of
divine action, spheres of divine emanation. They are, as it were, the

garments in which the Hidden God reveals Himself and acts in the universe, the channels through which His light is issued forth.

The names of the ten *Sefirot* are *Keter, Hochmah, Binah, Hesed, Geburah, Tiferet, Netsah, Hod, Yesod, Malkut.* The transition from divine latency to activity takes place in *Keter*, the "supreme crown" of God. This stage is inconceivable, absolute unity and beyond description. In the following *Sefirot, Hochmah* and *Binah*, the building and creation of the cosmos as well as that which divides things begins. They are parallel emanations from *Keter*, representing the active and the receptive principle.

While the first triad represents the transition from the divine to the spiritual reality, the second triad is the source of the moral order. *Hesed* stands for the love of God; *Geburah* for the power of justice manifested as severity or punishment. From the union of these emanates *Tiferet*, compassion or beauty of God, mediating between *Hesed* and *Geburah*, between the life-giving power and the contrary power, holding in check what would otherwise prove to be the excesses of love.

The next triad is the source of the psychic and physical existences—*Netsah* is the lasting endurance of God, *Hod* His majesty, and *Yesod* the stability of the universe, the seat of life and vitality. *Malkut* is the kingdom, the presence of the divine in the world. It is not a source of its own but the outflow of the other *Sefirot*: "Of itself lightless, it looks up to the others and reflects them as a lamp reflects the sun."[31] It is the point at which the external world comes in contact with the upper spheres, the final manifestations of the divine, the *Shekinah*, "the Mother of all Living."[32]

The recondite and unapproachable Self of God is usually thought of as transcendent to the *Sefirot*. There is only a diffusion of His light into the *Sefirot*. The *En Sof* and the realm of His manifestations are "linked together like the flame and the coal," the flame being a manifestation of what is latent in the coal. In the process of the emanation, the transition from the divine to the spiritual, from the spiritual to the moral, from the moral to the physical, reality takes place. The product of this manifestation is not only the visible universe but an endless number of spiritual worlds which exist beyond the physical universe in which we live. These worlds, the hidden cosmos, constitute a most complex structure, divided into various grades and forms which can be described only in symbols. These symbols are found in the Torah, which is the constitution of the cosmos. Every letter, word, or phrase in the Bible not only describes an event in the history of our world but also represents a symbol of some stage in the hidden cosmos. These are the so-called *Raze Torah*, the mysteries that can be discovered by the mystical method of interpretation.

The system of *Sefirot* can be visualized as a tree or a man or a circle, in three triads or in three columns. According to the last image, the *Sefirot* are divided into a *right* column, signifying Mercy, or light; a *left* column, signifying Severity, the absence of light; and a *central* column, signifying the synthesis of the right and the left. Each *Sefirah* is a world in itself, dynamic and full of complicated mutual relations with other *Sefirot*. There are many symbols by which each *Sefirah* can be expressed, e.g., the second triad is symbolized in the lives of each of the three patriarchs. The doctrine of *Sefirot* enables the kabbalists to perceive the bearings of God upon this world, to identify the divine substance of all objects and events. It offers the principles by means of which all things and events can be interpreted as divine manifestations.

The various parts of the day represent various aspects of divine manifestation. "From sunrise until the sun declines westward it is called 'day,' and the attribute of Mercy is in the ascendant; after that it is called 'evening,' which is the time for the attribute of Severity . . . It is for this reason that Isaac instituted the afternoon prayer (*minhah*), namely, to mitigate the severity of the approaching evening; whereas Abraham instituted morning prayer, corresponding to the attribute of mercy."[33]

The plurality into which the one divine manifestation is split symbolizes the state of imperfection into which God's relation to the world was thrown. Every good deed serves to restore the original unity of the *Sefirot*, while, on the other hand, "sinners impair the supernal world by causing a separation between the 'right' and the 'left.' They really cause harm only to themselves . . . as they prevent the descent of blessings from above . . . and the heaven keeps the blessings to itself." Thus the sinner's separation of the good inclination from the evil one by consciously cleaving to evil separates, as it were, the divine attribute of Grace from that of Judgment, the right from the left.[34]

THE DOCTRINE OF THE *SHEKINAH*

ORIGINALLY there was harmony between God and His final manifestations, between the upper *Sefirot* and the tenth *Sefirah*. All things were attached to God, and His power surged unhampered throughout all stages of being. Following the trespass of Adam, however, barriers evolved thwarting the emanation of His power. The creature became detached from the Creator, the fruit from the tree, the tree of knowledge from the tree of life, the male from the female, our universe from the world of unity, even the *Shekinah* or the tenth *Sefirah* from the upper *Sefirot*. Because of that separation, the world was thrown into disorder, the power of strict judgment increased, the power of love diminished, and the forces of evil released. Man, who was to exist in pure spiritual form as light in constant communication with the divine, was sunk into his present inferior state.

In spite of this separation, however, God has not withdrawn entirely from this world. Metaphorically, when Adam was driven out of Eden, an aspect of the divine, the *Shekinah*, followed him into captivity.[35] Thus there is a divine power that dwells in this world. It is the Divine Presence that went before Israel while they were going through the wilderness, that protects the virtuous man, that abides in his house and goes forth with him on his journeys, that dwells between a man and his wife.[36] The *Shekinah* "continually accompanies a man and leaves him not so long as he keeps the precepts of the Torah. Hence a man should be careful not to go on the road alone; that is to say, he should diligently keep the precepts of the Torah in order that he may not be deserted by the *Shekinah*, and so be forced to go alone without the accompaniment of the *Shekinah*."[37] The *Shekinah* follows Israel into exile and "always hovers over Israel like a mother over her children."[38] Moreover, it is because of Israel and its observance of the Torah that the *Shekinah* dwells on earth. Were they to corrupt their way, they would thrust the *Shekinah* out of this world and the earth would be left in a degenerate state.[39]

The doctrine of the *Shekinah* occupies a central place in the kabbalah. While emphasizing that in His essence "the Holy One and the *Shekinah* are one,"[40] it speaks of a cleavage, as it were, in the reality of the divine. The *Shekinah* is called figuratively the *Matrona* (symbolized by the divine name *Elohim*) that is separated from the King (symbolized by the ineffable name *Hashem*), and it signifies that God is, so to speak, involved in the tragic state of this world. In the light of this doctrine the suffering of Israel assumed new meaning. Not only Israel but the whole universe, even the *Shekinah*, "lies in dust"[41] and is in exile. Man's task is to bring about the restitution of the original state of the universe and the reunion of the *Shekinah* and the *En Sof*. This is the meaning of messianic salvation, the goal of all efforts.

"In time to come God will restore the *Shekinah* to its place and there will be a complete union. 'In that day shall the Lord be one and His Name one' (Zechariah 14:9). It may be said: Is He not now one? no; for now through sinners He is not really one. For the *Matrona* is removed from the King . . . and the King without the *Matrona* is not invested with His crown as before. But when He joins the *Matrona*, who crowns Him with many resplendent crowns, then the supernal Mother will also crown Him in a fitting manner. But now that the King is not with the *Matrona*, the supernal Mother keeps her crowns and withholds from Him the waters of the stream and He is not joined with her. Therefore, as it were, He is not one. But when the *Matrona* shall return to the place of the Temple and the King shall be wedded with her, then all will be joined together, without separation and regarding this it is written, 'In that day shall the Lord be One and His Name One.' Then there shall be such perfection in the world as had not been for all generations before, for then shall be completeness above and below, and all worlds shall be united in one bond."[42]

The restoration of unity is a constant process. It takes place through the study of the Torah, through prayer, and through the fulfillment of the commandments. "The only aim and object of the Holy One in sending man into this world is that he may know and understand that *Hashem* (God), signifying the *En Sof*, is *Elohim* (*Shekinah*). This is the sum of the whole mystery of the faith, of the whole Torah, of all that is above and below, of the written and the oral Torah, all together forming one unity."[43] "When a man sins it is as though he strips the *Shekinah* of her vestments, and that is why he is punished; and when he carries out the precepts of the Law, it is as though he clothes the *Shekinah* in her vestments. Hence we say that the fringes worn by the Israelites are, to the *Shekinah* in captivity, like the poor man's garments, of which it is said, 'For that is his only covering, it is his garment for his skin, wherein he shall sleep.' "[44]

MYSTIC EXPERIENCE

THE ULTIMATE goal of the kabbalist is not his own union with the Absolute but the union of all reality with God; one's own bliss is subordinated to the redemption of all: "We have to put all our being, all the members of our body, our complete devotion, into that thought so as to rise and attach ourselves to the *En Sof*, and thus achieve the oneness of the upper and lower worlds."[45]

What this service means in terms of personal living is described in the following way:

Happy is the portion of whoever can penetrate into the mysteries of his Master and become absorbed into Him, as it were. Especially does a man achieve this when he offers up his prayer to his Master in intense devotion, his will then becoming as the flame inseparable from the coal, and his mind concentrated on the unity of the lower firmaments, to unify them by means of a lower name, then on the unity of the higher firmaments, and finally on the absorption of them all into that most high firmament. Whilst a man's mouth and lips are moving, his heart and will must soar to the height of heights, so as to acknowledge the unity of the whole in virtue of the mystery of mysteries in which all ideas, all wills and all thoughts find their goal, to wit, the mystery of *En Sof*.[46]

The thirst for God is colored by the awareness of His holiness, of the endless distance that separates man from the Eternal One. Yet he who craves for God is not only a mortal being but also a part of the community of Israel; that is, the bride of God, endowed with a soul that is "a part of God." Shy in using endearing terms in his own name, the Jewish mystic feels and speaks in the plural. The allegory of the Song of Songs would be impertinent as an individual utterance, but as an expression of Israel's love for God it is among the finest of all expressions. "God is the soul and spirit of all, and Israel calls Him so and says: [My soul], I desire Thee in order to cleave to Thee and I seek Thee early to find Thy favor."[47]

Israel lives in mystic union with God, and the purpose of all its service is to strengthen this union: "O my dove that art in the clefts of the rock, in the covert of the cliff" (Song of Solomon 2:14). The "dove" here is the Community of Israel, which like a dove never forsakes her mate, the Holy One, blessed be He. "In the clefts of the rock": these are the students of the Torah, who have no ease in this world. "In the covert of the steep place": these are the specially pious among them, the saintly and God-fearing, from whom the Divine Presence never departs. The Holy One, blessed be He, inquires concerning them of the community of Israel, saying, "Let me see thy countenance, let me hear thy voice, for sweet is thy voice"; "for above only the voice of those who study the Torah is heard. We have learned that the likeness of all such is graven above before the Holy One, blessed be He, who delights Himself with them every day and watches them, and that voice rises and pierces its way through all firmaments until it stands before the Holy One, blessed be He."[48]

The concepts of the kabbalah cannot always be clearly defined and consistently interrelated. As the name of Jewish mysticism, "kabbalah" (lit.: "received lore"), indicates, it is a tradition of wisdom, supposed to have been revealed to elect sages in ancient times and preserved throughout the generations by an initiated few. The kabbalists accept at the outset the ideas on authority, not on the basis of analytical understanding.

Yet the lips of the teachers and the pages of the books are not the only sources of knowledge. The great kabbalists claimed to have received wisdom directly from the Beyond. Inspiration and Vision were as much a part of their life as contemplation and study. The prayer of Moses: "Show me, I pray Thee, Thy glory" (Exodus 33:18) has never died in the hearts of the kabbalists. The conception of the goal has changed but the quest for immediate cognition remained. The Merkaba mystics, following perhaps late prophetic traditions about the mysteries of the Divine Throne, were striving to behold the celestial sphere in which the secrets of creation and man's destiny are contained. In the course of the centuries the scope of such esoteric experiences embraced a variety of objectives. The awareness of the kabbalists that the place whereon they stood was holy ground kept them mostly silent about the wonder that was granted to them. Yet we possess sufficient evidence to justify the assumption that mystic events, particularly in the form of inner experiences, of spiritual communications rather than that of sense perceptions, were elements of their living. According to old rabbinic teachings, there have always been sages and saints upon whom the Holy Spirit rested, to whom wisdom was communicated from heaven by a voice, through the appearance of the spirit of Elijah, or in dreams. According to the *Zohar*, God reveals to the saints "profound secrets of the Holy Name which He does not reveal to the angels."[49] The disciples of Rabbi Simon ben Yohai are called prophets, "before whom both supernal and terrestrial beings tremble in awe."[50] Others pray that the inspiration of the Holy Spirit should come upon them.[51] The perception of the unearthly is recorded as an ordinary feature in the life of certain rabbis. "When R. Hamnuna the Ancient used to come out from the river on a Friday afternoon, he was wont to rest a little on the bank, and raising his eyes in gladness, he would say that he sat there in order to behold the joyous sight of the heavenly angels ascending and descending. At each arrival of the Sabbath, he said, man is caught up into the world of souls."[52] Not only may the human mind receive spiritual illuminations; the soul also may be bestowed upon higher powers. "Corresponding to the impulses of a man here are the influences which he attracts to himself from above. Should his impulse be toward holiness, he attracts to himself holiness from on high and so he becomes holy; but if this tendency is toward the side of impurity, he draws down toward himself the unclean spirit and so becomes polluted."[53]

Since the time of the prophet Joel the Jews have expected that at the end of days the Lord would "pour out His spirit upon all flesh" and all men would prophesy. In later times, it is believed, the light of that revelation of mysteries could already be perceived.

The mystics absorb even in this world "something of the odor of these secrets and mysteries."[54] Significantly, the Torah itself is conceived as a living source of inspiration, not as a fixed book. The Torah is a voice that "calls aloud" to men;[55] she calls them day by day to herself in love . . . "The Torah lets out a word and emerges for a little from her sheath, and then hides herself again. But she does this only for those who understand and obey her. She is like unto a beautiful and stately damsel, who is hidden in a secluded chamber of a palace and who has a lover of whom no one knows but she. Out of his love for her he constantly passes by her gate, turning his eyes toward all sides to find her. Knowing that he is always haunting the palace, what does she do? She opens a little door in her hidden palace, discloses for a moment her face to her lover, then swiftly hides it again. None but he notices it; but his heart and soul, and all that is in him are drawn to her, knowing as he does that she has revealed herself to him for a moment because she loves him. It is the same with the Torah, which reveals her hidden secrets only to those who love her. She knows that he who is wise of heart daily haunts the gates of her house. What does she do? She shows her face to him from her palace, making a sign of love to him, and straightaway returns to her hiding place again. No one understands her message save he alone, and he is drawn to her with heart and soul and all his being. Thus the Torah reveals herself momentarily in love to her lovers in order to awaken fresh love in them."[56]

THE TORAH—A MYSTIC REALITY

THE TORAH is an inexhaustible esoteric reality. To enter into its deep, hidden strata is in itself a mystic goal. The universe is an image of the Torah and the Torah is an image of God. For the Torah is "the Holy of Holies"; "it consists entirely of the name of the Holy One, blessed be He. Every letter in it is bound up with that Name."[57]

The Torah[58] is the main source from which man can draw the secret wisdom and power of insight into the essence of things. "It is called Torah (lit.: showing) because it shows and reveals that which is hidden and unknown; and all life from above is comprised in it and issues from it."[59] "The Torah contains all the deepest and most recondite mysteries; all sublime doctrines both disclosed and undisclosed; all essences both of the higher and the lower grades, of this world and of the world to come are to be found there."[60] The source of wisdom is accessible to all, yet only few resort to it. "How stupid are men that they take no pains to know the ways of the Almighty by which the world is maintained. What prevents them? Their stupidity, because they do not study the Torah; for if they were to study the Torah they would know the ways of the Holy One, blessed be He."[61]

The Torah has a double significance: literal and symbolic. Besides their plain, literal meaning, which is important, valid, and never to be over-looked, the verses of the Torah possess an esoteric significance, "comprehensible only to the wise who are familiar with the ways of the Torah."[62] "Happy is Israel to whom was given the sublime Torah, the Torah of truth. Perdition take anyone who maintains that any narrative in the Torah comes merely to tell us a piece of history and nothing more! If that were so, the Torah would not be what it assuredly is, to wit, the supernal Law, the Law of truth. Now, if it is not dignified for a king of flesh and blood to engage in common talk, much less to write it down, is it conceivable that the most high King, the Holy One, blessed be He, was short of sacred subjects with which to fill the Torah, so that He had to collect such commonplace topics as the anecdotes of Esau, and Hagar, Laban's talks to Jacob, the words of Balaam and his ass, those of Balak, and of Zimri, and such-like, and make of them a Torah? If so, why is it called the 'Law of Truth?' Why do we read 'The Law of the Lord is perfect . . . The testimony of the Lord is sure . . . The Ordinances of the Lord are true . . . More to be desired are they than gold, yea, than much fine gold' (Psalms 19:8–11). But assuredly each word of the Torah signifies sublime things, so that this or that narrative, besides its meaning in and for itself, throws light on the all-comprehensive Rule of the Torah."[63]

"Said Rabbi Simeon: 'Alas for the man who regards the Torah as a mere book of tales and everyday matters! If that were so, we, even we, could compose a Torah dealing with everyday affairs, and of even greater excellence. Nay, even the princes of the world possess books of greater worth which we could use as a model for composing some such Torah. The Torah, however, contains in all its words supernal truths and sublime mysteries. Observe the perfect balancing of the upper and lower worlds. Israel here below is balanced by the angels on high, of whom it says: 'who makest thine angels into winds' (Psalms 104:4). For the angels in descending on earth put on themselves earthly garments, as otherwise they could not stay in this world, nor could the world endure them.

"Now, if thus it is with the angels, how much more so must it be with the Torah—the Torah that created them, that created all the worlds and is the means by which these are sustained. Thus had the Torah not clothed herself in garments of this world the world could not endure it. The stories of the Torah are thus only her outer garments, and whoever looks upon that garment as being Torah itself, woe to that man—such a one will have no portion in the next world. David thus said: 'Open Thou mine eyes, that I may behold wondrous things out of Thy law' (Psalms 119:18); to wit, the things that are beneath the garment. Observe this. The garments worn by a man are the most visible part of him, and senseless people looking at the man do not seem to see more in him than the garments. But in truth the pride of the garments is the body of the man, and the pride of the body is the soul. Similarly the Torah has a body made up of the precepts of the Torah, called *gufe torah* (bodies, main principles of the Torah), and that body is enveloped in garments made up of worldly narratives. The senseless people see only the garment, the mere narrations; those who are somewhat wise penetrate as far as the body. But the really wise, the servants of the most high King, those who stood on Mt. Sinai, penetrate right through to the soul, the root principle of all, namely to the real Torah. In the future the same are destined to penetrate even to the super-soul (soul of the soul) of the Torah . . ."[64]

How assiduously should one ponder over each word of the Torah, for there is not a single word in it that does not contain allusions to the Supernal Holy Name, not a word that does not contain many mysteries, many aspects, many roots, many branches! Where now is this "book of the wars of the Lord"? What is meant, of course, is the Torah, for as the members of the fellowship have pointed out, he who is engaged in the battle of the Torah, struggling to penetrate into her mysteries, will wrest from his struggles an abundance of peace.[65]

THE MYSTIC WAY OF LIFE

A LONGING for the unearthly, a yearning for purity, the will to holiness, connected the conscience of the kabbalists with the strange current of mystic living. Being puzzled or inquisitive will not make a person mystery-stricken. The kabbalists were not set upon exploring or upon compelling the unseen to become visible. Their intention was to integrate their thoughts and deeds into the secret order, to assist God in undoing the evil, in redeeming the light that was concealed. Though working with fragile tools for a mighty end, they were sure of bringing about at the end the salvation of the universe and of this tormented world.

A new form of living was the consequence of the kabbalah. Everything was so replete with symbolic significance as to make it the potential heart of the spiritual universe. How carefully must all be approached. A moral rigorism that hardly leaves any room for waste or respite resulted in making the kabbalist more meticulous in studying and fulfilling the precepts of the Torah, in refining his moral conduct, in endowing everyday actions with solemn significance. For man represents God in this world. Even the parts of his body signify divine mysteries.

Everything a man does leaves its imprint on the world. "The Supernal Holy King does not permit anything to perish, not even the breath of the mouth. He has a place for everything, and makes it what He wills. Even a human word, yes, even the voice, is not void, but has its place and destination in the universe."[66] Every action here below, if it is done with the intention of serving the Holy King, produces a "breath" in the world above, and there is no breath which has no voice; and this voice ascends and crowns itself in the supernal world and becomes an intercessor before the Holy One, blessed be He. Contrariwise, every action which is not done with this purpose becomes a "breath" which floats about the world, and when the soul of the doer leaves his body, this "breath" rolls about like a stone in a sling, and it "breaks the spirit." The act done and the word spoken in the service of the Holy One, however, ascend high above the sun and become a holy breath, which is the seed sown by man in that world and is called *zedakah* (righteousness) or (loving-kindness), as it is written: "Sow to yourselves according to righteousness" (Hosea 10:12). This "breath" guides the departed soul and brings it into the region of the supernal glory, so that it is "bound in the bundle of life with the Lord thy God" (I Samuel 25:29). It is concerning this that it is written: "Thy righteousness shall go before thee; the glory of the Lord shall be thy reward" (Isaiah 58:8). That which is called "the glory of the Lord" gathers up the souls of that holy breath, and this is indeed ease and comfort for them; but the other is called "breaking of spirit." Blessed are the righteous whose works are "above the sun" and who sow a seed of righteousness which makes them worthy to enter the world to come.[67]

Everything a man does leaves its imprint upon the world: his breath, thought, speech. If it is evil, the air is defiled and he who comes close to that trace may be affected by it and led to do evil. By fulfilling the divine precepts man purifies the air and turns the "evil spirits" into "holy spirits." He should strive to spiritualize the body and to make it identical with the soul by fulfilling the 248 positive and 365 negative precepts which correspond to the 248 limbs and the 365 sinews of the human body. The precepts of the Torah contain "manifold sublime recondite teachings and radiances and resplendences,"[68] and can lift man to the supreme level of existence.

The purpose of man's service is to "give strength to God," not to attain one's own individual perfection. Man is able to stir the supernal spheres. "The terrestrial world is connected with the heavenly world, as the heavenly world is connected with the terrestrial one."[69] In fulfilling the good, the corresponding sphere on high is strengthened; in balking it, the sphere is weakened. This connection or correspondence can be made to operate in a creative manner by means of *kavanah*, or contemplation of the mysteries of which the words and precepts of the Torah are the symbols. In order to grasp the meaning of those words or to fulfill the purpose of those precepts, one has to resort to the divine names and qualities which are invested in those words and precepts, the mystic issues to which they refer, or, metaphorically, the gates of the celestial mansion which the spiritual content of their fulfillment has to enter. Thus, all deeds—study, prayer, and ceremonies—have to be performed not mechanically but while meditating upon their mystic significance.

Prayer is a powerful force in this service and a venture full of peril. He who prays is a priest at the temple that is the cosmos. With good prayer he may "build worlds"; with improper prayer he may "destroy worlds." "It is a miracle that a man survives the hour of worship," the Baal Shem said. "The significance of all our prayers and praises is that by means of them the upper fountain may be filled; and when it is so filled and attains completeness, then the universe below, and all that appertains thereto, is filled also and receives completeness from the completion which has been consummated in the upper sphere. The world below cannot, indeed, be in a state of harmony unless it receives that peace and perfection from above, even as the moon has no light in herself but shines with the reflected radiance of the sun. All our prayers and intercessions have this purpose, namely, that the region from whence light issues may be invigorated; for then from its reflection all below is supplied."[70] "Every word of prayer that issues from a man's mouth ascends aloft through all firmaments to a place where it is tested. If it is genuine, it is taken up before the Holy King to be fulfilled, but if not, it is rejected, and an alien spirit is evoked by it."[71] For example, "it is obligatory for every Israelite to relate the story of the Exodus on the Passover night. He who does so fervently and joyously, telling the tale with a high heart, shall be found worthy to rejoice in the *Shekinah* in the world to come, for rejoicing brings forth rejoicing; and the joy of Israel causes the Holy One Himself to be glad, so that He calls together all the family above and says unto them: 'Come ye and hearken unto the praises which my children bring unto me! Behold how they rejoice in my redemption!' Then all the angels and supernal beings gather round and observe Israel, how she sings and rejoices because of her Lord's own redemption—and seeing the rejoicings below, the supernal beings also break into jubilation, for that the Holy One possesses on earth a people so holy, whose joy in the Redemption of their Lord is so great and powerful. For all that terrestrial rejoicing increases the power of the Lord and His hosts in the regions above, just as an earthly king gains strength from the praises of his subjects, the fame of his glory being thus spread throughout the world."[72]

Worship came to be regarded as a pilgrimage into the supernal spheres, with the prayerbook as an itinerary, containing the course of the gradual ascent of the spirit. The essential goal of man's service is to bring about the lost unity of all that exists. To render praise unto Him is not the final purpose. "Does the God of Abraham need an exaltation? Is He not already exalted high above our comprehension? . . . Yet man can and must exalt Him in the sense of uniting in his mind all the attributes in the Holy Name, for this is the supremest form of worship."[73] By meditating upon the mysteries while performing the divine precepts, we act toward unifying all the supernal potencies in one will and bringing about the union of the Master and the *Matrona*.

Concerning the verse in Psalms 145:18, "The Lord is nigh to all them that call upon Him, to all that call upon Him in truth," the *Zohar* remarks that the words "in truth" mean in possession of the full knowledge which enables the worshipper perfectly "to unite the letters of the Holy Name in prayer . . . On the achievement of that unity hangs both celestial and terrestrial worship . . . If a man comes to unify the Holy Name, but without proper concentration of mind and devotion of heart, to the end that the supernal and terrestrial hosts should be blessed thereby, then his prayer is rejected and all beings denounce him, and he is numbered with those of whom the Holy One said, 'When ye come to see my countenance, who hath required this from your hand, to tread my courts?' All the 'countenances' of the King are hidden in the depths of darkness, but for those who know how perfectly to unite the Holy Name, all the walls of darkness are burst asunder, and the diverse 'countenances' of the King are made manifest, and shine upon all, bringing blessing to heavenly and earthly beings."[74]

The lower things are apparent, the higher things remain unrevealed. The higher an essence is, the greater is the degree of its concealment. To pray is "to draw blessings from the depth of the 'cistern,' from the source of all life . . . Prayer is the drawing of this blessing from above to below; for when the Ancient One, the All-Hidden, wishes to bless the universe, He lets His gifts of grace collect in that supernal depth, from whence they are to be drawn, through human prayer, into the 'cistern,' so that all the streams and brooks may be filled therefrom." The verse in Psalms 130:1, "Out of the depths have I called Thee," is said to mean not only that he who prays should do so from the depths of his soul; he must also invoke the blessing from the source of all sources.[75]

THE CONCERN FOR GOD

THE YEARNING for mystic living, the awareness of the ubiquitous mystery, the noble nostalgia for the nameless nucleus, have rarely subsided in the Jewish soul. This longing for the mystical has found many and varied expressions in ideas and doctrines, in customs and songs, in visions and aspirations. It is a part of the heritage of the psalmists and prophets.

There were divine commandments to fulfill, rituals to perform, laws to obey—but the psalmist did not feel as if he carried a yoke: "Thy statutes have been my songs" (119:54). The fulfillment of the *mitzvot* was felt to be not a mechanical compliance but a personal service in the palace of the King of Kings. Is mysticism alien to the spirit of Judaism? Listen to the psalmist: "As the hart panteth after the water brooks, so panteth my soul after Thee, O Lord. My soul thirsteth for God, for the Living God; when shall I come and appear before God?" (42:2–3). "My soul yearneth, yea even pineth for the courts of the Lord; my heart and my flesh sing for joy unto the Living God" (84:3). "For a day in Thy courts is better than a thousand" (84:11). "In Thy presence is fullness of joy" (16:11).

It has often been said that Judaism is an earthly religion, yet the psalmist states, "I am a sojourner in the earth" (119:19). "Whom have I in heaven but Thee? And besides Thee I desire none upon earth" (73:25). "My flesh and my heart faileth; but God is the rock of my heart and my portion forever" (73:26). "But as for me, the nearness of God is my good" (73:28). "O God, Thou art my God; earnestly will I seek Thee; my soul thirsteth for Thee, my flesh longeth for Thee in a dry and weary land, where no water is . . . for Thy loving-kindness is better than life. My soul is satisfied as with marrow and fatness . . . I remember Thee upon my couch and meditate on Thee in the nightwatches . . . My soul cleaveth unto Thee, Thy right hand holdeth me fast" (63:2, 4, 6, 7, 9).

In their efforts to say what God is and wills, the prophets sought to imbue Israel with two impulses: to realize that God is holy, different, and apart from all that exists and to bring into man's focus the dynamics that prevail between God and man. The first impulse placed the mind in the restful light of the knowledge of unity, omnipotence, and superiority of God to all other beings, while the second impulse turned the hearts toward the inexhaustible heavens of God's concern for man, at times brightened by His mercy, at times darkened by His anger. He is both transcendent, beyond human understanding, and at the same time full of love, compassion, grief, or anger. The prophets did not intend to afford man a view of heaven, to report about secret things they saw and heard but to disclose what happened in God in reference to Israel. What they preached was more than a concept of divine might and wisdom. They spoke of an inner life of God, of His love or anger, His mercy or disappointment, His interest or participation in the fate of Israel and other nations. God revealed Himself to the prophets in a specific state, in an emotional or passionate relationship to Israel. He not only demanded obedience but He was personally concerned and even stirred by the conduct of His people. Their actions aroused His joy, grief, or disappointment. His attitude was not objective but subjective. He was not only a judge but also a father. He is the lover, engaged to His people, who reacts to human life with a specific *pathos*, signified in the language of the prophets, in love, mercy, or anger. The divine pathos which the prophets tried to express in many ways was not a name for His essence but rather for the modes of this reaction to Israel's conduct which could be changed by a change in Israel's conduct. Such a change was often the object of the prophetic ministry.

The prophets discovered the holy dimension of living by which our right to live and to survive is measured. However, the holy dimension was not a mechanical magnitude, measurable by the yardstick of deed and reward, of crime and punishment, by a cold law of justice. They did not proclaim a universal moral mechanism but a spiritual order in which justice was the course but not the source. To them justice was not a static principle but a surge sweeping from the inwardness of God, in which the deeds of man find, as it were, approval or disapproval, joy or sorrow. There was a surge of divine pathos, which came to the souls of the prophets like a fierce passion, startling, shaking, burning, and led them forth to the perilous defiance of people's self-assurance and contentment. Beneath all songs and sermons they held conference with God's concern for the people, with the well out of which the tides of anger raged.

There is always a correspondence between what man is and what he knows about God. To a man of the *vita activa*, omnipotence is the most striking attribute of God. A man with an inner life, to whom thoughts and intuitions are not less real than things and deeds, will search for a concept of the inner life of God. The concept of inner life in the Divine Being is an idea upon which the mystic doctrines of Judaism hinge. The significance of prophetic revelation lies not in the inner experience of the prophet but in its character as a manifestation of what is in God. Prophetic revelation is primarily an event in the life of God. This is the outstanding difference between prophetic revelation and all other types of inspiration as reported by many mystics and poets. To the prophet it is not a psychic event but first of all a transcendent act, something that happens to God. The actual reality of revelation takes place outside the consciousness of the prophet. He experiences revelation, so to speak, as an ecstasy of God, who comes out of His imperceivable distance to reveal His will to man. Essentially, the act of revelation takes place in the Beyond; it is merely directed upon the prophet.

The knowledge about the inner state of the divine in its relationship to Israel determined the inner life of the prophets, engendering a passion for God, a *sympathy* for the divine pathos in their hearts. They loved Israel because God loved Israel, and they frowned upon Israel when they knew that such was the attitude of God. Thus the marriage of Hosea was an act of sympathy; the prophet had to go through the experience of being betrayed as Israel had betrayed God. He had to experience in his own life what it meant to be betrayed by a person whom he loved in order to gain an understanding of the inner life of God. In a similar way the sympathy for God was in the heart of Jeremiah like a "burning fire, shut up in my bones and I weary myself to hold it in, but cannot" (20:9).

The main doctrine of the prophets can be called pathetic theology. Their attitude toward what they knew about God can be described as religion of sympathy. The divine pathos, or as it was later called, the *Middot*, stood in the center of their consciousness. The life of the prophet revolved around the life of God. The prophets were not indifferent to whether God was in a state of anger or a state of mercy. They were most sensitive to what was going on in God.[76]

This is the pattern of Jewish mysticism: to have an open heart for the inner life of God. It is based on two assumptions: that there is an inner life in God and that the existence of man ought to revolve in a spiritual dynamic course around the life of God.[77]

1960

A Preface to an

Understanding of Revelation

WE HAVE NEVER BEEN the same since that day on which Abraham crushed his father's precious symbols, since the day on which the voice of God overwhelmed us at Sinai. It is forever impossible for us to retreat into an age that predates the Sinaitic event. Something unprecedented happened. God revealed His name to us, and we are named after Him. There are two Hebrew names for Jew: *Yehudi*, the first three letters of which are the first three letters of the Ineffable Name, and *Israel*, the end of which, *el*, means, in Hebrew, God.

If other religions can be characterized as a relation between man and God, Judaism must be described as a relation between *man with Torah* and *God*. The Jew is never alone in the face of God. The Torah is always with him. A Jew without the Torah is obsolete.

The Torah is not the wisdom but the destiny of Israel; not our literature but our essence. It was produced neither by way of speculation nor by way of poetic inspiration but by way of revelation. But what is revelation?

MANY PEOPLE reject the Bible because of a mistaken notion that revelation has proved to be scientifically impossible. It is all so very simple: there is no source of thought other than the human mind. The Bible is a book like any other book, and the prophets had no access to sources inaccessible to us. "The Bible is the national literature of the Jewish people." To the average mind, therefore, revelation is a sort of mental outcast, not qualified to be an issue for debate. At best, it is regarded as a fairy tale, on a par with the conception that lightning and thunder are signs of anger of sundry gods and demons, rather than the result of a sudden expansion of the air in the path of an electric discharge. Indeed, has not the issue been settled long ago by psychology and anthropology as primitive man's mistaking an illusion for a supernatural event?

The most serious obstacle which we encounter in entering a discussion about revelation, however, does not arise from our doubts whether the accounts of the prophets about their experiences are authentic; the most critical vindication of these accounts, even if it were possible, would be of little relevance. The most serious obstacle is the *absence of the problem.* An answer, to be meaningful, presupposes the awareness of a question, but the climate in which we live today is not genial to the growth of questions which have taken centuries to bloom. The Bible is an answer to the supreme question: What does God demand of us? Yet the question has gone out of the world. God is portrayed as a mass of vagueness behind a veil of enigmas, and His voice has become alien to our minds, to our hearts, to our souls. We have learned to listen to every ego except the "I" of God. The man of our time may proudly declare: Nothing animal is alien to me, but everything divine is. This is the status of the Bible in modern life: it is a great answer, but we do not know the question anymore. Unless we recover the question, there is no hope of understanding the Bible.

REVELATION is a complex issue, presupposing first of all certain assumptions about the existence and nature of God, who communicates His will to man. Even granting the existence of a Supreme Power, modern man, with his aloofness to what God means, would find it preposterous to assume that the Infinite Spirit should come down to commune with the feeble, finite mind of man, that man could be an ear to God. With the concept of the Absolute so far removed from the grasp of his mind, man is, at best, bewildered at the claim of the prophets, like an animal when confronted with the spectacle of human power. With his relative sense of values, with his mind conditioned by circumstances and reduced to the grasp of the piecemeal, constantly stumbling in his efforts to establish a system of universally integrated ideas, how can it be conceived that man was ever able to grasp the unconditioned?

The first thing, therefore, we ought to do is to find out whether, as many of us seem to think, revelation is an absurdity, whether the prophetic claim is an intellectual savagery.

IS IT MEANINGFUL to ask: Did God address Himself to man? Indeed, unless God is real and beyond definitions that confine Him; unless He is unfettered by such distinctions as transcendence and immanence; unless we feel that we are driven and pursued by His question, there is little meaning in starting our inquiry. But those who know that this life of ours takes place in a world that is not all to be explained in human terms; that every moment is a carefully concealed act of His creation, cannot but ask: Is there any event wherein His voice is not suppressed? Is there any moment wherein His presence is not concealed?

True, the claim of the prophets is staggering and almost incredible. But to us, living in this horribly beautiful world, God's thick silence is incomparably more staggering and totally incredible.

IS IT HISTORICAL curiosity that excites our interest in the problem of revelation? As an event of the past that subsequently affected the course of civilization, revelation would not engage the modern mind any more than the battle of Marathon or the Congress of Vienna. However, it concerns us not because of the impact it had upon past generations but as something which may or may not be of perpetual, unabating relevance. Thus, in entering this discourse, we do not conjure up the shadow of an archaic phenomenon but attempt to debate the question whether to believe that there is a voice in the world that pleads with man at all times or at some times in the name of God.

It is not only a personal issue but one that concerns the history of all men from the beginning of time to the end of days. No one who has, at least once in his life, sensed the terrifying seriousness of human history or the earnestness of individual existence can afford to ignore that problem. He must decide, he must choose between yes and no.

In thinking about the world, we cannot proceed without guidance, supplied by logic and scientific method. Thinking about the ultimate, climbing toward the invisible, leads along a path on which there are countless chasms and very few ledges. Faith, helping us take the first steps, is full of ardor but also blind; we are easily lost with our faith in misgivings which we cannot fully dispel. What could counteract the apprehension that it is utter futility to crave for contact with God?

Man in his spontaneity may reach out for the hidden God and with his mind try to pierce the darkness of His distance. But how will he know whether it is God he is reaching out for or some value personified? How will he know where or when God is found: in the ivory tower of space or at some distant moment in the future?

The certainty of being exposed to a Presence which is not the world's is a fact of human existence. But such certainty does not result in aesthetic indulgence in meditation; it stirs with a demand to live in a way which is worthy of that Presence.

The beginning of faith is not a feeling for the mystery of living or a sense of awe, wonder, or fear. The root of religion is the question what to do with the feeling for the mystery of living, what to do with awe, wonder, or fear. Religion, the end of isolation, begins with a consciousness that something is asked of us. It is in that tense, eternal asking in which the soul is caught and in which man's answer is elicited.[1] Who will tell us how to find a knowledge of the way? How do we know that the way we choose is the way He wants to pursue?

What a sculptor does to a block of marble, the Bible does to our finest intuitions. It is like raising the dead to life.

THE IDEALS we strive after, the values we try to fulfill, have they any significance in the realm of natural events? The sun spends its rays upon the just and the wicked, upon flowers and snakes alike. The heart beats normally within those who torture and kill. Is all goodness and striving for veracity but a fiction of the mind to which nothing corresponds in reality? Where are the spirit's values valid? Within the inner life of man? But the spirit is a stranger in the soul. A demand such as "Love thy neighbor as thyself" is not at home in the self.

We all have a terrible loneliness in common. Day after day a question arises desperately in our minds: Are we *alone* in the wilderness of the self, alone in this silent universe, of which we are a part, and in which we also feel like strangers?

It is such a situation that makes us ready to search for the voice of God in the world of man: the taste of utter loneliness; the discovery that unless the world is porous, the life of the spirit is a freak; that the world is a torso crying for its head; that the mind is insufficient to itself.

MODERN MAN used to think that the acceptance of revelation was an effrontery to the mind. Man must live by his intelligence alone; he is capable of both finding and attaining the aim of his existence. That man is not in need of superhuman authority or guidance was a major argument of the Deists against accepting the idea of prophecy. Social reforms, it was thought, would cure the ills and eliminate the evils from our world. Yet we have finally discovered what prophets and saints have always known: bread and beauty will not save humanity. There is a passion and drive for cruel deeds which only the fear of God can soothe; there is a suffocating sensuality in man which only holiness can ventilate.

It is, indeed, hard for the mind to believe that any member of a species which can organize or even witness the murder of millions and feel no regret should ever be endowed with the ability to receive a word of God. If man can remain callous to a horror as infinite as God, if man can be bloodstained and self-righteous, distort what the conscience tells, make soap of human flesh, then how did it happen that nations did not exterminate each other centuries ago?

Man rarely comprehends how dangerously great he is. The more power he attains, the greater his need for an ability to master his power. Unless a new source of spiritual energy is discovered commensurate with the source of atomic energy, a few men may throw all men into final disaster.

What stands in the way of accepting revelation is our refusal to accept its authority. Liberty is our security, and to accept the word of the prophets is to accept the sovereignty of God. Yet our understanding of man and his liberty has undergone a serious change in our time. The problem of man is more grave than we were able to realize a generation ago. What we used to sense in our worst fears turned out to have been a utopia compared with what has happened in our own days. We have discovered that reason may be perverse, that liberty is no security. Now we must learn that there is no liberty except the freedom bestowed upon us by God; that there is no liberty without sanctity.

Unless history is a vagary of nonsense, there must be a counterpart to the immense power of man to destroy, there must be a voice that says No to man, a voice not vague, faint, and inward, like qualms of conscience, but equal in spiritual might to man's power to destroy.

From time to time the turbulent drama is interrupted by a voice that says No to the recklessness of heart.

The voice speaks to the spirit of prophetic men in singular moments of their lives and cries to the masses through the horror of history. The prophets respond; the masses despair.

The Bible, speaking in the name of a Being that combines justice with omnipotence, is the never-ceasing outcry of No to humanity. In the midst of our applauding the feats of civilization, the Bible flings itself like a knife slashing our complacency, reminding us that God, too, has a voice in history. Only those who are satisfied with the state of affairs or those who choose the easy path of escaping from society rather than of staying within it and keeping themselves clean of the mud of vicious glories will resent its attack on human independence.

How did Abraham arrive at his certainty that there is a God who is concerned with the world? Said Rabbi Isaac: Abraham may be compared to a man who was traveling from place to place when he saw a *palace in flames.* "Is it possible that there is no one who cares for the palace?" he wondered. Until the owner of the building looked out and said, "I am the owner of the palace." Similarly, Abraham our father wondered, "Is it conceivable that the world is without a guide?" The Holy One, blessed be He, looked out and said, "I am the Guide, the Sovereign of the world."[2]

The world is in flames, consumed by evil. Is it possible that there is no one who cares?

THERE IS an abyss of not knowing God in many minds, with a rumor floating over it about an Ultimate Being, of which they know only that it is an immense unconscious mass of mystery. It is from the perspective of such knowledge that the prophets' claim seems preposterous.

Let us examine that perspective. By attributing immense mysteriousness to that Ultimate Being, we definitely claim to know it. Thus, the Ultimate Being is not an unknown but a known God. In other words, a God whom we know but one who does not know, the great Unknower. We proclaim the ignorance of God as well as our knowledge of His being ignorant!

This seems to be a part of our pagan heritage: to say the Supreme Being is a total mystery; and even having accepted the biblical God of creation, we still cling to the assumption: He who has the power to create a world is never able to utter a word. Yet why should we assume that the endless is forever imprisoned in silence? Why should we *a priori* exclude the power of expression from the Absolute Being? If the world is the work of God, isn't it conceivable that there would be within His work signs of His expression?

The idea of revelation remains an absurdity as long as we are unable to comprehend the impact with which the reality of God is pursuing man. Yet at those moments in which the fate of mankind is in the balance, even those who have never sensed how God turns to man suddenly realize that man—who has the power to devise both culture and crime, who is able to be a proxy for divine justice—is important enough to be the recipient of spiritual light at the rare dawns of his history.

God, Torah, and Israel

JUDAISM IS A COMPLEX STRUCTURE. It can be characterized exclusively neither as a theological doctrine nor as a way of living according to the Law nor as a community. A religious Jew is a person committed to God, to his concern and teaching (Torah), who lives as part of a covenant community (Israel). Judaism revolves around three sacred entities: God, Torah, Israel. The Jew never stands alone before God; the Torah and Israel are always with him.

God as an isolated concept may be exceedingly hidden, vague, and general. In Jewish experience the relation between God and man is established as a concrete and genuine situation in finding an answer to the questions: What are the acts and moments in which God becomes manifest to man? What are the acts and moments in which man becomes attached to God? To the Jew, the Torah is the answer.

Jewish existence is not only the adherence to particular doctrines and observances but primarily the living *in* the spiritual order of the Jewish people, the living *in* the Jews of the past and *with* the Jews of the present. Not only is it a certain quality in the souls of the individuals but it is primarily involvement and participation in the covenant and community of Israel. It is more than an experience or a creed, more than the possession of psychic traits or the acceptance of theological doctrine; it is, above all, the living in a holy dimension, in a spiritual order. Our share in holiness we acquire by living in the Jewish community. What we do as individuals may be a trivial episode; what we attain as Israel causes us to grow into the infinite.

This essay, originally written in Hebrew, was translated into English by Byron Sherwin and subsequently revised by the author.

Since sanctity is associated with each of these three entities, the question arises whether they are all on the same level of holiness, whether they form part of a hierarchy, or whether a dialectic relationship among them exists that is too subtle to be stated in a simple brief statement.

Because of the power and preciousness of the three entities, there is a tendency to extol and to overstate one at the expense of the other two. Various movements in modern Judaism have tended to indulge in such extravagance.

With some degree of justification it may be said that classical Reform Judaism has concentrated on ethical monotheism as the essence of Judaism. Secular nationalism has made the peoplehood of Israel its central concern, and neo-orthodoxy, in its eagerness to defend the traditional observances, has stressed the supremacy of the Torah and Law.

The purpose of this essay is an effort to clarify the relationship of God and Torah in the light of classical rabbinic literature, and to elucidate the classical rabbinic doctrine of the interdependence of the three entities.

GOD AND TORAH

THE TORAH, the comprehensive name for the revealed teachings of Judaism, has been an object of love and adoration. According to the school of Rabbi Akiba, the Torah has a concrete as well as a spiritual reality; it not only exists as a book in human possession; it also exists in heaven as well as on earth.[1] Indeed, the Hebrew term for revelation is literally "Torah from heaven."[2]

What is the relationship of Torah and God? What does the Torah mean to Israel?

The Torah is not only identified with the divine wisdom which preceded the existence of the world;[3] its worth surpasses the value of all things.

Two thousand years ago in Alexandria, we are told in a legend, a sage of the Greeks asked a sage of the Hebrews:

Why are you Jews so proud of your heritage? We Greeks have Homer, Plato, and Aristotle. What have you? Our sages have discovered the idea of the cosmos. What have yours done? How can you even venture to compare your intellectual heritage with ours?

"True," said the Jew, "you have discovered the cosmos. Yet what we have transcends even the mystery and vastness of the cosmos." "What can that be?" queried the Greek. Came the reply: "We have the Torah."[4]

This legend reflects a view not foreign to hyperbolic rabbinic thought. Not only does the Torah transcend the cosmos, but "any given part of the Torah is of greater importance than the cosmos."[5] The Torah determines both the essence and the existence of the universe. When God decided to create the universe, say the rabbis, he consulted the Torah. It served as his blueprint for creation.[6] The nature of creation was determined through the Torah. Even the initial existence of the cosmos is dependent upon the Torah. "The existence of the Torah is a necessary condition for the existence of the cosmos."[7]

How vast is the cosmos! Yet somewhere in the dimension of space lies its limit. Is there an entity without any limit? Yes, said the enthusiastic rabbis, the Torah.[8]

Not only was the existence of the Torah the necessary requirement for the creation of the cosmos; it is also the necessary condition for its continued existence. The world was created on approval. Unless the Torah was accepted at Sinai, the cosmos would have to be returned to chaos. There could be a cosmos only with the Torah. The absence of the Torah would imply the absence of the universe. With Torah comes the divine blessing of an ordered creation. Without it, there is danger of a return to the abyss of cosmic confusion. The Torah is the ground of all beings. The creatures of heaven and earth cannot exist without it.[9]

When one gives a gift in love to another, part of the giver is given with the gift. The Torah is God's gift to his creation and to his creatures. When God gives the Torah, it is as if he gives of himself.[10]

A parable:

Once there was a king who had an only daughter whom another king married. When the latter wished to return to his country and take his wife with him, the father said, "My daughter, whom I have given you in marriage, is my only child. My love for her is great. I cannot part from her. Yet I cannot ask you not to take her to your realm. It is now her proper home. Permit me this one request. To whatever distant place you take her now to live, always have a chamber ready for me that I may dwell with you and with her. For I can never consider really leaving my daughter."

So said God to Israel: "I have given you a Torah from which I cannot really part. I cannot tell you not to receive it in love. Yet I request only this. Wherever you go with it, make for me a house wherein I may sojourn. As it is written: Let them make me a sanctuary so that I may dwell among them" (Exodus 25:8).[11]

Is not a child both a part of and apart from its parent? So is the Torah part of and apart from God. When Israel accepts the Torah, she accepts God.

A child's presence testifies to the life of its parent. The Torah testifies for God.

Once a king had a daughter. He built her palaces with many great halls. His decree went forth: Whosoever is granted an audience with my daughter is to be considered as being in my presence. Whosoever dares to insult my daughter, it is as if he insulted me.[12]

The literary metaphors in which God's relation to the Torah is described may be compared to the rabbinic description of the relationship between the *Shekinah* (God's indwelling or presence) and the community of Israel. Participation in the same events links them, one to the other. It is almost as if the fate of one determined the fate of the other. As reflections about the relationship between God and Israel develop, the interdependence of God and Israel becomes more emphatic. As the love between them intensifies, the father becomes dependent upon the daughter for love, devotion, and care. In effect, the daughter assumes the role of mother. Israel remains no longer the receptive child. God's actions are in a way determined by and dependent upon those of the child.[13]

The parent bears the child. Yet elements of the parent are borne by the child. Similarly, the Torah, which comes from God, carries the presence of God within its words. Since God is the source of all wisdom, the Torah is the treasure house of all wisdom. *The spirit of God hovers over the waters*—these waters are the Torah. The Torah is all-inclusive. "Review its words again and again, all is contained in them."[14]

The child has qualities of the parent. Like God, the Torah transcends space and time. It is an element of heaven which was put upon the earth. It is eternity perceived through the given moment. Within it dwell secrets of perfection, visions of beatitude.

Perhaps the imagery describing the Torah is too exalting and consequently excessively audacious. Perhaps the image is too closely applied to the subject. Perhaps the Torah is identified too closely with divine wisdom, and there is a possibility of confusing the child with the parent. It is hardly acceptable, for example, to consider divine wisdom to be restricted to the Torah alone.

The tendency to assert a close identity between the Torah and God's wisdom may lead to the danger of making the Torah a substitute for God. One is tempted to understand the Torah not only as possessing a divine quality, as being saturated with divinity, but as being divinity itself, and consequently as being an object worthy of meditation and devotion in man's yearning to cleave to a higher reality than himself. In this view, divine wisdom is not only in the Torah; it is the Torah.

However, again and again we are admonished against taking a totalitarian view of the Torah. God is greater than the Torah. He who devotes himself only to Torah and does not cultivate awe of God is regarded as a failure.

Raba said:

When man is led in for judgment in the next life, he is asked, "Did you deal honestly in business? Did you fix times for the study of the Torah? Did you engage in procreation? Did you hope for salvation? Did you engage in the dialectics of wisdom? Did you learn by means of deductive reasoning? Even so, if 'the awe of the Lord is his treasure,' it is well. If not, it is not well."[15]

From this, Rabbi Joseph of Trani, a talmudist of the latter part of the sixteenth century, concludes: The study of Torah is worthless when not accompanied by awe and fear of heaven.[16]

There is an often-quoted remark that God has nothing else in this world but the four cubits of the Torah's Law,[17] as if the law were the only treasure cherished by God. Other statements, however, insist: "The Holy One, blessed be He, has nothing else in his world but awe and fear of heaven."[18] "The Holy One, blessed be He, has in his treasury nought except a store of awe of heaven."[19]

In the liturgy asking blessings for the new Hebrew month, according to the Western European Jewish ritual, we pray for both "love of Torah and awe of heaven." One complements the other. Jewish religious consciousness must embrace both.

For all the extreme praise of the Torah, its real preciousness is not in its qualities but in the fact that the Torah is God's Torah. The Torah is not an end in itself; it is transcended by God. The purpose of giving the Torah was to sanctify God's great name.[20]

The sanctity of the Torah is great. For example, one who leaves out or adds a letter to its text is compared to one who causes the entire world to be destroyed. Even so (says Rabbi Hiyya), it could still be asserted that it is better to remove a letter of the Torah than for God's name to be publicly desecrated.[21]

There are three cardinal sins: idolatry, adultery, and murder. More severe than they is the sin of desecrating God's name. "God shows indulgence toward idolatry . . . adultery . . . and murder . . . but does not show indulgence to him who has profaned his name."[22]

There were many debates concerning the scope of the study of the Torah. When the religious obligations were listed, the study of the Torah was counted among those which have no limit to their performance. He who does more becomes more praiseworthy. After all the religious obligations had been enumerated, it was concluded that the study of the Torah is equivalent to them all.[23] The ideal is study for "its own sake," meaning God's sake, and not for the sake of the Torah. Occupation with the Torah for its sake means "Because the Lord has commanded me, and not for the purpose of gaining recognition."[24]

Rabbi Bannah, a Palestinian *tanna* of the third century, used to say:

"Whoever occupies himself with the Torah for its own sake, his learning becomes an elixir of life for him . . . But whosoever occupies himself with the Torah not for its sake, it becomes for him a deadly poison."[25]

This emphasis upon the correct motivation applies to all other commandments as well as to the study of the Torah.

An accepted statement of rabbinic tradition is that not study but the deed is the most important thing.[26] Together with this, Rabbi José, a Palestinian *tanna* of the second century, said, "All one's deeds should be for the sake of heaven."[27] The *Mishnah*, after dwelling upon all details of the sacrificial laws of animal and meal offerings, concludes with the general principle: "It is the same whether a man offers much or little, so long as he directs his heart to heaven."[28] The great sage Hillel was not praised for his learning alone. His greatest merit was that "all his deeds were for the sake of heaven."[29] A favorite saying of Raba was "The goal of wisdom is repentance and good deeds . . . If one does good deeds for other motives than their own sake, it were better had he not been created."[30]

Rab, celebrated Babylonian *amora* and founder of the academy of Sura (died 247), said: "Always let a man be occupied with Torah and religious precepts even if not for their own sake. For observance not for their own sake will eventually become observance for their own sake."[31] Commenting on this, Rabbi Isaiah Horowitz (1555–1630?) wrote: "While one is studying Torah with ulterior motives, in the course of one's study, one will learn that the tradition teaches that to act in such a way is a great sin. He then becomes encouraged to observe for the sake of the commandments themselves. However, preoccupation with the Torah because of ulterior motives is a sin in itself."[32]

Though expressions such as "awe or fear of God," "awe of heaven," "fear of sin," are common in rabbinic literature, there is no such expression as "awe or fear of Torah." One must always live in the awe of God (Deuteronomy 6:13). To paraphrase an old rabbinic saying: One must not be in awe of the Torah but in awe of Him who gives the Torah.

In the Palestinian Talmud it is written:

Nehemiah of Emmaus, the teacher of Rabbi Akiba, who learned all the minute peculiarities and details of the methodology of rabbinic exegesis from Rabbi Akiba, once asked, "What is the meaning of the verse *One should be in awe of one's God*"? He said, "One must be in awe of God and his Torah."[33]

However, in the Babylonian Talmud, the story is reported differently:

Nehemiah of Emmaus interpreted the verse *One should be in awe of one's God* to mean that one would not allow the awe of God to be extended to anything other than God . . . Rabbi Akiba disagreed: The verse *One must be in awe of God* teaches that one should also be in awe of one's mentors. [34]

Should one be in awe of God's temple?

The verse reads, *You shall observe my Sabbaths and be in awe of my sanctuary* (Leviticus 19:30). The word "observe" was used in relation to the sanctuary . . . As in the case of "observance" used in relation to the Sabbath, one does not revere the Sabbath but Him who commanded the observance of the Sabbath, so in the case of "awe" used in relation to the sanctuary, one is not to be in awe of the sanctuary, but Him who gave the commandment concerning the sanctuary. [35]

Said Rabbi Abraham ben David of Posquieres (twelfth century), "One should be in awe of God while in the sanctuary. One's awe should be directed to God, not to the sanctuary." [36]

To whom then will you compare me, that I should be like him? says the Holy One (Isaiah 40:25). As God transcends the world, he transcends the Torah. Many rabbinic statements express this view. Suffice it here to note the general rule. The verse It is time for the Lord to act/They have made void thy Torah (Psalms 119:126) was interpreted to mean: It is time to act for the Lord, set aside the Torah! Sometimes one should annul parts of the Torah to act for the Lord. [37]

Rabbi Joshua ben Korha insisted that one must first take upon himself the authority of God before accepting the authority of the Torah. [38]

The Torah is not to be understood in its own terms. Love of the Torah and awe of God are interrelated. Acts of loving-kindness and study of Torah must go together. The Torah does not stand alone. It stands with God and with man. Love of Torah links awe of God with the individual performance of deeds of loving-kindness toward one's fellow men. The Torah is the knot wherein God and man are interlaced. However, he who accepts God's existence without accepting the authority of the Torah deviates from Judaism.

Rav Huna, Babylonian *amora* (ca. 216–ca. 296), said, "He who occupies himself only with the study of Torah is as if he had no God." [39] According to Rabbi José, "He who says he has an interest only in the Torah has no interest even in the Torah." [40]

He who suggests that the Torah has a supremacy, not exceeded by any other being, and that belief in God (or attachment to Israel) is of secondary importance is guilty of extreme distortion. Though the divine is within the Torah, it also transcends the Torah. Even Moses, who received the Torah and achieved the highest level of prophetic attainment, knew that his prophetic illumination and grasp of the wisdom of God were not perfect. [41]

Though the Torah that Moses received is God's wisdom, it is inconceivable, scholars of later generations maintained, that the Torah he received is exactly the way it was in God's wisdom. Perhaps Moses did not receive the whole Torah but only a small part of it,[42] only a small part of the all-inclusive store of God's wisdom was revealed on earth. "Fifty gates of understanding were created in the world and all were given to Moses, except one."[43] The Torah in our hands is some of God's wisdom but not all of his wisdom. The Torah we have is the unripened fruit of heavenly wisdom."[44] Scripture does not capture the totality of the divine personality. God's mercy, for example, transcends all biblical statements and expectations.

They asked Wisdom: What is the punishment of the sinner? Wisdom answered: *Evil pursues sinners* (Proverbs 13:21). They asked Prophecy. And Prophecy answered: *The soul that sins shall die* (Ezekiel 18:4). They then asked the Torah and she answered: Let him bring a guilt offering and it shall be forgiven unto him, as it says, *it may be acceptable in his behalf, in expiation for him* (Leviticus 1:4). Finally, they asked the Holy One, blessed be He, who answered: Let him do repentance and it shall be forgiven unto him. *For good and upright is the Lord; therefore he instructs sinners in the way* (toward repentance) (Psalms 25:8).[45]

A Palestinian *agadist*, whose chronology is unknown, argued strenuously against the fate of bastards; namely, their being excluded, according to the law, from the community:

Again I saw all the oppressions that are practiced under the sun. And behold, the tears of the oppressed, and they had no one to comfort them! On the side of their oppressors there was power, and there was no one to comfort them (Ecclesiastes 4:1). Daniel the Tailor interpreted the verse as applying to bastards. *And behold, the tears of the oppressed.* If the parents of these bastards committed transgression, why should their descendants suffer? If this man's father cohabited with a forbidden woman, what sin has his descendant committed and what concern is it of his? *And there was no one to comfort them!* But *on the side of their oppressors there was power.* This means Israel's Great Sanhedrin who comes to them with the power derived from the Torah and removes them from the fold, in virtue of the commandment *A bastard shall not enter into the assembly of the Lord* (Deuteronomy 23:3). *But they had no one to comfort them.* Says the Holy One, blessed be He, It shall be my task to comfort them. Though in this world there is dross in them, in the World to Come, says Zechariah (4:2), I have seen them all of pure gold.[46]

According to Nahmanides (born at Gerona, Spain, in 1194; died in Palestine about 1270), the Torah is not the all-inclusive guide to human behavior. "One can be a scoundrel within the letter of the Torah."[47]

It has been said: "He who is occupied with Torah is called a King and a Leader,"[48] and "He who studies Torah without ulterior motives, it is as though he built both the heavenly and the earthly Temple."[49] Nevertheless, it was believed that the rewards in the afterlife extended to the pious go beyond the attainment of wisdom and study of the Torah. A favorite saying of Rab was that in the future life "the pious will sit with their crowns on their heads feasting on the radiance of the divine presence."[50]

He who provides God with an image ascribes to Him imperfection and negates His transcendence. To equate God with the Torah would be a grave distortion.

It is clear that the suggestion to equate the essence of God with the essence of the Torah has never even enticed the minds of the authors of the Talmud. They considered the Torah to be God's creation, His property, not His essence.

"Five possessions has the Holy One, blessed be He, specifically declared His own in His world. These are: the Torah, the sanctuary, heaven and earth, Abraham, and Israel."[51] The Torah is God's creation and His property, His wisdom and His will, but not He Himself. Just as pantheism is foreign to the rabbinic mind, so would be the identification of God with the Torah. "With respect to the Holy One, blessed be He, the world is His and the Torah is His."[52]

In contrast to the Muslim view of the Koran as the eternal uncreated Word, Maimonides insisted that all Jews agree "that the Torah is a created entity," brought into being in the same manner as all other created beings.

However, in the development of Jewish mysticism we come upon one statement that seems to contradict Maimonides's observation, a statement by Rabbi Menahem Recanati (ca. 1300), for which I know no parallel in Jewish literature: "God is incomplete without the Torah. The Torah is not something outside Him, and He is not outside the Torah. Consequently, the mystic stated that God is the Torah."[53]

According to the *Zohar*, the Torah was emanated from divine wisdom. The Torah is connected to God. Therefore, "God is called the Torah"[54] since "the words of the Torah are in actuality the names of God."[55] Israel is the wick, the Torah the thread, and God's presence (*Shekinah*) is the fire.[56] These are three entities, each of which is connected to the other: God, the Torah, and Israel. "God and Israel, when together, are called one, but not when parted."[57] Similarly, "when a man separates himself from the Torah, he separates himself from God."[58]

The following statement is often quoted as having the *Zohar* for its source (late thirteenth century). Yet it is not found there. "The Torah, God, and Israel are one." The citation appears first among eighteenth-century authors.[59] The Torah and the world are God's possessions. The world is His, but He is not His world. The Torah is His, but He is not His Torah. The Torah is not in itself God, not His essence, but rather His wisdom and His will. Though the Torah preexisted creation, it is not an eternal existent. Israel's relationship to Torah, however, is a commitment more basic than loyalty to any particular commandment. "Rabbi

Jeremiah in the name of Rabbi Samuel bar Rabbi Isaac said: There are instances in which God excused Israel for the three cardinal sins of idolatry, adultery, and murder. Yet with regard to the sin of despising the Torah, we have no record of amnesty." How come? Paraphrasing the words of the prophet Jeremiah (16:11), They have forsaken me and have not kept my Torah. He continued: "Would that they had forsaken me and kept my Torah."[60]

To regard this passage, however, as a declaration of the primary if not exclusive importance of studying Torah over concern for God is to pervert the meaning of the passage. Such perversion is made possible by overlooking the second part of the passage, which reads as follows: "since by occupying themselves with the Torah, the light which she contains would have led them back *to me.*"[61] It was not an ideal that the rabbis envisaged but a last resort. Having forsaken all commandments, if the people had at least continued to study Torah, the light of the Torah would have brought them back to God.

It is, therefore, a distortion to interpret this passage to mean that Torah without fear or awe of God is acceptable, as if the importance of observance outweighs the centrality of faith.

The old rabbinic view that observance of Torah even without awe and fear of heaven is acceptable proposes that observance with improper ends in mind will lead to observance with proper ends in mind. "Rabbi Judah in the name of Rab said: A man should always occupy himself with Torah and good deeds, though it is not for their own sake, for out of doing good with an ulterior motive there comes about the service of God for its own sake, without an ulterior motive."[62]

Again and again we are taught that the Torah is not an end in itself. It is the gate through which one enters the court in which one finds awe of heaven. "Said Rabbi Yanni: Woe to him who has no court; woe to him who thinks the gate is the court . . . And Rabbi Jonathan said: Woe to those scholars who occupy themselves with Torah and have not awe of the Lord."[63]

In a medieval Midrash we come upon a complaint against those saintly and righteous men whose dedication to the Torah surpasses their craving for the messianic kingdom.[64]

Rabbi Solomon Alami, an ethical writer who lived in Portugal in the fourteenth and fifteenth centuries, was an eyewitness of the persecutions of the Jews of Catalonia, Castile, and Aragon in 1391. Attempting to explain why so much suffering befell his people, he wrote:

Let us search for the source of all these trials and sufferings, and we shall find that a state of dissolution prevails in the midst of us; that an evil spirit pervades our camp, which has split us into two parties. There are those of our brethren who expend all their energies in solving talmudic problems and in writing numberless commentaries and novellae dealing in minute distinctions and interpretations, full of useless subtleties as thin as cobwebs. They diffuse darkness instead of light, and lower respect for the law. Others, again, clothe the Torah in strange garments, deck it with Grecian and other anti-Jewish ornaments, and endeavor to harmonize it with philosophy, which can only be detrimental to religion and lead ultimately to its decay.[65]

Rabbi Jehudah Loewe ben Bezelel of Prague (died 1609) pointed to the problem involved in the exuberant love of the Torah. The scholar who while studying is passionately absorbed in the love of the Torah is unable at that very moment to experience the love of God, since it is impossible to experience two loves simultaneously.[66]

The relationship between *halacha* and *agada* in Judaism is reflected in the conception of the relationship between the Torah and God. Rabbi Mordechai Joseph of Isbitsa, a major figure in the history of the Hasidic movement, offers an important insight into this problem.

It has been foretold in the Bible that someday Ephraim will not be jealous of Judah and Judah will not harass Ephraim (Isaiah 11:13). These two types (tribes) are always in conflict. Ephraim has been appointed by God to concentrate himself on the Law and to be devoted to the commandments. This is why the prophet warns the people of Israel to observe the law strictly, *lest he break out like fire in the house of Joseph* (Amos 5:6).

Judah has been appointed to concentrate on God and to be attached to him in all his ways. Therefore Judah is not satisfied to know the mere Law but looks for God to reveal to him the depths of truth beyond the Law itself. (For it is possible in Law for a verdict to be correct according to the information which is available to the judges and yet to go against the truth. Cf. *Shevout* 29a, for example.) Judah refuses to be content with routine observance or perfunctory faith. Not content to do today what he did yesterday, he desires to find new light in His commandments every day. This insistence on fresh light sometimes drives Judah into doing actions for the sake of God which are against the strict law.

But in the future, we have been promised that Ephraim and Judah will no longer contend. God will show Ephraim that Judah's actions, even when they go outside the limits of the law, are always for His sake and not for any impure motive, and then there will be genuine understanding and peace between them.[67]

According to the method of "Judah," the Torah is not an end in itself. It has been said about the First Cause—"All existents need him and he does not need any one or all of them." Such a statement is not acceptable concerning the Torah. It needs us, it is not sufficient to itself.

GOD AND ISRAEL

ACCORDING TO rabbinic legend, the prophet Elijah, who did not die but ascended to heaven, not only was active as the helper in distress but also appeared to sages and saints assisting them in solving spiritual problems. Once, we are told, the following issue was submitted to him by a sage:

Two things I love wholeheartedly: the Torah and Israel. However, I am not sure which one I love more.

The response of Elijah was:

The accepted opinion seems to suggest that the Torah is most important, as the verse reads, with regard to the Torah, *The Lord made me as the beginning of his way* (Proverbs 8:22).* However, I think that not the Torah but Israel is most important. For the prophet has said: *Israel is holy to the Lord; the first fruits of his harvest* (Jeremiah 2:3).[68]

That which came first is to be cherished the most. Consequently, since the people Israel existed alone, first, without the Torah, it should be cherished more than the Torah. According to another source, reflecting apocalyptic thinking, Israel "existed (supernaturally) even before the world was created, as it says, Remember thy congregation which thou hast gotten of old" (Psalms 74:2).[69]

The extraordinary awareness of the endurance of Israel was expressed in an unsurpassed way by the prophet Jeremiah (31:35–37):

Thus says the Lord,
who gives the sun for light by day
   and the fixed order of the moon
      and the stars for light by night,
who stirs up the sea so that its waves roar—
   the Lord of hosts is his name:
"If this fixed order departs
   from before me, says the Lord,
then shall the descendants of Israel cease
   from being a nation before me for ever."

These extraordinary words were echoed in the statement of Rabbi Joshua ben Levian, *amora* of the first half of the third century, head of the school in Lydda in southern Palestine. "Israel can never die, neither in this world nor the world to come."[70] A world without Torah would be a world without

---

* There is an ancient belief in Judaism that wisdom, later identified with the Torah as well as with the name of the Messiah and other entities, was created before the creation of the world. See H. A. Wolfson, *The Philosophy of the Church Fathers*, Vol. I (Cambridge, England, 1956), pp. 156 ff.; Abraham J. Heschel, *op. cit.*, Vol. II, pp. 8 ff.

Israel, and a world without Israel would be a world without the God of Israel.

Rabbi Simon ben Yohai of the second century said, "It is written, *For as the days of a tree shall be the days of my people* (Isaiah 65:22). A 'tree' signifies the Torah, as it is stated, *It* (e.g., the Torah) *is a tree of life to them that lay hold upon it* (Proverbs 3:18). Now which was created for the sake of which? Was the Torah created for the sake of Israel or vice versa? Surely, the Torah was created for the sake of Israel. Thus if the Torah endures for all eternity, how much more must Israel for whose sake it was created endure for all eternity?"[71]

Though the law demands strict observance of the latter, teleological consideration may dictate its suspension, as, for example, for the purpose of saving human life, of saving the people. Perhaps the most striking expression of the relationship between the Torah and the people is the classical maxim by Rabbi Simeon ben Menasya, Palestinian Tanna of the second century, and contemporary of Rabbi Judah ha-Nasi, in his interpretation of Exodus 31:14, You shall keep the Sabbath therefore, for it is holy unto you. "The words 'unto you,' " he said, "imply that the Sabbath is given to you, and that you are not given to the Sabbath."[72]

The survival of Israel is an important consideration in dealing with the law.

Esther suggested to Mordechai: *Go gather all the Jews found in Sushan and fast for my sake. Do not eat or drink for three days* (4:16). This was during the month of Nissan (April). Mordechai answered Esther: "I cannot abrogate the law set down in the Scroll on Fasting in which it is written, From the first day of the month of Nissan until the eighteenth of the month one may not fast. You would break this law by insisting that we fast three days, beginning with the fourteenth?" She responded, "Are you the chief elder of Israel? Then consider, if Israel is annihilated (according to the decree of Haman), what good will God's commandments for Israel be? If there is no Israel, why should there be a Torah?" . . . And so Samuel said, Mordechai pretended he was unaware of the law and declared the fast.[73]

TORAH AND ISRAEL

IT IS CUSTOMARY to treat them as independent entities, as self-contained concepts with separate stature and independent validity. Nevertheless, these concepts are essentially related, one to the other. They are interdependent by virtue of their common source. Saadia Gaon was correct in asserting that Israel is a people only by virtue of its Torah,[74] that the only assurance for Israel's peoplehood is the Torah. On the other hand, Rabbi Halevi reminds us, "If there were no Jews, there would be no Torah."[75]

You are my witnesses, says the Lord, and I am God (Isaiah 43:12). Rabbi Simon ben Yohai (second century) took the sentence to mean: If you are my witnesses, I am God; if you cease to be my witnesses, I am not God.[76] This is a bold expression of the interdependence of God and Israel, a thought that occurs in various degrees of clarity in the history of Jewish theology. This particular statement maintains: If there are no witnesses, there is no God to be met. There is a mystery, an enigma, a darkness past finding out. For God to be present there have to be witnesses.[77]

The essence of Judaism is the awareness of the *reciprocity* of God and man, of man's *togetherness* with Him who abides in eternal otherness. For the task of living is His and ours, and so is the responsibility. We have rights, not only obligations; our ultimate commitment is our ultimate privilege.

In interpreting Mal. 3:18, Rabbi Aha ben Ada said: "Then shall ye again discern between the righteous and the wicked," meaning: "Between him who has faith and him who has not faith"; "between him that serveth God and him that serveth him not,"[78] meaning: "between him who serves God's *need* and him who does not serve God's *need*. One should not make of the Torah a spade with which to dig, a tool for personal use or a crown to magnify oneself."[79]

His need is a self-imposed concern. God is now in need of man, because He freely made him a partner in his enterprise, "a partner in the work of creation." "From the first day of creation the Holy One, blessed be He, longed to enter into *partnership* with the terrestrial world" to dwell with his creatures within the terrestrial world.[80] Expounding the verse in Genesis 17:1, the Midrash remarked: "In the view of Rabbi Johanan we need His honor; in the view of Rabbi Simeon ben Lakish He needs our honor."[81]

"When Israel performs the will of the Omnipresent, they add strength to the heavenly power; as it is said: *To God we render strength* (Psalms 60:14). When, however, Israel does not perform the will of the Omnipresent, they weaken— if it is possible to say so—the great power of Him who is above; as it is written, *Thou didst weaken the Rock that begot Thee* (Deuteronomy 32:18)."[82]

Man's relationship to God is not one of passive reliance upon His omnipotence but one of active assistance. "The impious rely on their gods . . . the righteous are the support of God."[83]

The patriarchs are therefore called "the chariot of the Lord."[84]

He glories in me, He delights in me;
My crown of beauty He shall be.
His glory rests on me, and mine on Him;
He is near to me, when I call on Him.

"The Hymn of Glory"

To repeat, Jewish existence is not only the adherence to particular doctrines and observances but primarily the living *in* the spiritual order of the Jewish people, the living *in* the Jews of the past and *with* the Jews of the present. It is not only a certain quality in the souls of the individuals; it is primarily involvement and participation in the covenant and community of Israel. It is more than an experience or a creed, more than the possession of psychic traits or the acceptance of theological doctrine; it is, above all, the living in a holy dimension, in a spiritual order. Our share in holiness we acquire by living within the community. What we do as individuals may be a trivial episode; what we attain as Israel causes us to grow into the infinite.

III

TOWARD A
JUST SOCIETY

The Meaning of This War

(World War II)

EMBLAZONED OVER the gates of the world in which we live is the escutcheon of the demons. The mark of Cain in the face of man has come to overshadow the likeness of God. There have never been so much guilt and distress, agony and terror. At no time has the earth been so soaked with blood. Fellow men turned out to be evil ghosts, monstrous and weird. Ashamed and dismayed, we ask: Who is responsible?

History is a pyramid of efforts and errors; yet at times it is the Holy Mountain on which God holds judgment over the nations. Few are privileged to discern God's judgment in history. But all may be guided by the words of the Baal Shem: If a man has beheld evil, he may know that it was shown to him in order that he learn his own guilt and repent; for what is shown to him is also within him.

We have trifled with the name of God. We have taken the ideals in vain. We have called for the Lord. He came. And was ignored. We have preached but eluded Him. We have praised but defied Him. Now we reap the fruits of our failure. Through centuries His voice cried in the wilderness. How skillfully it was trapped and imprisoned in the temples! How often it was drowned or distorted! Now we behold how it gradually withdraws, abandoning one people after another, departing from their souls, despising their wisdom. The taste for the good has all but gone from the earth. Men heap spite upon cruelty, malice upon atrocity.

The horrors of our time fill our souls with reproach and everlasting shame. We have profaned the word of God, and now we must give the wealth of our land, the ingenuity of our minds, and the dear lives of our youth to tragedy and perdition. There has never been more reason for man to be ashamed than now. Silence hovers mercilessly over many dreadful lands. The day of the Lord is a day without the Lord. Where is

God? Why dost Thou not halt the trains loaded with Jews being led to slaughter? It is so hard to rear a child, to nourish and to educate. Why dost Thou make it so easy to kill? Like Moses, we hide our face; for we are afraid to look upon *Elohim*, upon His power of judgment. Indeed, where were we when men learned to hate in the days of starvation? When raving madmen were sowing wrath in the hearts of the unemployed?

Let Fascism not serve as an alibi for our conscience. We have failed to fight for right, for justice, for goodness; as a result we must fight against wrong, against injustice, against evil. We have failed to offer sacrifices on the altar of peace; now we must offer sacrifices on the altar of war. A tale is told of a band of inexperienced mountain climbers. Without guides, they struck recklessly into the wilderness. Suddenly a rocky ledge gave way beneath their feet and they were tumbled headlong into a dismal pit. In the darkness of the pit they recovered from their shock, only to find themselves set upon by a swarm of angry snakes. Every crevice became alive with fanged, hissing things. For each snake the desperate men slew, ten more seemed to lash out in its place. Strangely enough, one man seemed to stand aside from the fight. When the indignant voices of his struggling companions reproached him for not fighting, he called back: If we remain here, we shall be dead before the snakes. I am searching for a way of escape from the pit for all of us.

OUR WORLD seems not unlike a pit of snakes. We did not sink into the pit in 1939, or even in 1933. We had descended into it generations ago, and the snakes have sent their venom into the bloodstream of humanity, gradually paralyzing us, numbing nerve after nerve, dulling our minds, darkening our vision. Good and evil, which were once as real as day and night, have become a blurred mist. In our everyday life we worshipped force, despised compassion, and obeyed no law but our unappeasable appetite. The vision of the sacred has all but died in the soul of man. And when greed, envy, and the reckless will to power, the serpents that were cherished in the bosom of our civilization, came to maturity, they broke out of their dens to fall upon the helpless nations.

The outbreak of this war was no surprise. It came as a long expected sequel to a spiritual disaster. Instilled with the gospel that truth is mere advantage and reverence weakness, people succumbed to the bigger advantage of a lie—"The Jew is our misfortune"—and to the power of arrogance—"Tomorrow the whole world shall be ours." The roar of bombers over Rotterdam, Warsaw, was but the echo of thoughts bred for years by individual brains, and later applauded by entire nations. It was through our failure that people started to suspect that science is a device for exploitation; parliaments pulpits for hypocrisy, and religion a pretext for a bad conscience. In the tantalized souls of those who had faith in ideals, suspicion became a dogma and contempt the only solace. Mistaking the abortions of their conscience for intellectual heroism, many thinkers employed clever pens to scold and to scorn the reverence for life, the awe for truth, the loyalty to justice. Man, about to hang himself, discovered it was easier to hang others.

THE CONSCIENCE of the world was destroyed by those who were wont to blame others rather than themselves. Let us remember, we revered the instincts but distrusted ideals. We labored to perfect engines and let our inner life go to wreck. We ridiculed superstition until we lost our ability to believe. We have helped to extinguish the light our fathers had kindled. We have bartered holiness for convenience, loyalty for success, love for power, wisdom for diplomas, prayer for sermon, wisdom for information, tradition for fashion.

We cannot dwell at ease under the sun of our civilization as our ancestors thought we could. What was in the minds of our martyred brothers in Poland in their last hours? They died with disdain and scorn for a civilization in which the killing of civilians could become a carnival of fun, for a civilization which gave us mastery over the forces of nature but lost control over the forces of our self. A messenger recently came and conveyed the following message from all the European Jews who are being slaughtered in the hell of Poland: "We, Jews, despise all those who live in safety and do nothing to save us."

Tanks and planes cannot redeem humanity. A man with a gun is like a beast without a gun. The killing of snakes will save us for the moment but not forever. The war will outlast the victory of arms if we fail to conquer the infamy of the soul: the indifference to crime, when committed against others. For evil is indivisible. It is the same in thought and in speech, in private and in social life. The greatest task of our time is to take the souls of men out of the pit. The world has experienced that God is involved. Let us forever remember that the sense for the sacred is as vital to us as the light of the sun. There can be no nature without spirit, no world without the Torah, no brotherhood without a father, no humanity without God.

God will return to us when we are willing to let Him in—into our banks and factories, into our Congress and clubs, into our homes and theaters. For God is everywhere or nowhere, the father of all men or no man, concerned about everything or nothing. Only in His presence shall we learn that the glory of man is not in his will to power but in his power of compassion. Man reflects either the image of His presence or that of a beast. Will the voices of those who in this very hour are pushing tumbrels with shriveled, bare-bone corpses of Jews to a huge grave outside the ghetto walls reach the ears of statesmen?

Soldiers in the horror of battle offer solemn testimony that life is not a hunt for pleasure but an engagement for service; that there are things more valuable than life; that the world is not a vacuum. Either we make it an altar for God or it is invaded by demons. There can be no neutrality. Either we are ministers of the sacred or slaves of evil. Let the blasphemy of our time not become an eternal scandal. Let future generations not loathe us for having failed to preserve what prophets and saints, martyrs and scholars have created in thousands of years. The Fascists have shown that they are great in evil. Let us reveal that we can be as great in goodness. We will survive if we are as fine and sacrificial in our homes and offices, in our Congress and clubs as our soldiers are on the fields of battle.

THERE IS a divine dream which the prophets and rabbis have cherished and which fills our prayers and permeates the acts of Jewish piety. It is the dream of a world, rid of evil by the efforts of man, by his will to serve what goes beyond his own interests. God is waiting for us to redeem the world. We should not spend our life hunting for trivial satisfactions while God is waiting constantly and keenly for our effort and devotion.

The Almighty has not created the universe that we may have opportunities to satisfy our greed, envy, and ambition. Israel has not survived that we may waste our years in vulgar vanities. The martyrdom of millions in this very hour demands that we consecrate ourselves to the fulfillment of God's dream of salvation. Israel did not accept the Torah of their own free will. When Israel approached Sinai, God lifted up the mountain and held it over their heads saying: "Either you accept the Torah or be crushed beneath the mountain."

The mountain of history is over our heads again. Shall we renew the covenant with God?

The Plight of Russian Jews

A PERSON CANNOT BE religious *and* indifferent to other human beings' plight and suffering. In fact, the tragedy of man is that so much of our history is a history of indifference, dominated by a famous statement, Am I my brother's keeper?

We are involved in the great battle for equal rights being waged in our country, and this great and victorious drama has electrified many millions of Americans. But another drama is being enacted which is agonizing, heart-rending, tragic, and ignored: the plight of the Jews in Soviet Russia.

The essence of a Jew is his involvement in the plight of other people, as God is involved. This is the secret of our legacy, that God is implied in the human situation and man must be involved in it. Here we face a major religious problem. For many years a systematic process of spiritual liquidation of millions of Jews has been going on in Soviet Russia. It is above all and first of all at this moment of central religious concern to me. How can I call myself a Jew and remain indifferent to the spiritual extinction of so many Jews?

They are left alone. They don't even believe that there are Jews outside Soviet Russia. To quote a Russian Jew: "I don't believe Jews live in America, because had there been Jews in America, they wouldn't have been indifferent to our plight." Russian Jews are isolated. They feel abandoned. The prophet says that Zion complains, The Lord has forsaken me. My Lord has forgotten me. Russian Jewry says, The Jewish people have forsaken me. The Jewish people have forgotten me. Russian Jews are the forgotten Jews.

According to our tradition, whoever forgets one segment of the Torah commits a great sin. How much more is a person guilty if he remains careless to the agony of one human being! The Torah tells us, You shall not stand by the blood of your neighbor. To be sure, there is a risk to be taken whenever we undertake to challenge the policy or the acts of a mighty power, particularly now when we are hoping and praying whole-heartedly that a new era of mutual understanding and reconciliation between the world's two Great Powers will take place. But risk is involved in every decision and in every action. Weighing the risk that the Jewish community may assume in fighting with moral and spiritual means for the rights of the Jews in Russia, we must be ready to suffer ourselves in order to assure their survival. The commandment You shall not stand by the blood of your neighbor implies that one is obliged to render help even at the cost of personal danger.

There is no other people in the world which is so absolutely committed to the sanctity of human rights and equality of all men as our people. Our history is the most emphatic testimony that injustice to *some* men spells the doom of *all* men. Prejudice is like a hydra, a monster which has many heads, an evil which requires many efforts to overcome. One head sends forth poison against the people of a different race, another against people of a different religion or culture. Thus the evil of prejudice is indivisible. Discrimination against the political rights of the Negro in America and discrimination against the religious and cultural rights of the Jews in the Soviet Union are indivisible.

We live in the darkest century of Jewish history. The Jewish world as it existed in 1914 is now a vast cemetery. Living in this country, one doesn't know whether it is a privilege or a punishment to be among those who have been saved from the Holocaust. Six million Jews are no more, and three million Jews are in the process of systematic spiritual liquidation. Those who really sense it live in dismay, while the majority of Jews in America don't even know about it and are at best indifferent. What we must do above all is to create an atmosphere of concern for what is happening in Soviet Russia, where there are practically no synagogues left where a Jew may enter to say his prayers, where Jews cannot meet together as Jews, where a Bible is not available, where a prayerbook is the most rare book, where matzos cannot be baked, where there are no kosher meat shops, no teachers, no schools, where only one rabbinical seminary exists—its student body consisting of one single student.

We have been long indifferent to the plight of the Jews in Soviet Russia. Time is running out. *A few years from now there may be no more Jews left in Russia to be saved.* We have forgotten the Jews of Russia. This is our major sin. You shall not stand by the blood of your neighbor. You will say it is impossible, nothing can be achieved, all efforts will remain futile. To do the impossible is the beginning of faith. Judaism is the art of the impossible. There is much that can be done as individuals, as citizens of America. What we can do, first of all, for our own selves is not to sink forever in the mire of indifference. If there is an actual atmosphere of concern, if little children in the religious schools learn to say a prayer for their brethren and the little children of Russia who are deprived of studying the holy tongue, something great will happen to the souls of our children right here.

It is a burning sin that we remain indifferent. What is happening in our own days in America proves beyond doubt that a strong voice, ringing with force and dignity, has the power to pierce the iron shield of dormant conscience. We will get support from the Protestant and Catholic leadership, from the Negro leadership, in our effort to help save the Russian Jews from complete extinction.

What is called for is not a silent sigh but a voice of moral compassion and indignation, the sublime and inspired screaming of a prophet uttered by a whole community.

The Negro problem, I believe, is on the way to a solution because of the decision of the Supreme Court. Spirit has power. The voice of justice is stronger than bigotry. Yet, if not for personal involvement, if not for action on the part of the Negroes, the decision of the Supreme Court would have remained a still small voice; and the hour calls for the voice of justice as well as for concerted and incessant action.

The Moral Dilemma of

the Space Age

WE ARE IN AN ERA of great scientific and technological advancement. Science has pried from the atom forces of tremendous power that hold both promise and peril for mankind; technology has developed vehicles that can be used to destroy the earth or search out the secrets of the universe. In this Space Age, to a greater degree than ever before, we all face the dilemma expressed by Moses: "I have put before you life and death, blessing and curse. Choose life."

Man has been endowed by God with the greatest and most awesome of freedoms: the freedom of choice. The deeper meaning of this freedom, applied to our programs in space, compels us to consider their political and social consequences from a moral perspective. The choices presented pose their greatest challenge to religion—a moral challenge, which is not being met. This goes beyond the question most often put; namely, whether space exploration is against God's will. There is no commandment or prohibition forbidding the exploration of space. But the fact that an action is not forbidden does not necessarily justify its pursuit. Nor does it make it morally right. The deeper meaning of the gift of free choice is that it is not always a question of choosing between good and evil, but also of choosing between two good things.

It is from this perspective that I question the enthusiasm with which many people rejoice in our scientific and technological achievements in space. Some religious leaders have praised them as a great triumph of the spirit of man. A more realistic appraisal is that the triumph belongs to science and technology, which threatens the enslavement of the spirit of man by inhibiting freedom of choice. For the sheer dynamics of modern scientific and technological developments interfere with the human capacity for decision. This would be true even if our only objective in space was to discover truths about the universe, which it is not. We are exploring space, not so much to seek scientific truths or because we are motivated by ennobling philosophic insight, but largely because space exploration has political and military value for the state.

In the past, science was subservient to the church. Its emancipation from the church—its freedom from the dominance of religious dogma—was a cause of pride and celebration. Now, for the first time in history, science has become the handmaiden of the state. Now science must satisfy the demand of the state, and that demand is power. Therein lies the danger of its secular subservience and the cause of its conflict with humanity. For power, even if prompted by moral objectives, tends to become self-justifying and creates moral imperatives of its own.

Our objective in advancing our capability in space is, as stated by our political leaders, to demonstrate power that will assure the security and maintenance of our democratic institutions. On this basis, the conquest of space has been given top priority; and a great portion of the nation's wealth and talent is dedicated to such programs as manned lunar exploration and the search for extraterrestrial life.

Some of our most thoughtful scientists allege that the discovery of life elsewhere in the universe would be the most important and rewarding achievement of mankind. If I question this, it is not because such discovery would not be in harmony with our belief in God. On the contrary, if God in creating the universe has created life elsewhere than on our planet earth, this is in perfect harmony with the Judaic understanding of the might and wisdom of God. I challenge the high value placed on the search for extraterrestrial life only because it is being made at the expense of life and humanity here on earth. It is on this basis, too, that I object to the high price being paid for manned lunar exploration.

Is the discovery of some form of life on Mars or Venus or man's conquest of the moon really as important to humanity as the conquest of poverty, disease, prejudice, and superstition? Of what value will it be to land a few men on the wilderness of the moon if we neglect the needs of millions of men on earth? The conflict we face is between the exploration of space and the more basic needs of the human race. In their contributions to its resolution, religious leaders and teachers have an obligation to challenge the dominance of science over human affairs. They must defy the establishment of science as God. It is an instrument of God which we must not permit to be misused.

It is our duty to point out that in placing lunar exploration above more fundamental human values there is a loss of self-respect, a sort of cheapening of human life. While there is no theological prohibition against doing research beyond the confines of this planet, what is really involved is the matter of doing the right thing at the right time. In my judgment, this is not the right time to invest more than $5 billion annually in space, measured against the less than half a billion we are allotting over a four-year period for the retraining of men and women whose productive capacities have been made obsolete by a mushrooming technology, or the less than $1 billion that President Johnson has recommended to fight the poverty that keeps more than one-fourth of our nation ill clothed, ill housed, and ill fed. On any moral or ethical basis, when we can overlook the suffering of humanity in our childish delight in our ability to place monkeys and men in orbit around the earth, we are ill prepared spiritually and morally for the vast accumulation of power which we are achieving through science.

God has a stake in the life of every man. He never exposes humanity to a challenge without giving humanity the spiritual power to face that challenge. Admittedly the challenge today is enormously great. We live in a time when we are going through several revolutions simultaneously: political, social, scientific, technological, and spatial. This has never happened in history before. But we must exert the spiritual will to focus the attention of our minds and hearts on the problems we face. We cannot avoid them by reaching for the moon or grasping for life elsewhere. We must turn our efforts to rediscovering the true value and dignity of man, what man's life means as a totality in its great dimensions, his great potential for the creative arts, for the advancement of science in the search for peace and understanding, for acts of charity.

The tragedy of man is that he is so great and that he fails to recognize his greatness. Jean-Paul Sartre has said, "Man is condemned to be free." God has given him "choice"—the greatest obligation of freedom. He is waiting for man to exercise that choice. Man no longer can afford to compromise by accommodations not premised on moral values. The choice for man and humanity in this Space Age lies not in the stars but right here on this blessed planet earth. Will mankind fulfill its great destiny? Who can predict? We can only hope, pray, and demand.

Required:

A Moral Ombundsman

A MILITARY COURT has declared Captain Calley guilty of manslaughter and for a few days the nation was in a state of dismay.

The question which agonized many people was: Who else is guilty? The tragedy revealed at the trial of Captain Calley should engender lasting turmoil in the conscience and self-esteem of every sensitive American.

The wound is open, the hurt is deep. To ignore an open wound is to court contamination, further infection, and the diffusive influence of a vicious example.

To whitewash our deeds simply by maintaining our innocence is to defy God, who hears the cry of the guiltless killed in Vietnam. Jeremiah expressed it (2:14–15): "On your shirt is found the life-blood of guiltless poor. Yet in spite of all these things, you say: 'I am innocent.' Behold I will bring you to judgment for saying: 'I have not sinned.' "

To offer easy forgiveness would be not only self-complacency but self-abasement. Easy forgiveness implies that an individual who has shot and killed men, women, and children is devoid of responsibility. Yet the individual's moral responsibility is the heart of the dignity of man. At a time of increasing dehumanization and mechanization of human existence, such an attitude would be a mortal blow to the humanity of man.

Of the many problems involved, religious leaders face a special problem. How were such crimes possible?

Ten or twenty years ago no one would have believed that American boys could have acted in such a way. But they did. Who else is guilty? Who else is to blame?

Did our religious leaders not fail to instill in our people an absolute, unconditional sense of horror for murder?

Relativity of values, permissiveness, is today a powerful trend in living and thinking. This trend tends to become universal, embracing all thoughts and all actions. It may also embrace homicide or even genocide. There is one issue in regard to which no permissiveness or relativity must be tolerated, and that is *murder*!

The sense of sanctity of human life is subsiding. Let us at least preserve the sense of horror of murder!

The image of America, once the great promise and the marvelous hope of humanity, has been tragically tarnished. America was built on religious foundations. She declares herself to be a "nation under God." Obviously, we who are teachers of religion have failed to impress upon the people of America that God is the father of all individuals, of all races, that murder is the supreme abomination.

By now the trial of Captain Calley has sunk into oblivion. How few remember it! How few feel the agony of the victims on their conscience!

I cannot reconcile myself to the fact that a large segment of the American people rushed to support, uphold, and even champion the cause of a man convicted of multiple premeditated murders of men, women, and children; a killer who described his action: "It was not a big deal . . ." To proceed on the principle that "Calley is all of us; he is every single citizen in our graceless land" (Dean Francis B. Sayre) is to slash any understanding of what crime means and to tear out the heart of human dignity. For the heart of human dignity is, I repeat, the ability to be responsible.

At this hour a major lesson implied in the teaching of the ancient prophets of Israel assumes renewed validity: *Few are guilty, but all are responsible.*

It is important that we distinguish between guilt and responsibility. It is dangerous to confuse these two distinct terms. Guilt which originally denoted a crime or sin implies a connection with or involvement in a misdeed of a grave or serious character; the fact of having committed a breach of conduct, especially such as violates law and involves penalty.

Responsibility is the capability of being called upon to answer, or to make amends, to someone for something, without necessarily being directly connected with or involved in a criminal act.

The war in Indochina was and continues to be a heinous affair. But in addition to my sense of outrage at what we have done, I am haunted by a nightmare of what its aftereffects may be: the war in Indochina as the great example of how wars should be waged, Captain Calley a national hero or a revered martyr.

We stand at the crossroads of our history. The atrocities we have committed are part of our record, of our consciousness. Either we accept and vindicate it and establish techniques of atrocities as a legitimate mode of national policy or repent earnestly, confessing our sins, making amends, and adopting measures that would prevent similar crimes from happening in the future.

Repentance can come about only in a state of utter hopelessness. For how dare we hope for God's forgiveness? Confronted with the results of our crimes—multitudes of people killed, crippled, demoralized, orphaned, widowed—can we expect the God of justice to forgive us?

We must first pass through a theology of hopelessness before we can dare to pray for pardon!

The issue we should all ponder is moral, not legal; responsibility, rather than guilt; *prevention*, rather than punishment.

What steps must be taken by our leaders to prevent the possibility of our people committing war crimes in the future?

If we remain silent in the face of this challenge, greater atrocities will take place in the days to come. I therefore propose that in order to prevent occurrences of similar acts in the future, we appeal to the President of the United States, the Commander in Chief of the Armed Forces, to appoint a guardian or commissioner of moral discipline whose responsibility it would be to see to it that military operations be carried out in accordance with international rules of warfare as accepted by the American government.

Such an office is needed not because military men are inherently malevolent but because all dedicated self-perpetuating institutions tend to become victims of their single-mindedness and self-centeredness. Utilitarian considerations and professionalism tend to assume that all means are justified by the end, thus overriding inhibitions imposed by law. The voice of outside critics is too feeble to overturn their decisions and is expressed too late to prevent what has often already taken place. What is called for is a mechanism which would prevent official misjudgment and deviation.

I do not have in mind only the establishment of grievance bureaus to which an aggrieved person may choose to take his case, an office of ombundsman which would function as a complaint department. What I call for is the creation primarily of an office of guardian of legality as part of the Defense Department, whose task would be to monitor and survey the army's adherence to international rules of war.

He should have the authority not only to call to judgment those who have transgressed the rules of international law but also to anticipate and to prevent such transgression. The knowledge that there is constant scrutiny would help deter violence.

There are precedents for setting up such an office, as, for example, the General Accounting Office, whose task is to discover whether moneys

Congress appropriates are being spent for congressionally approved purposes and no others. The Office of the Inspector General at the Department of Agriculture is authorized to conduct not only conventional audits and studies but also evaluations and investigations of programs and departmental personnel.

The office which I am proposing would not create new restraints and restrictions that may jeopardize good administration. Its task would be to see to it that the restraints and restrictions already accepted by the army will be observed.

I fully realize that the awareness that someone is constantly peering over their shoulders may cause some military commanders to be too timid instead of too bold. But perhaps this is the heart of the contemporary military situation: being too bold—the possibility of releasing hydrogen bombs and intercontinental missiles—creates greater danger of disaster than being too timid.

A person of high competence as a jurist is needed, one who has the authority to inhibit, to restrain operations carried out by people whose principal standard is efficiency. Professional competence, political independence, and moral sensitivity would be required qualities of the guardian of moral discipline. He should have the ear of the President and the Congress, the privilege of informing directly the Commander in Chief or the Supreme Court when detecting failure on the part of the military forces.

The creation of such an office in the United States of America would stimulate the establishment of similar sources of moral authority in other countries and contribute to the cause of world peace.

There is another burden on our conscience. Many of us who have served as teachers at theological seminaries have prepared and even encouraged our students to enter the chaplaincy of the armed forces. It comes as a shock to us that none of the chaplains has cried out during these many years of waging war in Indochina about the atrocities committed there. The war crimes were disclosed by reporters and privates rather than by ministers, priests, and rabbis. What a jolt to our expectation of the role of religious people in modern society!

If the chaplaincy is to be saved and cleansed from its terrible sin of silence, it ought to become a voice calling for the establishment of such an authority, a legal and moral authority as proposed above.

After the conquest of ancient Palestine, the Babylonian king, Nebuchadnezzar, appointed Gedaliah, a distinguished Jewish citizen, to be governor of Judea. As a result of a conspiracy, Gedaliah was assassinated.

More than 2,500 years have passed and Jews continue on the day following the New Year's Festival to observe a fast day in commemoration of the sad event, in which only one single man was murdered.

May I propose that at least a minute of silence be observed every year in mourning and repentance of crimes of our times in Indochina.

The Reasons for My Involvement

in the Peace Movement

FOR MANY YEARS I lived by the conviction that my destiny is to serve in the realm of privacy, to be concerned with the ultimate issues and involved in attempting to clarify them in thought and in word. Loneliness was both a burden and a blessing, and above all indispensable for achieving a kind of stillness in which perplexities could be faced without fear.

Three events changed my attitude. One was the countless onslaughts upon my inner life, depriving me of the ability to sustain inner stillness. The second event was the discovery that indifference to evil is worse than evil itself. Even the high worth of reflection in the cultivation of inner truth cannot justify remaining calm in the face of cruelties that make the hope of effectiveness of pure intellectual endeavors seem grotesque. Isolationism is frequently an unconscious pretext for carelessness, whether among statesmen or among scholars.

The most wicked men must be regarded as great teachers, for they often set forth precisely an example of that which is unqualifiedly evil. Cain's question "Am I my brother's keeper?" (Genesis 4:9) and his implied negative response must be regarded among the great fundamental evil maxims of the world.

The third event that changed my attitude was my study of the prophets of ancient Israel, a study on which I worked for several years until its publication in 1962. From them I learned the niggardliness of our moral comprehension, the incapacity to sense the depth of misery caused by our own failures. It became quite clear to me that while our eyes are witness to the callousness and cruelty of man, our heart tries to obliterate the memories, to calm the nerves, and to silence our conscience.

There is immense silent agony in the world, and the task of man is to be a voice for the plundered poor, to prevent the desecration of the soul and the violation of our dream of honesty.

The more deeply immersed I became in the thinking of the prophets, the more powerfully it became clear to me what the lives of the prophets sought to convey: that morally speaking there is no limit to the concern one must feel for the suffering of human beings. It also became clear to me that in regard to cruelties committed in the name of a free society, some are guilty, while all are responsible. I did not feel guilty as an individual American for the bloodshed in Vietnam, but I felt deeply responsible. "Thou shalt not stand idly by the blood of thy neighbor" (Leviticus 19:15). This is not a recommendation but an imperative, a supreme commandment. And so I decided to change my mode of living and to become active in the cause of peace in Vietnam.*

The more carefully I studied the situation in Vietnam, the more obvious it became to me that the root problem there was not the conflict between North and South Vietnam but the misery and corruption and despair of the population in South Vietnam, which to a large degree was brought about by colonial exploitation. The answer to that misery was not in killing the rebels but in seeking a just solution to the economic and political issues of that land.

To my dismay I discovered that the people in this country who made decisions on waging the war in Vietnam thought almost exclusively in terms of generalizations—for example, Communism was seen as the devil and the only source of evil in the world. These decision-makers also had an exceedingly superficial knowledge of the economic, cultural, and psychological conditions of that country. Americans who went to Vietnam to take over the running of affairs there were not even able to speak the Vietnamese language, and as a result could not communicate except through interpreters who were often biased, self-seeking, and even corrupt. Devoid of understanding, burdened with prejudice and pride, mighty America sank into the quagmire of this most obscure and complex conflict.

When I concluded in 1965 that waging war in Vietnam was an evil act, I was also convinced that immediate and complete withdrawal from Vietnam would be the wisest act. Realizing the hopelessness that such a proposal would ever be accepted by the then-current administration, I formulated my thought by saying: True, it is very difficult to withdraw from Vietnam today, but it will be even more difficult to withdraw from Vietnam tomorrow. Above all, it was a war that couldn't be morally justified, for war under all circumstances is a supreme atrocity and is justified only when there is a necessity to defend one's own survival. It is politically illogical, I thought, to assume that Communism in South

---

* "Clergy Concerned About Vietnam." The assembly elected three co-chairmen, Daniel Berrigan, Richard Neuhaus, and the writer of this essay. One of the results of this meeting was Daniel Berrigan's involvement in the movement for peace in Vietnam (see the essay "The Priest Who Stayed Out in the Cold," *The New York Times*, June 28, 1970).

Vietnam would be a greater threat to the security of the United States than Communism in Hungary or Czechoslovakia.

As much as I abhor many of the principles of Communism, I also abhor Fascism and the use of violence in suppressing those who fight against oppression by greedy or corrupt overlords. In addition, the war in Vietnam by its very nature was a war that could not be waged according to the international law to which America is committed, which protects civilians from being killed by military forces. I very early discovered that large numbers of innocent civilians were being killed by the indiscriminate bombing and shooting of our own military forces, that numerous war crimes were being committed, that the very fabric of Vietnamese society was being destroyed, traditions desecrated, and honored ways of living defiled. Such discoveries revealed the war as being exceedingly unjust. As a result, my concern to stop the war became a *central religious* concern.

Although Jewish tradition enjoins our people to obey scrupulously the decrees issued by the government of the land, whenever a decree is unambiguously immoral, one nevertheless has a duty to disobey it.

When President Johnson expressed to veterans his consternation at the fact that so many citizens protested against his decisions in Vietnam, in spite of his authority as President and the vast amount of information at his disposal, I responded, at the request of John Cogley of *The New York Times*, that when the Lord was considering destroying Sodom and Gomorrah, Abraham did not hesitate to challenge the Lord's judgment and to carry on an argument with Him whether His decision was just. Can it be that the Judge of the entire universe would fail to act justly? For all the majesty of the office of the President of the United States, he cannot claim greater majesty than God Himself.

1973

In Search of Exaltation

IN MY CHILDHOOD and in my youth I was the recipient of many blessings. I lived in the presence of quite a number of extraordinary persons I could revere. And just as I lived as a child in their presence, their presence continues to live in me as an adult. And yet I am not just a dwelling place for other people, an echo of the past. I am guided by the principle that the future is wiser than the present. I am basically an optimist. I am an optimist against my better judgment.

I seek to understand the present and the future while I disagree with those who think of the present in the past tense. I consider in my own intellectual existence that the greatest danger is to become obsolete. I try not to be stale, I try to remain young. I have one talent and that is the capacity to be tremendously surprised, surprised at life, at ideas. This is to me the supreme Hasidic imperative: Don't be old. Don't be stale. See life as all doors. Some are open, some are closed. You have to know how to open them.

But what is the key? The key is a song. As was the case with the Jew in the Hasidic story who is suddenly taken by surprise. A Cossack comes to his house and says: "I hear you are a cantor. Sing me a song." The poor Jew does not understand Russian, but fortunately his wife does. "He wants you to sing a *niggun*, a song," she tells her husband. The Jew is frightened, but still he sings a *niggun*; not a sad song, but an honest one. And when he finishes the Cossack beats him up. "Why does he beat me?" he asks his wife in bewilderment. She in turn asks the Cossack, who replies that he didn't like that *niggun*, he wants another. The Jew sings another *niggun* and the Cossack doesn't like that one either. And the Jew gets another beating.

Maybe this is my life. I always try to sing a *niggun*. I write one book and the Cossack gives me a beating. So I try to write another. The Cossack may well be my greatest benefactor.

Perhaps the Cossack can be important to America, too. Nowadays when I think about the destiny of America I am very sad. Having lived in Poland and later in Germany, I know what America really means. For generations America was the great promise, the great joy, the last hope of humanity. Ten years ago if I had said to students that America is a great blessing and an example to the world, they would have laughed at me. Why speak such banalities? Today one of the saddest experiences of my life is to observe what is happening to America morally. The world once had a great hope, a great model: America. What is going to happen to America?

And here I return to the subject of blessings and how they come sometimes as blessings and sometimes in the guise of a curse. Like that Cossack.

We have a major curse in America today, the epidemic of drug addiction. Sometimes I have a strange feeling that this problem may be a blessing in the form of a curse. Perhaps this will wake us up to discover that we have gone the wrong way.

I interpret the young people's escape to drugs as coming from their driving desire to experience moments of exaltation. In my youth, growing up in a Jewish milieu, there was one thing we did not have to look for and that was exaltation. Every moment is great, we were taught, every moment is unique. Every moment can do such great things.

Jewish education may not have trained us in the art of relaxation, but our tradition did teach us something else. If I was rich as a child and as a young man, it was because I was offered numerous moments of exaltation, one after the other, in my home, in the synagogue, among my family and elders. Today, in America, Jews may have learned how to relax, but we have not learned the sources of exaltation. Man cannot live by sedatives alone. He needs not only tranquilizers and sedatives, he also needs stimulants.

In search of exaltation man is ready to burn Rome, even to destroy himself. It is difficult for a human being to live on the same level, shallow, placid, repetitious, uniform, ordinary, unchanged. The classical form of exaltation is worship. Prayer lifts a person above himself. Life without genuine prayer is a wasteland.

But exaltation is gone from the synagogue, from the church, and also from many a classroom and university. The cardinal sin is boredom, and the major failure the denial to our young of moments of exaltation. We have shaped our lives around the practical, the utilitarian, devoid of dreams and vision, higher concerns and enthusiasms. And our religious leadership suffers from a me-too attitude toward fad and fashion, accommodation and progressive surrender.

Our life thus devours the wisdom of religious tradition without deriving from it sources of renewal and uplift. Reduced to a matter of expediency, the entire image of man becomes flat. The sickness of our technological civilization has at least reached our consciousness, although the depths of that sickness have yet to be plumbed.

Young people are being driven into the inferno of the drug culture in search of high moments. Add to this the tremendous discontent of youth and its cry for justice for the disadvantaged, its disgust with halfhearted commitments and hypocrisies, and we may have the beginning of a thirst for the noble and the spiritual. The drug addict may well turn out to be the tragic witness who will guide adults into the realization that man without God eventually becomes insane.

Man is born to be concerned with ultimate issues. When he refuses to care, he ceases to be human. In this country, from top to bottom, from philosophy department to kindergarten, there is a violent disregard of such issues in favor of preoccupation with linguistic subtleties and semantics. The country at large is in frantic search of immediate comfort, instant pleasure, instant satisfaction, quick achievement.

This is the challenge. The new witnesses for a revival of the spirit in America may well be those poor miserable young men and women who are victims of the narcotics epidemic. If we will but heed the warning and try to understand their misguided search for exaltation, we can begin the task of turning curse into blessing.

A Prayer for Peace

Ours is an assembly of shock, contrition, and dismay. Who would have believed that we life-loving Americans are capable of bringing death and destruction to so many innocent people? We are startled to discover how unmerciful, how beastly we ourselves can be. So we implore you, our Father in heaven, help us to banish the beast from our hearts, the beast of cruelty, the beast of callousness.

Since the beginning of history evil has been going forth from nation to nation. The lords of the flocks issue proclamations, and the sheep of all nations indulge in devastation. But who would have believed that our own nation at the height of its career as the leader of free nations, the hope for peace in the world, whose unprecedented greatness was achieved through "liberty and justice for all," should abdicate its wisdom, suppress its compassion, and permit guns to become its symbols?

America's resources, moral and material, are immense. We have the means and know the ways of dispelling prejudice and lies, of overcoming poverty and disease. We have the capacity to lead the world in seeking to overcome international hostility. Must napalm stand in the way of our power to aid and to inspire the world?

To be sure, just as we feel deeply the citizen's dilemma, we are equally sensitive to the dilemma confronting the leaders of our government. Our government seems to recognize the tragic error and futility of the escalation of our involvement but feels that we cannot extricate ourselves without public embarrassment of such dimension as to cause damage to America's prestige. But the mire in which we flounder threatens us with an even greater danger. It is the dilemma of either losing face or losing our soul.

At this hour Vietnam is our most urgent, our most disturbing religious problem, a challenge to the whole nation as well as a challenge to every one of us as an individual. When a person is sick, in danger, or in misery, all religious duties recede, all rituals are suspended, except one: to save life and relieve pain.

Vietnam is a personal problem. To speak about God and remain silent on Vietnam is blasphemous.

> When you spread forth your hands
> I will hide my eyes from you;
> Yea, when you make many prayers,
> I will not hear—
> Your hands are not clean.

In the sight of so many thousands of civilians and soldiers slain, injured, crippled, of bodies emaciated, of forests destroyed by fire, God confronts us with this question: Where are you?

Is there no compassion in the world? No sense of discernment to realize that this is a war that refutes any conceivable justification of war? The sword is the pride of man; arsenals, military bases, nuclear weapons lend supremacy to nations. War is the climax of ingenuity, the object of supreme dedication. Men slaughtering each other, cities battered into ruins: such insanity has plunged many nations into an abyss of disgrace. Will America, the promise of peace to the world, fail to uphold its magnificent destiny?

The most basic way in which all men may be divided is between those who believe that war is unnecessary and those who believe that war is inevitable; between those to whom the sword is the symbol of honor and those to whom seeking to convert swords into plowshares is the only way to keep our civilization from disaster.

Most of us prefer to disregard the dreadful deeds we do over there. The atrocities committed in our name are too horrible to be credible. It is beyond our power to react vividly to the ongoing nightmare, day after day, night after night. So we bear graciously other people's suffering.

O Lord, we confess our sins, we are ashamed of the inadequacy of our anguish, of how faint and slight is our mercy. We are a generation that has lost the capacity for outrage. We must continue to remind ourselves that in a free society all are involved in what some are doing. *Some are guilty, all are responsible.*

Prayer is our greatest privilege. To pray is to stake our very existence, our right to live, on the truth and on the supreme importance of that which we pray for. Prayer, then, is radical commitment, a dangerous involvement in the life of God. In such awareness we pray . . .

We do not stand alone. Millions of Americans, millions of people all over the world are with us. At this moment, praying for peace in Vietnam, we are spiritually Vietnamese. Their agony is our affliction, their hope is our commitment.

God is present wherever men are afflicted. Where is God present now? We do not know how to cry, we do not know how to pray! Our conscience is so timid, our words so faint, our mercy so feeble. O Father, have mercy upon us.

Our God, add our cries uttered here to the cries of the bereaved, crippled, and dying over there. Have mercy upon all of us.

Help us to overcome the arrogance of power. Guide and inspire the President of the United States in finding a speedy, generous, and peaceful end to the war in Vietnam.

The intensity of the agony is high, the hour is late, the outrage may reach a stage where repentance will be too late, repair beyond any nation's power.

We call for a covenant of peace, for reconciliation of America and all of Vietnam. To paraphrase the words of the prophet Isaiah (62:1):

> *For Vietnam's sake I will not keep silent,*
> *For America's sake I will not rest,*
> *Until the vindication of humanity goes forth as brightness,*
> *And peace for all men is a burning torch.*

Here is the experience of a child of seven who was reading in school the chapter which tells of the sacrifice of Isaac on the way to Mt. Moriah with his father. "He lay on the altar, bound, waiting to be sacrificed. My heart began to beat even faster; it actually sobbed with pity for Isaac. Behold, Abraham now lifted the knife. And now my heart froze within me with fright. Suddenly the voice of the angel was heard: 'Abraham, lay not your hand upon the lad, for now I know that you fear God.' And here I broke out in tears and wept aloud. 'Why are you crying?' asked the rabbi. 'You know that Isaac was not killed.' And I said to him, still weeping, 'But, Rabbi, supposing the angel had come a second too late?' The rabbi comforted me and calmed me by telling me that an angel cannot come late."

An angel cannot be late, but man, made of flesh and blood, may be.

IV

NO RELIGION

IS AN ISLAND

No Religion Is an Island

I SPEAK AS a member of a congregation whose founder was Abraham, and the name of my rabbi is Moses.

I speak as a person who was able to leave Warsaw, the city in which I was born, just six weeks before the disaster began. My destination was New York; it would have been Auschwitz or Treblinka. I am a brand plucked from the fire in which my people was burned to death. I am a brand plucked from the fire of an altar of Satan on which millions of human lives were exterminated to evil's greater glory, and on which so much else was consumed: the divine image of so many human beings, many people's faith in the God of justice and compassion, and much of the secret and power of attachment to the Bible bred and cherished in the hearts of men for nearly two thousand years.

I speak as a person who is often afraid and terribly alarmed lest God has turned away from us in disgust and even deprived us of the power to understand His word. In the words Isaiah perceived in his vision (6:9–10):

Then I said, "Here I am! Send me." And he said, "Go, and say to this people: Hear and hear, but do not understand; see and see, but do not perceive. Make the heart of this people fat, and their ears heavy, and shut their eyes; lest they see with their eyes, and hear with their ears, and understand with their hearts, and turn and be healed."

Some of us are like patients in the state of final agony—who scream in delirium: The doctor is dead, the doctor is dead.

I speak as a person who is convinced that the fate of the Jewish people and the fate of the Hebrew Bible are intertwined. The recognition of our status as Jews, the legitimacy of our survival, is possible only in a world in which the God of Abraham is revered.

Nazism in its very roots was a rebellion against the Bible, against the God of Abraham. Realizing that it was Christianity that implanted attachment to the God of Abraham and involvement with the Hebrew Bible in the hearts of Western man, Nazism resolved that it must both exterminate the Jews and eliminate Christianity, and bring about instead a revival of Teutonic paganism.

Nazism has suffered a defeat, but the process of eliminating the Bible from the consciousness of the Western world goes on. It is on the issue of saving the radiance of the Hebrew Bible in the minds of man that Jews and Christians are called upon to work together. *None of us can do it alone.* Both of us must realize that in our age anti-Semitism is anti-Christianity and that anti-Christianity is anti-Semitism.

Man is never as open to fellowship as he is in moments of misery and distress. The people of New York City have never experienced such fellowship, such awareness of being one, as they did last night in the midst of darkness. *

Indeed, there is a light in the midst of the darkness of this hour. But, alas, most of us have no eyes.

Is Judaism, is Christianity, ready to face the challenge? When I speak about the radiance of the Bible in the minds of man, I do not mean its being a theme for *Information, Please* but rather an openness to *God's presence in the Bible,* the continuous ongoing effort for a breakthrough in the soul of man, the guarding of the precarious position of being human, even a little higher than human, despite defiance and in face of despair.

The supreme issue is today not the *halacha* for the Jew or the Church for the Christian—but the premise underlying both religions, namely, whether there is a *pathos,* a divine reality concerned with the destiny of man which mysteriously impinges upon history; the supreme issue is whether we are alive or dead to the challenge and the expectation of the living God. The crisis engulfs all of us. The misery and fear of alienation from God make Jew and Christian cry together.

Jews must realize that the spokesmen of the Enlightenment who attacked Christianity were no less negative in their attitude toward Judaism. They often blamed Judaism for the misdeeds of the daughter religion. The casualties of the devastation caused by the continuous onslaughts on biblical religion in modern times are to be found among Jews as well as among Christians.

---

* This essay was originally delivered as the inaugural lecture for the Harry Emerson Fosdick Visiting Professorship at Union Theological Seminary, which my father held during the academic year 1965–66. He delivered the lecture the evening of November 10, 1965, and referred in his speech to the widespread electrical power failure in New York City that had occurred the night before.

On the other hand, the community of Israel must always be mindful of the mystery of aloneness and uniqueness of its own being. "There is a people that dwells apart, not reckoned among the nations" (Numbers 23:19), says the Gentile prophet Balaam. Is it not safer for us to remain in isolation and to refrain from sharing perplexities and certainties with Christians?

Our era marks the end of complacency, the end of evasion, the end of self-reliance. Jews and Christians share the perils and the fears; we stand on the brink of the abyss together. Interdependence of political and economic conditions all over the world is a basic fact of our situation. Disorder in a small obscure country in any part of the world evokes anxiety in people all over the world.

Parochialism has become untenable. There was a time when you could not pry out of a Boston man that the Boston state house is not the hub of the solar system or that one's own denomination has not the monopoly of the holy spirit. Today we know that even the solar system is not the hub of the universe.

The religions of the world are no more self-sufficient, no more independent, no more isolated than individuals or nations. Energies, experiences, and ideas that come to life outside the boundaries of a particular religion or all religions continue to challenge and to affect every religion.

Horizons are wider, dangers are greater . . . *No religion is an island.* We are all involved with one another. Spiritual betrayal on the part of one of us affects the faith of all of us. Views adopted in one community have an impact on other communities. Today religious isolationism is a myth. For all the profound differences in perspective and substance, Judaism is sooner or later affected by the intellectual, moral, and spiritual events within the Christian society, and vice versa.

We fail to realize that while different exponents of faith in the world of religion continue to be wary of the ecumenical movement, there is another ecumenical movement, worldwide in extent and influence: nihilism. We must choose between interfaith and internihilism. Cynicism is not parochial. Should religions insist upon the illusion of complete isolation? Should we refuse to be on speaking terms with one another and hope for each other's failure? Or should we pray for each other's health and help one another in preserving one's respective legacy, in preserving a common legacy?

The Jewish Diaspora today, almost completely to be found in the Western world, is certainly not immune to the spiritual climate and the state of religious faith in the general society. We do not live in isolation, and the way in which non-Jews either relate or bid defiance to God has a profound impact on the minds and souls of the Jews. Even in the Middle

Ages, when most Jews lived in relative isolation, such impact was acknowledged. To quote: "The usage of the Jews is in accordance with that of the non-Jews. If the non-Jews of a certain town are moral, the Jews born there will be so as well." Rabbi Joseph Yaabez, a victim of the Spanish Inquisition, in the midst of the Inquisition was able to say that "the Christians believe in Creation, the excellence of the patriarchs, revelation, retribution and resurrection. Blessed is the Lord, God of Israel, who left this remnant after the destruction of the second Temple. But for these Christian nations we might ourselves become infirm in our faith."

We are heirs to a long history of mutual contempt among religions and religious denominations, of religious coercion, strife, and persecutions. Even in periods of peace, the relationship that obtains between representatives of different religions is not just reciprocity of ignorance; it is an abyss, a source of detraction and distrust, casting suspicion and undoing efforts of many an honest and noble expression of good will.

The psalmist's great joy is in proclaiming: "Truth and mercy have met together" (Psalms 85:11). Yet frequently faith and the lack of mercy enter a union, out of which bigotry is born, the presumption that my faith, my motivation, is pure and holy, while the faith of those who differ in creed—even those in my own community—is impure and unholy. How can we be cured of bigotry, presumption, and the foolishness of believing that we have been triumphant while we have all been defeated?

Is it not clear that in spite of fundamental disagreements there is a convergence of some of our commitments, of some of our views, tasks we have in common, evils we must fight together, goals we share, a predicament afflicting us all?

On what basis do we people of different religious commitments meet one another?

First and foremost, we meet as human beings who have much in common: a heart, a face, a voice, the presence of a soul, fears, hope, the ability to trust, a capacity for compassion and understanding, the kinship of being human. My first task in every encounter is to comprehend the personhood of the human being I face, to sense the kinship of being human, solidarity of being.

To meet a human being is a major challenge to mind and heart. I must recall what I normally forget. A person is not just a specimen of the species called *Homo sapiens*. He is all of humanity in one, and whenever one man is hurt, we are all injured. The human is a disclosure of the divine, and all men are one in God's care for man. Many things on earth are precious, some are holy, humanity is holy of holies.

To meet a human being is an opportunity to sense the image of God, the *presence* of God. According to a rabbinical interpretation, the Lord said to Moses: "Wherever you see the trace of man there I stand before you . . ."

When engaged in a conversation with a person of different religious commitment, if I discover that we disagree in matters sacred to us, does the image of God I face disappear? Does God cease to stand before me? Does the difference in commitment destroy the kinship of being human? Does the fact that we differ in our conceptions of God cancel what we have in common: the image of God?

For this reason was man created single (whereas of every other species many were created) . . . that there should be peace among human beings: one cannot say to his neighbor, my ancestor was nobler than thine (*Sanhedrin* 37 a).

The primary aim of these reflections is to inquire how a Jew out of his commitment and a Christian out of his commitment can find a religious basis for communication and cooperation on matters relevant to their moral and spiritual concern in spite of disagreement.

There are four dimensions of religious existence, four necessary components of man's relationships to God: (a) the teaching, the essentials of which are summarized in the form of a creed, which serve as guiding principles in our thinking about matters temporal or eternal, the dimension of the doctrine; (b) faith, inwardness, the direction of one's heart, the intimacy of religion, the dimension of privacy; (c) the law, or the sacred act to be carried out in the sanctuary in society or at home, the dimension of the deed; (d) the context in which creed, faith, and ritual come to pass, such as the community or the covenant, history, tradition, the dimension of transcendence.

In the dimension of the deed there are obviously vast areas for cooperation among men of different commitments in terms of intellectual communication, of sharing concern and knowledge in applied religion, particularly as they relate to social action.

In the dimension of faith, the encounter proceeds in terms of personal witness and example, sharing insights, confessing inadequacy. On the level of doctrine we seek to convey the content of what we believe in; on the level of faith we experience in one another the presence of a person radiant with reflections of a greater presence.

I suggest that the most significant basis for meeting of men of different religious traditions is the level of fear and trembling, of humility and contrition, where our individual moments of faith are mere waves in the endless ocean of mankind's reaching out for God, where all formulations and articulations appear as understatements, where our souls are swept away by the awareness of the urgency of answering God's commandment, while stripped of pretension and conceit we sense the tragic insufficiency of human faith.

What divides us? What unites us? We disagree in law and creed, in commitments which lie at the very heart of our religious existence. We say no to one another in some doctrines essential and sacred to us. What unites us? Our being accountable to God, our being objects of God's concern, precious in His eyes. Our conceptions of what ails us may be different, but the anxiety is the same. The language, the imagination, the concretization of our hopes are different, but the embarrassment is the same, and so is the sigh, the sorrow, and the necessity to obey.

We may disagree about the ways of achieving fear and trembling, but the fear and trembling are the same. The demands are different, but the conscience is the same, and so is arrogance, iniquity. The proclamations are different, the callousness is the same, and so is the challenge we face in many moments of spiritual agony.

Above all, while dogmas and forms of worship are divergent, God is the same. What unites us? A commitment to the Hebrew Bible as Holy Scripture. Faith in the Creator, the God of Abraham; commitment to many of His commandments, to justice and mercy; a sense of contrition; sensitivity to the sanctity of life and to the involvement of God in history; the conviction that without the holy the good will be defeated; prayer that history may not end before the end of days; and so much more.

There are moments when we all stand together and see our faces in the mirror: the anguish of humanity and its helplessness; the perplexity of the individual and the need of divine guidance; being called to praise and to do what is required.

In conversations with Protestant and Catholic theologians I have more than once come upon an attitude of condescension to Judaism, a sort of pity for those who have not yet seen the light; tolerance instead of reverence. On the other hand, I cannot forget that when Paul Tillich, Gustave Weigel, and I were invited by the Ford Foundation to speak from the same platform on the religious situation in America, we not only found ourselves in deep accord in disclosing what ails us but, above all, without prior consultation, the three of us confessed that our guides in this critical age are the prophets of Israel, not Aristotle, not Karl Marx, but Amos and Isaiah.

The theme of these reflections is not a doctrine or an institution called Christianity but human beings all over the world, both present and past, who worship God as followers of Jesus, and my problem is how I should relate myself to them spiritually. The issue I am called upon to respond to is not the truth of dogma but the faith and the spiritual power of the commitment of Christians. In facing the claim and the dogma of the

Church, Jews and Christians are strangers and stand in disagreement with one another. Yet there are levels of existence where Jews and Christians meet as sons and brothers. "Alas, in heaven's name, are we not your brothers, are we not the sons of one father and are we not the sons of one mother?"

To be sure, all men are sons of one father, but they have also the power to forfeit their birthright, to turn rebels, voluntary bastards, "children with no faithfulness in them" (Deuteronomy 32:20). It is not flesh and blood but honor and obedience that save the right of sonship. We claim brotherhood by being subject to His commandments. We are sons when we hearken to the Father, when we praise and honor Him.

The recognition that we are sons in obeying God and praising Him is the starting point of my reflection. "I am a companion of all who fear Thee, of those who keep Thy precepts" (Psalms 119:63). I rejoice wherever His name is praised, His presence sensed, His commandment done.

The first and most important prerequisite of interfaith is faith. It is only out of the depth of involvement in the unending drama that began with Abraham that we can help one another toward an understanding of our situation. Interfaith must come out of depth, not out of a void absence of faith. It is not an enterprise for those who are half learned or spiritually immature. If it is not to lead to the confusion of the many, it must remain a prerogative of the few.

Faith and the power of insight and devotion can only grow in privacy. Exposing one's inner life may engender the danger of desecration, distortion, and confusion. Syncretism is a perpetual possibility. Moreover, at a time of paucity of faith, interfaith may become a substitute for faith, suppressing authenticity for the sake of compromise. In a world of conformity, religions can easily be leveled down to the lowest common denominator.

Both communication and separation are necessary. We must preserve our individuality as well as foster care for one another, reverence, understanding, cooperation. In the world of economics, science, and technology, cooperation exists and continues to grow. Even political states, though different in culture and competing with one another, maintain diplomatic relations and strive for coexistence. Only religions are not on speaking terms. Over a hundred countries are willing to be part of the United Nations; yet no religion is ready to be part of a movement for United Religions. Or should I say, not yet ready? Ignorance, distrust, and disdain often characterize their relations to one another. Is disdain for the opposition indigenous to the religious position? Granted that Judaism and Christianity are committed to contradictory claims, is it impossible to carry on a controversy without acrimony, criticism without loss of respect, disagreement without disrespect? The problem to be faced is how to combine loyalty to one's own tradition with reverence for different traditions. How is mutual esteem between Christian and Jew possible?

A Christian ought to ponder seriously the tremendous implications of a process begun in early Christian history. I mean the conscious or unconscious de-Judaization of Christianity, affecting the Church's way of thinking, its inner life as well as its relationship to the past and present reality of Israel—the father and mother of the very being of Christianity. The children did not arise to call the mother blessed; instead, they called the mother blind. Some theologians continue to act as if they did not know the meaning of "Honor your father and mother"; others, anxious to prove the superiority of the Church, speak as if they suffered from a spiritual Oedipus complex.

A Christian ought to realize that a world without Israel would be a world without the God of Israel. A Jew, on the other hand, ought to acknowledge the eminent role and part of Christianity in God's design for the redemption of all men.

Modern Jews who have come out of the state of political seclusion and are involved in the historic process of Western mankind cannot afford to be indifferent to the religious situation of our fellow men. Opposition to Christianity must be challenged by the question: What religious alternative do we envisage for the Christian world? Did we not refrain for almost two thousand years from preaching Judaism to the nations?

A Jew ought to ponder seriously the responsibility involved in Jewish history for having been the mother of two world religions. Does not the failure of children reflect upon their mother? Do not the sharp deviations from Jewish tradition on the part of the early Christians who were Jews indicate some failure of communication within the spiritual climate of first-century Palestine?

Judaism is the mother of the Christian faith. It has a stake in the destiny of Christianity. Should a mother ignore her child, even a wayward, rebellious one? On the other hand, the Church should acknowledge that we Jews, in loyalty to our tradition, have a stake in its faith, recognize our vocation to preserve and to teach the legacy of the Hebrew Scripture, accept our aid in fighting anti-Marcionite trends as an act of love.

Is it not our duty to help one another in trying to overcome hardness of heart, in cultivating a sense of wonder and mystery, in unlocking doors to holiness in time, in opening minds to the challenge of the Hebrew Bible, in seeking to respond to the voice of the prophets?

No honest religious person can fail to admire the outpouring of the love of man and the love of God, the marvels of worship, the magnificence of spiritual insight, the piety, charity, and sanctity in the lives of countless men and women, manifested in the history of Christianity. Have not Pascal, Kierkegaard, Immanuel Kant, and Reinhold Niebuhr been a source of inspiration to many Jews?

Over and above mutual respect we must acknowledge indebtedness to one another. It is our duty to remember that it was the Church that brought the knowledge of the God of Abraham to the Gentiles. It was the Church that made Hebrew Scripture available to mankind. This we Jews must acknowledge with a grateful heart.

The Septuagint, the works of Philo, Josephus, as well as the Apocrypha and Pseudepigrapha, and the *Fons vitae* by Ibn Gabirol would have been lost had they not been preserved in monasteries. Credit for major achievements in modern scholarship in the field of Bible, in biblical as well as Hellenistic Jewish history, goes primarily to Protestant scholars.

The purpose of religious communication among human beings of different commitments is mutual enrichment and enhancement of respect and appreciation rather than the hope that the person spoken to will prove to be wrong in what he regards as sacred.

Dialogue must not degenerate into a dispute, into an effort on the part of each to get the upper hand. There is an unfortunate history of Christian-Jewish disputations, motivated by the desire to prove how blind the Jews are and carried on in a spirit of opposition, which eventually degenerated into enmity. Thus any conversation between Christian and Jew in which abandonment of the other partner's faith is a silent hope must be regarded as offensive to one's religious and human dignity.

Let there be an end to disputation and polemic, an end to disparagement. We honestly and profoundly disagree in matters of creed and dogma. Indeed, there is a deep chasm between Christians and Jews concerning, e.g., the divinity and messiahship of Jesus. But across the chasm we can extend our hands to one another.

Religion is a means, not an end. It becomes idolatrous when regarded as an end in itself. Over and above all being stands the Creator and Lord of history, He who transcends all. To equate religion and God is idolatry.

Does not the all-inclusiveness of God contradict the exclusiveness of any particular religion? The prospect of all men embracing one form of religion remains an eschatological hope. What about here and now? Is it not blasphemous to say: I alone have all the truth and the grace, and all those who differ live in darkness and are abandoned by the grace of God?

Is it really our desire to build a monolithic society: one party, one view, one leader, and no opposition? Is religious uniformity desirable or even possible? Has it really proved to be a blessing for a country when all its citizens belonged to one denomination? Or has any denomination attained a spiritual climax when it had the adherence of the entire population?

Does not the task of preparing the Kingdom of God require a diversity of talents, a variety of rituals, soul-searching as well as opposition?

Perhaps it is the will of God that in this eon there should be diversity in our forms of devotion and commitment to Him. In this eon diversity of religions is the will of God.

In the story of the building of the Tower of Babel we read: "The Lord said: They are one people, and they have all one language, and this is what they begin to do" (Genesis 11:6). These words are interpreted by an ancient rabbi to mean: What has caused them to rebel against me? The fact that they are one people and they have all one language . . .

For from the rising of the sun to its setting my name is great among the nations, and in every place incense is offered to my name, and a pure offering; for my name is great among the nations, says the Lord of hosts (Malachi 1:11).

This statement refers undoubtedly to the contemporaries of the prophet. But who were these worshippers of one God? At the time of Malachi there was hardly a large number of proselytes. Yet the statement declares: All those who worship their gods do not know it, but they are really worshipping me.

It seems that the prophet proclaims that men all over the world, though they confess different conceptions of God, are really worshipping one God, the father of all men, though they may not be aware of it.

Religions, I repeat, true to their own convictions, disagree profoundly and are in opposition to one another on matters of doctrine. However, if we accept the prophet's thesis that they all worship one God, even without knowing it, if we accept the principle that the majesty of God transcends the dignity of religion, should we not regard a divergent religion as His Majesty's loyal opposition? However, does not every religion maintain the claim to be true, and is not truth exclusive?

The ultimate truth is not capable of being fully and adequately expressed in concepts and words. The ultimate truth is about the situation that pertains between God and man. "The Torah speaks in the language of man." Revelation is always an accommodation to the capacity of man. No two minds are alike, just as no two faces are alike. The voice of God reaches the spirit of man in a variety of ways, in a multiplicity of languages. One truth comes to expression in many ways of understanding.

A major factor in our religious predicament is due to self-righteousness and to the assumption that faith is found only in him who has arrived, while it is absent in him who is on the way. Religion is often inherently guilty of the sin of pride and presumption. To paraphrase the prophet's words, the exultant religion dwelt secure and said in her heart: "I am, and there is no one besides me."

Humility and contrition seem to be absent where most required—in theology. But humility is the beginning and end of religious thinking, the secret test of faith. There is no truth without humility, no certainty without contrition.

Ezra the Scribe, the great renovator of Judaism, of whom the rabbis said that he was worthy of receiving the Torah had it not been already given through Moses, confessed his lack of perfect faith. He tells us that after he had received a royal *firman* from King Artaxerxes granting him permission to lead a group of exiles from Babylonia: "I proclaimed a fast there at the river Ahava, that we might afflict ourselves before our God, to seek of Him a right way for us, and for our little ones, and for all substance. For I was ashamed to require of the king a band of soldiers and horsemen to help us against the enemy in the way: because we had spoken unto the king, saying, The hand of God is upon all them for good that seek Him" (8:21–22).

Human faith is never final, never an arrival, but rather an endless pilgrimage, a being on the way. We have no answers to all problems. Even some of our sacred answers are both emphatic and qualified, final and tentative; final within our own position in history, tentative because we can speak only in the tentative language of man.

Heresy is often a roundabout expression of faith, and sojourning in the wilderness is a preparation for entering the Promised Land.

Is the failure, the impotence of all religions, due exclusively to human transgression? Or perhaps to the mystery of God's withholding His grace, of His concealing even while revealing? Disclosing the fullness of His glory would be an impact that would surpass the power of human endurance.

His thoughts are not our thoughts. Whatever is revealed is abundance compared with our soul and a pittance compared with His treasures. No word is God's last word, no word is God's ultimate word.

Following the revelation at Sinai, the people said to Moses: "You speak to us, and we will hear; let not God speak to us, lest we die" (Exodus 20:19).

The Torah as given to Moses, an ancient rabbi maintains, is but an unripened fruit of the heavenly tree of wisdom. At the end of days, much that is concealed will be revealed.

The mission to the Jews is a call to the individual Jew to betray the fellowship, the dignity, the sacred history of his people. Very few Christians seem to comprehend what is morally and spiritually involved in supporting such activities. We are Jews as we are men. The alternative to our existence as Jews is spiritual suicide, extinction. It is not a change into something else. Judaism has allies but no substitutes.

The wonder of Israel, the marvel of Jewish existence, the survival of holiness in the history of the Jews is a continuous verification of the marvel of the Bible. Revelation to Israel continues as a revelation through Israel.

The Protestant pastor Christian Furchtegott Gellert was asked by Frederick the Great, "Herr Professor, give me proof of the Bible, but briefly, for I have little time." Gellert answered, "Your Majesty, the Jews."

Indeed, is not the existence of the Jews a witness to the God of Abraham? Is not our loyalty to the Law of Moses a light that continues to illumine the lives of those who observe it as well as the lives of those who are aware of it?

Gustave Weigel spent the last evening of his life in my study at the Jewish Theological Seminary. We opened our hearts to one another in prayer and contrition and spoke of our own deficiencies, failures, hopes. At one moment I posed the question: Is it really the will of God that there be no more Judaism in the world? Would it really be the triumph of God if the scrolls of the Torah were no longer taken out of the Ark and the Torah no longer read in the synagogue, our ancient Hebrew prayers in which Jesus himself worshipped no more recited, the Passover Seder no longer celebrated in our lives, the Law of Moses no longer observed in our homes? Would it really be *ad Majorem Dei gloriam* to have a world without Jews?

My life is shaped by many loyalties—to my family, to my friends, to my people, to the U.S. Constitution, etc. Each of my loyalties has its ultimate root in one ultimate relationship: loyalty to God, the loyalty of all my loyalties. That relationship is the Covenant of Sinai. All we are we owe to Him. He has enriched us with gifts of insight, with the joy of moments full of blessing. He has also suffered with us in years of agony and distress.

None of us pretends to be God's accountant, and His design for history and redemption remains a mystery before which we must stand in awe. It is as arrogant to maintain that the Jews' refusal to accept Jesus as the Messiah is due to their stubbornness or blindness as it would be pre-sumptuous for the Jews not to acknowledge the glory and holiness in the lives of countless Christians. "The Lord is near to all who call upon Him, to all who call upon Him in truth" (Psalm 145:18).

Fortunately there are some important Christian voices who expressed themselves to the effect that the missionary activities to the Jews be given up. Reinhold Niebuhr may have been the first Christian theologian who at a joint meeting of the faculties of the Union Theological Seminary and the Jewish Theological Seminary declared that the missionary activities are wrong not only because they are futile and have little fruit to boast for their exertions. They are wrong because the two faiths despite differences are sufficiently alike for the Jew to find God more easily in terms of his own religious heritage than by subjecting himself to the hazards of guilt feelings involved in conversion to a faith which, whatever its excellencies, must appear to him as a symbol of an oppressive majority culture . . . Practically nothing can purify the symbol of Christ as the image of God in the imagination of the Jew from the taint with which ages of Christian oppression in the name of Christ have tainted it.[1]

Tillich has said,

Many Christians feel that it is a questionable thing, for instance, to try to convert Jews. They have lived and spoken with their Jewish friends for decades. They have not converted them, but they have created a community of conversation which has changed both sides of the dialogue.[2]

And a statement on "relations with the Roman Catholic Church" adopted by the Central Committee of the World Council of Churches, in its meeting in Rochester, New York, in August 1963, mentions proselytism as a "cause of offence," an issue "which must be frankly faced if true dialogue is to be possible."[3]

The ancient rabbis proclaimed: "Pious men of all nations have a share in the life to come."

"I call heaven and earth to witness that the Holy Spirit rests upon each person, Jew or Gentile, man or woman, master or slave, in consonance with his deeds."

Holiness is not the monopoly of any particular religion or tradition. Wherever a deed is done in accord with the will of God, wherever a thought of man is directed toward Him, there is the holy.

The Jews do not maintain that the way of the Torah is the only way of serving God. "Let all the peoples walk each one in the name of its god, but we will walk in the name of the Lord our God for ever and ever" (Micah 4:5).

"God loves the Saint" (Psalms 146:8)—"They love me, and I love them . . . If a person wishes to be a Levite or a priest, he cannot become a saint, even if he is a Gentile, he may become one. For saints do not derive their saintliness from their ancestry; they become saints because they dedicate themselves to God and love Him." Conversion to Judaism is no prerequisite for sanctity. In his Code Maimonides asserts: "Not only is the tribe of Levi (God's portion) sanctified in the highest degree, but any man among all the dwellers on earth whose heart prompts him and whose mind instructs him to dedicate himself to the services of God and to walk uprightly as God intended him to, and who disencumbers himself of the load of the many pursuits which men invent for themselves." "God asks for the heart, everything depends upon the intention of the heart . . . all men have a share in eternal life if they attain according to their ability knowledge of the Creator and have ennobled themselves by noble qualities. There is no doubt that he who has thus trained himself morally and intellectually to acquire faith in the Creator will certainly have a share in the life to come. This is why our rabbis taught: A Gentile who studies the Torah of Moses is (spiritually) equal to the High Priest at the Temple in Jerusalem."

Leading Jewish authorities, such as Yehudah Halevi and Maimonides, acknowledge Christianity to be *preparatio messianica*, while the Church regarded ancient Judaism to have been a *preparatio evangelica*. Thus, whereas the Christian doctrine has often regarded Judaism as having outlived its usefulness and the Jews as candidates for conversion, the Jewish attitude enables us to acknowledge the presence of a divine plan in the role of Christianity within the history of redemption. Yehudah Halevi, though criticizing Christianity and Islam for retaining relics of ancient idolatry and feast days—"They also revere places sacred to idols"—compares Christians and Mohammedans to proselytes who adopted the roots but not all the branches (or the logical conclusions of the divine commandments).

The wise providence of God towards Israel may be compared to the planting of a seed of corn. It is placed in the earth, where it seems to be changed into soil, and water, and rottenness, and the seed can no longer be recognized. But in very truth it is the seed that has changed the earth and water into its own nature, and then the seed raises itself from one stage to another, transforms the elements, and throws out shoots and leaves . . . Thus it is with Christians and Muslims. The Law of Moses has changed them that come into contact with it, even though they seem to have cast the Law aside. These religions are the preparation and the preface to the Messiah we expect, who is the fruit himself of the seed originally sown, and all men, too, will be fruit of God's seed when they acknowledge Him, and all become one mighty tree.

A similar view is set forth by Maimonides in his authoritative Code:

It is beyond the human mind to fathom the designs of the Creator; for our ways are not His ways, neither are our thoughts His thoughts. All these matters relating to Jesus of Nazareth and the Ishmaelite (Mohammed) who came after him served to clear the way for King Messiah, to prepare the whole world to worship God with one accord, as it is written, "For then will I turn to the peoples a pure language, that they may all call upon the name of the Lord to serve Him with one consent" (Zephaniah 3:9). Thus the messianic hope, the Torah, and the commandments have become familiar topics—topics of conversation (among the inhabitants) of the far isles and many peoples . . .

Christianity and Islam, far from being accidents of history or purely human phenomena, are regarded as part of God's design for the redemption of all men. Christianity is accorded ultimate significance by acknowledging that "all these matters relating to Jesus of Nazareth and [Mohammed] . . . served to clear the way for King Messiah." In addition to the role of these religions in the plan of redemption, their achievements within history are explicitly affirmed. Through them "the messianic hope, the Torah, and the commandments have become familiar topics . . . (among the inhabitants) of the far isles and many peoples." Elsewhere Maimonides acknowledges that "the Christians believe and profess that the Torah is God's revelation (torah min ha-shamayim) and given to Moses in the form in which it has been preserved; they have it completely written down, though they frequently interpret it differently."

Rabbi Johanan Ha-Sandelar, a disciple of Rabbi Akiba, says: "Every community which is established for the sake of heaven will in the end endure; but one which is not for the sake of heaven will not endure in the end."

Rabbi Jacob Emden maintains that heretical Jewish sects such as the Karaites and the Sabbatians belong to the second category, whereas Christianity and Islam are in the category of "a community which is for the sake of heaven" and which will "in the end endure." They have emerged out of Judaism and accepted "the fundamentals of our divine religion . . . to make known God among the nations . . . to proclaim that there is a Master in heaven and earth, divine providence, reward and punishment . . . Who bestows the gift of prophecy . . . and communicates through the prophets laws and statutes to live by . . . This is why their community endures . . . Since their intention is for the sake of heaven, reward will not be withheld from them." He also praises many Christian scholars who have come to the rescue of Jews and their literature.

Rabbi Israel Lifschutz of Danzig (1782–1860) speaks of the Christians, "our brethren, the Gentiles, who acknowledge the one God and revere His Torah which they deem divine and observe, as is required of them, the seven commandments of Noah . . ."

What, then, is the purpose of interreligious cooperation?

It is neither to flatter nor to refute one another, but to help one another; to share insight and learning, to cooperate in academic ventures on the highest scholarly level and, what is even more important, to search in the wilderness for wellsprings of devotion, for treasures of stillness, for the power of love and care for man. What is urgently needed are ways of helping one another in the terrible predicament of here and now by the courage to believe that the word of the Lord endures forever as well as here and now; to cooperate in trying to bring about a resurrection of sensitivity, a revival of conscience; to keep alive the divine sparks in our souls, to nurture openness to the spirit of the Psalms, reverence for the words of the prophets, and faithfulness to the Living God.

Choose Life!

I WOULD SAY that the major religious problem today is the systematic liquidation of man's sensitivity to the challenge of God. Let me try to explain that. We cannot understand man in his own terms. Man is not to be understood in the image of nature, in the image of an animal, or in the image of a machine. He has to be understood in terms of a transcendence, and that transcendence is not a passive thing; it is a challenging transcendence. Man is always being challenged; a question is always being asked of him. The moment man disavows the living transcendence, he is contracted; he is reduced to a level on which his distinction as a human being gradually disappears. What makes a man human is his openness to transcendence, which lifts him to a level higher than himself. Overwhelmed by the power he has achieved, man now has the illusion of sovereignty; he has become blind to his own situation, and deaf to the question being asked of him.

To destroy the illusion that man is his own center cannot be done easily. In order to understand, and to cultivate an openness to transcendence, many prerequisites are necessary, prerequisites of the mind and of the heart. However, our society, our education, all continue to corrode men's sensibilities. I am not optimistic; we are getting poorer by the day. To give you an example: Man does not feel a sense of outrage anymore, even in the face of crime. We are getting used to it. We are getting accustomed to evil. We are surrendering to that which we call inevitable. That is fatalism; it is pagan. The message of the Bible is that man is capable of making a choice. Choose life—but instead we choose death, blindness, callousness, helplessness, despair.

Religion, if taught as religion, has no life. In order to understand what the Bible says, one has to understand life as seen by the Bible, all of life.

My understanding of the meaning of God depends on my way of looking at this very table, at this very desk, at everything, at creation. The tragedy of religion is partly due to its isolation from life, as if God could be segregated. God has become an alibi for our conscience, for real faith. He has become a sort of after-life insurance policy.

Just as we are commanded to love man, we are also called upon to be sensitive to the grandeur of God's creation. We are infatuated with our great technological achievements; we have forgotten the mystery of being, of being alive. We have lost our sense of wonder, our sense of radical amazement at sheer being. We have forgotten the meaning of being human and the deep responsibility involved in just being alive. Shakespeare's Hamlet said: "To be or not to be, that is the question." But that is no problem. We all want to be. The real problem, biblically speaking, is *how to be* and how *not* to be; that is our challenge, and it is what makes the difference between the human and the animal. The animal also wants to be. For us, it is the problem of *how to be* and how *not* to be, on the levels of existence. Now, what is the meaning of God? The meaning of God is precisely the challenge of "how to be." And this is, in a sense, the meaning of Jewish Law—how to be. It occurred to me only recently that the difference between old-fashioned Jewish education and modern education is this: What was old-fashioned Jewish education? The study of the Law, the Talmud, the Law, the Law. There was a preoccupation with the Law in Jewish study. Personally I feel that old Jewish education went much too far, because there are other ways of approaching being besides through the Law. But it suddenly dawned on me that, in secular education, the secular Law is not even taught—there is no place for Law in education. We teach students the arts and sciences and the humanities, but not the Law. We do not study the Law and we do not instill in young people the glory and the ethos of the Law. Therefore, there is no real understanding of the meaning of the Law.

ONE OF THE GREAT experiences of my life has been to see the response of Americans to the challenge of civil rights. In 1963 I was privileged to deliver the keynote address at the National Conference on Religion and Race in Chicago, and I recall vividly my great anxiety. At the time I wasn't sure whether the nation would respond to the challenge of racial justice. Prejudices are deeply rooted; vested interests are strong. But I must say that, by and large, and until recently, this great revolution has been accomplished peacefully. Try to imagine what would have happened in certain other civilizations—there would have been a great deal of bloodshed. The fact is that great steps forward have been taken with a minimum of violence; it is really a great sign, to be sure. But when I look at the total picture, I see a number of disappointing features. First, although people have accepted the civil-rights movement as legitimate, they do not seem to have perceived the movement's implications. Their lives continue without awareness of the spiritual implications that civil rights demand, without a sense of the deeper meaning of human dignity. The implications of such dignity must be translated into daily action and the way we live. In a sense, the civil-rights movement is of concern not only for the Negro but for the white people. I have not seen much repentance, or a renewed understanding of what it means to be human, regardless of color. Instead, I see that indifference continues. We are getting used to scandals, to outrage, even to terrible danger. There is an apathy about nuclear bombs, for example, and about Vietnam. I don't blame anybody. There are too many dangers, too many events. Every day another outrage. How long can we be tense and sensitive? Herein is the great danger. Now we are told that the German Army had nuclear warheads. It was kept a secret; the American people didn't know about it. I should go out and cry and scream at this scandal. But I don't. Now I read in the newspaper that nuclear weapons are being driven through the streets of New York in the middle of the night. I wasn't even aware of it. Can I go around screaming every day, ten times a day? No, of course not. So I get accustomed to these things; I get used to them; I get callous. One of the dreadful aspects of today's existence is that we seem to be doing things we hate to do. No one wants the nuclear bomb, but we are spending fortunes on it. Frankly, no one wants these satellites in the air, but we are building them. No one wants the war in Vietnam, but we are fighting it. It is as if we have lost all vision, all wisdom, and there is very little comfort. If this goes on, we will lose all initiative, all insight, all conviction and commitment, and the power to sacrifice ourselves.

JEWISH-CHRISTIAN relations have improved beautifully. There is certainly a new atmosphere and increasing mutual esteem. I now teach Protestant students (and there are also some Catholic students in my classes), and it is possible for my students, for my colleagues, and for me to speak out of depth and out of sincere mutual respect. We have a great deal in common, and at the same time we are ready to acknowledge our differences. I think there is a great deal to be done in this field. One way is just to meet one another; even this is a great contribution. The image of the Jew in Western history has been distorted, stained. The history of Jewish-Christian relations has been sordid. There are a great many wonderful, important, and influential Christians who never had an opportunity to speak to a religious Jew. But now Christians are discovering that there is a religious voice and a human voice in the Jew. Usually we know about each other in clichés, sometimes bad clichés. Therefore, acknowledging one another is of great importance, on several levels. The first is our humanity. We have so much in common—a face, a heart, anguish, seeking, hoping. They are all common to us as human beings; we share the kinship of being human. We also have the image of God in common; man is created in the image of God. "Wherever you see the trace of man, there I stand before you," says God, according to the rabbis. Christians and Jews have that conception of man in common. Regardless of whether I am a believer or I am against religion, I still have the image of God. So, first we meet as human beings, and though we discover that our dogmas differ, does God's presence disappear? Does He not stand in front of me anymore? Also, Christians and Jews believe in the same God, the God of Abraham. We acknowledge the Bible as sacred Scripture, and so many other things. I am convinced that we ought to express our differences, but we must also learn from one another. I usually distinguish between theology and depth-theology, between creed and faith, between the very depth of a person and the way he articulates his faith. On the level of dogma we differ, we say no to one another; but on the level of faith, on the level of depth, we meet. Our creeds are different, but our fear and trembling are the same. So is our sighing, our sin, and our embarrassment. In dogma we are different, but in failure we are the same. Although I respect dogmas, creed, and doctrine, I feel that no doctrine and no dogma ever articulates fully what is ineffable. Differences should be retained; it is my conviction that religious diversity is the will of God. It is certainly not our dream to have one Führer, one view and one theology. I have no information about what will happen at the end of days, but for now we ought to accept our diversity, and at the same time try to learn from one another. There are vast areas where we could cooperate. For instance, is Vietnam a Catholic problem? A Protestant problem? A Jewish problem? It is *our* problem, the whole civilized world's problem.

AS SOON AS the Vatican Council is mentioned, the name of Pope John comes to mind. Pope John was a great miracle. Contrary to all expectations, a Roman pontiff all of a sudden captured the heart of everybody, Christian and non-Christian. How that happened, we don't know. It didn't happen through any philosophy. It happened through the sheer humanity and love of one human being. I don't know of any other human being, except Kennedy perhaps, who has captured the hearts of so many people. But Pope John's appeal was much deeper than Kennedy's. Now, what motivated him? From the conversations I have had with many Catholics involved in the ecumenical movement, I would say that, first of all, it was a sudden realization that no edifice, no religion, magnificent as it may be, can survive without repair from time to time. Just as a human being must repent, so a religious institution must always examine itself and repent if necessary. Only God is perfect. Everything else, when it becomes its own end, runs a risk of being idolatrous; it is under judgment and in need of repentance and self-examination. John understood that, just as others in the ecumenical movement have understood it. Second, John realized that there is always the danger of self-segregation, of not seeing the world, not seeing one's fellow man, of not acknowledging the bonds that come from without, of placing the answer before the question, the cart before the horse. Furthermore, spontaneity, intellectual spontaneity and spontaneity of the conscience, was frequently suppressed by the sheer weight of doctrine and institution. But with John and the Council hearts were opened—not only windows but hearts. Suddenly there was an outpouring of freshness, new devotion, and understanding. This was a great moment in the eyes of non-Catholics—a great phenomenon. And in the ecumenical movement as a whole, there has been, I believe, a discovery of the humanity we share, regardless of our religious affiliation or religious commitment. Above all, I believe that some of those who became involved were inspired by prophetic teaching. The impact of the study of the Hebrew Bible, particularly the prophets, upon some leaders of the ecumenical movement is undeniable. Therefore I would say that that movement is one of the greatest consolations of our time.

WHAT IS NEEDED at this very moment is to mobilize all human beings for one great task, to achieve world peace. As long as we do not make the problem of world peace a matter of absolute priority, I cannot be optimistic. Here is a parable: If my pockets are full of money, and I pass by a store which sells useless things, I will somehow be driven by all the money in my pockets to buy something, however useless. In the same way, we have so many atomic bombs now, do you think that we will not be tempted to use them?

I cannot say that I feel complacent about our chances for peace. Our terrible sin is in not giving peace absolute priority and in failing to realize that to attain peace, we have to make sacrifices. We are ready to make sacrifices for the sake of war, but not, apparently, for the sake of peace.

Let us assume that the religions represent moral powers in the world. They could do something, but they are scarcely on speaking terms. The ecumenical movement has made some progress in human relations, but on the top level I don't see much progress. It is conceivable for states to get together and have a United Nations, but it is still inconceivable to have a United Religions. The question is, Why do we not see the writing on the wall? The situation is very grave, and though many individuals feel it, most of us say, "Business as usual." What we must do is to alarm the world. People become more complacent and more involved in daily affairs, and their sensitivity, as I said before, is decreasing all the time. We continue to be ignorant of one another, of our fellow human beings; we really don't know what is happening in Vietnam, for example. Just recently I spoke to someone who is very important in the press in New York, and he admitted that he himself doesn't know what is going on in Vietnam. But we are apathetic. We bought toys for Christmas, and we celebrated Chanukkah while people were dying, while civilians were being killed. When Rotterdam was being invaded by German planes and civilians were being killed we were capable of a sense of outrage. But now American bombers are killing civilians, and we are getting used to it. We ought to mobilize *all* our forces *everywhere* in the service of trying to find ways to achieve peace. The problems are complex: power is involved, industry is involved, trade is involved. But what about life itself? What about humanity itself? We are doing too little, next to nothing, about peace. We leave it to a few individuals in Washington. Do they have the wisdom? Can I turn over my soul and conscience to them? Peace is our most important challenge and task, from every point of view and for all religions. But we leave it to others. We have delegated our conscience to a few diplomats and generals, and this is a very, very grave sin.

On Prayer

PRIMARILY MY THEME is not liturgy, public worship, public ritual, but rather private worship, prayer as an enterprise of the individual self, as a personal engagement, as an intimate, confidential act.

Public worship is an act of the highest importance. However, it tends in our days to become a spectacle in which the congregation remain passive, inert spectators. But prayer is action; it requires complete mobilization of heart, mind, and soul. What is the worth of attending public worship when mind and soul are not involved? Renewal of liturgy involves renewal of prayer.

There is, in addition, a malady indigenous or congenital to liturgy. Liturgy as an act of prayer is an outcome and distillation of the inner life. Although its purpose is to exalt the life which engenders it, it harbors a tendency to follow a direction and rhythm of its own, independent of and divorced from the energies of life which brought prayer into being. At the beginning, liturgy is intimately related to the life which calls it into being. But as liturgy unfolds, it enters a state of stubborn disconnection, even into a state of opposition. Liturgy is bound to become rigid, to stand by itself, and to take on a measure of imperviousness. It tends to become timeless, transpersonal; liturgy for the sake of liturgy. Personal presence is replaced by mere attendance; instead of erecting a sanctuary of time in the realm of the soul, liturgy attracts masses of people to a sanctuary in the realm of space.

I do not wish to set up a dichotomy of prayer and liturgy. This would contradict the spirit of devotion. I merely wish to concentrate my thoughts on prayer as a personal affair, as an act of supreme importance. I plead for the primacy of prayer in our inner existence. The test of authentic theology is the degree to which it reflects and enhances the power of prayer, the way of worship.

In antiquity as well as in the Middle Ages, due to the scarcity of parchment, people would often write new texts on top of earlier written parchments. The term denoting such writings is "palimpsest." Metaphorically, I suggest that authentic theology is a palimpsest: scholarly, disciplined thinking grafted upon prayer.

Prayer is either exceedingly urgent, exceedingly relevant, or inane and useless. Our first task is to learn to comprehend why prayer is an ontological necessity. God is hiding, and man is defying. Every moment God is creating and self-concealing. Prayer is disclosing or at least preventing irreversible concealing. God is ensconced in mystery, hidden in the depths. Prayer is pleading with God to come out of the depths. "Out of the depths have I called Thee, O Lord" (Psalms 130:1).

We have lost sensitivity to truth and purity of heart in the wasteland of opportunism. It is, however, a loss that rebounds to afflict us with anguish. Such anguish, when converted into prayer, into a prayer for truth, may evoke the dawn of God. Our agony over God's concealment is sharing in redeeming God's agony over man's concealment.

Prayer as an episode, as a cursory incident, will not establish a home in the land of oblivion. Prayer must pervade as a climate of living, and all our acts must be carried out as variations on the theme of prayer. A deed of charity, an act of kindness, a ritual moment—each is prayer in the form of a deed. Such prayer involves a minimum or even absence of outwardness, and an abundance of inwardness.

PRAYER IS NOT a stratagem for occasional use, a refuge to resort to now and then. It is rather like an established residence for the innermost self. All things have a home: the bird has a nest, the fox has a hole, the bee has a hive. A soul without prayer is a soul without a home. Weary, sobbing, the soul, after roaming through a world festered with aimlessness, falsehoods, and absurdities, seeks a moment in which to gather up its scattered life, in which to divest itself of enforced pretensions and camouflage, in which to simplify complexities, in which to call for help without being a coward. Such a home is prayer. Continuity, permanence, intimacy, authenticity, earnestness are its attributes. For the soul, home is where prayer is.

In his cottage, even the poorest man may bid defiance to misery and malice. That cottage may be frail, its roof may shake, the wind may blow through it, the storms may enter it, but there is where the soul expects to be understood. Just as the body, so is the soul in need of a home.

Everybody must build his own home; everybody must guard the independence and the privacy of his prayers. It is the source of security for the integrity of conscience, for whatever inkling we attain of eternity. At home I have a Father who judges and cares, who has regard for me, and, when I fail and go astray, misses me. I will never give up my home.

What is a soul without prayer? A soul runaway or a soul evicted from its own home. To those who have abandoned their home: The road may be hard and dark and far, yet do not be afraid to steer back. If you prize grace and eternal meaning, you will discover them upon arrival.

How marvelous is my home. I enter as a suppliant and emerge as a witness; I enter as a stranger and emerge as next of kin. I may enter spiritually shapeless, inwardly disfigured, and emerge wholly changed. It is in moments of prayer that my image is forged, that my striving is fashioned. To understand the world I must love my home. It is difficult to perceive luminosity anywhere if there is no light in my own home. It is in the light of prayer's radiance that I find my way even in the dark. It is prayer that illumines my way. As my prayers, so is my understanding.

PRAYER SERVES many aims. It serves to save the inward life from oblivion. It serves to alleviate anguish. It serves to partake of God's mysterious grace and guidance. Yet, ultimately, prayer must not be experienced as an act for the sake of something else. We pray in order to pray.

Prayer is a perspective from which to behold, from which to respond to, the challenges we face. Man in prayer does not seek to impose his will upon God; he seeks to impose God's will and mercy upon himself. Prayer is necessary to make us aware of our failures, backsliding, transgressions, sins.

Prayer is more than paying attention to the holy. Prayer comes about as an event. It consists of two inner acts: an act of turning and an act of direction. I leave the world behind as well as all interests of the self. Divested of all concerns, I am overwhelmed by only one desire: to place my heart upon the altar of God.

God is beyond the reach of finite notions, diametrically opposed to our power of comprehension. In theory He seems to be neither here nor now. He is so far away, an outcast, a refugee in His own world. It is as if all doors were closed to Him. To pray is to open a door, where both God and soul may enter. Prayer is arrival, for Him and for us. To pray is to overcome distance, to shatter screens, to render obliquities straight, to heal the break between God and the world. A dreadful oblivion prevails in the world. The world has forgotten what it means to be human. The gap is widening, the abyss is within the self.

Though often I do not know how to pray, I can still say: Redeem me from the agony of not knowing what to strive for, from the agony of not knowing how my inner life is falling apart.

A candle of the Lord is the soul of man, but the soul can become a holocaust, a fury, a rage. The only cure is to discover that over and above the anonymous stillness in the world there is a name and a waiting.

Many young people suffer from a fear of the self. They do not feel at home in their own selves. The inner life is a place of dereliction, a no-man's-land, inconsolate, weird. The self has become a place from which to flee. The use of narcotic drugs is a search for a home.

Human distress—wretchedness, agony—is a signal of a universal distress. It is a sign of human misery; it also proclaims a divine predicament. God's mercy is too great to permit the innocent to suffer. But there are forces that interfere with God's mercy, with God's power. This is a dreadful mystery as well as a challenge: God is held in captivity.

I pray because God, the *Shekinah*, is an outcast. I pray because God is in exile, because we all conspire to blur all signs of His presence in the present or in the past. I pray because I refuse to despair, because extreme denials and defiance are refuted in the confrontation of my own presumption and the mystery all around me. *I pray because I am unable to pray.*

And suddenly I am forced to do what I seem unable to do. Even callousness to the mystery is not immortal. There are moments when the clamor of all sirens dies, presumption is depleted, and even the bricks in the walls are waiting for a song. The door is closed, the key is lost. Yet the new sadness of my soul is about to open the door.

Some souls are born with a scar, others are endowed with anesthesia. Satisfaction with the world is base and the ultimate callousness. The remedy for absurdity is still to be revealed. The irreconcilable opposites which agonize human existence are the outcry, the prayer. Every one of us is a cantor; every one of us is called to intone a song, to put into prayer the anguish of all.

God is in captivity in this world, in the oblivion of our lives. God is in search of man, in search of a home in the soul and deeds of man. God is not at home in our world. Our task is to hallow time, to enable Him to enter our moments, to be at home in our time, in what we do with time.

Ultimately, prayer in Judaism is an act in the messianic drama. We utter the words of the *Kaddish: Magnified and sanctified be His great name in the world which He has created according to His will.* Our hope is to enact, to make real the magnification and sanctification of this name here and now.

A great mystery has become a reality in our own days, as God's response to a people's prayer. After nearly two thousand years, the city of David, the city of Jerusalem, is now restored to the people of Israel. This marvelous event proclaims a call for the renewal of worship, for the revival of prayer. We did not enter the city of Jerusalem on our own in 1967.

Streams of endless craving, endless praying, clinging, dreaming, day and night, midnights, years, decades, centuries, millennia, streams of tears, pledging, waiting—from all over the world, from all corners of the earth, carried us of this generation to the Wall, to the city of Jerusalem.

PRAYER MUST NOT be dissonant with the rest of living. The mercifulness, gentleness, which pervades us in moments of prayer is but a ruse or a bluff if it is inconsistent with the way we live at other moments. The divorce of liturgy and living, of prayer and practice, is more than a scandal; it is a disaster. A word uttered in prayer is a promise, an earnest, a commitment. If the promise is not kept, we are guilty of violating a promise. A liturgical revival cannot come about in isolation. Worship is the quintessence of living. Perversion or suppression of the sensibilities that constitute being human will convert worship into a farce. What is handicapping prayer is not the antiquity of the Psalms but our own crudity and spiritual immaturity.

The hour calls for a revision of fundamental religious concerns. The wall of separation between the sacred and the secular has become a wall of separation between the conscience and God. In the Pentateuch, the relation of man to things of space, to money, to property is a fundamental religious problem. In the affluent society sins committed with money may be as grievous as sins committed with our tongue. We will give account for what we have done, for what we have failed to do.

Religion as an establishment must remain separated from the government. Yet prayer as a voice of mercy, as a cry for justice, as a plea for gentleness, must not be kept apart. Let the spirit of prayer dominate the world. Let the spirit of prayer interfere in the affairs of man. Prayer is private, a service of the heart; but let concern and compassion, born out of prayer, dominate public life.

Prayer is a confrontation with Him who demands justice and compassion, with Him who despises flattery and abhors iniquity. Prayer calls for self-reflection, for contrition and repentance, examining and readjusting deeds and motivations, for recanting the ugly compulsions we follow, the tyranny of acquisitiveness, hatred, envy, resentment. We face not only things—continents, oceans, planets. We also face a claim, an expectation.

God reaches us as a claim. Religious responsibility is responsiveness to the claim. He brought us into being; He brought us out of slavery. And He demands.

Heaven and earth were known to all men. Israel was given a third reality, the reality of the claim of the word of God. The task of the Jew is a life in which the word becomes deed. A sacred deed is where heaven and earth meet.

We have no triumphs to report except the slow, painstaking effort to redeem single moments in the lives of single men, in the lives of small communities. We do not come on the clouds of heaven but grope through the mists of history.

There is a pressing urgency to the work of justice and compassion. As long as there is a shred of hatred in a human heart, as long as there is a vacuum without compassion anywhere in the world, there is an emergency.

Why do people rage? People rage and hurt and do not know how to regret, how to repent. The problem is not that people have doubts but rather that people may not even care to doubt. The charity we may do is terribly diminutive compared with what is required. You and I have prayed, have craved to be able to make gentleness a certainty, and have so often failed. But there are in the world so many eyes streaming with tears, hearts dumb with fears, that to be discouraged would be treason.

THE PREDICAMENT of prayer is twofold: Not only do we not know how to pray; we do not know what to pray for.

We have lost the ability to be shocked.

The malignity of our situation is increasing rapidly, the magnitude of evil is spreading furiously, surpassing our ability to be shocked. The human soul is too limited to experience dismay in proportion to what has happened in Auschwitz, in Hiroshima.

We do not know what to pray for. Should we not pray for the ability to be shocked at atrocities committed by man, for the capacity to be dismayed at our inability to be dismayed?

Prayer should be an act of catharsis, of purgation of emotions, as well as a process of self-clarification, of examining priorities, of elucidating responsibility. Prayer not verified by conduct is an act of desecration and blasphemy. Do not take a word of prayer in vain. Our deeds must not be a refutation of our prayers.

It is with shame and anguish that I recall that it was possible for a Roman Catholic church adjoining the extermination camp in Auschwitz to offer communion to the officers of the camp, to people who day after day drove thousands of people to be killed in the gas chambers.

Let there be an end to the separation of church and God, of sacrament and callousness, of religion and justice, of prayer and compassion.

A home is more than an exclusive habitat, mine and never yours. A residence devoid of hospitality is a den or a hole, not a home. Prayer must never be a citadel for selfish concerns but rather a place for deepening concern over other people's plight. Prayer is a privilege. Unless we learn how to be worthy, we forfeit the right and ability to pray.

Prayer is meaningless unless it is subversive, unless it seeks to overthrow and to ruin the pyramids of callousness, hatred, opportunism, falsehoods.

The liturgical movement must become a revolutionary movement, seeking to overthrow the forces that continue to destroy the promise, the hope, the vision.

The world is aflame with evil and atrocity; the scandal of perpetual desecration of the world cries to high heaven. And we, coming face to face with it, are either involved as callous participants or, at best, remain indifferent onlookers. The relentless pursuit of our interests makes us oblivious of reality itself. Nothing we experience has value in itself; nothing counts unless it can be turned to our advantage, into a means for serving our self-interests.

We pray because the disproportion of human misery and human compassion is so enormous. We pray because our grasp of the depth of suffering is comparable to the scope of perception of a butterfly flying over the Grand Canyon. We pray because of the experience of the dreadful incompatibility of how we live and what we sense.

Dark is the world to me, for all its cities and stars. If not for my faith that God in His silence still listens to a cry, who could stand such agony?

Prayer will not come about by default. It requires education, training, reflection, contemplation. It is not enough to join others; it is necessary to build a sanctuary within, brick by brick, instants of meditation, moments of devotion. This is particularly true in an age when overwhelming forces seem to conspire at destroying our ability to pray.

THE BEGINNING of prayer is praise. The power of worship is song. First we sing, then we understand. First we praise, then we believe. Praise and song open eyes to the grandeur of reality that transcends the self. Song restores the soul; praise repairs spiritual deficiency.

To praise is to make Him present to our minds, to our hearts, to vivify the understanding that beyond all questions, protests, and pain at God's dreadful silence is His mercy and humility. We are stunned when we try to think of His essence; we are exalted when intuiting His presence.

While it is true that being human is verified in relations between man and man, depth and authenticity of existence are disclosed in moments of worship.

Worship is more than paying homage. To worship is to join the cosmos in praising God. The whole cosmos, every living being sings, the psalmists insist. Neither joy nor sorrow but song is the ground plan of being. It is the quintessence of life. To praise is to call forth the promise and presence of the divine. We live for the sake of a song. We praise for the privilege of being. Worship is the climax of living. There is no knowledge without love, no truth without praise. At the beginning was the song, and praise is man's response to the never-ending beginning.

The alternative to praise is disenchantment, dismay.

Society today is no longer in revolt against particular laws which it finds alien, unjust, and imposed, but against law as such, against the principle of law. And yet we must not regard this revolt as entirely negative. The energy that rejects many obsolete laws is an entirely positive impulse for renewal of life and law.

"Choose life!" is the great legacy of the Hebrew Bible, and the cult of life is affirmed in contemporary theology. However, life is not a thing, static and final. Life means living, and in living you have to choose a road, direction, goals. Pragmatists who believe that life itself can provide us with the criteria for truth overlook the fact that forces of suicide and destruction are also inherent in life.

The essence of living as a human being is being challenged, being tempted, being called. We pray for wisdom, for laws of knowing how to respond to our being challenged. Living is not enough by itself. Just to be is a blessing. Just to live is holy. And yet being alive is no answer to the problems of living. To be or not to be is *not* the question. The vital question is: how to be and how not to be?

The tendency to forget this vital question is the tragic disease of contemporary man, a disease that may prove fatal, that may end in disaster. To pray is to recollect *passionately* the perpetual urgency of this vital question.

ONE OF THE results of the rapid depersonalization of our age is a crisis of speech, profanation of language. We have trifled with the name of God, we have taken the name and the word of the Holy in vain. Language has been reduced to labels, talk has become double-talk. We are in the process of losing faith in the reality of words.

Yet prayer can happen only when words reverberate with power and inner life, when uttered as an earnest, as a promise. On the other hand, there is a high degree of obsolescence in the traditional language of the theology of prayer. Renewal of prayer calls for renewal of language, of cleansing the words, of revival of meanings.

The strength of faith is in silence, and in words that hibernate and wait. Uttered faith must come out as surplus of silence, as the fruit of lived faith, of enduring intimacy.

Theological education must deepen privacy, strive for daily renewal of innerness, cultivate ingredients of religious existence, *reverence* and *responsibility*.

We live in an age of self-dissipation, of depersonalization. Should we adjust our vision of existence to our paucity, make a virtue of obtuseness, glorify evasion?

My own sense of the reality of food depends upon my being hungry, upon my own craving for food. Had I grown up on intravenous food injections, apples and beans would be as relevant to me as pebbles and garbage.

Do we know how to thirst for God? Do we know what it means to starve?

O God, thou art my God, I seek Thee,
*   my soul thirsts for Thee;*
*   my flesh faints for Thee,*
*   as in a dry and weary land where no water is.*
So I have looked upon Thee in the sanctuary,
*   beholding Thy power and glory.*
Because Thy steadfast love is better than life,
*   my lips will praise Thee.*
So I will bless Thee as long as I live;
*   I will lift up my hands and call on Thy name.*

—Psalms 63:2–4

As a hart longs for flowing streams,
*   so longs my soul for Thee, O God.*
My soul thirsts for God,
*   for the living God.*
When shall I come and behold the face of God?
My tears have been my food day and night,
*   while men say to me continually,*
*   "Where is your God?"*

—Psalms 42:2–4

Religion is critique of all satisfaction. Its end is joy, but its beginning is discontent, detesting boasts, smashing idols. It began in Ur Kasdim, in the seat of a magnificent civilization. Yet Abraham said, "No," breaking the idols, breaking away. And so every one of us must begin saying no to all visible, definable entities pretending to be triumphant, ultimate. The ultimate is a challenge, not an assertion. Dogmas are allusions, not descriptions.

Standing before Mt. Sinai, Israel was told: "Take heed that you do not go up to the mountain and touch the border of it." Take heed that you do not go up to the mountain and only touch the border. Go to the peak! Once you start going, proceed to the very end. Don't stop in the middle of the road.

This is the predicament of man. All souls descend a ladder from heaven to this world. Then the ladders are taken away. Once they are in this world, they are called upon from heaven to rise, to come back. It is a call that goes out again and again. Each soul seeks the ladder in order to ascend above; but the ladder cannot be found. Most people make no effort to ascend, claiming, How can one rise to heaven without a ladder? However, there are souls which resolve to leap upwards, without a ladder. So they jump and fall down. They jump and fall down, until they stop.

Wise people think that since no ladder exists, there must be another way. We must face the challenge and act. Be what it may, one must leap until God, in His mercy, makes exultation come about.

What do we claim? That religious commitment is not just an ingredient of the social order, an adjunct or reinforcement of existence, but rather the heart and core of being human; its exaltation, its verification being manifest in the social order, in daily deeds.

We begin with a sense of wonder and arrive at radical amazement. The first response is reverence and awe, openness to the mystery that surrounds us. We are led to be overwhelmed by the awareness of eternity in daily living.

Religious existence is living in solidarity with God. Yet to maintain such solidarity involves knowing how to rise, how to cross an abyss. Vested interests are more numerous than locusts, and of solidarity of character there is only a smattering. Too much devotion is really too little. It is grave self-deception to assume that our destiny is just to be human. In order to be human, one must be more than human. A person must never stand still. He must always rise, he must always climb. Be stronger than you are.

Well-trodden ways lead into swamps. There are no easy ways, there are no simple solutions. What comes easy is not worth a straw. It is a tragic error to assume that the world is flat, that our direction is horizontal. The way is always vertical. It is either up or down; we either climb or fall. Religious existence means struggle uphill.

LIFE IS A DRAMA, and religion has become routine. The soul calls for exaltation, and religion offers repetition. Honesty, veracity, does not come about by itself. Freshness, depth have to be acquired. One must work on them constantly.

To be moderate in the face of God would be a profanation. The goal is not an accommodation but a transformation. A mediocre response to immensity, to eternity, is offensive.

The tragedy of our time is that we have moved out of the dimension of the holy, that we have abandoned the intimacy in which relationship to God can be patiently, honestly, persistently nourished. Intimate inner life is forsaken. Yet the soul can never remain a vacuum. It is either a vessel for grace or it is occupied by demons.

At first men sought mutual understanding by taking counsel with one another, but now we understand one another less and less. There is a gap between the generations. It will soon widen to be an abyss. The only bridge is to pray together, to consult God before seeking counsel with one another. Prayer brings down the walls which we have erected between man and man, between man and God.

For centuries Jerusalem lay in ruins; of the ancient glory of King David and Solomon only a wall remained, a stone wall left standing after the Temple was destroyed by the Romans. For centuries Jews would go on a pilgrimage to Jerusalem in order to pour out their hearts at the Wailing Wall.

A wall stands between man and God, and at the wall we must pray, searching for a cleft, for a crevice, through which our words can enter and reach God behind the wall. In prayer we must often knock our heads against the stone wall. But God's silence does not go on forever. While man is busy setting up screens, thickening the wall, prayer may also succeed in penetrating the wall.

The tragedy is that many of us do not even know how to find the way leading to the wall. We of this generation are afflicted with a severe case of dulling or loss of vision. Is it the result of our own intoxication, or is it the result of God's deliberate concealment of visible lights?

The spiritual memory of many people is empty, words are diluted, incentives are drained, inspiration is exhausted. Is God to be blamed for all this? Is it not man who has driven Him out of our hearts and minds? Has not our system of religious education been an abysmal failure?

The spiritual blackout is increasing daily. Opportunism prevails, callousness expands, the sense of the holy is melting away. We no longer know how to resist the vulgar, how to say no in the name of a higher yes. Our roots are in a state of decay. We have lost the sense of the holy.

This is an age of spiritual blackout, a blackout of God. We have entered not only the dark night of the soul, but also the dark night of society. We must seek out ways of preserving the strong and deep truth of a living God theology in the midst of the blackout.

For the darkness is neither final nor complete. Our power is first in waiting for the end of darkness, for the defeat of evil; and our power is also in coming upon single sparks and occasional rays, upon moments full of God's grace and radiance.

We are called to bring together the sparks to preserve single moments of radiance and keep them alive in our lives, to defy absurdity and despair, and to wait for God to say again: Let there be light.

And there will be light.

The God of Israel

and Christian Renewal

THE TITLE OF MY LECTURE as proposed in the original invitation read like this: "The God of Israel and Christian Renewal." On reading these words, I first recoiled. Who am I to speak with such a voice? Upon second thought, I realized that to decline such an invitation would be an act of irreverence. Is it not a moment of blessing that this congress of illustrious Catholic theologians is willing to submit the great movement of Christian renewal to a confrontation with Jewish understanding of the meaning of the God of Israel?

On the way to the printer, the power of the title was emasculated. The magnificent biblical saying "the God of Israel" was replaced by a scholastic mis-saying, "the Jewish notion of God." Realism was replaced by notionalism. Biblical words were pushed out by the jargon of manuals.

"The God of Israel" is a *name*, not a notion, and the difference between the two is perhaps the difference between Jerusalem and Athens. A notion applies to all objects of similar properties; a name applies to an individual. The name "God of Israel" applies to the one and only God of all men. A notion describes; a name evokes. A notion is attained through generalization; a name is learned through acquaintance. A notion is conceived; a name is called. Indeed, the terms "notion" and "the God of Israel" are profoundly incompatible. All notions crumble when applied to Him. A more appropriate title might be: "The Jewish Experience of the Collapse of All Notions in Relation to God." The God of Israel is a "devouring fire" (Deuteronomy 4:24), not an object of abstraction or generalization.

To be sure, we are given certain ways of understanding God, ways that point to Him, that lead to Him. "Hear, O Israel, the Lord is our God, the Lord is One" (Deuteronomy 6:4). "The Lord, the Lord, a God merciful and gracious, slow to anger and abounding in love and faithfulness"

(Exodus 34:6). Yet the adequacy of our understanding these ways depends upon our sensitivity to its inadequacy.

A notion is definitive, finished, final, while understanding is an act, the intention of which is to receive, register, record, reflect, and reiterate; an act that goes on forever. Having a notion of friendship is not the same as having a friend or living with a friend, and the story of a friendship cannot be fully told by what one friend thinks of the being and attributes of the other friend. The process of forming an idea is one of generalization and abstraction. Yet such a process implies a split between situation and idea, a disregard for the fullness of what transpires, and the danger of regarding the part as the whole. An idea or a theory of God can easily become a substitute for God, impressive to the mind when God as a living reality is absent from the soul.

The prophets of Israel had no theory or "notion" of God. What they had was an *understanding*. Their God-understanding was not the result of a theoretical inquiry, of a groping in the midst of alternatives. To the prophets, God was overwhelmingly real and shatteringly present. They never spoke of Him from a distance. They lived as witnesses, struck by the words of God, rather than as explorers engaged in an effort to ascertain the nature of God; their utterances were the unloading of a burden rather than glimpses obtained in the fog of groping. To them, the attributes of God were drives, challenges, commandments, rather than timeless notions detached from His Being. They did not offer an exposition of the nature of God, but rather an exposition of God's insight into man and His concern for man. They disclosed attitudes *of* God rather than notions *about* God.

I am not going to speak about notions. To quote from Isaiah: "You are my witnesses, says the Lord, I am the Lord" (43:10–11).

There are no proofs for the existence of the God of Israel. There are only witnesses. You can think of Him only by seeking to be present to Him. You cannot define Him, you can only invoke Him. He is not a notion but a name.

Now there are voices in our own days, all over the country, suggesting that we eliminate and get rid of the traditional name God to refer to the ultimate Presence. After all, who needs that word, that name? This is being done for the telephone exchanges in the United States: to get rid of names! So let us abolish names altogether. Let us call every human being by a number, and worship zero.

You know what goes on in our days about words. Certain chapters from certain books are considered obsolete because the words are not understandable anymore. For example, "The Lord is my shepherd; I shall not want." An impossible verse; who has seen a shepherd? Children grow up without ever having heard of a shepherd. I therefore offer an emendation and suggest that we read: "The Lord is my plumber, I shall not want." In the same spirit, artificial fertilization may substitute the test tube for the mother. There will be no mothers. All men will be organization members.

The supreme issue is not the question whether in the infinite darkness there is a ground of being which is an object of man's ultimate concern but whether the reality of God confronts us with a pathos—God's ultimate concern with good and evil; whether God is mysteriously present in the events of history; whether being is transcended by creation; whether creation is transcended by care; whether my life is dependent on God's care; whether in the course of my life I come upon a trace of His guidance.

God is either of no importance or of supreme importance. God is He whose regard for me is more precious than life. Otherwise, He is not God. God is the meaning beyond the mystery.

How can I speak of a notion? To speak adequately about God one would have to sense all the horrors and all the joys of all creatures since the beginning of time, and to intuit how God is relevant to all this.

The ambiguities are numerous and drive us to despair—almost. Yet the God of Israel does not leave us to ourselves. Even when He throws us into darkness, we know that it is *His* darkness, that we have been cast into it by *Him*. Thus we do not pretend to know His secrets or to understand His ways. Yet we are certain of knowing His name, of living by His love and receiving His grace, as we are certain of receiving His blows and dying according to His will. Such is our loyalty, a loyalty that lives as a surprise in a world of staggering vapidity, in an hour of triumphant disloyalty.

The Covenant is a holy dimension of existence. Faith is the consciousness of living in that dimension, rather than an assent to propositions. Important as is the intellectual crystallization of faith in terms of creed, what characterizes Judaism, I believe, is the primacy of faith over creed.

Faith is both certainty and trial: certainty in spite of perplexities, a trial demanding sacrifice, strain, wrestling. For certainty without trial becomes complacency, lethargy, while trial without certainty is chaos, presumption, as if God had never reached us, as if history were always a monologue. Faith is a mode of being alive to the meaning beyond the mystery, commitment of total existence, and the dynamics of faith is the ongoing shaping and modification of one's existence. Faith also involves fear: fear lest He discard us, lest He forsake us. Then we must learn how to despise the convenience of belief. We have again and again experienced His wrath. "Thou hast made us like sheep for slaughter . . ." (Psalms 44:12–13).

We remain faithful in spite of the demonic darkness that often engulfs us, in spite of the vapidity of the holy that often affects us. God is one, but man is torn to pieces by temptation and ambiguity. We are both haunted and exalted by the words of Job: "Though He slay me yet will I trust in Him" (Job 13:15).

Faith is a high ladder and at times all the rungs seem to have been taken away. Can we replace the rungs? Can we recover the will to rise? And if the rungs cannot be replaced, shall we learn how to reach the truth at the top of the ladder?

Let me illustrate. In 1492, the Jews of Spain were given the choice: to be converted or to be expelled. The overwhelming majority left their homeland. Ships overcrowded with fugitives found difficulty landing, because disease had broken out among them on board ship. One of the boats was infested with the plague, and the captain of the boat put the passengers ashore at some uninhabited place. There most of them died of starvation, while some of them gathered up all their strength and set out on foot in search of some settlement. There was one Jew among them who struggled on foot together with his wife and two sons. The wife grew faint and died, not being accustomed to so much difficult walking. The husband picked up his children and carried them in his arms until he and they fainted from hunger. When he regained consciousness, he found that his sons had died also. In great grief he rose to his feet, raised his eyes to the heavens, and cried out: "Lord of the universe, much have you done to make me desert my faith. But know this of a certainty, that a Jew I am and a Jew I shall remain! And nothing which you have brought upon me, or are likely to bring upon me, will be of any avail!"

THE MEANING of the saying "the God of Israel" differs essentially from a phrase such as "the God of Aristotle" or "the God of Kant." It does not mean a doctrine of God conceived of or taught by Israel. It means God with whom Israel is vitally, intimately involved, an involvement transcending the realm of thinking, not reducible to human consistency, and one which does not simplify itself in order to accommodate common sense.

Furthermore, the saying "God of Israel" has no possessive or exclusive connotation: God belonging to Israel alone. Its true meaning is that the God of all men has entered a Covenant with one people for the sake of all people. It is furthermore clear that "Israel" in this saying does not mean the Israel of the past, a people living in ancient Palestine which has long ceased to exist. Israel is a people in whom the past endures in the present tense. The Exodus occurs now. We are still on the way, and cannot accept any event as a final event. We are God's stake in human history, regardless of merit and often against our will.

Israel is a people that shares the name of God. Of the two words in Hebrew for the Jews, "Israel" and "Yehudi," the "*el*" in Israel means "God," whereas the Hebrew word for "Jew," "*Yehud*," has the three letters that combine to make up the four in the ineffable name. It is a people that can endure only in a world in which the name of God is revered. The disappearance of God would mean the disappearance of the Jew. But we know of God's commitment and of His faithfulness.

THE TERM "renewal" has many meanings, but I shall suggest only briefly that what is taking place in the movement of Christian renewal is certainly a shift from evasion to confrontation, a willingness to recognize the validity of principles long disparaged or disregarded, which it is unnecessary to enumerate here.

It is clear, however, that renewal is not an act carried out once and for all, but rather a constant happening, *semper a novo incipere*. It is furthermore a process, not only in relation to others, but above all one that affects the inner life and substance of the Christian.

I believe that one of the achievements of this age will be the realization that in our age religious pluralism is the will of God, that the relationship between Judaism and Christianity will be one of mutual reverence, that without denying profound divergencies, Jew and Christian will seek to help each other in understanding each one's respective commitment and in deepening appreciation of what God means. And I should like to make some suggestions in the hope they will be taken in the right spirit. Although I may be critical, I shall be offering the critique of a friend.

My own suggestion, first, is that Christian renewal should imply confrontation with Judaism out of which it emerged. Separated from its source, Christianity is easily exposed to principles alien to its spirit. The vital challenge for the Church is to decide whether Christianity came to overcome, to abolish, or to continue the Jewish way by bringing the God of Abraham and His will to the Gentiles.

Now, in a real sense, I believe there is a battle going on in this twentieth century which centers around the Hebrew Bible. The prohibition and suppression of the Hebrew Bible in Soviet Russia is symbolic of that battle.

There is an old challenge to the Christian Church going back to Marcion, a challenge that has never died out. The recurrent tendency to bring about a disengagement of the New Testament from the context of Judaism in which it came into being is evidence of what may be an unresolved tension. Marcion's spirit resounds in words recently uttered by a distinguished Catholic writer, that "it would be inexact . . . to suppose that the Christian *Theos* is the same" as the God of the Old Testament.[1] Marcion's criticism of the Old Testament or the Hebrew Bible proceeded from his conviction that the Gospel was something absolutely and utterly new. However, the Catholic Church of the second century appreciated the heritage, and rejected the one-sidedness of Marcion's doctrines.

Although I do not presume to judge matters of Christian doctrine, it seems utterly strange to assert that the community of Israel, "the Synagogue," did not have the capacity to determine the canonicity of Holy Scripture. If this were the case, there could not have been any legitimacy in the scriptural text which the New Testament, and Jesus as depicted in it, quoted to authenticate their claims. Without the existence of a scriptural canon which is presupposed by the New Testament, the arguments of Jesus would be bereft of their foundation. And to turn a disagreement about the identity of this "Anointed" to an act of apostasy from God Himself seems to me neither logical nor charitable.

I would go beyond that and make a suggestion that what I believe the hour calls for is a renewal of understanding, renewed acknowledgment of the primacy of the Hebrew Bible. It was the Torah and the prophets that Jesus himself expounded, preached about. It was the Torah and the prophets that he revered as sacred Scripture, and it is in the words of the psalmist that Christians pray. To be sure, according to conciliar doctrine, equal reverence is required for all books, both of the Hebrew Bible and of the New Testament. And still, what lingers on in theology is the assumption that the worth of the Hebrew Bible is in its being a preparation, a prehistory, not in its own grandeur.

Let me mention an example. At Vatican Council II each morning after Mass an ancient copy of the Gospel was carried down the nave of St. Peter's Church and deposited on a golden throne on the altar. It was the Gospel only and no other book.[2]

According to Karl Rahner, "Ultimately God effected the production of the Old Testament books to the extent that they were to have a certain function and authority in regard to the New Testament,"[*] not in their own majesty and preciousness, but only to the degree to which they plan a role in the New Testament. Now this statement reminds me of the proof of Divine Providence that was offered in the seventeenth century by an Anglican bishop. He said, "You see, you can see Divine Providence in the fact that wherever there is a city, Providence supplied a river . . ." I

---

[*] *Inquiries* (New York, 1964), p. 56. Equally astonishing is Rahner's statement: "Now the Synagogue, unlike the Church, does not have the authority to testify infallibly to the inspiration of the Scriptures. Even prior to the death of Christ, there existed no authoritative teaching *office* in the Old Testament, in the sense of a permanent institution formally endowed with inerrancy. There were individual prophets, but no infallible Church, for the eschatological event, the final and irreversible salvation act of God, had not yet occurred. It was possible for the Synagogue to apostatize from God, to turn a "No" to him and to his "Anointed" into its own official "truth," thus bringing about its own end as a divine institution" (*ibid.*, p. 54).

think this is a perspective that makes the infinite power of the Hebrew Bible conform to a rather narrow ecclesiastic principle.

Why is the Hebrew Bible indispensable to our existence? It is because the Bible urges us to ask and to listen: What does God require of me? And if there is any validity to my claim to be human, it is the fact that I am aware of this problem: What does God require of me? It is through the Bible that I learn how to say "Here I am!"

The place and power of the Hebrew Bible is so important because all subsequent manifestations and doctrines, whether in Judaism or Christianity, derive their truth from it and, unless they are continually judged and purified by it, tend to obscure and distort the living relationship of God to the world.

Now, the Bible is absent from contemporary thinking. It is quoted for edification, as a pretext for a sermon. It does not live as a power judging our lives. The Bible is respected as a source of dogma, not as living history. The Psalms are read, but the prophets are not. They are revered as forerunners, not as guides and teachers.

The Bible is ongoing disclosure. Yet the word will not speak in a vacuum. It is a sledgehammer to the prophet, when he knows how to be an anvil. The words speak. The words are not signs, but outcries. The words stand for Him, they extend from Him, pleading unceasingly. The words are gates disclosing possibilities, possibilities of engagement to Him and the staccato of His presence and His concealments.

An important root of contemporary nihilism is the age-old resistance to the Hebrew view of the world and of man. The Hebrew Bible has destroyed an illusion, the illusion that one can be an innocent bystander or spectator in this world. It is not enough to be a consumer in order to be a believer. The Bible has destroyed the ancient tradition in which the relation to the gods came with ease, in which gods accommodated themselves to our notions and standards, in which religion was above all a *guarantee*.

God is Judge and Creator, and not only Revealer and Redeemer. Detached from the Hebrew Bible, people began to cherish one perspective of the meaning of God, preferably His promise as Redeemer, and become oblivious to His demanding presence as Judge, to His sublime transcendence as Creator. The insistence upon His love without realizing His wrath, the teaching of His immanence without stressing His transcendence, the certainty of His miracles without an awareness of the infinite darkness of His absence—these are dangerous distortions. To believe too much is more perilous than to believe too little.

With your permission, I should like to say that it is difficult for a Jew to understand when Christians worship Jesus as the Lord, and this Lordship takes the place of the Lordship of God the Creator. It is difficult for a Jew to understand when theology becomes reduced to Christology. It is significant that quite a number of theologians today consider it possible to say, "We can do without God and hold to Jesus of Nazareth."[3]

THE OVERRIDING issue of this hour in the world and Western civilization is the *humanity of man*. Man is losing his true image and shaping his life in the image of anti-man. Is there anything in the human situation today that makes reverence and responsibility a vital necessity? Is being human a supreme purpose? Does not man cease to be human if reverence and responsibility are gone?

The task of Christian renewal, I should like to hope, is above all the renewal of man, and the renewal of man is the *renewal of reverence*. How shall we prevent and heal man's discarding the power of freedom, his massive disposal of his power to decide? How shall we teach him to be involved in living engagement with the challenge and mystery of what being alive demands of him? The task is to deliver the mind from the illusion that availability and transparency are the exclusive attributes of being. False lucidity misguides us more than plain obscurity.

THE RENEWAL of man involves a renewal of language. To the man of our age, nothing is as familiar and trite as words. Of all things they are the cheapest, most abused, and least esteemed. They are the objects of perpetual defilement. We all live in them, feel in them, think in them, but since we fail to uphold their independent dignity, they turn waif, elusive—a mouthful of dust. When placed before the Bible, the words of which are like dwellings made of rock, we do not know how to find the door. There is no understanding the God of Israel without deep sensitivity to the holiness in words. For what is the Bible? Holiness in words. And we destroy all the gates of the Bible by the ongoing desecration of the power of the word. The effect, I believe, is that we are all engaged, all involved, in the process of liquidating the English language. Promiscuity of expression, loss of sensitivity to words, has nearly destroyed the fortress of the spirit. And the fortress of the spirit is the *dabar*, the word. Words have become slums. What we need is a renewal of words.

The hour calls for the *renewal of the antecedents of faith*. The task is pre-theological. Revival and cultivation of basic antecedents of faith will help us to rediscover the image of man.

The renewal of man involves renewal of the sense of wonder and mystery of being alive, taking notice of the moment as a surprise. The renewal of man must begin with rebellion against reducing existence to mere fact or function. Why do I speak about the renewal of man? Because the Hebrew

Bible is not a book about God. It is a book about man. Paradoxical as the Bible is, we must accept its essential premise: that God is concerned about man. If God had asked me for advice, I would have told him right after the first experience with Adam and Eve, "Don't bother with that species." But He goes on patiently, waiting for man. I say we need a revival of the premises and antecedents of faith because it is useless to offer conclusions of faith to those who do not possess the prerequisites of faith. It is useless to speak of the holy to those who have failed to cultivate the ingredients of being human.

Prior to theology is depth theology; prior to faith are premises or pre-requisites of faith, such as a sense of wonder, radical amazement, reverence, a sense of mystery of all being. Man must learn, for example, to question his false sense of sovereignty.

The biblical message remains unacceptable unless seen in the context of essential attitudes and sensibilities. The tendency to rely completely, in our religious thinking, upon the so-called contemporary experience must be questioned. Contemporary experience is stunted experience, it is largely devoid of the higher qualities of experience.

Human beings have never been so bewildered about issues that challenge them most deeply. The famous dictum of Dietrich Bonhoeffer "that a world that has come of age . . . could live without the tutelage" of God presupposes a view of our world which is, I believe, naïve. Can you regard a world of Auschwitz and Hiroshima, of Vietnam and intercontinental ballistic missiles, as a world that has come of age?

The most radical question we face does not really concern God but man—has not man proved to be incompatible or incongruous with the civilization that has emerged? Contemporary consciousness has not come to terms with its own experience. Overwhelmed by the rapid advancement in technology, it has failed to develop an adequate anthropology, a way of ensuring the independence of the human being in the face of forces hostile to it.

The level of experience is wide but shallow. Man is gradually losing his ability to be in charge of his own life. He is beginning to regard himself not only as a self-contradiction but as an impossibility. To what degree is the predicament of man of this civilization, which is shaped by Judaism and Christianity, due to the failure of the Jewish and the Christian faiths? Too many events happening too rapidly bombard our consciousness too frequently for us to be able to ponder their significance. Contemporary experience is lacking in adequate corresponding reflection. In facing the tension between faith and the everyday world, we must not forget that our everyday experience is a problem rather than a norm. It is not assumed that we must renounce technology but rather that we must ask whether man's image can be derived from technology.

I mention all this because, where ancient religions were concerned with a single aspect or some aspects of the human, the Hebrew Bible is concerned with all of human existence. In a sense, there is no preoccupation with the "religious" in the Bible; in the Bible what counts is the secular.

I SHOULD LIKE here to touch briefly on a few other subjects I believe are of concern to us here. Men of faith frequently succumb to a spectacular temptation: to personalize faith, to localize the holy, to isolate commitment. Detached from and irrelevant to all emergencies of being, the holy may segregate the divine.

Is the world of faith a realm of its own, an oasis of peace in the wilderness of the world? Is its task accomplished in being concerned for the holy, in offering spiritual comfort, while remaining aloof from the material and secular issues of this world?

In Israel there are two orientations, I believe, two directions of living for the sake of God, exemplified by the prophet and by the psalmist. I would suggest, therefore, that the right goal would be to bring about some kind of balance or polarity—the proper polarity of the sacramental and the prophetic.

The psalmist is mostly guided by personal impulse. His own life, his concern for his spiritual situation, form the background of his experiences. His attainments, his insights, and his purification constitute self-enhancement of significance to his existence as an individual. He exemplifies the individual's secret love affair with God.

The prophet's existence, by contrast, involves public affairs. Its content, aim, and events have an eminently super-personal character. Prophecy is not a private affair of the experiencer. The prophet is not concerned with his own salvation. His aim is not personal illumination but the illumination of the people; not spiritual self-enhancement but leading the people to the service of God. The prophet is nothing without his people. The prophet is a person who holds God and man in one thought at one time—and at all times.

When the people Israel arrived at the wilderness of Sinai, the Lord called to them out of the mountain, saying: "You shall be to me a kingdom of priests and a holy nation" (Exodus 19:6). A whole nation of priests? A people who so recently were slaves are told to be priests! And yet to Moses, our teacher, the charge was not radical enough. His vision of what the people ought to be was of a grandeur unsurpassed in the history of self-reflection. When Joshua the son of Nun, the minister of Moses, appealed to him to curb the prophetic outpourings of Eldad and Medad, Moses said to him: "Would that all the Lord's people were prophets, that the Lord would put His spirit upon them!" (Numbers 11:29).

The two central ideas proclaimed in the Bible are *demand* and *promise*.

Theologically, the demand precedes the promise. God first said to Abraham: "Go from your country . . . to the land that I will show you," and then ". . . and I will make of you a great nation . . ." (Genesis 12:1–2).

Existentially, the commandment is the link of man to God. Man's existence has a touch of eternity if God is waiting for his deeds. God's expectation, God's waiting for man, comes to expression in His commandments. Indeed, the transcendence alluded to in man's existence is that mysterious waiting, that divine expectation.

The Hebrew Bible records God's "mighty acts" in history. What is overlooked is that on every page of the Bible we come upon God's hoping and waiting for *man's* mighty acts.

This is the meaning of human existence.

The world is unredeemed and deficient, and God is in need of man to be a partner in completing, in aiding, in redeeming. Of all the forms of living, doing is the most patent way of aiding. Action is truth. The deed is elucidation of existence, expressing thirst for God with body and soul. The Jewish *mitzvah* is a prayer in the form of a deed. The *mitzvot* are the Jewish sacraments, sacraments that may be performed in common deeds of kindness. Their nature is intelligible if seen in the light of God's care for man. The good act, ritual as well as moral, is a *mitzvah*, a divine offer, a divine representative.

Ultimate issues confront us in immediate situations. What is urgent for the Jew is not the acceptance of salvation but the preparing of redemption, the preparing *for* redemption.

The prophet Samuel would not abide in the security of his own home, of his piety. He moved from place to place, mixing with those who were not pious. In sharp contrast, Noah stayed at home, waiting for others to come to him. He and his family were saved, while his generation perished.

The urgent issue is not personal salvation but the prevention of mankind's surrender to the demonic. The sanctuary has no walls; the opportunity to praise or to aid has no limits. When God is silent, man must speak in His place. When God is hiding His compassion, man must reveal His love in this name.

Words become stale, and faith is tired. Unless we labor in helping God to carry out His promise—to be a father to those who are forsaken, a light to those who despair in secret darkness—we may all be forsaken by Him. Man must be involved in redeeming the promise: Nation shall not lift up sword against nation, and there shall be no war anymore.

From the Jewish point of view, any doctrine that downgrades the demands and merely proclaims the promise is a distortion. An influential Protestant theologian has said: "The key to the ethics in the New Testament is contained in the following passages: Romans 6, 7, and the beginnings of Romans 8. Here, as nowhere else, we perceive in great clearness and detail the identity of the central points in dogmatics and in ethics. The Sermon on the Mount, on the other hand, although it is the necessary presupposition of Christian ethics, is not its foundation. Its relation to Romans 6 is that of the Law to the Gospel."[4] I cite this viewpoint because it is utterly alien to the Jewish mind.

I SHOULD LIKE to offer a rather controversial—and perhaps heretical—idea: that Christians have become less and less messianic; there is very little waiting. I may be mistaken. I hope I am. In primitive Christianity, there was a waiting for the Second Coming. In the consciousness of the Christian today, there seems to be no such awareness, no such waiting. Where is the promise of redemption?

Perhaps I can illustrate my point with a story told by a Christian pilgrim in the great drama by Maxim Gorki. There was once a man who was very poor and very old, who lived in Siberia. Things went badly for him, so badly that soon nothing remained for him to do but to lie down and die. But still he did not lose courage. He often laughed and said to himself, "It makes no difference—I can bear it! A little longer yet will I wait, and then I will throw this life aside and go into the Land of Justice." It was his only pleasure, this Land of Justice. At that time there was brought to Siberia an exile, a man of learning, with books and maps of all sorts. And that poor old sick man said to this great sage: "Tell me, I implore you, where lies the Land of Justice? How can one succeed in getting there?" Then the learned man opened his books, spread out his maps, and searched and searched, but nowhere could he find the Land of Justice. Everything else was correct, all the countries were shown, only the Land of Justice was not to be found.

The old man would not believe him. "It must be there," he said. "Look more closely! For all your books and maps," said he, "are not worth a whistle if the Land of Justice is not shown on them." The learned man felt himself insulted. "My maps," said he, "are absolutely correct, and a Land of Justice nowhere exists." The other was furious. "What," he cried, "have I now lived and lived and lived, endured and endured, and always believed there was such a country. And according to your maps there is none! That is robbery, you good-for-nothing knave! You are a cheat and no sage." Then he gave him a sound blow over the skull, and still another. And then he went home and choked himself. "There must be a Land of Justice," he said, "there must be and will be an Age of Justice."[5]

I WOULD LIKE to conclude with one more point. We Jews have gone through an event in our history which is like biblical history continued.

The Jewish people everywhere have entered a new era in history. Jerusalem, the city of David, has been restored to the state of Israel. It is an event of high significance in the history of redemption. It is therefore proper, I believe, for me to share a few remarks with you on the subject.

But first, how should a Christian view this event?

According to the Book of Acts, right at the very beginning, the disciples to whom Jesus presented himself alive after his Passion asked him: "Lord, will you at this time restore the kingdom to Israel?" And he said to them: "It is not for you to know times or seasons which the Father has fixed by his own authority" (Acts 1:6–7).

Now, what is the meaning of this question and this answer? It was a time when Jerusalem was taken away from the Jewish people, the holy Temple was destroyed, Jews were sold into slavery. Pagan Rome ruled in the Holy Land.

But there was a hope, a hope of deliverance from the pagans; there was the promise offered by the prophets that Jerusalem would be returned to the kingdom of Israel. So, when the disciples saw Jesus for the first time in these extraordinary circumstances, it is understandable this was the first question they asked, their supreme concern: "Will you at this time restore the kingdom?" In other words, they asked the question about the restoration.

Jesus' answer was that the time of the fulfillment of the divine promise was a matter which lay within the Father's sole authority. So, earlier, he had assured them that he himself did not know the day or the hour of his Parousia. "But of that day or that hour no one knows, not even the angels in heaven, nor the Son, but only the Father" (Mark 13:32). A similar awareness is common in rabbinic literature. "Nobody knows when the house of David will be restored."[6] According to Rabbi Shimeon Lakish (c. 250), "I have revealed it to my heart, but not to the angels."[7] Jesus' answer is as characteristic of the rabbinic mind of the age as is the question itself.

However, this passage is generally interpreted in a different way. Reflecting a dichotomy in early Christian thinking, the position of the Galilean disciples was different from that of the Hellenistic Christians. The original hope of the disciples was that the kingdom was at hand in the apocalyptic sense, but the Hellenistic Christians, who in the end conquered the empire, preached the Gospel as having present importance for each individual apart from the eschatological kingdom.

Thus Augustine explains that the meaning of the question was that, after the resurrection, Jesus was visible only to his followers, and that they were asking whether he would now make himself visible to everyone.[8] Calvin maintains that "there are as many errors in this question as there are words."* Modern commentators assert that the question reflects the spiritual ignorance and hardness of hearts of the disciples,† "the darkened utterance of carnal and uninspired minds,"[9] and that the answer of Jesus was a rebuke.[10]

However, the simple meaning of the entire passage has a perfect *Sitz im Leben*, and both question and answer read like a *Midrash*. The Apostles were Jews and evidently shared the hope of their people of seeing the Kingdom of God realized in the restoration of Israel's national independence. So now, hearing their Master speak of the new age, they asked if this was to be the occasion for restoring the kingdom to Israel. We can scarcely fail to realize or to understand the naturalness of their question. The expectation was burned into their very being by the tyranny of the Roman rule. The answer confirms the expectation that the kingdom will be restored to Israel—an expectation expressed again and again in ancient Jewish liturgy. It is the point in history at which that restoration will take place that remains the secret of the Father.[11]

It is very likely that, following Daniel and Esdras, calculations were made to predict the time of the coming of the restoration. However, most rabbis disapproved such computations which deal with "a time, two times, and half a time" of Daniel 7:25. Jesus' answer is not a rebuke of the

---

* He points out that apostles were gathered together when this question was posed, "to show us that it was not raised through the foolishness of one or two but through the concern of all. Yet their blindness is remarkable, that when they had been so fully and carefully instructed over a period of three years, they betrayed no less ignorance than if they had never heard a word. There are as many errors in this question as there are words. They ask Him concerning the kingdom; but they dream of an earthly kingdom, dependent upon wealth, luxury, outward peace, and the blessings of this nature. And while they assign the present as the time for restoring this kingdom, they desire to enjoy the triumph before fighting the battle. Before setting hands to the work for which they are ordained they desire their wages; they also are mistaken in this, that they confine to Israel after the flesh the kingdom of Christ which is to be extended to the farthest parts of the world. The whole question is at fault in this, that they desire to know things which are not right for them to know. No doubt they were well aware of what the prophets had said about the restoration of the kingdom of David, for they had often heard Christ speaking of this, and it was a common saying that in the depths of the captivity of the people every man's spirit was revived by the hope of the kingdom to come. They hoped that this restoration would take place at the coming of the Messiah, and so the apostles, when they saw Christ raised from the dead, at once turned their thoughts to this. But in so doing they betrayed what poor progress they had made under so good a Master. Therefore Christ in His short reply briefly reprimands their errors one by one, as I shall presently indicate. To "restore" in this passage means to set up again that which was broken down and disfigured by many ruins. For out of the dry stock of Jesse should spring a branch, and the tabernacle of David which was miserably laid waste should rise again. *Calvin's Commentaries, The Acts of the Apostles* (Edinburgh, 1965), p. 29.

† "The hardness of the disciples' hearts is apparent here as in Mark's Gospel; they awaited a material kingdom, for the Spirit was not yet poured out on them to give them a more enlightened conception of it." C. S. C. Williams, *A Commentary on the Acts of the Apostles* (London, 1964), p. 56.

apostles' hope; it is rather a discouragement of messianic calculations (see Luke 17:20–21).

Jesus' expectation that Jerusalem would be restored to Israel is implied in his prediction that *Jerusalem will be trodden down by the Gentiles, until the times of the Gentiles are fulfilled* (Luke 21:24). Some commentators see in these words a prediction of "the re-establishment of Jerusalem as a capital of the Jewish nation." By "the times of the Gentiles" is probably meant "the period God has fixed for the punishment of the Jews."[12]

Several weeks ago I was privileged to be in Jerusalem, and upon my return I wrote my impressions of Jerusalem and particularly of what the Wailing Wall, the western Wall means to us. In the following personal remarks, I shall attempt to show what Jerusalem means to my people.

I HAVE discovered a new land. Israel is not the same as before. There is a great astonishment in the soul. It is as though the prophets had risen from their graves. Their words have a new ring. Jerusalem is everywhere; she hovers over the whole country. There is a new radiance, a new awe.

The great quality of a spiritual moment is not in its being an unexpected, unbelievable event in which the presence of the holy bursts forth, but in its happening to human beings who are profoundly astonished at such an outburst.

My astonishment is mixed with anxiety. Am I worthy? Am I able to appreciate the marvel?

I did not enter the city of Jerusalem on my own. Streams of endless craving, clinging, dreaming, flowing, days and nights, midnights, years, decades, centuries, millennia, streams of tears, of pledging, of waiting— from all over the world, from all corners of the earth—carried us of this generation to the Wall. My ancestors could only dream of you, to my people in Auschwitz you were more remote than the moon—but I can touch your stones! Am I worthy? How shall I ever repay for these moments?

The martyrs of all ages are sitting at the gate of heaven, having refused to enter the world to come lest they forget Israel's pledge given in and for this world: "If I forget thee, O Jerusalem, let my right hand forget its cunning!" They would rather be without heaven than forget the glory of Jerusalem. From time to time they would go on a pilgrimage to the souls of the Jewish people, reminding them that God Himself is in exile, that He will not enter the heavenly Jerusalem until His people Israel enter Jerusalem here.

Jerusalem, I always try to see the inner force that emanates from you, enveloping and transcending all weariness and travail. I try to use my eyes, and there is a cloud. Is Jerusalem higher than the road I walk on? Does she hover in the air above me? No: in Jerusalem, past is present and heaven is almost here. For an instant I am close to Hillel, who is here. All of history is present.

You see Jerusalem only when you hear. She has been an ear when no one else heard, an ear open to the prophets' denunciations, to the prophets' consolations, to the lamentations of the ages, to the hopes of countless sages and saints, and to the prayers flowing from distant places. And she is more than an ear. Jerusalem is a *witness*, an echo of eternity. Stand still and listen. We know Isaiah's voice from hearsay; but these stones have heard what he said concerning Judah and Jerusalem:

> It shall come to pass in latter days . . .
> out of Zion shall go forth the law,
> and the word of the Lord from Jerusalem.
> He shall judge between the nations,
> and shall decide for many peoples;
> nation shall not lift up sword against nation,
> neither shall they learn war any more.

> —Isaiah 2:3–4

Jerusalem was stopped in the middle of her speech. She is a voice interrupted. Let Jerusalem speak again to our people, to all people.

The words have gone out of here and have entered the pages of holy books. And yet Jerusalem has not given herself away. There is so much more in store. Jerusalem is never at the end of the road. She is the city where the expectation of God was born, where the anticipation of lasting peace came into being. Jerusalem is waiting for the prologue, for the new beginning.

What is the secret of Jerusalem? Her past is a prelude. Her power is in reviving. Her silence is prediction; the walls are in suspense. It may happen any moment: a shoot may come forth from the stump of Jesse; a branch may grow out of his roots (Isaiah 11:1).

AT FIRST I fainted. Then I saw: a wall of frozen tears, a cloud of sighs.

The Wall. Palimpsests hiding books, secret names. The stones are seals.

The Wall. The old mother crying for all of us. Stubborn, loving, waiting for redemption. The ground on which I stand is Amen. My words become echoes. All of our history is waiting here.

The Wall. No comeliness to be acclaimed, no beauty to be relished. But a heart and an ear. Its very being is compassion. You stand still and hear: stones of sorrow, acquaintance with grief. We all hide our faces from agony, shun the afflicted. The Wall is compassion, its face is open only to those smitten with grief.

When Jerusalem was destroyed, we were driven out; like sheep we have gone astray; we have turned, each one to his own way. The Wall alone stayed on.

What is the Wall? The unceasing marvel. Expectation. The Wall will not perish. The redeemer will come.

Silence. I embrace the stones. I pray: "O Rock of Israel, make our faith strong and your words luminous in our hearts and minds. No image. Pour holiness into our moments."

Once you have lived a moment at the Wall, you never go away.

For more than three thousand years we have been in love with Jerusalem. She has occupied our hearts, filled our prayers, pervaded our dreams. Continually moaning her loss, our grief was not subdued when celebrating festivities, when arranging a dinner table, when painting our homes. No meal was concluded without imploring, "Build Jerusalem, speedily, in our own days . . ." The two most dramatic occasions of the year, Seder on Passover and the Day of Atonement, found their climax in the proclamation: "Next year in Jerusalem." And on the Sabbath we implored Him:

> *When will you reign in Zion?*
> *Speedily, in our own days*
> *dwell there, and forever!*
> *May you be magnified and sanctified*
> *in the midst of Jerusalem Thy city*
> *throughout all generations and all eternity.*
> *Let our eyes behold Thy kingdom . . .*

Jerusalem, our hearts went out to you whenever we prayed, whenever we pondered the destiny of the world. For so many ages we have been lovesick. "My beloved is mine, and I am his," Jerusalem whispered. We waited unbearably long, despite frustration and derision.

In our own days the miracle occurred. Jerusalem has proclaimed loudly: "My beloved is mine and I am his" (Song of Solomon 2:16).

How shall we live with Jerusalem? She is a queen demanding high standards. What does she expect of us, living in an age of spiritual obtuseness, near-exhaustion? What sort of light should glow in Zion? What words, what thoughts, what vision should come out of Zion?

The eyes of history are upon the city of David, upon "the faithful city"; authenticity cannot be borrowed.

What is the mystery of Jerusalem? A promise: peace and God's presence.

First there was a vision. God's vision of the human being. Then He created man according to His vision, according to His image. But man's resemblance to God's image is fading rapidly.

God had a vision of restoring the image of man. He created a city in heaven and called it Jerusalem, hoping and praying that the Jerusalem on earth might resemble the Jerusalem in heaven.

Jerusalem is a recalling, an insisting, a waiting for the answer to God's hope.

> *Your eyes will see Jerusalem,*
> *a quiet habitation, an immovable tent,*
> *whose stakes will never be plucked up,*
> *nor will any of its cords be broken.*
> *But there the Lord in majesty will be for us*
> *a place of broad rivers and streams,*
> *where no galley with oars can go,*
> *nor stately ship can pass.*

—Isaiah 33:20–21

At that time Jerusalem shall be called the throne of the Lord, and all nations shall gather to it, to the presence of the Lord in Jerusalem . . .

—Jeremiah 3:17

. . . my house shall be called a house of prayer for all peoples.

—Isaiah 56:7

What Ecumenism Is

WHEN ISRAEL APPROACHED Sinai, God lifted up the mountain and held it over their heads, saying: "Either you accept the Torah or be crushed beneath the mountain."

The mountain of history is over our heads again. Shall we renew the Covenant with God?

In the words of Isaiah: "The envoys of peace weep bitterly . . . Covenants are broken, witnesses are despised, there is no regard for man" (33:7–8).

Men all over the world have a dreadful sense in common, the fear of absolute evil, the fear of total annihilation. An apocalyptic monster has descended upon the world, and there is nowhere to go, nowhere to hide.

This is an hour when even men of reason call for accommodation to absolute evil and preparation for disaster, maintaining that certain international problems are weird, demonic, beyond solution.

Dark is the world for us, for all its cities and stars. If not for Thee, O Lord, who could stand such anguish, such disgrace?

The gap between the words we preach and the lives we live threatens to become an abyss. How long will we tolerate a situation that refutes what we confess?

Is it not true that God and nuclear stockpiles cannot dwell together in one world? Is it not true that facing disaster together we must all unite to defy despair, to prevent surrender to the demonic?

The minds are sick. The hearts are mad. Humanity is drunk with a sense of absolute sovereignty. Our pride is hurt by each other's arrogance.

The dreadful predicament is not due to economic conflicts. It is due to a spiritual paralysis.

This is an age of suspicion, when most of us seem to live by the rule: Suspect thy neighbor as thyself. Such radical suspicion leads to despair of man's capacity to be free and to eventual surrender to demonic forces, surrender to idols of power, to the monsters of self-righteous ideologies.

What will save us is a revival of reverence for man, unmitigable indignation at acts of violence, burning compassion for all who are deprived, the wisdom of the heart. Before imputing guilt to others, let us examine our own failures.

What all men have in common is poverty, anguish, insecurity. What all religions have in common is power to refute the fallacy of absolute expediency, insistence that the dignity of man is in his power of compassion, in his capacity for sacrifice, self-denial.

Our era marks the end of complacency. We all face the dilemma expressed by Moses: "I have put before you life and death, blessing and curse. Choose life." Religion's task is to cultivate disgust for violence and lies, sensitivity to other people's suffering, the love of peace. God has a stake in the life of every man. He never exposes humanity to a challenge without giving humanity the power to face the challenge.

Different are the languages of prayer, but the tears are the same. We have a vision in common of Him in whose compassion all men's prayers meet.

In the words of the prophet Malachi: "From the rising of the sun to its setting my name is great among the nations, in every place incense is offered to my name, and a pure offering; for my name is great among the nations, says the *Lord of hosts*" (1:11). It seems to me that the prophet proclaims that men all over the world, though they confess different conceptions of God, are really worshipping one God, the father of all men, though they may not even be aware of it.

What will save us? God, and our faith in man's relevance to God.

This is the agony of history: bigotry, the failure to respect each other's commitment, each other's faith. We must insist upon loyalty to the unique and holy treasures of our own tradition and at the same time acknowledge that in this eon religious diversity may be the providence of God.

Respect for each other's commitment, respect for each other's faith, is more than a political and social imperative. It is born of the insight that God is greater than religion, that faith is deeper than dogma, that theology has its roots in depth theology.

The ecumenical perspective is the realization that religious truth does not shine in a vacuum, that the primary issue of theology is pre-theological, and that religion involves the total situation of man, his attitudes and deeds, and must therefore never be kept in isolation.

It is customary to blame secular science and anti-religious philosophy for the eclipse of religion in modern society. It would be more honest to blame religion for its own defeats. Religion declined not because it was refuted but because it became irrelevant, dull, oppressive, insipid. When faith is completely replaced by creed, worship by discipline, love by habit; when the crisis of today is ignored because of the splendor of the past; when faith becomes an heirloom rather than a living fountain; when religion speaks only in the name of authority rather than with the voice of compassion—its message becomes meaningless.

The great spiritual renewal within the Roman Catholic Church, inspired by Pope John XXIII, is a manifestation of the dimension of depth of religious existence. It already has opened many hearts and unlocked many precious insights.

There is a longing for peace in the hearts of man. But peace is not the same as the absence of war. Peace among men depends upon a relationship of reverence for each other.

Reverence for man means reverence for man's freedom. God has a stake in the life of man, of every man.

It was in the spirit of depth theology that Cardinal Bea announced his intention to prepare a constitution on religious liberty for presentation at the Vatican Council, in which the Fathers would be asked to come out emphatically with a public recognition of the inviolability of the human conscience as the final right of every man, no matter what his religious beliefs or ideological allegiance. Cardinal Bea stated further that the axiom "Error has no right to exist," which is used so glibly by certain Catholic apologists, is sheer nonsense, for error is an abstract concept incapable of either rights or obligations. It is persons who have rights, and even when they are in error, their right to freedom of conscience is absolute.

To quote from classic rabbinic literature: "Pious men of all nations have a share in the world to come," and are promised the reward of eternal life. "I call heaven and earth to witness that the Holy Spirit rests upon each person, Jew or Gentile, man or woman, master or slave, in consonance with his deeds."

God's voice speaks in many languages, communicating itself in a diversity of intuitions.

The word of God never comes to an end. No word is God's last word.

Man's greatest task is to comprehend God's respect and regard for the freedom of man, freedom, the supreme manifestation of God's regard for man.

In the words of Pope John's Encyclical, *Pacem in Terris*: "Every human being has the right to freedom in searching for truth and in expressing and communicating his opinions . . . Every human being has the right to honor God according to the dictates of an upright conscience."

Man's most precious thought is God, but God's most precious thought is man.

A religious man is a person who holds God and man in one thought at one time, at all times, who suffers in himself harm done to others, whose greatest passion is compassion, whose greatest strength is love and defiance of despair.

What We Might Do Together

A FAMOUS FOUR-VOLUME work on the history of atheism in the West, published sixty years ago, begins with the statement: "God has died. The time has come to write His history." Today, no historian would regard such a project as urgent; our major anxiety today seems to be diametrically opposed. Man may be dying and there will be no one to write his history. This is the problem that shatters all complacency: "Is man obsolete?" A generation ago people maintained: Technological civilization contradicts religion. Today we are wondering: Does technological civilization contradict man? The striking feature of our age is not the presence of anxiety but the inadequacy of anxiety, the insufficient awareness of what is at stake in the human situation. It is as if the nightmare of our fears surpassed our capacity for fear.

Men all over the world see the writing on the wall but are too illiterate to understand what it says. We all have that sense of dread for what may be in store for us, it is a fear of absolute evil, a fear of total destruction. It is more than an emotion. An apocalyptic monster has descended upon the world, and there is nowhere to go, nowhere to hide. What is the nature of that monster? Is it a demon the power of which is ultimate; in the presence of which there is only despair?

This is a time in which it is considered unreasonable to believe in the presence of the divine but quite reasonable to believe in the presence of the demonic. And yet, as a Jew, I recoil from the belief in the demonic. Over and against the belief in the ultimate power of the demon stands the admonition of Moses: "Know, therefore, this day and believe in your heart, that the Lord is God in heaven above, on the earth beneath; there is no one else." There are no demonic forces.

The great act of redemption brought about by Moses and the prophets of Israel was the elimination of the demons, the gods, and demigods from the consciousness of man; the demons which populated the world of ancient man are dead in the Bible. And yet even Moses knew that man is endowed with the power to make a god; he has an uncanny ability to create or to revive a demon. Indeed, man's worship of power has resurrected the demon of power.

IT IS NOT a coincidence that the three of us who are participating in this evening's panel discussion also serve as co-chairmen of the National Committee of Clergy and Laymen Concerned about Vietnam. The meeting place of this evening's discussion should be not the Palmer House in Chicago but somewhere in the jungles of Vietnam. An ecumenical nightmare—Christians, Jews, Buddhists, dying together, killing one another. So soon after Auschwitz, so soon after Hitler.

The question about Auschwitz to be asked is not "Where was God?" but rather "Where was man?" The God of Abraham has never promised always to hold back Cain's hand from killing his brother. To equate God and history is idolatry. God is present when man's heart is alive. When the heart turns to stone, when man is absent, God is banished, and history, disengaged, is distress.

What should have been humanity's answer to the Nazi atrocities? Repentance, a revival of the conscience, a sense of unceasing, burning shame, a persistent effort to be worthy of the name human, to prevent the justification of a death-of-man theology, to control the urge to cruelty.

Is it not a desecration of our commitment to act as if that agony never happened, to go on with religion as usual at a time when nuclear disaster is being made a serious possibility?

We should have learned at least one lesson: *Don't hate!*

Today is the anniversary of the death of President Kennedy. His assassination shook the world. Yet it made no impact on our laws and customs. No lesson was learned, no conclusion was drawn. Guns are still available c.o.d. Mass killing in Chicago, in Houston, in Arizona, and elsewhere is becoming a favorite pastime of young boys.

The Pentagons of the world are temples. Within their hallowed walls the great decisions come about: How many shall live, how many shall die.

The envoys of peace weep bitterly.
The highways lie waste . . .
Covenants are broken,
Witnesses are despised,
There is no regard for man.

—Isaiah 33:8

Jonah is running to Tarshish, while Nineveh is tottering on the brink. Are we not all guilty of Jonah's failure? We have been running to Tarshish when the call is to go to Nineveh.

"What is the use of running when you are on the wrong road?" What are the traps and spiritual pitfalls that account for the outrage of the war in Vietnam? What is the use of social security when you have a surplus of nuclear weapons?

Religion cannot be the same after Auschwitz and Hiroshima. Its teachings must be pondered not only in the halls of learning but also in the presence of inmates in extermination camps, and in the sight of the mushroom of a nuclear explosion.

The new situation in the world has plunged every one of us into unknown regions of responsibility. Unprepared, perplexed, misguided, the world is a spiritual no-man's-land. Men all over the world are waiting for a way out of distress, for a new certainty of the meaning of being human. Will help come out of those who seek to keep alive the words of the prophets?

This is, indeed, a grave hour for those who are committed to honor the name of God.

THE ULTIMATE standards of living, according to Jewish teaching, are *Kiddush Hashem* and *Hillul Hashem*. The one means that everything within one's power should be done to glorify the name of God before the world, the other that everything should be avoided to reflect dishonor upon the religion and thereby desecrate the name of God.

According to the ancient rabbis, the Lord said to Israel: "I have brought you out of Egypt upon the condition that you sacrifice your very lives should the honor of my name require it" (*Sifre*, ed. Weiss, 99d).

"All sins may be atoned for by repentance, by means of the Day of Atonement, or through the chastening power of affliction, but acts which cause the desecration of the name of God will not be forgiven. 'Surely this iniquity will not be forgiven you till you die, says the Lord of hosts'" (Isaiah 23:14).

In the light of these principles, e.g., a slight act of injustice is regarded as a grave offense when committed by a person whose religious leadership is acknowledged and of whose conduct an example is expected.

God had trust in us and gave us His word, some of His wisdom, and some of His power. But we have distorted His word, His wisdom, and abused His gift of power.

Those who pray tremble when they realize how staggering are the debts of the religions of the West. We have mortgaged our souls and borrowed so much grace, patience, and forgiveness. We have promised charity, love, guidance, and a way of redemption, and now we are challenged to keep the promise, to honor the pledge. How shall we prevent bankruptcy in the presence of God and man?

God has moved out of the fortress of pedestrian certainties and is dwelling in perplexities. He has abandoned our complacencies and has entered our spiritual agony, upsetting dogmas, discrediting articulations. Beyond all doctrines and greater than human faith stands God, God's question of man, God's waiting for man, for every man, God in search of man. Deeper than all our understanding is our bold certainty that God is with us in distress, hiding in the scandal of our ambiguities. And now God may send those whom we have expected least "to do His deed—strange is His deed; to carry out his work—alien is His work" (Isaiah 28:21).

What is the use of running to Tarshish when the call is to go to Nineveh?

We must learn how to labor in the affairs of the world with fear and trembling. While involved in public affairs, we must not cease to cultivate the secrets of religious privacy.

Abraham, who despised the spirit of Sodom and Gomorrah as much as Washington despises the ideology of Red China, was nevertheless horrified by the Lord's design to rain napalm, brimstone, and fire upon the sinful cities. But why? Destruction of Sodom and Gomorrah would be a spectacular manifestation of God's power in the world! So why did Abraham oppose an action which would have been a great triumph for "religion"? It is said in that story: "Abraham is still standing before the Lord" (Genesis 18:22). To this very day, Abraham is still pleading, still standing before the Lord "in fear and trembling."

It is necessary to go to Nineveh; it is also vital to learn how to stand before God. For many of us the march from Selma to Montgomery was both protest and prayer. Legs are not lips, and walking is not kneeling. And yet our legs uttered songs. Even without words, our march was worship.

Unlike Jonah, Jeremiah did not go into the desert of loneliness. He remained a solitary dissenter in the midst of his people. Defied by his contemporaries, bewildered by the ways of the Lord, he would rather be defeated with God than victorious without him.

The cardinal problem is not the survival of religion but the survival of man. What is required is a continuous effort to overcome hardness of heart, callousness, and above all to inspire the world with the biblical image of man, not to forget that man without God is a torso, to prevent the dehumanization of man. For the opposite of human is not the animal. *The opposite of human is the demonic.*

CONTEMPORARY MAN is a being afflicted with contradictions and perplexities, living in anguish in an affluent society. His anxiety makes a mockery of his boasts. Passing through several revolutions simultaneously, his thinking is behind the times. High standards of living, vulgar standards of thinking, too feeble to stop the process of the spiritual liquidation of man. Man is becoming obsolete, computers are taking over.

The issue we face is not secularization but total *mechanization, militarization. The issue is not empty pews but empty hearts.*

If the ultimate goal is power, then modern man has come of age. However, if the ultimate goal is meaning of existence, then man has already descended into a new infancy.

At times it is as if our normal consciousness were a state of partly suspended animation. Our perceptivity limited, our categories one-sided.

Things that matter most are of no relevance to many of us. Pedestrian categories will not lead us to the summit; to attain understanding for realness of God we have to rise to a higher level of thinking and experience.

This is an age in which even our common sense is tainted with commercialism and expediency. To recover sensitivity to the divine, we must develop in uncommon sense, rebel against seemingly relevant, against conventional validity; to unthink many thoughts, to abandon many habits, to sacrifice many pretensions.

The Temple in Jerusalem has been destroyed. All that is left is a Wailing Wall. A stone wall stands between God and man. Is there a way of piercing the wall?

Is there a way of surmounting the wall?

What is the substance of which that wall is made? Is it, as the prophets maintain, man's heart of stone? Or is it, as Isaiah also claims, the hiding of God? The darkening of his presence?

Perhaps this is the chief vocation of man: to scale the wall, to sense what is revealed wherever he is concealed, to realize that even a wall cannot separate man from God, that the darkness is but a challenge and a passageway.

We have pulled down the shutters and locked the doors. No light should enter, no echo should disturb our complacency. Man is the master, all else is a void. Religion came to be understood in commercial terms. We will pay our dues, and He will offer protection.

God has not complied with our expectations. So we sulk and call it quits. Who is to blame? Is God simply wicked—has He failed to keep the deal?

The hour calls for a penetration through the splendid platitudes that dominate our thinking, for efforts to counteract the systematic deflation of man, for a commitment to recall the dimension of depth within which the central issues of human existence can be seen in a way compatible with the dangerous grandeur of the human condition.

CHARACTERISTIC of our own religious situation is an awareness that theology is out of context, irrelevant to the emergencies engulfing us, pitifully incongruous with the energies technology has released, and unrelated to our anguish.

The word "heaven" is a problem, and so is the living, loving God, and so is the humanity in man a grave problem. There are two ways of dealing with a problem: one is an effort to solve it; the other is an effort to dissolve it, to kill it . . .

Let us not make a virtue of spiritual obtuseness. Why canonize deficiencies? Why glorify failure?

The crisis is wider, the anguish is deeper. What is at stake is not only articles of the creeds, paragraphs of the law; what is at stake is the humanity of man, the nearness of God.

What do we claim? *That religious commitment is not just an ingredient of the social order, an adjunct or reinforcement of existence, but rather the heart and core of being human.*

We have been preoccupied with issues, some marginal, some obsolete, evading urgent problems, offering answers to questions no longer asked, adjusting to demands of intellectual comfort, cherishing solutions that disregard emergencies.

We suffer from the fact that our understanding of religion today has been reduced to ritual, doctrine, institution, symbol, theology, detached from the *pre-theological* situation, the pre-symbolic depth of existence. To redirect the trend, we must lay bare what is involved in religious existence; we must recover the situations which both precede and correspond to the theological formulations; we must recall the questions which religious doctrines are trying to answer, the antecedents of religious commitment, the presuppositions of faith. What are the prerequisites, conditions, qualifications for being sensitive to God? Are we always ready to talk about Him?

There are levels of thinking where God is irrelevant, categories that stifle all intimations of the holy.

We are inclined to quantify quality as we are to canonize prejudice. Just as primitive man sought to personalize the impersonal, contemporary man seeks to depersonalize the personal, to think in average ways, yet every thought pertaining to God can be conceived only in uncommon ways.

God is *not a word but a name. It can be uttered only in astonishment.* Astonishment is the result of openness to the true mystery, of sensing the ineffable. It is through openness to the mystery that we are present to the presence of God, open to the ineffable name.

The urgent problem is not only the truth of religion, but *man's capacity to sense the truth of religion, the authenticity of religious concern.* Religious truth does not shine in a vacuum. It is certainly not comprehensible when the antecedents of religious insight and commitment are wasted away; when the mind is dazzled by ideologies which either obscure or misrepresent man's ultimate questions; when life is lived in a way which tends to abuse and to squander the gold mines, the challenging resources of human existence. The primary issue of theology is *pre-theological*; it is the total situation of man and his attitudes toward life and the world.

What is necessary is a recall to those ultimate sources of the spirit's life which commonplace thinking never touches. Theology must begin in *depth-theology.* Knowing must be preceded by listening to the call: "Do not come closer. Remove your sandals from your feet, for the place on which you stand is holy ground."

No one attains faith without first achieving the prerequisites of faith. First we praise, then we believe. We begin with a sense of wonder and arrive at radical amazement. The first response is reverence and awe, openness to the mystery that surrounds, and we are led to be overwhelmed by the glory.

God is not a concept produced by deliberation. God is an outcry wrung from heart and mind; God is never an explanation, it is always a challenge. It can only be uttered in astonishment.

Religious existence is a pilgrimage rather than an arrival. Its teaching —a challenge rather than an intellectual establishment, an encyclopedia of ready-made answers.

Perhaps the grave error in theology is the *claim to finality*, to absolute truth, as if all of God's wisdom were revealed to us completely and once and for all, as if God had nothing more to say.

God is a problem alive when the mind is in communion with the conscience, when realizing that in depth we are receivers rather than manipulators. The word "God" is an assault, a thunder in the soul, not a notion to play with. Prayer is the premise, moments of devotion are prerequisites of reflection. A word about God must not be born out of wedlock of heart and mind. It must not be uttered unless it has the stamp of one's own soul.

Detachment of doctrine from devotion, detachment of reason from reverence, of scrutiny from the sense of the ineffable reduces God as a challenge to a logical hypothesis, theoretically important but not overwhelmingly urgent. God is relevant only when overwhelmingly urgent.

It is a fatal mistake to think that believing in God is gained with ease or sustained without strain.

Faith is steadfastness in spite of failure. It is defiance and persistence in the face of frustration.

The most fruitful level for interreligious discussion is not that of dog-matic theology but that of *depth-theology*.

THERE ARE four dimensions of religious existence, four necessary com-ponents of man's relationship to God: (a) *the teaching*, the essentials of which are summarized in the form of a creed, which serve as guiding principles in our thinking about matters temporal or eternal, the dimension of the doctrine; (b) *faith*, inwardness, the direction of one's heart, the intimacy of religion, the dimension of privacy; (c) *the Law*, or the sacred act to be carried out in the sanctuary in society or at home, the dimension of the deed; (d) *the context* in which creed, faith, and ritual come to pass, such as the community or the Covenant, history, tradition, the dimension of transcendence.

In the dimension of the deed there are obviously vast areas for coop-eration among men of different commitments in terms of intellectual communication, of sharing concern and knowledge in applied religion, particularly as they relate to social action.

In the dimension of faith, the encounter proceeds in terms of personal witness and example, sharing insights, confessing inadequacy. On the level of doctrine we seek to convey the content of what we believe in; on the level of faith we experience in one another the presence of a person radiant with reflections of a greater presence.

I suggest that the most significant basis for the meeting of men of different religious traditions is the level of fear and trembling, of humility and contrition, where our individual moments of faith are mere waves in the endless ocean of mankind's reaching out for God, where all formu-lations and articulations appear as understatements, where our souls are swept away by the awareness of the urgency of answering God's com-mandment, while stripped of pretension and conceit we sense the tragic insufficiency of human faith.

What divides us? What unites us? We disagree in law and creed, in commitments which lie at the very heart of our religious existence. We say no to one another in some doctrines essential and sacred to us. What unites us? Our being accountable to God, our being objects of God's concern, precious in His eyes. Our conceptions of what ails us may be different, but the anxiety is the same. The language, the imagi-nation, the concretization of our hopes are different, but the embarrass-ment is the same, and so is the sigh, the sorrow, and the necessity to obey.

We may disagree about the ways of achieving fear and trembling, but the fear and trembling are the same. The demands are different, but the conscience is the same, and so is arrogance, iniquity. The proclamations are different, the callousness is the same, and so is the challenge we face in many moments of spiritual agony.

Above all, while dogmas and forms of worship are divergent, God is the same. What unites us? A commitment to the Hebrew Bible as Holy Scripture. Faith in the Creator, the God of Abraham, commitment to many of His commandments, to justice and mercy, a sense of contrition, sensitivity to the sanctity of life and to the involvement of God in history, the conviction that without the holy the good will be defeated, prayer that history may not end before the end of days, and so much more.

There are moments when we all stand together and see our faces in the mirror: the anguish of humanity and its helplessness; the perplexity of the individual and the need of divine guidance; being called to praise and to do what is required.

MANY OF our people still think in terms of an age in which Judaism wrapped itself in spiritual *isolation*. In our days, however, for the majority of our people *involvement* has replaced *isolation*.

The emancipation has brought us to the *very heart* of the total society. It has not only given us *rights*, it has imposed *obligations*. It has expanded the scope of our responsibility and concern. Whether we like it or not, the words we utter and the actions in which we are engaged affect the life of the total community.

We *affirm* the principle of separation of church and state; we *reject* the separation of religion and the human situation. We abhor the equation of state and society, of power and conscience, and perceive society in the image of human beings comprising it. The human individual is beset with needs and is called upon to serve ends.

To what religious ends must my fellow men be guided?

The world we live in has become a single neighborhood, and the role of religious commitment, of reverence and compassion, in the thinking of our fellow men is becoming a domestic issue. What goes on in the Christian world affects us deeply. Unless we learn how to help one another, we may only hurt each other.

Our society is in crisis not because we intensely disagree but because we feebly agree. "The clash of doctrines is not a disaster, it is an opportunity" (Alfred Whitehead).

The survival of mankind is in balance. One wave of hatred, callousness, or contempt may bring in its wake the destruction of all mankind. Vicious deeds are but an aftermath of what is conceived in the hearts and minds of man. It is from the inner life of man and from the articulation of evil thoughts that evil actions take their rise. It is therefore of extreme importance that the sinfulness of thoughts of suspicion and hatred and particularly the sinfulness of any contemptuous utterance, however flippantly it is meant, be made clear to all mankind. This applies in particular to thoughts and utterances about individuals or groups of other religions, races, and nations. Speech has power and few men realize that words do not fade. What starts out as a sound ends in a deed.

In an age in which the spiritual premises of our existence are both questioned and even militantly removed, the urgent problem is not the competition among some religions but the condition of all religions, the condition of man, crassness, chaos, darkness, despair.

THERE IS much we can do together in matters of supreme concern and relevance to both Judaism and Christianity.

The world is too small for anything but mutual care and deep respect; the world is too great for anything but responsibility for one another.

A full awareness and appreciation of our fellow men's spiritual commitments becomes a moral obligation for all of us.

A Jew who hears what he prays cannot be indifferent to whether God's way is known in the world, to whether the Gentiles know how to praise. In our liturgy we proclaim every day:

> Give thanks to the Lord,
> Call upon Him,
> Make known His deeds among the peoples!
>
> —*Psalms* 105:1

In the Omer liturgy it is customary to recite Psalm 67:

May God be gracious to us and bless us and make His face to shine upon us, that Thy way may be known upon earth, Thy saving power among all nations. Let the peoples praise Thee, O God; let all the peoples praise Thee!

What is our task as Jews in relation to Gentiles? I rely upon the words of an inspired Hasidic sage in expounding Deuteronomy 28:9ff: "The Lord shall establish you as His holy people . . . if you keep the commandments . . . and walk in His ways. And all the peoples of the earth shall see that the Lord's name is proclaimed upon you, and they will acquire reverence through you."

The real bond between people of different creeds is the awe and fear of God they have in common. It is easy to speak about the different dogmas we are committed to; it is hard to communicate the fear and reverence. It is easy to communicate the learning we have inherited; it is hard to communicate the praise, the contrition, and the sense of the ineffable. But souls which are in accord with what is precious in the eyes of God, souls to whom God's love for them is more precious than their own lives, will always meet in the presence of Him whose glory fills the hearts and transcends the minds.

What, then, is the purpose of interreligious cooperation?

It is neither to flatter nor to refute one another but to help one another; to share insight and learning, to cooperate in academic ventures on the highest scholarly level, and, what is even more important, to search in the wilderness for wellsprings of devotion, for treasures of stillness, for the power of love and care for man. What is urgently needed are ways of helping one another in the terrible predicament of here and now by the courage to believe that the word of the Lord endures forever as well as here and now; to work for peace in Vietnam, for racial justice in our own land, to purify the minds from contempt, suspicion, and hatred; to co-operate in trying to bring about a resurrection of sensitivity, a revival of conscience; to keep alive the divine sparks in our souls, to nurture openness to the spirit of the Psalms, reverence for the words of the prophets, and faithfulness to the Living God.

There ought to be standards and rules for interreligious dialogue. An example of such a rule for Catholics and Protestants would be not to discuss the supremacy of the bishop of Rome or papacy; an example of such a rule for Christians and Jews would be not to discuss Christology.

The God of Abraham, the Creator of heaven and earth, deemed it wise to conceal His presence in the world in which we live. He did not make it easy for us to have faith in Him, to remain faithful to Him.

This is our tragedy: the insecurity of faith, the unbearable burden of our commitment. The facts that deny the divine are mighty in-deed; the arguments of agnosticism are eloquent, the events that defy Him are spectacular. Our faith is too often tinged with arrogance, self-righteousness. It is even capable of becoming demonic . . . Even the creeds we proclaim are in danger of becoming idolatry. Our faith is fragile, never immune to error, distortion, or deception.

There are no final proofs for the existence of God, Father and Creator of all. There are only witnesses. Supreme among them are the prophets of Israel.

Humanity is an unfinished task, and so is religion. The Law, the creed, the teaching and the wisdom are here, yet without the outburst of prophetic demands coming upon us again and again, religion may become fossilized.

Reinhold Niebuhr

THIS IS A CRITICAL MOMENT in the lives of many of us, in the history of religion in America: to say farewell to the physical existence of the master and to pray: Abide, continue to dwell in our midst, spirit of Reinhold Niebuhr. Do not depart from us; we need your power, we need your guidance, in faith, in conscience.

For many of us the world will be darker without you. Reinhold Niebuhr, your spirituality combined heaven and earth, as it were. Your life was an example of one who did justly, loved mercy, and walked humbly with his God, an example of unity of worship and living. You reminded us that evil will be conquered by the One, while you stirred us to help conquer evils one by one.

A FULL APPRECIATION of the greatness of Reinhold Niebuhr will have to take into account not only his teachings but also his supreme integrity as a person. It will turn not only to his books but also to his deeds. For all his profundity, prophetic radicalism, insight into the ultimate aspects of human destiny, Reinhold Niebuhr maintained a concern for the immediate problems of justice in society and politics, of the here and now.

In boldness of penetration, depth of insight, fullness of vision, Reinhold Niebuhr's system excels any other system produced by an American theologian to this very day. He has helped us all in striving for human integrity in religious terms. He has, to quote his words, "sought to strengthen the Hebraic prophetic content of the Christian tradition."

A lover of Zion and Jerusalem, imbued with the spirit of the Hebrew Bible, he was a staunch friend of the Jewish people and the state of Israel, of the poor and the downtrodden here and everywhere.

His legacy is rich, precious, vital: purity of heart, disgust with intellectual falsehood, with spiritual sham, whether in the Congress or in our own sanctuaries.

SHALL WE remember his legacy?

How shall we thank you, Reinhold Niebuhr, for the light you have brought into our lives? For the strength you have given to our faith? For the wisdom you have imparted in our minds?

HE BEGAN his teaching at a time when religious thinking in America was shallow, insipid, impotent—bringing life and power to theology, to the understanding of the human situation, changing the lives of many Christians and Jews.

He appeared among us like a sublime figure out of the Hebrew Bible. Intent on intensifying responsibility, he was impatient of excuse, contemptuous of pretense and self-pity.

IT IS DEEPLY meaningful to ponder at this hour some words of the Hebrew Bible. With Job, we say:

> *The Lord has given,*
> *The Lord has taken,*
> *Praised be the name of the Lord.*
> *My flesh and my heart may fail,*
> *But God is the strength of my heart.*
> *He is my portion forever.*

Niebuhr's life was a song in the form of deeds, a song that will go on forever.

REVERED, beloved Reinhold: In the words of the psalmist:

> *You are the fairest of the sons of men,*
> *Grace is poured upon your lips*
> *Therefore God has blessed you forever.*

And now your soul is entering life eternal, a beautiful princess. And with the words of the psalmist, I conclude:

> *With joy and gladness*
> *She is led along*
> *As she enters the*
> *Palace of the King.*

V

THE HOLY

DIMENSION

An Analysis of Piety

FROM TIME IMMEMORIAL, piety has been esteemed as one of the more precious ideals of human character. At all times, and in all places, men have striven to acquire piety, and no effort or sacrifice has seemed too costly to this end. Was this merely an illusion on their part, a flight of the imagination? No! It was a real virtue—something solid, clearly to be seen, and of real power. Thus, as a specific fact of existence met with in life, it is something which indisputably deserves examination. That it is commonly neglected or overlooked by scientific research is due partly to the methodological difficulties involved in an approach to such a subject, but more fundamentally to the fact that it has theological connections which are somewhat repellent to the modern mind. To some, piety suggests escape from normal life, an abandonment of the world, seclusion, a denial of cultural interests, and is associated with an old-fashioned, clerical, unctuous pattern of behavior. To others, the word suggests prudishness, if not hypocrisy and fanaticism, or seems symptomatic of an attitude toward life which is unhealthy and, indeed, absurd. In the interests of mental health and spiritual freedom, they feel that such an attitude to life as that of piety is to be rejected.

Yet the pious man is still with us. He has not vanished from the earth, and indeed more frequently than is generally realized, situations in normal life are to be encountered which are full of the evidence of pious devotion. The presence of piety among us is thus an incontestable fact, so why should prejudice deter us from investigating this phenomenon and, at least, endeavoring to understand it?

To begin with, we may ask, What is piety? Is it some psychical disposition or quality of the spirit? Is it a state of mind? or an attitude? or a praxis? What are its essential features? What is its meaning and value?

What is its significance? What are its aspirations? Is it a unique phenomenon, or is it an accidental circumstance concomitant with other events of human life? What is the inner life of a pious man like? What are the underlying concepts, and what are the apprehensions that are realized in acts of piety?

We are not discussing here that implicit faith which is involved in general systems of faith and worship but is not acquired independently by individuals, nor is it our intention to scrutinize critically any doctrine or creed. Our purpose, rather, is to analyze the pious man, and to examine, not his position with regard to any specific form of institutionalized religion, but his attitudes toward the elemental forces of reality. What does God mean in his life? What is his attitude toward the world, toward life, toward his inner forces as well as toward his possessions?

Piety is not a psychological concept. The word belongs as little to psychological nomenclature as do the logical concepts of true and false, the ethical concepts of right and wrong, or the aesthetic concepts of beautiful and ugly. Piety does not denote a function but an ideal of the soul. Like wisdom or truthfulness, it is something attainable, and is subject to the individual character of a man, being colored by his qualities. Thus there is a passionate as well as a sober type of piety, an active as well as a quietistic type, an emotional as well as an intellectual one. Yet, in spite of the fact that it is never independent of the psychical structure of the individual, it is futile to attempt to explain piety by any bent or bias of the mental life. It is far from being the result of any psychical dispositions or organic functions. Certain dispositions may influence or intensify it, but they do not create it.

As an actuality, it belongs to the stream of the psychical life, but its content, its spiritual aspect, is as independent of the psychical chain of causation as the acceptance of the Pythagorean theorem is independent of the individual temper. Ideas are not to be confused with the psychical setting in which they appear. It is fallacious to identify knowledge with the processes of its acquisition or realization. The spiritual content is not identical with the act itself, nor are concepts tantamount to functions of the mind. The spiritual objective content is universal, and should be distinguished from the subjective psychical function. Piety is an objective spiritual entity. There have been times in which piety was as common as knowledge of the multiplication table is today.

Our objective in this paper is an analysis of the consciousness that accompanies the acts of a pious man, and a classification of the concepts latent in his mind. There is hardly need for us to emphasize the fact that the validity of such an analysis is not impaired by the possibility that the concepts derived from a general inquiry may not be found in every act or example of piety. The fact that a poet proves to be unacquainted with the rules that govern his art, or does not apply them in every poem, does not mean that there are no rules of poetry.

We are not here concerned primarily with the psychological aspects of the question. These have their own importance, but would require a special investigation. Our purpose is to direct our attention to those essential, constitutive elements that are common to different types of piety, disregarding accidental colorings and the unimportant accompanying circumstances which may differ in different cases. Our task will be to describe piety as it is, without claiming to explain it or to suggest its derivation from other phenomena. We shall not analyze psychologically the course it runs, or its peculiarities as they appear in the life of an individual. We shall not attempt to trace historically its development through the ages and in the matrix of different civilizations, but shall, rather, try to expound its spiritual content, and set forth its concepts and its manifestations in relation to the main realities of common life.

To label piety as an ability, a potential quality of the soul, would be like defining architecture as a skill. It is impossible to understand facts by mere speculation as to their origins. We should likewise go astray if we label it as a mood, an emotional state, a flutter of romantic feeling. To do this would be like characterizing the light of the moon as melancholy, or judging navigation by its danger to human life. Again, to call it a moral or intellectual virtue would be like trying to nail down the shadow of an escaping horse, and so securing neither horse nor shadow. Piety does not consist in isolated acts, in sporadic, ephemeral experiences, nor is it limited to a single stratum of the soul. Although it manifests itself in particular acts, it is beyond the distinctions between intellect and emotion, will and action. Its source seems to lie deeper than the reach of reason and to range wider than consciousness. While it reveals itself in single attitudes such as devotion, reverence, or the desire to serve, its essential forces lie in a stratum of the soul far deeper than the orbit of any of these. It is something unremitting, persistent, unchanging in the soul, a perpetual inner attitude of the whole man. Like a breeze in the atmosphere, it runs as a drift through all the deeds, utterances, and thoughts; it is a tenor of life betraying itself in each trait of character, each mode of action.

Piety points to something beyond itself. As it works in the inner life, it is ever referring us to something that transcends man, something that goes beyond the present instant, something that surmounts what is visible and available. Steadily preventing man from immersing himself in sensation or ambition, it stands staunchly as the champion of something more important than interest and desires, than passion or career. While not denying the beauty and grandeur of the world, the pious man realizes that life takes place under wide horizons, horizons that range beyond the span of an individual life or even the life of a nation, of a generation or even of an era. His sight perceives something indicative of the divine. In the small things he senses the significant, in the common and the simple he senses the ultimate; in the rush of the passing he feels the stillness of the eternal. While piety stands in relation to what man knows and feels about the horizons of life, it exceeds by far the sum total reached by adding up his diverse intellectual and emotional experiences. Its essence, in fact, stands for something more than a theory, a sentiment, or a conviction. To those who adhere to it, piety is compliance with destiny, the only life worth living, the only course of life that does not eventually throw man into bestial chaos.

Piety is thus a mode of living. It is the orientation of human inwardness toward the holy. It is a predominant interest in the ultimate value of all acts and feelings and thoughts. With his heart open to and attracted by some spiritual gravitation, the pious man moves, as it were, toward the center of a universal stillness, and his conscience is so placed as to listen to the voice of God.

Every man's life is dominated by certain interests, and is essentially determined by the aspiration for those things which matter to him to a greater or a lesser degree. The pious man's main interest is concern for the will of God, which thus becomes the driving force controlling the course of his actions and decisions, molding his aspirations and behavior. It is fallacious to see in isolated acts of perception or consideration the decisive elements in human behavior. Actually, it is the direction of mind and heart, the general interest of a person, that leads him to see or discover certain situations and to overlook others. Interest is a selective apprehension based on prior ideas, preceding insights, recognitions, or predilections. The interest of a pious man is determined by his faith, so that piety is faith translated into life, spirit embodied in a personality.

Piety is the direct opposite of selfishness. Living as he does in the vision of the unutterably pure, the pious man turns his back on his own human vanity, and his longing is to surrender the forces of egotism to the might of God. He is aware of both the shabbiness of human life and the meagerness and insufficiency of human service, and so, to protect the inner wholesomeness and purity of devotion from being defiled by interference from the petty self, he strives toward self-exclusion, self-forgetfulness, and an inner anonymity of service. He desires to be unconscious that it is he who is consecrating himself to the service of God. The pious man lays no claim to reward. He hates show, or being conspicuous in any way, and is shy of displaying his qualities even to his own mind. He is engrossed in the beauty of that which he worships, and dedicates himself to ends the greatness of which exceeds his capacity for adoration.

Piety is not a habit, something running along in a familiar groove. It is rather an impulse, a spurt, a stirring of the self. Apart from a certain ardor, zeal, intentness, vigor, or exertion, it becomes a stunted thing. No one who has even once been impelled by its force will ever entirely shake off its pursuing drive. In moments of stress the pious man may stumble, he may blunder or go astray, he may at moments succumb in his weakness to the agreeable instead of holding to the true, follow the ostentatious instead of the simple and hard, but his adherence to the holy will only slacken, it will never break away. Such lapses, indeed, are often followed by a new sweep toward the goal, the lapse providing new momentum.

Although piety implies a certain spiritual profundity, it is not an outgrowth of innate intelligence. Its forces spring from purity of heart rather than from acumen of mind. To be pious does not necessarily mean to be sagacious or judicious. It does, however, as a prevailing trend show features that are peculiar to wisdom, in the ancient sense of that word. Both piety and wisdom involve self-command, self-conquest, self-denial, strength of will, and firmness of purpose. But though these qualities are instrumental in the pursuit of piety, they are not its nature. It is the regard for the transcendent, the devotion to God, that constitute its essence. To the pious man, as to the wise one, mastery over self is a necessity of life. However, unlike the wise man, the pious man feels that he himself is not the autonomous master but is rather a mediator who administers his life in the name of God.

Piety and faith are not one and the same thing. They have differences from each other and are not necessarily concurrent. There can be faith without piety, just as there can be piety without faith. Unlike faith, piety not only accepts the mystery but attempts to match it in human endeavor, venturing to lift the human to the level of the spiritual. This should not be called an experience but the acting upon experience, not a concern about meaning and its exploration but an attempt to make life balance with an accepted meaning. In other words, it is neither a search nor a quest, neither a discovery of new truth nor a new viewpoint, nor is it some new insight into latent forces or possibilities.

The pious man is alive to what is solemn in the simple, to what is sublime in the sensuous, but he is not aiming to penetrate into the sacred. Rather, he is striving to be himself, penetrated and actuated by the sacred, eager to yield to its force, to identify himself with every trend in the world which is toward the divine. To piety it is not the outlook that carries weight but the impression, not the notion but the sentiment, not acquaintance but appreciation, not knowledge but veracity. Piety is not a thinking about coming but a real approach. It is not identical with the performance of rites and ceremonies but is rather the care and affection put into their performance, the personal touch therein, the offering of life. Piety is the realization and verification of the transcendent in human life.

Faith is a way of thinking, and thus a matter of the mind; piety is a matter of life. Faith is a sense for the reality of the transcendent; piety is the taking of an adequate attitude toward it. Faith is vision, knowledge, belief; piety is relation, adjustment, an answer to a call, a mode of life. Faith belongs to the objective realm; piety stands entirely within the subjective and originates in human initiative. Piety is usually preceded by faith, and it is then faith's achievement, an effort to put faith's ideas into effect, to follow its suggestions. It desires not merely to learn faith's truth but to agree with it; not merely to meet God but to abide by Him, agree with His will, echo His words, and respond to His voice.

It is through piety that there comes the real revelation of the self, the disclosure of what is most delicate in the human soul, the unfolding of the purest elements in the human venture. Essentially it is an attitude toward God and the world, toward men and things, toward life and destiny, and in what follows we shall make an attempt to outline a few examples of this.

The pious man is possessed by his awareness of the presence and nearness of God. Everywhere and at all times he lives as in His sight, whether he remains always heedful of His proximity or not. He feels embraced by God's mercy as by a vast encircling space. Awareness of God is as close to him as the throbbing of his own heart, often deep and calm, but at times overwhelming, intoxicating, setting the soul afire. The momentous reality of God stands there as peace, power, and endless tranquillity, as an inexhaustible source of help, as boundless compassion, as an open gate awaiting prayer. It sometimes happens that the life of a pious man becomes so involved in God that his heart overflows as though it were a cup in the hand of God. This presence of God is not like the proximity of a mountain or the vicinity of an ocean, the view of which one may relinquish by closing the eyes or removing from the place. Rather is this convergence with God unavoidable, inescapable; like air in space it is always being breathed in, even though one is not at all times aware of continuous respiration.

To dwell upon those things that are stepping-stones on the path to the holy, to be preoccupied with the great and wondrous vision of His presence, does not necessarily mean an avoidance of the common ways of life, or involve losing sight of worldly beauty or profane values. Piety's love of the Creator does not exclude love of the creation, but it does involve a specific approach to all values. Between man and world stands God. He is before all things, and all values are looked at through Him. Mere splendor of appearance does not appeal to the man of piety. He is fond of what is good in the eyes of God and holds as valuable that which stands in accord with His peace. He is not deceived by the specious or dissuaded by the unseemly. Shining garments, a smiling countenance, or miracles of art do not enchant him when they cover vice or blasphemy. The most magnificent edifices, most beautiful temples and monuments of worldly glory are repulsive to him when they are built by the sweat and tears of suffering slaves or erected through injustice and fraud. Hypocrisy and pretence of devoutness are more distasteful to him than open iniquity. But in the roughened, dirty hands of devoted parents, or in the maimed bodies and bruised faces of those who have been persecuted but have kept faith with God, he may detect the last great light on earth.

Whatever the pious man does is linked to the divine; each smallest trifle is tangential to His course. In breathing he uses His force; in thinking he wields His power. He moves always under the unseen canopy of remembrance, and the wonderful weight of the name of God rests steadily on his mind. The word of God is as vital to him as air or food. He is never alone, never companionless, for God is within reach of his heart. Under affliction or some sudden shock he may feel temporarily as though he were on a desolate path, but a slight turn of his eyes is sufficient for him to discover that his grief is outflanked by the compassion of God. The pious man needs no miraculous communication to make him aware of God's presence, nor is a crisis necessary to awaken him to the meaning and appeal of that presence. His awareness may momentarily be overlaid or concealed by some violent shift in consciousness, but it never fades away. It is this awareness of ever living under the watchful eye of God that leads the pious man to see hints of God in the varied things he encounters in his daily walk, so that many a simple event can be accepted by him both for what it is and also as a gentle hint or kindly reminder of things divine. In this mindfulness he eats and drinks, works and plays, talks and thinks, for piety is a life compatible with God's presence.

This compatibility reveals itself in the way in which he regards and evaluates all phenomena. Man is by nature inclined to evaluate things and events according to the purpose they serve. In the economic life a man is estimated according to his efficiency, by his worth in labor, and by his social standing. Here every object in the universe is regarded as a commodity or a tool, its value being determined by the amount of work it can perform or the degree of pleasantness it can confer, so that utilization is the measure of all things. But was the universe created merely for the use of man, for the satisfaction of his animal desires? Surely it is obvious how crude and, indeed, thoughtless it is to subject other beings to the service of our interests, seeing that every existence has its own inner value, and to utilize such without regard to their individual essence is to desecrate them and despise their real dignity. The folly of this instrumental approach is manifest in the vengeance which inevitably follows. In treating everything else as an instrument, man eventually makes himself the instrument of something he does not understand. By enslaving others, he plunges himself into serfdom, serving warlords or those prejudices which come to be imposed upon him. Often, indeed, he wastes his life in serving passions which others shrewdly excite in him, fondly believing that this is his indulgence of his freedom.

The inner value of any entity—men or women, trees or stars, ideas or things—is, as a matter of fact, not entirely subject to any purposes of ours. They have a value in themselves quite apart from any function which makes them useful to our purposes. This is particularly true of man, for it is his essence, that secret of his being in which both existence and meaning are rooted, that commands our respect, so that even though we know no way in which he might be useful, or no means of subordinating him to any end or purpose, we should esteem him for that alone.

Further, piety is an attitude toward reality in its entirety. It is alert to the dignity of every human being, and to those bearings upon the spiritual value which even inanimate things inalienably possess. The pious man, being able to sense the relations of things to transcendent values, will be incapable of disparaging any of them by enslaving them to his own service. The secret of every being is in the divine care and concern that are invested in it. In every event there is something sacred at stake, and it is for this reason that the approach of the pious man to reality is in reverence. This explains his solemnity and his conscientiousness in dealing with things both great and small.

Reverence is a specific attitude toward something that is precious and valuable, toward someone who is superior. It is a salute of the soul, an awareness of value without enjoyment of that value or seeking any personal advantage from it. There is a unique kind of transparence about things and events. The world is seen through, and no veil can conceal God completely. So the pious man is ever alert to see behind the appearance of things a trace of the divine, and thus his attitude toward life is one of expectant reverence.

Because of this attitude of reverence, the pious man is at peace with life, in spite of its conflicts. He patiently acquiesces in life's vicissitudes, because he glimpses spiritually their potential meaning. Every experience opens the door into a temple of new light, although the vestibule may be dark and dismal. The pious man accepts life's ordeals and its meed of anguish, because he recognizes these as belonging to the totality of life. This does not mean complacency or fatalistic resignation. He is not insensitive. On the contrary, he is keenly sensitive to pain and suffering, to adversity and evil in his own life and in that of others, but he has the inner strength to rise above grief, and with his understanding of what these sorrows really are, grief seems to him a sort of arrogance. We never know the ultimate meaning of things, and so a sharp distinction between what we deem good or bad in experience is unfair. It is a greater thing to love than to grieve, and with love's awareness of the far-reachingness of all that affects our lives, the pious man will never overestimate the seeming weight of momentary happenings.

The natural man feels a genuine joy at receiving a gift, in obtaining something he has not earned. The pious man knows that nothing he has has been earned, not even his perceptions, his thoughts and words, or even his life, are his by desert. He knows that he has no claim to anything with which he is endowed. Knowing, therefore, that he merits little, he never arrogates anything to himself. His thankfulness being stronger than his wants and desires, he can live in joy and with a quiet spirit. Being conscious of the evidences of God's blessing in nature and in history, he pays tribute to the values of that blessing in all that he receives. The natural man has two attitudes to life, joy and gloom. The pious man has but one, for to him gloom represents an overbearing and presumptuous depreciation of underlying realities. Gloom implies that man thinks he has a right to a better, more pleasing world. Gloom is a refusal, not an offer, a snub not an appreciation, a retreat instead of a pursuit. Gloom's roots are in pretentiousness, fastidiousness, and a disregard of the good. The gloomy man, living in irritation and a constant quarrel with his destiny, senses hostility everywhere, and seems never to be aware of the illegitimacy of his own complaints. He has a fine sense for the incongruities of life but stubbornly refuses to recognize the delicate grace of existence.

The pious man does not take life for granted. The weighty business of living does not cloud for him the miracle that we live through God. No routine of social or economic life dulls his mindfulness of this—the ineffably wonderful in nature and history. History to him is a perpetual improvisation by the Creator, which is being continually and violently interfered with by man, and his heart is fixed on this great Mystery that is being played by God and man. Thus his main asset is not some singular experience but life itself. Any exceptional experience serves only as a keyhole for the key of his belief. He does not depend on the exceptional, for to him common deeds are adventures in the domain of the spiritual, and all his normal thoughts are, as it were, sensations of the holy. He feels the hidden warmth of good in all things, and finds hints of God cropping up in almost every ordinary thing on which he gazes. It is for this reason that his words bring hope into a sordid and despairing world.

The scope of that in which the pious man feels himself involved is not a single realm, as, for instance, that of ethical acts, but covers the whole of life. Life to him is a liability, and a liability from which he can never be free. No evasion on his part can escape it, and no sphere of action, no period of life, can be withdrawn from it. So piety cannot consist only in specific acts, such as prayer or ritual observance, but is something bound up with all actions, concomitant with all doings, accompanying and shaping all life's activities. Man's responsibility to God is not an excursion into spirituality, an episode of spiritual rhapsody, but the scaffold on which he stands as daily he goes on building life. His every deed, every incident of mind, takes place on this stage, so that unremittingly man is at work either building up or tearing down his life, his home, his hope of God.

Responsibility implies freedom, and man, who is in bondage to environment, to social ties, to inner disposition, may yet enjoy freedom before God. Only before God is man truly independent and truly free. But freedom in its turn implies responsibility, and man is responsible for the way in which he utilizes nature. It is amazing how thoughtless modern man is of his responsibility in relation to his world. He finds before him a world crammed to overflowing with wonderful materials and forces, and without hesitation or scruple he grasps at whatever is within his range. Omnivorous in his desire, unrestrained in his efforts, tenacious in his purpose, he is gradually changing the face of the earth, and there seems to be none to deny him or challenge his mastery. Deluded by this easy mastery, we give no thought to the question of what basis there is to our assumed right to possess our universe. Our own wayward desires and impulses, however natural they may be, are no title to ownership. Unmindful of this we take our title for granted and grasp at everything, never questioning whether this may be robbery. Powerhouse, factory, and department store make us familiar with the exploitation of nature for our benefit. And lured by familiarity, the invisible trap for the mind, we easily yield to the illusion that these things are rightfully at our disposal, thinking little of the sun, the rainfall, the watercourses, as sources by no means rightfully ours. It is only when we suddenly come up against things obviously beyond the scope of human domination or jurisdiction, such as mountains or oceans, or uncontrollable events like sudden death, earthquake, or other catastrophes, which clearly indicate that man is neither lord of the universe nor master of his own destiny, that we are somewhat shaken out of our illusions.

In reality man has not unlimited powers over the earth, as he has not over stars or winds. He has not even complete power over himself. In the absolute sense, neither the world nor his own life belongs to him. And of the things he does more or less control, he controls not the essence but only the appearance, as is evident to anyone who has ever looked with unclouded vision in the face even of a flower or a stone. The question then is, Who is the lord? Who owns all that exists? The universe is not a waif, nor is life a derelict, abandoned and unclaimed. All things belong to God. So the pious man regards the forces of nature, the thoughts of his own mind, life, and destiny as the property of God. This governs his attitude toward all things. He does not grumble when calamities befall him, or lapse into despair, for he knows that all in life is a concern of the divine because all is in the divine possession.

Thus the pious man realizes, also, that whatever he may have at his disposal has been bestowed upon him as a gift. And there is a difference between a possession and a gift. Possession is loneliness. The very word excludes others from the use of the possessed object without the consent of the possessor, and those who insist on possession ultimately perish in self-excommunication and loneliness. On the contrary, in receiving a gift, the recipient obtains, besides the present, the love of the giver. A gift is thus the vessel that contains the affection, which is destroyed as soon as one begins to look on it as a possession. The pious man avers that he has a perpetual gift from God, for in all that comes to him he feels the love of God. In all the thousand and one experiences that make up a day, he is conscious of that love intervening in his life.

The ordinary man is inclined to disregard all indications in life of the presence of the divine. In his conceit and vainglory he thinks of himself as the possessor. But this is sacrilege to the pious man, and his method of saving himself from such hallucinations is by asceticism and sacrifice. He rids himself of all sense of being a possessor by giving up for God's sake things that are desired or valued, and depriving himself of those things that are precious to him for the sake of others who need his help. Thus, to sacrifice is not to abandon what has been granted to us, to throw away the gifts of life. It is, on the contrary, giving back to God what we have received from Him by employing it in His service in the cause of good. Such giving is a form of thanksgiving.

Both self-dispossession and offering are essential elements of sacrifice. Mere offering without self-dispossession would be without personal participation and would easily lapse into a superficial ritual act in which the mechanical aspect is more important than the personal. It would result in externalization and perfunctoriness of sacrifice, as has so often happened in religious history. On the other hand, self-dispossession alone tends to make asceticism an end in itself, and when turned into an end in itself, it loses its bearing on God. True asceticism is not merely depriving ourselves but is giving to God what was precious to us.

Poverty has often been an ideal for pious men, but one may be poor in material goods while yet clinging the more tenaciously to one's ambitions and intellectual goods. Mere poverty in itself is not a good, for the bitterness of poverty often upsets the balance of values in human character, while the delight of the righteous in the gifts of God affords him strength in service and the means to give. Purpose of sacrifice does not lie in pauperization as such but in the yielding of all aspirations to God, thus creating space for Him in the heart. Moreover it is an *imitatio Dei*, for it is done after the manner of the Divine Giver, and reminds man that he is created in the divine image, and is thus related to God.

This, however, presents another problem. How are we to understand this kinship of man with the divine? One indication of man's affinity with God is his persistent aspiration to go beyond himself. He has an ability to devote himself to a higher aim, the potentiality of a will to serve, to dedicate himself to a task which goes beyond his own interests and his own life, to live for an ideal. This ideal may be the family, a friend, a group, the nation, or it may be art, science, or social service. In many persons this will to serve is kept under, but in the pious man it blooms and flourishes. In many lives these ideals seem blind alleys, but in the pious man they are thoroughfares to God. If these ideals become idols, ends in themselves, they close in the soul, but to the pious man they are openings letting in the light from far places to illumine many a small particular thing. To him ideals are strides on the way, but they are never the destination.

Piety, finally, is allegiance to the will of God. Whether that will is understood or not, it is accepted as good and holy, and is obeyed in faith. Life is a mandate, not the enjoyment of an annuity; a task, not a game; a command, not a favor. So, to the pious man, life never appears as a fatal chain of events following necessarily one on another, but comes as a voice with an appeal. It is a flow of opportunity for service, every experience giving the cue to a new duty, so that all that enters life is for him a means of devotion. Piety is, thus, not an excess of enthusiasm, but implies a resolve to follow a definite course of life in pursuit of the will of God. All the pious man's thoughts and plans revolve around this concern, and nothing can distract him or turn him from the way. Whoever sets out on this way soon learns how imperious is the spirit. He senses the compulsion to serve, and though at times he may attempt to escape, the strength of this compulsion will bring him back inevitably to the right way in search of the will of God. Before he acts, he will pause to weigh the effects of his act on the scales of God. Before he speaks, he will consider whether his words will be well pleasing to Him. Thus in self-conquest and earnest endeavor, with sacrifice and single-mindedness, through prayer and grace, he proceeds on his way, and to him the way is more important than the goal. It is not his destiny to accomplish but to contribute, and his will to serve shapes his entire conduct. His preoccupation with the will of God is not limited to a section of his activities; his great desire is to place his whole life at the disposal of God, and in this he finds the real meaning of life. He would feel wretched and lost without the certainty that his life, insignificant though it be, is of some purpose in the great plan, and life takes on enhanced value when he feels himself engaged in fulfilling purposes which lead him away from himself. In this way he feels that in whatever he does he is ascending step by step a ladder leading to the ultimate. In aiding a creature, he is helping the Creator. In succoring the poor, he is taking care of something that concerns God. In admiring the good, he is revering the spirit of God. In loving the pure, he is being drawn to Him. In promoting the right, he is directing things toward His will, in which all aims must terminate. Ascending by this ladder, the pious man reaches the state of self-forgetfulness, sacrificing not only his desires but also his will, for he realizes that it is the will of God that matters and not his own perfection or salvation. Thus the glory of man's devotion to the good becomes a treasure of God on earth.

Yet it is not his desire to serve as a slave. Man's task is to reconcile liberty with service, reason with faith. This is the deepest wisdom man can attain. It is our destiny to serve, to surrender. We have to conquer in order to succumb; we have to acquire in order to give away; we have to triumph in order to be overwhelmed. Man has to understand in order to believe, to know in order to accept. The aspiration is to obtain; the perfection is to dispense. This is the meaning of death: the ultimate self-dedication to the divine. Death so understood will not be distorted by the craving for immortality, for this act of giving away is reciprocity on man's part for God's gift of life. For the pious man it is a privilege to die.

The Holy Dimension

TO LOOK UPON RELIGION as upon a star, sublime, distant, and inaccessible, while at the same time handling it as if it were a bank account, a matter of calculation, wherein every detail is explainable and every transaction a computable operation, is an extravagant inconsistency. To apply a paleontological method to religion as if it were a fossil chiseled from the shale is intellectual violence. Indeed, the routine of our scientific procedure threatens to confine living religion in a frozen system of concepts, treating it as if it were a plant brought home by an expedition from exotic lands. But will observations made on a plant that is uprooted from its soil, removed from its native winds, sunrays, and vegetal surroundings, and kept in a hothouse disclose its primordial nature? The growth in the inwardness of man that reaches and curves toward the light of God can hardly be transplanted into the shallowness of mere reflection. When taken out of the depths of piety, it exists mostly in a symbiosis with other values like beauty, justice, or truth. Torn out of its medium in human life, it is metamorphosed like a rose pressed between the pages of a book. Reduced to terms and definitions, to concepts and moral principles, religion is like a desiccated remnant of a living reality.

Religion should be studied in its natural habitat of faith and piety, in a soul where the divine is within reach of all its thoughts. From the point of view of a critical mind, to which the enigmatic holiness of religion is not a certainty but a problem, we can hardly expect more than a telescopic examination, a glimpse from afar of what is to the pious man compellingly present and overwhelmingly close. A questionnaire submitted to a chance audience will not yield the evidence we need. It is fallacious to idealize neutral and indifferent informants. Vacancy of experience cannot be compensated for by lack of bias. How do we gain an adequate concept of history or astronomy? We do not turn to the man in the street but to those who devote their life to research, to those who are trained in scientific thought and have absorbed all the data about the subject. For an adequate concept of religion we likewise should turn to those whose mind is bent upon the spiritual, whose life *is* religion, and who are able to discern between truth and happiness, between spirit and emotion, between faith and self-reliance. Only those will apprehend religion who can probe its depth with unhalting precision, who can combine the intuition of love with rigor of method, who are able to translate the ineffable into thought and to forge the imponderable into words. It is not enough to describe the given content of religious consciousness. We have to press the man of piety with questions, compelling him to understand and unravel the meaning of what is taking place in his life as it stands at the divine horizon. While penetrating the consciousness of the pious man, we may conceive the reality behind it.

Every investigation springs out of a basic question, which sets the rudder of our mind. Yet the number of questions available for our research is limited. They are conventionally repeated in almost every scientific investigation. Like tools, they are handed down from one scholar to another. Not through our own eyes but through lenses ground by our intellectual ancestry do we look at the world. But our eyes are strained and tired of staring through spectacles worn by another generation. We are tired of overlooking entities, of squinting at their relations to other things. We want to face reality as it is and not ask only: What is its cause? What is its relation to its sources? To society? To psychological motives? We are tired of dating and comparing. Indeed, when the questions that were once keen and penetrating are worn out, the investigated object no longer reacts to the inquiry. Much depends upon the driving force of a new question. The question is an invocation of the enigma, a challenge to the examined object, provoking the answer. A new question is more than the projection or vision of a new goal; it is the first step toward it. To know what we want to know is the first prerequisite of research.

Modern man seldom faces things as they are. In the interpretation of religion our eyes are bent toward its bearing upon various realms of life rather than upon its own essence and reality. We investigate the relation of religion to economics, history, art, libido. We ask for the origin and development, for its effect upon psychical, social, and political life. We look upon religion as if it were an instrument only, not an entity. We forget to inquire: What is religion itself? In our contemplations religion as such is left in the background. In the foreground looms large and salient its subjective supplement, the human response to religion. We heed the resonance and ignore the bell, we peer into religiousness and forget religion, we behold the experience and disregard the reality that antecedes the experience. But to understand religion through the analysis of the sentiments it instills is as if instead of describing the inner value of a work of art we were to apprehend it by its effects on our mind or feelings. The essence of a thing is neither tantamount to nor commensurable with the impression it produces; what is reflected in the imagination of an individual is something altogether different from the original. The stratum of inner experience and the realm of objective reality do not lie on the same level.

IT IS HARD to dismiss the popular concept that religion is a function of human nature, an avenue in the wide estate of civilization. We have been indoctrinated with the idea that religion is man's own response to a need, the result of craving for immortality, or the attempt to conquer fear. But are we not like the dwellers in the desert who, never having seen rivers, presume that they are canals devised and constructed by man for navigation? It is true that economic needs and political factors have taught him to exploit the riverways. But are the rivers the product of human genius?

Most people assume that we feed our body to ease the pangs of hunger, to calm the irritated nerves of the empty stomach. As a matter of fact, we do not eat because we feel hungry but because the intake of food is essential for the maintenance of life, supplying the energy necessary for the various functions of the body. Hunger is the signal for eating, its occasion and regulator, not its true cause. Let us not confound the river with navigation, nutrition with hunger, or religion with the use which man makes of it.

To restrict religion to the realm of human endeavor or consciousness would imply that a person who refuses to take notice of God could isolate himself from the Omnipresent. But there is no neutrality before God; to ignore means to defy him. Even the emptiness of indifference breeds a concern, and the bitterness of blasphemy is a perversion of a regard for God. There is no vacuum of religion. Religion is neither the outgrowth of imagination nor the product of will. It is not an inner process, a feeling, or a thought, and should not be looked upon as a bundle of episodes in the life of man. To assume that religion is limited to specific acts of man, that man is religious for the duration of an experience, meditation, or performance of a ritual is absurd. Religion is not a cursory activity. What is going on between God and man is for the duration of life.

We do not see the forest for the trees. We hear, see, feel, and think, but are unaware of our soul; we devise systems of ideas and we organize society and nature but do not comprehend the purpose of our life. Our life seems to be a confused jumble of spasmodic and disconnected events. The overwhelming desire of yesterday is forgotten today, and the monumental achievement of today will be obliterated tomorrow. Does our soul live in dispersion? Is there nothing but a medley of facts unrelated to one another, chaos camouflaged by civilization?

The pious man believes that there is a secret interrelationship among all events, that the sweep of all we are doing reaches beyond the horizon of our comprehension, that there is a history of God and man in which everything is involved.

Religion is the light in which even the momentous appears as a detail. It is the ultimateness in the face of which everything seems premature, preliminary, and transitory. The pious man lives in esteem for ultimateness, in devotion to the final amid the mortal and evanescent. Religion to him is the integration of the detail into the whole, the infusion of the momentary into the lasting. As time and space in any perception, so is the totality of life implied in every act of piety. There is an objective coherency that holds all episodes together. A man may commit a crime now and teach mathematics perfectly an hour later. But when a man prays, all he has done in his life enters his prayer.

His own heart is not the source of that light in which the pious man sees his simple words becoming signals of eternity. Hands do not build the citadel in which the pious man takes shelter when all towers reared by man are tottering. Man does not produce what is overwhelming and holy. The wonder occurs to him when he is ready to accept it.

Religion is neither a state of mind nor an achievement of the intellect. It does not rule hearts by the grace of man; its roots lie not in his inwardness. It is not an event in the soul but a matter of fact outside the soul. Even what starts as an experience *in* man transcends the human sphere, becoming an objective event outside him. In this power of transcending the soul, time, and space, the pious man sees the distinction of religious acts. If prayer were only the articulation of words, of nothing but psychological relevance and of no metaphysical resonance, nobody would in an hour of crisis waste his time by praying in self-delusion.

Religion is a bestowal, a divine grant to man. It did not come into existence to console the desperate, to guarantee immortality, or to protect society. It is a reality in itself, not a function of man.

Religion is not an exclusive event in the course of time but a permanent condition, an invisible continuity. It is not a conclusion won from an inquiry into the nature of the universe, not an explanation of a riddle, but the living in the riddle, the effort to be the answer to the riddle oneself.

The domain of religion is the entire world, all of history, the vast as well as the tiny, the glorious as well as the trite. Everything in the universe throws its weight upon the scales of God's balance. Every deed denotes a degree in the gauge of the holy, irrespective of whether the man who performs it is aiming at this goal or not. It is just the nonritual, the secular conditions, which the prophets of Israel regarded as being a divine concern. To them the totality of human activities, social and individual, all inner and external circumstances, are the divine sphere of interest.

The desire of a pious man is not to acquire knowledge of God but to abide by him, to dedicate to him the entire life. How does he conceive the possibility of such devotion? How can man be near to God?

RELIGION in itself, the state which exists between God and man, is neither produced by man nor dependent upon his belief; it is neither a display of human spirit nor the outgrowth of his conscience. Religion exists even if it is in this moment not realized, perceived, or acknowledged by anybody, and those who reject or betray it do not diminish its validity. Religion is more than a creed or a doctrine, more than faith or piety; it is an everlasting fact in the universe, something that exists outside knowledge and experience, an *order of being*, the *holy dimension* of existence. It does not emanate from the affections and moods, aspirations and visions of the soul. It is not a divine force in us, a mere possibility, left to the initiative of man, something that may or may not take place, but an actuality, the inner constitution of the universe, the system of divine values involved in every being and exposed to the activity of man, the ultimate in our reality. As an absolute implication of being, as an ontological entity, not as an adorning veneer for a psychical wish or for a material want, religion cannot be totally described in psychological or sociological terms.

All actions are not only agencies in the endless series of cause and effect; they also affect and concern God, with or without human intention, with or without human consent. All existence stands in a holy dimension. All existence stands before God—not only men—here and everywhere, now and at all times. Not only a vow or conversion, not only the focusing of the mind upon God, engages man to Him. Life is enlistment in His service; all deeds, thoughts, feelings, and events become His concern.

Religion is, as it were, the space for perpetual contact between God and the universe. This condition outlasts catastrophes and apostasies and constitutes God's covenant with mankind and the universe.

Man does not possess religion; he exists *in* religion. This religious existence precedes his religious experience. Creed and aspiration are the adjustments of consciousness to the holy dimension. Religion is not an election; it is the destiny of man.

Man can know God only because God knows him. Our love of God is a scant reflection of God's love for us. For every soul is a wave in the endless stream that flows out of the heart of God.

Man is an animal at heart, carnal, covetous, selfish, and vain; yet spiritual in his destiny: a vision beheld by God in the darkness of flesh and blood. Only eyes vigilant and fortified against the glaring and superficial can still perceive God's vision in the soul's horror-stricken night of falsehood, hatred, and malice.

We are prone to be impressed by the ostentatious, the obvious. The strident caterwaul of the animal fills the air, while the still, small voice of the spirit is heard only in the rare hours of prayer and devotion. From the streetcar window we may see the hunt for wealth and pleasure, the onslaught upon the weak, faces expressing suspicion or contempt. On the other hand, the holy lives only in the depths. What is noble retires from sight when exposed to light, humility is extinguished in the awareness of it, and the willingness for martyrdom rests in the secrecy of the things to be. Walking upon clay, we live in nature, surrendering to impulse and passion, to vanity and arrogance, while our eyes reach out to the lasting light of truth. We are subject to terrestrial gravitation, yet we are faced by God.

In the holy dimension the spiritual is a bridge flung across a frightful abyss, while in the realm of nature the spiritual hovers like the wafted clouds, too tenuous to bear man across the abyss. When a vessel sails into a typhoon and the maw of the boiling maelstrom opens to envelop the tottering prey, it is not the pious man, engrossed in supplication, but the helmsman who intervenes in the proper sphere with proper means, fighting with physical tools against physical powers. What sense is there in imploring the mercy of God? Words do not stem the flood nor does meditation banish the storm. Prayer never entwines directly with the chain of physical cause and effect; the spiritual does not interfere with the natural order of things. The fact that man with undaunted sincerity pours into prayer the ichor of his soul springs from the conviction that there is a realm in which the acts of faith are puissant and potent, that there is an order in which things of spirit can be of momentous consequence.

There are phenomena which appear irrelevant and accidental in the realm of nature but are of great meaning in religion. To worship violence, to use brutal force, is natural, while sacrifice, humility, and martyrdom are absurd from the point of view of nature. It is in the domain of religion that a thought or a sentiment may stand out as an everlasting approach to truth, where prayers are steps toward him that never retreat.

Just as man lives in the realm of nature and is subject to its laws, so does he find himself in religion; and just as it is impossible to take leave of nature, so it is impossible to escape the bounds of religion. Whatever happens to man, he will sever himself from the dimension of the divine neither by sin nor by stupidity, neither by apostasy nor by ignorance.

It has become a general habit to denote religion as the relationship between God and man. However, relationship expresses only a particular aspect in the existence of a subject, while religion is an essence, the meaning and totality of existence. Relationships do not touch the quick of life. Man's being related to state, society, family, etc., does not penetrate all strata of his personality. In his final solitude, in the hour of approaching death, they are blown away like chaff. It is in religion, in the holy dimension, that he abides whatever befalls him.

There is no relationship *ex nihilo*, no relationship in a void. Every relationship presupposes a setting in which it can take place, the common ground to those associated in it. In this setting the relationship is potentially contained even before it comes into effect. It is the setting, origin, and possibility of the relationship between God and man that we call religion.

Man's life is not imprisoned in a realm wherein causality, struggle for existence, will to power, *libido sexualis*, and the craving for prestige are the only springs of action. Life is not permanently enslaved to these variable motives. It is woven into relations which run far beyond that realm. Besides the struggle for physical existence there is an effort to acquire meaning and value, an endeavor to preserve what is lasting in man, to maintain the essential in all the vicissitudes and changes. But what is the lasting in man? What is the meaning of the whole life, not of particular actions or of single episodes which happen now and then, but of existence as such?

WHAT DO we mean by the concept of existence? In ascribing existence to a person, we imply that the person is more than a mere word, name, or idea, and that he exists independent of us and our thinking, while what is denoted as a product of our imagination, like the chimerical Brobdingnags or the Yahoos, depends entirely on our mind; it is nonexistent when we do not think of it. However, existence so described is a negative concept, asserting what the existing is not or indicating the relation of the existing to us. What is the positive and direct meaning of existence? Even if we add that existence always implies some minimum of continuity or permanence, we gain nothing but an insight into the relation between existence and time, saying that the existing has some sequence in time. The concept of what is most fundamental is thus impregnable to analysis. It is even immune to a question, for to ask what *is* existence is almost a tautology. However, we may ask: What does existence mean to us? How do we understand our own existence?

We usually ignore the problem; it is an intellectual adventure that few dare. Yet we are harrowed with wonder and awe when swept by the awareness of our existence. When death wipes away what has once been dear, mighty, and independent, the rock and riddle of life fall upon us, and we learn that life is not a matter of course, that it cannot be taken for granted. Why are we in existence instead of nothing? Is life the offspring of nothingness or the germ of immortality? What is the course of the shuttle that runs but once between birth and death?

Our existence seesaws between what is more and what is less than existence. Death stands behind each of us, while before us is the open door of the divine exchequer, where we lay up the sterling coin of piety and spirit, the immortal remains of our dying lives. We are constantly in the mills of death, while for a limited time the contemporaries of God.

The island of existence is washed by the two oceans of eternity and nothingness, eroding it into what is less and elevating it into what is more than existence, into nothingness and into a higher reality, namely, the identity of event and value, the unity of being and meaning.

Existence, the domain of things and facts, is not the ultimate realm. There is a reality of spirit. The realm of values that illumine our lives— justice, beauty, goodness, purity, holiness—did not evolve from nature. Values cannot be derived from being nor can being be derived from nature. Both originate in a higher source. Values are ideals that ought to be realized, a challenge to nature, not a part of nature. Values are not laws of being that express a regularity in the life of nature like the laws of physics. They never fully agree with natural reality. Being as such is neutral and indifferent to values. The physician is not concerned with the question whether the heart of his patient is "good" or "bad" in a moral sense. He is interested only in a diagnosis of the physical condition. The cosmic tragedy is the abyss between being and value. It is incumbent upon us to build the bridge, to invade life with spirit, and to anoint the slaves of selfishness princes of spirit.

The universe, the apex of our abstractive thinking, is a concept of totality that implies not only the sum of parts but some sort of unity or system, in which each part has its specific function, in which each particular is related to the whole. Totality, the arrangement of being according to a purpose, is neither a quantity nor a relation; it is a quality *sui generis* that is not contained in the parts. "The human body contains a sufficient amount of fat to make seven cakes of soap, enough iron to make a medium-sized nail, a sufficient amount of phosphorus to equip two thousand matchheads; enough sulphur to rid oneself of one's fleas." But man as such is more than the mere addition of these elements. The parts did not exist prior to the whole; their character is derived from and conditioned by the whole. Totality is an essence, a value. But being valuable, it points toward something that is beyond itself. Things can be valuable only for something or somebody. The universe has a value that transcends its being; its totality is prior to its parts.

There is a connection between being and value. No being is without relation to value. The universe is not without windows. But where do they lead if not to God? Religion is the value of the universe, the inner unity of all being, a cosmic disposition toward what is more than being and value. As totality is implied in every part, so is the value of the universe involved in every event, in every phenomenon. The care for the universal in the particular, for the complete in the part, is the essence of piety. Piety is emancipation from the absurdity of the particular.

There is no existence in itself. Existence always belongs to an existing but is not identical with it. Every existence belongs to something that is by itself less than existence. But this relationship between existence and existing is transitory, mortal. All beings are perishable, passing, and always dependent upon external conditions. The very essence of existence reveals the inner impotence of being *qua* being. For existence implies, as we have seen, belonging to somebody as well as permanence and independence; but there is neither independence nor true permanence in the existence of an existing. This want manifests the dualism of being and value. Independence and permanence are values, the freedom from what is less than being, namely, nothingness. Existence as such is devoid of value and borders on nothingness. Hence existence must also imply another relationship that is permanent and independent; it must stand in a relationship to something that is devoid of nothingness. Existence without what is more than existence is an abstraction.

To exist is to belong to an existing as well as to something that is more than existence. Existence has two sides: one is directed to us; the other is open to God. To be means to belong to God and to man. This dual ownership is the value of life. In visions of wisdom, in devotion to the good, in submission to beauty, and when overwhelmed by the holy, we awake to behold existence in this relationship. In reverence, suffering, and humility we discover our existence and find the bridge that leads from existence to God. And this is religion.

Life is something that visits matter. It is a transcendent loan, hidden to man and faced by God. Since it is present in our body, we are inclined to take it for granted. To the unbiased mind it is a revelation of a transcendent sphere. Being neither physical nor emotional, neither material nor rational, it remains a mystery in spite of its reality. Human will never creates life. In generating life, man is the tool, not the master. Science can produce a machine but not an organism. The old dream of a homunculus, a man produced artificially, has been renounced by science. We know that something animates and inspirits a living body. But how? And whence does life come?

Nothing can exist or be conceived of as being apart from the holy dimension. Through our very existence we possess duration in the divine knowledge. Existence is our contact with God. In existence man discovers God. We do not infer ourself through a syllogism or through any reasoning but through our existence. So we approach God not only through our thoughts but, first of all, through our life.

Religion is the interest of God in man, his covenant with the universe. Our task is to concur with his interest, to live in accordance with God's vision of man. Piety is the response of man to the holy dimension, the subjective correlative of objective religion.[1]

We live not only in time and space but also in the knowledge of God. The events in the world reflect in him, and all existence is coexistence with God. Time and space are not the limits of the world. Our life occurs here and in the knowledge of God.

Faith

ONE OF THE GREATEST SHOCKS that we experience in our childhood comes with the discovery that our deeds and desires are not always approved by our fellow men, that the world is not mere food for our delight. The resistance we encounter, the refusals we meet with, open our eyes to the existence of a world outside ourselves. But, growing older and stronger, we gradually recover from that shock, forget its dolorous lesson, and apply most of our ingenuity to enforcing our will on nature and men. No recollection of our past experience is capable of upsetting the arrogance that guides the traffic in our mind. Dazzled by the brilliant achievements of the intellect in science and technique, we have been deluded into believing that we are the masters of the earth and our will the ultimate judge of what is right and wrong. However, the universe is not a waif and life is not a derelict. Man is neither the lord of the universe nor even the master of his own destiny. Our life is not our own property but a possession of God. And it is this divine ownership that makes life a sacred thing.

The world that we have long considered to be ours has exploded in our hands, and a stream of guilt and misery has been unloosed, which leaves no conscience unblemished. Will this flood of wretchedness sweep away our monstrous conceit? Will we comprehend that the sense for the sacred is as vital to us as the light of the sun? The enjoyment of beauty, possession, and safety in civilized society depends on man's sense for the sacredness of life, on his reverence for this spark of light in the darkness of selfishness. Permit this spark to be quenched and the darkness falls upon us like thunder.

We are impressed by the towering buildings of New York City. Yet not the rock of Manhattan nor the steel of Pittsburgh but the law that came from Sinai is their ultimate foundation. The true foundation upon which our cities stand is a handful of spiritual ideas. All of our life hangs by a thread—the faithfulness of man to the will of God.

The course in which human life moves is, like the orbit of heavenly bodies, an ellipse, not a circle. We are attached to two centers: to the focus of our self and to the focus of what is beyond our self. Even the intelligence is driven by two forces—by a force that comes as an instinct from within and by a force that comes with ideals from without. The inner force generates the impulse to acquire, to enjoy, to possess; the outer force arouses an urge to respond, to yield, to give.

It seems as though we have arrived at a point in history, closest to instincts and remotest from ideals, where the self stands like a wall between God and man. It is the period of a divine eclipse. We sail the seas, we count the stars, we split the atom, but never ask: Is there nothing but a dead universe and our reckless curiosity?

Primitive man's humble ear was alert to the inwardness of the world, while the modern man is presumptuous enough to claim that he has the sole monopoly over soul and spirit, that he is the only thing alive in the universe. A little crust of bread holds so much of goodness, of secret harmony, of tacit submission to purpose. Why should our minds be crowded by so much deceit, folly, and supercilious vanity?

BUT THERE is a dawn of wonder and surprise in our souls, when the things that surround us suddenly slip off the triteness with which we have endowed them, and their strangeness opens like a gap between them and our mind, a gap that no words can fill. How does it happen that I am using this pen and writing these lines? Who am I to scan the holy stars, to witness the settings of the sun, to have the service of the spring for my survival? How shall I ever reciprocate for breathing, thinking, for sight and hearing, for love and dreaming? Some delicate cognition weans us then from mistaking the benignity of the world for ownerlessness, its symbolic living for dull order.

What is the incense of self-esteem to him who tastes in all things the flavor of the utterly unknown, the fragrance of what is beyond our senses? There are neither skies nor oceans, neither birds nor trees—there are only signs of what can never be perceived. And all power and beauty are mere straws in the fire of a pure man's vision.

He who chooses a life of utmost striving for the utmost stake, the vital, matchless stake of God, feels as though the spirit of God comes to rest upon his lids—so close to his eyes and yet never seen. He who has ever been confronted with the ultimate and has realized that sun and stars and souls do not ramble in a vacuum will keep his heart in readiness for the hour when the world is entranced, and awaits a soul to breathe in the mystery that all things exhale in their craving for salvation. For things are not mute. The stillness is full of demands. Out of the world comes a behest to instill into the air a rapturous song for God, to incarnate in the stones a message of humble beauty, and to instill a prayer for goodness in the hearts of all children.

Beliefs are hanging over our souls like stars, remote and guiding: the freedom of God is the spring of all things; the life of man can sometimes be a mirror that God holds before His face; the destiny of Israel is to remain clean amid the mud of splendor and madness. The tenets shine through dark and dangerous ages. Their reflection can be seen in the ways of contemporaries whose life is like a fountain of conscience and memory in the desert of careless living.

Since those basic principles of Jewish life have moved into our mind, the wonder has never left our eyes. Heedfully we stare through the telescope of ancient rites lest we lose the sight of the promise of God, the perpetual brightness at the edge of our soul. Our mind has not kindled the flame, has not produced these principles. Still our thoughts glow with their light. What is the nature of this glow, of this faith? and how is it acquired?

FAITH IS sensitiveness to what transcends nature, knowledge, and will, awareness of the ultimate, alertness to the holy dimension of all reality.[1] Faith is a force in man, lying deeper than the stratum of reason and its nature cannot be defined in abstract, static terms. To have faith is not to infer the beyond from the wretched here, but to perceive the wonder that is here and to be stirred by the desire to integrate the self into the holy order of living. It is not a deduction but an intuition, not a form of knowledge, of being convinced without proof, but the attitude of mind toward ideas whose scope is wider than its own capacity to grasp.

Such alertness grows with the sense for the meaningful, for the marvel of matter, for the core of thoughts. It is begotten in passionate love for the significance of all reality, in devotion to the ultimate meaning which is only God. By our very existence we are in dire need of meaning, and anything that calls for meaning is always an allusion to Him. We live by the certainty that we are not as dust in the wind, that our life is related to the ultimate, the meaning of all meanings. And the system of meanings that permeates the universe is like an endless flight of stairs. Even when the upper steps are beyond our sight, we constantly rise toward the distant goal.

Strange and scattered are the wells from which we draw the transport of faith. Some of us are sickened by the dismay over living constantly for naught, by the dread of an unprepared death; some are thrilled by the innocence of limbs and words, misused by our whims and sins and insolence. Others are charmed by the sanctity of living for His laws. Instead of indulging in jealousy, greed, in relishing themselves, there are men who keep their hearts alert to the stillness in which time rolls on and leaves us behind. It is only God who would never desert us, who sues for our devotion, audibly, constantly, persistently.

Forgoing beauty for goodness, power for love, grief for gratitude, entreating the Lord for help to understand our hopes, for strength to resist our fears, we shall receive a gentle sense for the holiness that permeates the air like a strangeness that cannot be removed. Crying out of the pitfall of our selfishness for purity of devotion will usher in the dawn of faith in the mist of honest tears. For those who are open to the wonder will not miss it. Faith is found in solicitude for faith, in an inner care for the wonder that is everywhere.

Highest in the list of virtues, this anxious caring extends not only to the moral sphere but to all realms of life, to oneself and to others, to words and to thoughts, to events and to deeds. Unawed by the prevailing narrowness of mind, it persists as an attitude toward the whole of reality; to hold small things great, to take light matters seriously, to think of the common and the passing from the aspect of the lasting.

Timid knocking at distant gates of silence, inquiring whether or not God is dwelling somewhere, the exuberant growth of evil notwithstanding, is not a move of faith. Only straight discovering in the nearest stone or tree, sound or thought, the shelter of His often desecrated goodness, the treasury of His waiting for man's heart to affiliate with His will—this is the rapture of faith. It is an echo to a pleading voice, a reply to the inconceivable in all beauty. The tumult of strife and envy, insidious selfishness, inflation of cruelty, is a poor setting for the plain unfolding of the divine. Yet a force from beyond our conscience cries at the insolent haughtiness of man, reminding and admonishing that the wanton will fail in rebellion against the good. He who listens to this voice opens his life to the sight of the unseen in the desert of indifference.

IS FAITH just another feature of man's mentality, the self-effacement of curiosity, the asceticism of reason? No, it is not an inner, private quality that concerns the character of man alone, but rather the extension of man's love to what God may approve, a wave in the tide of His thoughts, rising to the dry and desolate shore of man's despair. Faith is real only when it is not one-sided but reciprocal. Man can rely on God, if God can rely on man. We may trust in Him because He trusts in us. Our trustworthiness for God is the measure of the integrity of our faith. Thus faith is an awareness of divine mutuality and companionship, a form of communion between God and man. It is not a psychical quality, something that exists in the mind only, but a force from the beyond.

Faith is not the clinging to a shrine but the endless, tameless pilgrimage of hearts. Audacious longing, calling, calling, burning songs, daring thoughts, an impulse overwhelming the heart, usurping the mind—it is all a stalwart driving to the precious serving of Him who rings our hearts like a bell, wishing to enter our empty perishing life. What others call readiness to suffer, willingness to relinquish, is felt here as bestowal of joy, as granting of greatness. Is it a surrender to confide? Is it a sacrifice to believe? True, beliefs are not secured by demonstration nor impregnable to objection. But does goodness mean serving only as long as rewarding lasts? Towers are more apt to be shaken than graves. Insistent doubt, contest, and frustration may stultify the trustworthy mind, may turn temples into shambles. But those of faith who plant sacred thoughts in the uplands of time, the secret gardeners of the Lord in mankind's desolate hopes, may slacken and tarry but rarely betray their vocation.

Faith is always exposed to failure. We often submit to the forces that draw us down to where a small desire seems to outweigh the noblest aspiration. There is the network of the false into which we easily slip. There is the enjoyment of the vile that vitiates the taste for the true. We must not cease to be vigilant, careful and anxious to keep our inner ear open to the holy.

Faith is not a languid attitude of resignation toward the chances of life, a fatalistic apotheosis of all events. To regard all that happens as workings of Providence is to deny human responsibility. We must not idolize history. This world is more frequently subject to the power of man than to the love of God.

Faith comes over us like a force urging for action. It often begins by pledging us to constancy of devotion, by committing us to the presence of God, and remains an affiliation for life, an allegiance involving restraint, submission, self-control, and courage. Its power is revealed when man is able to exercise defiance in the face of adversity.

We cannot stem the tempest of evil by taking refuge in temples, by fervently adoring the restrained omnipotence of God. Our task is to act not only to enjoy; to change not only to accept; to augment not only to discover the glory of God. And life is refulgent with possibilities of creating the good.

He whose soul is charged with awareness of God earns his inner livelihood by a passionate desire to pour his life into the eternal wells of love. What is it that makes us worthy of life, if not our compassion and ability to help? We do not exist for our own sake. Life would be preposterous if not for the love it confers.

Faith implies no denial of evil, no disregard of danger, no whitewashing of the abominable. He whose heart is given to faith is mindful of the obstructive and awry, of the sinister and pernicious. It is God's strange dominion over both good and evil on which he relies. But even this reliance is not an indefeasible bridge across ravines and precipices, a viaduct over the valley of death. To rely only on our faith would be idol worship. We have only the right to rely on God, on His love and mercy. Faith is not a mechanical insurance but a dynamic, personal act, flowing between the heart of man and the love of God.

Yet life is not all action. Our body and soul, the sun and the air we breathe are not the products of our will. We receive more than we give. We find in nature both motion and stillness, stir and tranquillity, initiative and acquiescence. The attitude of faith is that the totality of being is not chaos but order, that there is often more dignity in acceptance than in rebellion. The man of faith will know when to consent and when to defy.

NOT THE individual man nor a single generation by its own power can erect the bridge that leads to God. Faith is the achievement of many generations, an effort accumulated over centuries. Many of its ideas are as the light of the star that left its source a long time ago. Many enigmatic songs, unfathomable today, are the resonance of voices of bygone times. There is a collective memory of God in the human spirit, and it is this memory which is the main source of our faith.

However, faith is not a stagnant pool. It is, rather, a fountain that rises with the influx of personal experience. Personal faith flows out of an experience and a pledge. For faith is not a thing that comes into being out of nothing. It originates in an event. In the spiritual vacancy of life something may suddenly occur that is like lifting the veil at the horizon of knowledge. A simple episode may open a sight of the eternal. A shift of conceptions, boisterous like a tempest or soft as a breeze, may swerve the mind for an instant or forever. For God is not wholly silent and man is not always deaf. God's willingness to call men to His service and man's responsiveness to the divine indications in things and events are for faith what sun and soil are for the plant.

That experience survives as a recollection of how we have once been blessed by the manifestation of divine presence in our life. The remembrance of that experience and the loyalty to the pledge given at that moment are the forces that sustain us in our faith.

For the riches of a soul are stored up in its memory. This is the test of character, not whether a man follows the daily fashion, but whether the past is alive in his present. If we want to understand ourselves, to find out what is most precious in our lives, we should search into our memory.

Only those who are spiritually imitators, only people who are afraid to be grateful and too weak to be loyal, have nothing but the present moment. The mark of nobility is inherited possession. To a noble person it is a holy joy to remember, an overwhelming thrill to be grateful, while to a person whose character is neither rich nor strong, gratitude is a most painful sensation. The secret of wisdom is never to get lost in a momentary mood or passion, never to forget friendship over a momentary grievance, never to lose sight of the lasting values over a transitory episode. The tide of things which sweeps through our daily life should never be a whirlpool devouring our energies, but a fountain from which to draw visions and ideas to enrich the treasury of our soul, our memory. That only is valuable in our experience which is worth remembering. Remembrance is the touchstone of all our actions.

An exquisite feature of the Jewish mentality is its phenomenal power of recollection. With a passionate tenacity we have retained through the ages the recollection of what happened to our people. Once a light had been kindled in the temple of our history, it was never extinguished. We are the keepers of ancient events. The immortal past of our people has survived with sustaining vitality in our thoughts, in our hearts, in our ritual. To us, recollection is a holy act; we sanctify the present by re-membering the past. To us Jews, the essence of faith is memory. To believe is to remember. For what is the function of faith? Each of us has at least once in his life experienced the momentous reality of God. Each of us has once caught a glimpse of the beauty, peace, and power that flow through the souls of those who are devoted to God. But such ex-periences or inspirations are rare events. To some people they are like shooting stars, passing and unremembered. In others they kindle a light that is never quenched. Faith is loyalty to an experience. Faith is loyalty to an inspiration that has occurred to us. Jewish faith is recollection of that which occurred to our ancestors, of that which happened to Israel in the past. The events in which the spirit of God became a reality of history stood before our eyes painted in colors that never fade. Much of what the Bible demands can be comprised in one imperative: Remember!

IN THE LIGHT of faith we do not seek to unveil or to explain but to perceive and to absorb the rarities of mystery that are gleaming softly from all things; not to know more, but to know what is more than anything we can grasp. Only those who maintain that all things in life and death are within reach of their will will try to place the world in the frame of their knowledge. But how can our soul be insensitive to the fragrance of the unknown that is bestowed upon our life? What is most dear and real is neither known nor knowable.

With the gentle sense for the depth of all existence, for the sacred relevance of all being, the man of faith can afford to forgo the joy of knowing, the thrill of perceiving, bent upon by the ears, eyes, and mind. For he who loves the grandeur of what faith is alive to dwells at a distance from his goal, shuns familiarity with the necessarily hidden, and looks for neither proofs nor miracles. God's existence can never be tested by human thought. All proofs are mere demonstrations of our thirst for Him. Does the thirsty need a proof for his thirst?

The realm toward which faith is directed can be approached, but not penetrated; approximated, but not entered; aspired to, but not grasped; sensed, but not understood. For to believe is to abide rationally outside, while spiritually within the mystery.

Faith is an act of spirit. The spirit can afford to acknowledge the superiority of the divine: it has the fortitude to realize the greatness of the transcendent, to love its superiority. The man of faith is not enticed by the ostensible. He abstains from intellectual arrogance and spurns the triumph of the merely obvious. He knows that possession of truth is devotion to it. He rejoices more in giving than in acquiring, more in believing than in perceiving. He can afford to disregard the deficiencies of reason. This is the secret of the spirit which is not disclosed to reason: the adaptation of the mind to the sacred. The spirit surrenders to the mystery of the spirit, not in resignation or despair, but with honor and in love. Exposing its destiny to the Ultimate, it enters into an intimate relation with God. Faith is intellectual humility, devotion of the mind, a true offering, the finest feat the heart can perform.

Some men go without knowing on a hunger strike in the prison of the mind, starving for God. There is joy, ancient and sudden, in this starving. There is reward, grasp of the intangible, in the flaming reverie breaking through the latticework of notions.

FAITH AS the act of believing should be distinguished from creed as the content, as that in which we believe. Faith, itself as little rational as love of beauty or motherly affection, becomes a dogma or a doctrine when pressed into an opinion. Our creed is, like music, a translation of the unutterable into sounds, thoughts, words, deeds. The original is known to God alone. And what is expressed and taught as a creed is but the adaptation of the uncommon spirit to the common sense. Yet it is the creed that keeps the flame when our thoughts go out and we lose the sight of our beloved dreams. For the words of our great sages, full of never aging grace, are to us like a mother that never forgets, that is not impatient of folly or failing.

There are many creeds but only one faith. Creeds may change, develop, and grow flat, while the substance of faith remains the same in all ages. The overgrowth of creed may bring about the disintegration of that substance. The proper relation is a minimum of creed and a maximum of faith.

Driven by soaring faith to the delight of reaching out for God, men of faith have often been stabbed in the back by the idea that faith is not an elevation but a depression, a lower form of thinking, a substitute befitting the poor in the kingdom of reason. Strangely enough, many went down to reach the height, descending to insipid formulas, to words that were shells without feeling.

Those who are prone to evaluate music with their tongue and the shades of color with their fingers may be consistent in trying to compare faith with reason and to embroider religion on the academic gown of logicians. And who is not guilty of attempting to understand love as a syllogism and beauty as an algebraic equation? Only rarely has man resisted the temptation to aid faith by gaining approval for its claim from any impertinent science. In fact, the fascination that goes with the gentle power of faith lies in its defiance of our limitations.

The force that inspires the heart to believe is not identical with the impulse that stimulates the mind to reason. The thoughts that breed beauty in the songs of faith may fashion shackles around the reckless wrists of scholars. The purity of which we never cease to dream, the untold things we so insatiably love, the vision of the good for which we either die or perish alive—no reason can hold. It is faith from which we draw the sweetness of life, the taste of the sacred, the joy of the imperishably dear. It is faith that offers us a share in eternity. It is faith in which the great things occur.

We rarely manage to cross the gulf between heart's believing and mind's plain knowing. There is no common basis for comparing religion and science. It is impossible to render the visions of faith in terms of speculation, and its truth cannot be proved by logical arguments. Its certainty is intuitive, not speculative. Its apparent demonstration has often resulted in its frustration. Unlike knowledge, which is a quiet possession of the intellect, faith is an overwhelming force that enables man to perceive the reality of the transcendent. It is not only the assent to a proposition but the staking of the whole life on the truth of an invisible reality.

Formulated belief is an attempt to translate into words an unutterable spiritual reality. We should never forget that any attempt to vindicate belief does not deal with the original reality but with the translation; it tries to integrate an imitation into the system of original logical symbols. Moreover, from a rational justification of faith, we may gain the idea that the existence of God is as probable as ether in physics or phlogiston in chemistry, a hypothesis that can easily be refuted or rendered superfluous by a change of premises. Such a supposition is an impotent expression for the most powerful idea of the human soul. It tries to fill out the universe with a tiny abstract figure of speech.

In the realm of faith, God is not a hypothesis derived from logical assumptions but an immediate insight, self-evident as light. To rationalists He is something after which they seek in the darkness with the light of their reason. To men of faith He *is* the light.

Faith is not an act of thinking logically and consecutively. Its ripe fruit is not a cold judgment, valid and correct when estimated from any point of view. There may be a great deal of vagueness in faith, lacking both distinctness and precision. Its body is too fine to be retained in the logician's sieve when sifted for formulas. Rational terms in which faith is expressed as a creed remain a varnish and do not render its essence.

The perceivable and temporal we grasp with our reason, the sacred and everlasting we approach through faith. It belongs to the genius of man to believe, to look up to what transcends his faculty to know, to perceive the things in their relation to the ultimate, to the eternally valid. However, since there is no borderline that keeps apart the temporal from the everlasting, the scope of faith can hardly be circumscribed.

Knowledge is the integration of the unknown with the known; faith is the integration of the known with the unknown. The historian explains the suffering of Israel with the geographical condition of Palestine, which, situated astride the crossroad of three continents, was exposed to the ambitions of conquerors. The prophet speaks of a divine plan to let Israel be afflicted in order to atone not for his own sins but for the sins of the heathens.

Faith is something that comes out of the soul. It is not a piece of information that is absorbed but an attitude, existing prior to the formulation of any creed. It is the insight that life is not a self-maintaining, private affair, not a chaos of whims and instincts, but an aspiration, a way not a refuge. In the impact of our forces—body, intellect, will, imagination, emotion—with reality, we stumble upon the poverty of our justice and glimpse the richness of values we can dream of.

REASON IS NOT the measure of all things, not the all-inclusive power in the inner life of man. The powers of will and emotion, the realm of the subconscious lie beyond the scope of knowledge. The rush of reason is an effort of limited strength.

Faith is not a miniature of thinking but its model, not its shadow but its root. It is a spiritual force in man, not dealing with the given, concrete, limited, but directed upon the transcendent. It is the spring of our creative actions.

In believing we anticipate what reason, will, and emotion may grasp afterward. The evaporation of believing sheds drops of reason into the mind. All action is vicarious faith.

Reality is not exhausted by knowledge. Inaccessible to research are the ultimate facts. All scientific conclusions are based upon axioms, all reasoning depends ultimately upon faith. Faith is virgin thinking, preceding and transcending all knowledge. To believe is to abide at the extremities of spirit.

Are we able to prove the principles upon which we rely in our actions? The things we accept are more numerous than the things we gain by our own inquiries. Our knowledge contains more that is inherited than explored. As individuals we owe more to tradition than to our own research.

For the reality, which man has at his disposal here and now, is narrow and limited. What will happen in the next instant, what is beyond the scope of his direct experience, what lies ahead in time or remote in space, is behind a veil, recondite and obscure. Nobody can prove that the sun will rise tomorrow. Man has to take into consideration latencies and uncertainties, contingencies, surprises, and chances. He may be shaken and he may recoil before the perilous impact of possibilities, he may hesitate to go forward, suspend the next step, and live bewildered, in a quandary. Or he may take the leap in the dark haphazardly. Were men not in possession of courage, foresight, and trust, which are the general conditions of faith, there would be no activity.

Man has to venture, to risk, not to be afraid of possible failures, but be defiant of peril, ready to suffer without thinking, willing to take upon himself grief and anguish, pain and sorrow. Man needs foresight in order to sense what is behind the veil, to anticipate the potential, to scent from afar the qualities and values of reality. Only weariness and fear counteract these forces, stemming and hindering man's efforts and strivings.

There is neither advance nor service without faith. Nobody can rationally explain why he should sacrifice his life and happiness for the sake of the good. The conviction that I must obey the ethical imperatives is not derived from logical arguments but originates in an intuitive certitude, in a certitude of faith.

There is no conspiracy against reason, no random obstinacy, no sluggish inertia of mind or smug self-assurance entrenched behind the walls of believing. Faith does not detach man from thinking, it does not suspend reason. It is opposed not to knowledge but to backwardness and dullness, to indifferent aloofness to the essence of living. It is not an isolated trend of the mind, but is in need of clarification and of a corrective in order to establish the contents and objects of belief, to secure its inner consistency. It is a distortion to regard reason and faith as alternatives. Reason is a necessary coefficient of faith. Faith without explication by reason is mute, reason without faith is deaf. There can be a true symbiosis of reason and faith.

The account of our experiences, the record of debit and credit, is reflected in the amount of trust or distrust we display toward life and humanity. There are those who maintain that the good is within our reach everywhere; you have but to stretch out your arms and you will grasp it. But there are others who, intimidated by fraud and ugliness, sense scorn and ambushes everywhere and misgive all things to come. Those who trust develop a finer sense for the good, even at the high cost of blighted hopes. Charmed by the spell of love, faith is, as it were, imposed upon their heart.

Actually, trust is the core of human relationships, of gregariousness among men. Friendship, a puzzle to the syllogistic and critical mentality, is not based on experiments or tests of another person's qualities but on trust. It is not critical knowledge but a risk of the heart which initiates affection and preserves loyalty to our fellow men.

Faith does not spring out of nothing. It comes with the discovery of the holy dimension of our existence. Suddenly we become aware that our lips touch the veil that hangs before the Holy of Holies. Our face is lit up for a time with the light from behind the veil. Faith opens our hearts for the entrance of the holy. It is almost as though God were thinking for us.

Prayer

ABOUT A HUNDRED YEARS AGO, Rabbi Isaac Meir Alter of Ger pondered the question of what a certain shoemaker of his acquaintance should do about his morning prayer. His customers were poor men who owned only one pair of shoes. The shoemaker used to pick up their shoes at a late evening hour and work on them the whole night and part of the morning, in order to deliver them before their owners had to go to work. When should the shoemaker say his morning prayer? Should he pray quickly the first thing in the morning and then go back to work? Or should he continue his work, let the appointed hour of prayer go by, and, every once in a while, raising his hammer from the shoes, utter a sigh: "Woe unto me, I haven't prayed yet!"? Perhaps that sigh is worth more than prayer itself.

We, too, face this dilemma of wholehearted regret or perfunctory fulfillment. Many of us regretfully refrain from habitual prayer, waiting for an urge that is complete, sudden, and unexampled. But the unexampled is scarce, and perpetual refraining can easily grow into a habit—idle, sullen, and stolid. We may even come to forget what to regret, what to miss.

PRAYER AS AN ANSWER

WE DO NOT refuse to pray. We merely feel that our tongue is tied, our mind inert, our inner vision dim, when we are about to enter the door that leads to prayer. We do not refuse to pray; we abstain from it. We ring the hollow bell of selfishness, rather than absorb the stillness that surrounds the world, that hovers over all the restlessness and fear of life —the secret stillness that precedes our birth and follows our death. Futile self-indulgence brings us out of tune with the gentle song of nature's waiting, of mankind's striving for salvation. Is not listening to the pulse of wonder worth silence and abstinence from self-assertion? Why do we not set apart an hour of living for devotion to God by surrendering to stillness? We dwell on the edge of mystery and ignore it, wasting our souls, risking our stake in God. We constantly pour our inner light away from Him, setting up the thick screen of self between Him and us, adding more shadows to the darkness that already hovers between Him and our wayward reason. Accepting surmises as dogmas and prejudices as solutions, we ridicule the evidence of life for what is more than life. Our mind has ceased to be sensitive to the wonder. Deprived of the power of devotion to what is more important than our individual fate, steeped in passionate anxiety to survive, we lose sight of what fate is, of what living is. Rushing through the ecstasies of ambition, we awake only when plunged into dread or grief. In darkness, then, we grope for solace, for meaning, for prayer.

But there is a wider, voluntary entrance to prayer than sorrow and despair—the opening of our thoughts to God. We cannot make Him visible to us, but we can make ourselves visible to Him. So we open our thoughts to Him—feeble our tongue, but sensitive our heart. We see more than we can say. The trees stand like guards of the Everlasting; the flowers like signposts of His goodness—only *we* have failed to be testimonies to His presence, tokens of His trust. How could we have lived in the shadow of greatness and defied it?

Mindfulness of God rises slowly, a thought at a time. Suddenly we are there. Or is He here, at the margin of our soul? When we begin to feel a qualm of diffidence lest we hurt what is holy, lest we break what is whole, then we discover that He is not austere. He answers with love our trembling awe. Repentant of forgetting Him even for a while, we become sharers of gentle joy; we would like to dedicate ourselves forever to the unfolding of His final order.

To pray is to take notice of the wonder, to regain the sense of the mystery that animates all beings, the divine margin in all attainments. Prayer is our humble answer to the inconceivable surprise of living. It is all we can offer in return for the mystery by which we live. Who is worthy to be present at the constant unfolding of time? Amid the meditation of mountains, the humility of flowers—wiser than all alphabets—clouds that die constantly for the sake of beauty, *we* are hating, hunting, hurting. Suddenly we feel ashamed of our clashes and complaints in the face of the tacit greatness in nature. It is so embarrassing to live! How strange we are in the world, and how presumptuous our doings! Only one response can maintain us: gratefulness for witnessing the wonder, for the gift of our unearned right to serve, to adore, and to fulfill. It is gratefulness which makes the soul great.

However, we often lack the strength to be grateful, the courage to answer, the ability to pray. To escape from the mean and penurious, from calculating and scheming, is at times the parching desire of man. Tired of discord, he longs to escape from his own mind—and for the peace of prayer. How good it is to wrap oneself in prayer, spinning a deep softness of gratitude to God around all thoughts, enveloping oneself in the silk of a song! But how can man draw songs out of his heart if his consciousness is a woeful turmoil of fear and ambition? He has nothing to offer but disgust, and the weariness of wasting the soul. Accustomed to winding strands of thoughts, to twisting phrases in order to reap praise, he is incapable of finding simple, straight words. His language abounds in traps and decoys, in shams and tricks, in gibes and sneers. In the teeth of such powerful distractions he has to focus all the powers of his mind on one concern. In the midst of universal agitation how can there be tranquillity?

Trembling in the realization that we are a blend of modesty and insolence, of self-denial and bias, we beseech God for rescue, for help in the control of our thoughts, words, and deeds. We lay all our forces before Him. Prayer is arrival at the border. "The dominion is Thine. Take away from me all that may not enter Thy realm."

PRAYER AND THE SPIRITUAL LIFE

AS A TREE torn from the soil, as a river separated from its source, the human soul wanes when detached from what is greater than itself. Without the ideal, the real turns chaotic; without the universal, the individual becomes accidental. It is the pattern of the impeccable which makes the average possible. It is the attachment to what is spiritually superior: loyalty to a sacred person or idea, devotion to a noble friend or teacher, love for a people or for mankind, which holds our inner life together. But any ideal, human, social, or artistic, if it forms a roof over all of life, shuts us off from the light. Even the palm of one hand may bar the light of the entire sun. Indeed, we must be open to the remote in order to perceive the near. Unless we aspire to the utmost, we shrink to inferiority.

Prayer is our attachment to the utmost. Without God in sight, we are like the scattered rungs of a broken ladder. To pray is to become a ladder on which thoughts mount to God to join the movement toward Him which surges unnoticed throughout the entire universe. We do not step out of the world when we pray; we merely see the world in a different setting. The self is not the hub, but the spoke of the revolving wheel. In prayer we shift the center of living from self-consciousness to self-surrender. God is the center toward which all forces tend. He is the source, and we are the flowing of His force, the ebb and flow of His tides.

Prayer takes the mind out of the narrowness of self-interest and enables us to see the world in the mirror of the holy. For when we betake ourselves to the extreme opposite of the ego, we can behold a situation from the aspect of God. Prayer is a way to master what is inferior in us, to discern between the signal and the trivial, between the vital and the futile, by taking counsel with what we know about the will of God, by seeing our fate in proportion to God. Prayer clarifies our hopes and intentions. It helps us discover our true aspirations, the pangs we ignore, the longings we forget. It is an act of self-purification, a quarantine for the soul. It gives us the opportunity to be honest, to say what we believe, and to stand for what we say. For the accord of assertion and conviction, of thought and conscience, is the basis of all prayer.

Prayer teaches us what to aspire for. So often we do not know what to cling to. Prayer implants in us the ideals we ought to cherish. Salvation, purity of mind and tongue, or willingness to help may hover as ideas before our mind, but the idea becomes a concern, something to long for, a goal to be reached, when we pray: "Guard my tongue from evil and my lips from speaking guile; and in the face of those who curse me, let my soul be silent."

Prayer is the essence of spiritual living. Its spell is present in every spiritual experience. Its drive enables us to delve into what is beneath our beliefs and desires, and to emerge with a renewed taste for the endless simplicity of the good. On the globe of the microcosm the flow of prayer is like the Gulf Stream, imparting warmth to all that is cold, melting all that is hard in our life. For even loyalties may freeze to indifference if detached from the stream which carries the strength to be loyal. How often does justice lapse into cruelty and righteousness into hypocrisy. Prayer revives and keeps alive the rare greatness of some past experience in which things glowed with meaning and blessing. It remains important, even when we ignore it for a while, like a candlestick set aside for the day. Night will come, and we shall again gather round its tiny flame. Our affection for the trifles of living will be mixed with longing for the comfort of all men.

However, prayer is no panacea, no substitute for action. It is, rather, like a beam thrown from a flashlight before us into the darkness. It is in this light that we who grope, stumble, and climb discover where we stand, what surrounds us, and the course which we should choose. Prayer makes visible the right, and reveals the hampering and the false. In its radiance we behold the worth of our efforts, the range of our hopes, and the meaning of our deeds. Envy and fear, despair and resentment, anguish and grief, which lie heavily upon the heart, are dispelled like shadows by its light.

Sometimes prayer is more than a light before us; it is a light within us. Those who have once been resplendent with this light find little meaning in speculations about the efficacy of prayer. A story is told about a rabbi who once entered heaven in a dream. He was permitted to approach the temple in Paradise where the great sages of the Talmud, the *tannaim*, were spending their eternal lives. He saw that they were just sitting around tables studying the Talmud. The disappointed rabbi wondered, "Is this all there is to Paradise?" But suddenly he heard a voice, "You are mistaken. The *tannaim* are not in Paradise. Paradise is in the *tannaim*."

SUFFERING — THE SOURCE OF PRAYER?

IN THOSE SOULS in which prayer is a rare flower, enchanting, surprising, and scarce, it seems to come to pass by the lucky chance of misfortune, as an inevitable or adventitious by-product of affliction. But suffering is not the source of prayer. A motive does not bring about an act as a cause produces an effect; it merely stimulates the potential into becoming the actual. Peril or want may clear the ground for its growth, stubbing up the weeds of self-assurance, ridding the heart of the hard and obdurate, but it can never raise prayer.

To a farmer about to prepare a seedbed, the prerequisite for his undertaking is not the accidental need of a crop. His need of food does not endow him with skill in cultivating the earth; it merely affords the stimulus and purpose for his undertaking. It is his knowledge, his possession of the idea of tillage, which enables him to raise crops. The same principle applies to prayer. The natural loyalty of living, fertilized by faith saved through a lifetime, is the soil on which prayer can grow. Laden with secret fertility, and patient discreetness concerning things to be and things forever unknown, the soil of the soul nourishes and holds the roots of prayer. But the soil by itself does not produce crops. There must also be the idea of prayer to make the soul yield its amazing fruit.

The idea of prayer may seem to be the assumption of man's ability to accost God, to lay our hopes, sorrows, and wishes before Him. But this assumption is a paraphrase rather than a precise expression of what we believe. We do not feel that we possess a magic power of speaking to the Infinite; we merely witness the wonder of prayer, the wonder of man addressing himself to the Eternal. Contact with Him is not our achievement. It is a gift, coming down to us from on high like a meteor, rather than rising up like a rocket. Before the words of prayer come to the lips, the mind must believe in God's willingness to draw near to us, and in our ability to clear the path for His approach. Such belief is the idea that leads us toward prayer.

Prayer is not a soliloquy. But is it a dialogue with God? Does man address Him person to person? It is incorrect to describe prayer with the analogy of human conversation; we do not communicate with God. We only make ourselves communicable to Him. Prayer is an emanation of what is most precious in us toward Him, the outpouring of the heart before Him. It is not a relationship between person and person, between subject and subject, but an endeavor to become the object of His thought.

Prayer is like the light from a burning glass in which all the rays that emanate from the soul are gathered to a focus. There are hours when we are resplendent with the glowing awareness of our share in His secret interests on earth. We pray. We are carried forward to Him who is coming close to us. We endeavor to divine His will, not merely His command. Prayer is an answer to God: "Here am I. And this is the record of my days. Look into my heart, into my hopes and my regrets." We depart in shame and joy. Yet prayer never ends, for faith endows us with a bold craving that He draw near to us and approach us as a father—not only as a ruler, not only through our walking in His ways, but through His entering into our ways. The purpose of prayer is to be brought to His attention, to be listened to, to be understood by Him; not to know Him, but to *be known* to Him. To pray is to behold life not only as a result of His power but as a concern of His will, or to strive to make it a divine concern. For the ultimate aspiration of man is to be not a master but an object of His knowledge. To live "in the light of His countenance," to become a thought of God—this is the true career of man.

But are we worthy of being known, of entering into His mercy, of being a matter of concern to Him? It seems as if the meaning of prayer lies in man's aspiration to be thought of by God as one who is thinking of Him. Man waxes in God when serving the sacred, and wanes when he betrays his task. Man lives in His mind when He abides in human life.

There is no human misery more strongly felt than the state of being forsaken by God. Nothing is so terrible as rejection by Him. It is a horror to live deserted by God, effaced from His mind. The fear of being forgotten even for an instant is a powerful spur to a pious man to bring himself to the attention of God, to keep his life *worth* being known to Him. He prefers to be smitten by His punishment rather than to be left alone. In all his prayers he begs, explicitly or implicitly, "Do not forsake me, O Lord."

The man who betrays Him day after day, drunk with vanity, resentment, or reckless ambition, lives in a ghostly mist of misgivings. Having ruined love with greed, he is still wondering about the lack of tenderness. His soul contains a hiding place for an escaping conscience. He has torn his ties to God into shreds of shrieking dread, and his ear is dull and callous. Spoiler of his own lot, he walks the earth a skeleton of a soul, raving about missed delight.

God is not alone when discarded by man. But man is alone. To avoid prayer constantly is to dig a gap between man and God which can widen into an abyss. But sometimes, awakening on the edge of despair to weep, and arising from forgetfulness, we feel how yearning moves in softly to become the lord of a restless breast, and we pass over the gap with the lightness of a dream.

THE NATURE OF KAVANAH

A RABBI once remarked on the passage in the Amidah "For Thou hearkenest in mercy to the prayer of every mouth" that we would expect the phrase to be "the prayer of every heart." But the passage wishes to remind us that it is the mercy of God to accept even prayers that come only from the mouth as lip service, without inner devotion. However, this remark in no way denies the principle that *kavanah*, or inner participation, is indispensable to prayer, the principle which found a precise expression in the medieval saying: "Prayer without *kavanah* is like a body without a soul."

Yet what is the nature of kavanah? Is it paying attention to the context of the fixed texts? Thinking? Prayer is not thinking. To the thinker, God is an object; to the man who prays, He is the subject. Awaking in the presence of God, our aim is not to acquire objective knowledge but to deepen the mutual allegiance of man and God. What we want is not to know Him but to be known to Him; not to form judgments about Him but to be judged by Him; not to make the world an object of our mind but to let it come to His attention, to augment His, rather than our knowledge. We endeavor to disclose ourselves to the Sustainer of all, rather than to enclose the world in ourselves.

To most people, thinking is a thing that grows in the hothouse of logic, separated from the atmosphere of character and of everyday living. They consider it possible for a man to be unscrupulous and yet to write well about righteousness. Others may disagree with this view. However, all of us, mindful of the ancient distinction between lip service and the service of the heart, agree that prayer is not a hothouse plant of temples but a shoot that grows in the soil of life, springing from widespread roots hidden in all our needs and deeds. Vicious needs, wicked deeds, felt or committed today, are like rot cankering the roots of tomorrow's prayer. A hand used in crime is an ax laid to the roots of worship. It is as Isaiah said: "And when ye spread forth your hands, I will hide mine eyes from you; Yea, when ye make many prayers, I will not hear; your hands are full of blood." Life is fashioned by prayer, and prayer is the quintessence of life.

The laws of science we comprehend as a rational concept in critical understanding, while the mercy and greatness of the Infinite we absorb as a mystery. Prayer is a spiritual source in itself. Though not born of an urge to learn, it often endows us with insights not attainable by speculation. It is in prayer that we obtain the subsidy of God for the failing efforts of our wisdom.

But prayer goes beyond the scope of emotion; it is the approach of the human to the transcendent. Prayer makes man a relative to the sublime, initiating him into the mystery. The will, at times, is an outsider to the sanctuary of the soul. It ushers in great things, but does not always control them. The will to pray opens the gates, but what enters is not its product. The will is not a creative but an auxiliary power, the servant of the soul. Creative forces may be discharged, but not engendered, by the will. Thus, inclination to pray is not prayer. Deeper forces and qualities of the soul must be mobilized before prayer can be accomplished. To pray is to pull oneself together, to pour our perception, volition, memory, thought, hope, feeling, dreams, all that is moving in us, into one tone. Not the words we utter, the service of the lips, but the way in which it is performed, the devotion of the heart to what the words contain, the consciousness of speaking under His eyes, is the pith of prayer.

For neither the lips nor the brain is the limit of the scene on which prayer takes place. Speech and devotion are functions auxiliary to a metaphysical process. Common to all men who pray is the certainty that prayer is an act which makes the heart audible to God. Who would pour his most precious hopes into a deaf abyss? Essential is the metaphysical rather than the psychical dimension of prayer. Prayer is not a thought that rambles alone in the world but an event that starts in man and ends in God. What goes on in our heart is a humble preliminary to an event in God.

The passage of hours, almost unnoticeable, but leaving behind the feeling of loss or omission, is either an invitation to despair or a ladder to eternity. This little time in our hands melts away ere it can be formed. Before our eyes man and maid, spring and splendor, slide into oblivion. However, there are hours that perish and hours that join the everlasting. Prayer is a crucible in which time is cast in the likeness of the eternal. Man hands over his time to God in the secrecy of single words. When anointed by prayer, his thoughts and deeds do not sink into nothingness but merge into the endless knowledge of an all-embracing God. We yield our thoughts to Him who endowed us with a chain of days for the duration of life.

THE ESSENCE OF PRAYER

TO MANY psychologists, prayer is but a function, a shadow cast by the circumstances of our lives, growing and diminishing along with our needs and wants. Consequently, to understand the nature of prayer, it is enough to become familiar with the various occasions on which it is offered. But is it possible to determine the value of a work of art by discovering the occasion of its creation? Assuming that we can ascertain whether Cervantes wrote his *Don Quixote* in order to pay his debts or to attain fame and impress his friends, would that have any bearing upon either the intrinsic value or our appreciation of his art? Nor is the factor which induces a person to pray the substance of prayer. The essence of prayer is inherent in the act of prayer itself. It can be detected only inside the consciousness of man during the act of worship.

The drive toward practical consequences is not the force that inspires a person at the moment of his chanting praise to God. Even in supplication, the thought of aid or protection does not constitute the inner act of prayer. The hope of results may be the motive that leads the mind into prayer, but not the content which fills the worshipper's consciousness in the essential moment of prayer. The artist may give a concert for the sake of the promised remuneration, but in the moment when he is passionately seeking with his fingertips the vast swarm of swift and secret sounds, the consideration of subsequent reward is far from his mind. His whole being is immersed in the music. The slightest shift of attention, the emergence of any ulterior motive, would break his intense concentration, and his single-minded devotion would collapse, his control of the instrument would fail. Even an artisan can never be true to his task unless he is motivated by love of the work for its own sake. Only by wholehearted devotion to his trade can he produce a consummate piece of craftsmanship. Prayer, too, is primarily *kavanah*, the yielding of the entire being to one goal, the gathering of the soul into focus.

The focus of prayer is not the self. A man may spend hours meditating about himself, or be stirred by the deepest sympathy for his fellow man, and no prayer will come to pass. Prayer comes to pass in a complete turning of the heart toward God, toward His goodness and power. It is the momentary disregard of our personal concerns, the absence of self-centered thoughts, which constitute the act of prayer. Feeling becomes prayer in the moment in which we forget ourselves and become aware of God. When we analyze the consciousness of a supplicant, we discover that it is not concentrated upon his own interests but on something beyond the self. The thought of personal need is absent, and the thought of divine grace alone is present in his mind. Thus, in beseeching Him for bread, there is *one* instant, at least, in which our mind is directed neither to our hunger nor to food but to His mercy. This instant is prayer.

We start with a personal concern and live to feel the utmost, for the fate of the individual is a counterpoint in a larger theme. In prayer we come close to hearing the eternal theme and discerning our place in it. It is as if our life were a seamless garment, continuous with the Infinite. Our poverty is His. His property is ours. Overwhelmed with awe of His share in our lives, we extend ourselves to Him, expose our goals to His goodness, exchange our will for His wisdom. For this reason, the analogy between prayer and petitioning another human being is like the analogy between the ocean and a cup of water. For the essence of prayer lies in man's self-transcending, in his surpassing the limits of what is human, in his relating the natural to the divine.

Prayer is an invitation to God to intervene in our lives, to let His will prevail in our affairs; it is the opening of a window to Him in our will, an effort to make Him the Lord of our soul. We submit our interests to His concern and seek to be allied with what is ultimately right. Our approach to the holy is not an intrusion but an answer. Between the dawn of childhood and the door of death, man encounters things and events out of which comes a whisper of truth, not much louder than stillness, but exhorting and persistent. Yet man listens to his fears and his whims, rather than to the soft petitions of God. The Lord of the universe is suing for the favor of man, but man fails to realize his own importance. It is the disentanglement of our heart from cant, bias, and ambition, the staving in of the bulk of stupid conceit, the cracking of hollow self-reliance, that enables us to respond to this request for our service.

THE TWO MAIN TYPES OF PRAYER

AT FIRST SIGHT prayer appears to be a communication of ideas or feelings through spoken words. Every one of us bears a vast accumulation of unuttered sorrows, scruples, hopes, and yearnings, frozen in the muteness of his nature. In prayer the ice breaks, our feelings begin to move our mind, striving for an outlet. It is not an expression of things accidentally stored up in our minds but an emanation of what is most personal in us, an act of self-expression.

Yet, in a sense, prayer starts where expression fails. The words that reach our lips are often but waves of an overflowing stream touching the shore. We often seek and miss, struggle and fail to adjust our unique feelings to the patterns of texts. The soul, then, intimates its persistent striving, the riddle of its unhappiness, the strain of living twixt hope and fear. Where is the tree that can utter fully the silent passion of the soil? Words can only open the door, and we can only weep on the threshold of our incommunicable thirst after the incomprehensible. A certain passage in the morning prayer was interpreted by the Kotzker rabbi to mean that God loves what is left over at the bottom of the heart and cannot be expressed in words. It is the ineffable feeling which reaches God rather than the expressed feeling.

Various attempts have been made to classify prayer. The division into supplication and praise pays attention to the theme but not to the inner dynamics of prayer. This inner dynamics takes its course between the soul of man and the words. From this point of view, we have to distinguish between two main types of prayer: prayer as an act of expression and prayer as an act of empathy. The first type takes place when there is a strong feeling within that leads to prayer, when we are stirred by something and seek words to express our state of mind. But the more common type of prayer is an act of empathy. There need be no prayerful mood in us when we begin to pray. It is through our reading and feeling the words of the prayers, through imaginative projection of our consciousness into the meaning of the words, and through empathy into the ideas with which the words are pregnant, that this type of prayer comes to pass.

The ability to express what is hidden in the heart is a rare gift and cannot be counted upon by all men. What, then, makes it possible for us to pray is our ability to affiliate our own minds with the pattern of fixed texts, to unlock our hearts to the words, and to surrender to their meanings. For words are not dead tools but living entities full of spiritual power. The power of words often surpasses the power of our minds. The word is often the giver, and man the recipient. Thus man submits to the words. They inspire his mind and awaken his heart. We do not turn the light of prayer on and off at will, as we control sober speculation; we are seized by the overwhelming spell of His name. It is amazement, not understanding; awe, not reasoning; a challenge, a sweep of emotion, the tide of a mood, an identification of our wills with the living will of God.

What do most of us know about the substance of words? Estranged from the soil of the soul, our words do not grow as fruits of joy but are found as sapless clichés, refuse in the back yard of the intelligence. There can be no prayer without a sense of the dignity of words. Everyone feels the binding force of the uttered word, the reality of an oath, vow, or promise, but rarely do we ponder on the nature of the secret power stored up in words. When the heart, cooperating with the forces of faith against tumult and anxiety, succeeds in keeping alive the inner stillness, we feel how great and gentle words can be. Strength and pride come from their sounds. They soften the harshness of fear and unfold the wings of hope. Our thoughts, tiny and feeble, become powerful in their wake.

There is always the opportunity of realizing the holy, but when we fail to use it, there are words to remind the mind what to draw from the depth of every hour. Words are like mountain peaks pointing to the unfathomable. Ascending their trails we arrive at prayer. They are like notes of music. It is the strength of our inner life which makes the symbols live; it is the fullness of our heart which lends force to words. By our feeling we make manifest and real what is indicated in the texts. In prayer, we discover what moves us unawares, what is urgent in our lives, what in us is related to the ultimate.

Is it the outburst of eloquence which makes the Infinite listen to our feeble voice? Prayer is not a sermon delivered to God. Essential in prayer is the intention, not the technical skill. In oratory, as in any other work of art, we endeavor to lend an adequate form to an idea; we apply all our care to adjusting the form to the content. But prayer is almost pure content; the form is unimportant. It makes no difference whether we stammer or are eloquent. We can concentrate entirely on our inner devotion.

Two brief stories may be told relative to the two main types of prayer, the expressive and the empathic. One of these, told in *Sefer Hasidim*, concerns a young shepherd who was unable to read the Hebrew prayers. The only way in which he worshipped God was to say: "O Lord, I should like to pray, but I cannot read Hebrew. There is only one thing I can do for you—if you would give me your sheep, I would take care of them for nothing." One day a learned man passing by heard the shepherd pronounce his offer and shouted at him: "You are blasphemous!" He told the boy that he should read the daily Hebrew prayers instead of uttering irreverent words. When the shepherd told him that he could not read Hebrew, he took him to his house and began to teach him to read the prayerbook. One night the learned man had a dream in which he was told that there was great sadness in heaven because the young shepherd had ceased to say his usual prayer. He was commanded to advise the boy to return to his old way of praying.

Now, many of us are so much on the side of the shepherd boy as to be opposed to the institution of regular prayer, claiming that we should pray only when and as we feel inspired to do so. For such there is a story, told by Rabbi Israel Friedman, the Rizhiner, about a small Jewish town far off from the main roads of the land. But it had all the necessary municipal institutions: a bathhouse, a cemetery, a hospital, and a law court; as well as all sorts of craftsmen—tailors, shoemakers, carpenters, and masons. One trade, however, was lacking; there was no watchmaker.

In the course of years many of the clocks became so annoyingly inaccurate that their owners just decided to let them run down and ignore them altogether. There were others, however, who maintained that as long as the clocks ran they should not be abandoned. So they wound their clocks day after day, though they knew that they were not accurate. One day the news spread through the town that a watchmaker had arrived, and everyone rushed to him with their clocks. But the only ones he could repair were those that had been kept running—the abandoned clocks had grown too rusty!

THE VISION OF PRAYER

THE THIRST for companionship, which drives us so often into error and adventure, indicates the intense loneliness from which we suffer. We are alone even with our friends. The smattering of understanding which a human being has to offer is not enough to satisfy our need of sympathy. Human eyes can see the foam, but not the seething at the bottom. In the hour of greatest agony we are alone. It is such a sense of solitude which prompts the heart to seek the companionship of God. He alone can know the motives of our actions; He alone can be truly trusted. Prayer is confidence, unbosoming oneself to God. For man is incapable of being alone. His incurable, inconsolable loneliness forces him to look for things yet unattained, for people yet unknown. He often runs after a sop, but soon retires discontented from all false or feeble companionship. Prayer may follow such retirement.

What is pride worth if it does not add to the glory of God? We forfeit our dignity when we abandon loyalty to what is sacred; our existence dwindles to trifles. We barter life for oblivion and pay the price of toil and pain in the pursuit of aimlessness. Only concern for our inalienable share in the unknown holds our inner life together. It enables us to grasp the utopia of faith, to divine what is desirable to God, aspiring to be, not only a part of nature, but a partner of God. The sacred is a necessity in our lives, and prayer is born of this necessity. Through prayer we sanctify ourselves, our feelings, our ideas. Everyday things become sacred when prayed for to God.

The privilege of praying is man's greatest distinction. For what is there in man to induce reverence, to make his life sacred and his rights inalienable? The possession of knowledge, wealth, or skill does not compose the dignity of man. A person possessing none of these gifts may still lay claim to dignity. Our reverence for man is aroused by something in him beyond his own and our reach, something that no one can deprive him of. It is his right to pray, his ability to worship, to utter the cry that can reach God: "If they cry at all unto me, I will surely hear their cry."

The main ends of prayer are to move God, to let Him participate in our lives, and to interest ourselves in Him. What is the meaning of praise if not to make His concern our own? Worship is an act of inner agreement with God. We can petition Him for things we need only when we are sure of His sympathy for us. To praise is to feel God's concern; to petition is to let Him feel our concern. In prayer we establish a living contact with God, between our concern and His will, between despair and promise, want and abundance. We affirm our adherence by invoking His love.

Prayer is spiritual ecstasy. It is as if all our vital thoughts in fierce ardor should burst the mind to stream toward God. A keen single force draws our yearning for the utmost out of the seclusion of the soul. We try to see our visions in His light, to feel our life as His affair. We begin by letting the thought of Him engage our minds, by realizing His name and entering into a reverie which leads through beauty and stillness, from feeling to thought, and from understanding to devotion. For the coins of prayer bear the image of God's dreams and wishes for fear-haunted man.

At the beginning of all action is an inner vision in which things to be are experienced as real. Prayer, too, is frequently an inner vision, an intense dreaming for God—the reflection of the divine intentions in the soul of man. We dream of a time "when the world will be perfected under the Kingdom of God, and all the children of flesh will call upon Thy name, when Thou wilt turn unto Thyself all the wicked of the earth." We anticipate the fulfillment of the hope shared by both God and man. To pray is to dream in league with God, to envision His holy visions.

The Biblical View of Reality

PHILOSOPHY OF RELIGION is primarily not the philosophy of a philosophy, the philosophy of a doctrine, the interpretations of a dogma, but
the philosophy of concrete events, acts, insights, of that which is immediately given with the pious man. The dogmas are merely a catalogue,
an indispensable index. For religion is more than a creed or an ideology
and cannot be understood when detached from actual living. It comes to
light in moments in which one's soul is shaken with unmitigated concern
about the meaning of all meaning, about one's ultimate commitment,
which is integrated with one's very existence; in moments in which all
foregone conclusions, all life-stifling trivialities are suspended, in which
the soul is starved for an inkling of eternal reality; in moments of discerning
the indestructibly sudden within the perishably constant.[1]

Thus the issue which must be discussed first is not belief, ritual, or the
religious experience but the source of these phenomena: the total situation
of man; not what or how he experiences the supernatural, but why he
experiences and accepts it. What necessitates religion in my life and yours.

In our quest for an answer it is important to inquire: What was the
source of the faith of the people of the Bible? Is it correct to define their
faith as an act of relying upon an inherited doctrine? Is it correct to say
that the records of revelation were the only direct source of faith, or that
Judaism derived its religious vitality exclusively from loyalty to the events
that happened in the days of Moses and from obedience to Scripture, in
which those events were recorded? Such an assumption seems to overlook
the nature of man and his faith. A great event, miraculous as it may be,
if it happened only once will hardly be able to dominate forever the minds
of men. The mere remembrance of such an event is too weak to hold in
its spell the soul of man with its restlessness and vitality. There must have
been a continuous stream out of which Jewish faith was drawn.

The prophets appeal to the spiritual power in man: "Know therefore this day, and lay it to your heart, that the Lord is God in heaven above and on the earth beneath; there is no other" (Deuteronomy 4:39). The psalmist calls upon us: "O *taste* and see that the Lord is good" (34:9).* How does one know? How does one taste?

Indeed, the belief of the people of Israel was not an act of blind acceptance of dogmas but rather the result of insight, the outcome of their being exposed to the power and presence of God in the world.

There is in the Bible God's word to man, but there is also man's word to God; man's insight, not only God's approach. To recapture that insight is to delve into the inside of the religious drama of Israel, to grasp what it was that enabled Job to say:

As for me, I know that my Redeemer lives,
that He will witness at the last upon the dust.
After my skin has been destroyed,
from my flesh I shall see God.
My own eyes shall behold, not another's.
My heart faints within me.

Job 19:25–27

Yet how does a man reach a stage of thinking where he can "see God from his flesh"? What are the ways that lead to the certainty of this existence, to the perception of His presence?

The Bible contains within its words the answer to our questions. Yet that answer is rarely spelled out, and we must learn to ascertain the reasons for that certainty, the perception behind the utterance. This means going to the roots of biblical experience and asking: Is there anything within the world that would enable us to sense the existence and presence of Him who creates the world? To answer this question we must first ask: What is the world to the biblical man?

There are three aspects of nature that command man's attention: *power, loveliness, grandeur.* Power he exploits, loveliness he enjoys, grandeur fills him with awe. It is according to how deeply man is drawn to one of these aspects that his particular way of knowledge is developed. Western knowledge of the last four centuries may be characterized by the famous principle of Bacon: *Knowledge is power.* The goal of that knowledge is neither to portray the beauty nor to convey the grandeur of the world, but to exploit its resources. Man, proud to be *Homo faber*, regards the world as a source of satisfaction of his needs. He is willing to define his

---

* The verb *tacam* always means to perceive, to taste. The noun is also used in the sense of judgment. In our passage Targum renders the word *ta amu* with "realize"; the Septuagint, *geisasthe* with "taste." Compare Seforno's commentary *ad locum*, "taste, namely, feel with your sense and *see* with the eye of reason that God is good."

essence as "a seeker after the greatest degree of comfort for the least necessary expenditure of energy." His hero is the technician rather than the artist, the philosopher, or the prophet. Out of such a system of knowledge it is hard to find a way to the reality of God. Nature as power is a world that does not point beyond itself. It is when nature is sensed as mystery and grandeur that it calls upon us to look beyond it. Similarly, when nature is sensed as beauty, we become infatuated by her grace and look to her for answers to problems she is incapable of giving. It is when nature is sensed as mystery and grandeur that we discover that nature herself is the problem.

Significantly, the theme of biblical poetry is not the charm or beauty of nature; it is the *sublime* aspect of nature which is constantly referred to.

What was the world, what was reality to the biblical man? The Hebrew word *olam*, which in post-biblical times came to denote the world, is, according to many scholars, derived from the root *alam*, which means to hide, to conceal.[2] The world is hiddenness; its essence is mystery. In the Bible, where the word *olam* expresses a conception of time, the world is never taken for granted or regarded as an instrument of the human will.

In awe and amazement the prophets stand before the mystery of the universe:

Who has measured the waters in the hollow of his hand,
And marked off the heavens with a span,
Enclosed the dust of the earth in a measure,
And weighed the mountains in scales,
And the hills in a balance?

Isaiah 40:12

An even deeper sense of humility is expressed in the words of Agur:

Surely I am too stupid to be a man.
I have not the understanding of a man.
I have not learned wisdom,
Nor have I knowledge of the Holy One.
Who has ascended to heaven and come down?
Who has gathered the wind in his fists?
Who has wrapped up the waters in a garment?
Who has established all the ends of the earth?
What is his name, and what is his son's name,
If thou knowest?

Proverbs 30:2–4

Such an attitude toward the mystery and grandeur of nature affected, of course, the biblical understanding of the meaning and scope of human knowledge and wisdom.

Philosophy is the love and quest of wisdom. To attain wisdom is one of the highest aspirations.

But where shall wisdom be found?
Where is the place of understanding?
Man does not know the way to it;
It is not found in the land of the living.
The deep says, "It is not in me";
The sea says, "It is not with me . . ."
Whence then comes wisdom?
And where is the place of understanding?
It is hidden from the eyes of all living,
And concealed from the birds of the air.
Destruction and Death say,
"We have heard a rumor of it with our ears."
God understands the way to it,
He knows its place.
For He looks to the ends of the earth,
And sees everything under the heavens.
When He gave to the wind its weight,
And meted out the waters by measure;
When He made a decree for the rain,
And a way for the lightning of the thunder;
Then He saw it and declared it;
He established it, and searched it out.
And He said to man,
"Behold, the fear of the Lord, that is wisdom;
And to depart from evil is understanding."

Job 28:12–14, 20–28

In another book of the Bible, in Ecclesiastes, we read the account of a man who sought wisdom, who searched for insight into the world and its meaning. "I said, I will be wise" (7:23) and "I applied my mind to know wisdom and to see what is done on earth" (8:16). Did he succeed? He claims, "I have acquired great wisdom, surpassing all who were over Jerusalem before me" (1:16). And yet he ultimately realized "that *man cannot find out* the work that is done under the sun. However much man may toil in seeking, he will not find it out; even though a wise man claims to know, he cannot find it out" (8:17).

"I said, *I will be wise*, but it was far from me. *That which is is far off and deep, exceeding deep. Who can find it out?*" (7:23–24). Ecclesiastes is not only saying that "the world's wise are not wise" but something more radical. What *is* is more than what you see; what is is "far off and deep, exceeding deep." *Being is mysterious.*

This is one of Ecclesiastes' central insights: "I have seen the task that God has given to the sons of men . . . He has made everything beautiful in its time; but He has *also implanted* in the hearts of men the *mystery*, so that man cannot find out what God has done from the beginning to the end" (3:10–11).

Wisdom is beyond our reach. We are unable to attain insight into the ultimate meaning and purpose of things. Man does not even know the thoughts of his own mind; nor is he able to understand the meaning of his own dreams. (See Daniel 2:27.)

These are the last words in the Book of Job:

> *Who is this that hides counsel without knowledge?*
> *Therefore have I uttered what I did not understand,*
> *Things too wonderful for me, which I did not know.*
> *Hear, and I will speak;*
> *I will question you, and you declare to me.*
> *I had heard of Thee by the hearing of the ear;*
> *But now my eye sees Thee;*
> *Therefore I despise myself, and repent in dust and ashes.*
>
> Job 42:3–6

What have Job, Agur, Ecclesiastes discovered in their search? They have discovered that the existence of the world is a most mysterious fact. Referring not to miracles, to startling phenomena, but to the natural order of things, they insist that the world of the known is a world unknown, of hiddenness, of mystery. Not the apparent but the hidden is the apparent; not the order but the mystery of the order that prevails in the universe is what man is called upon to behold. The prophet, like Job and Agur, alludes to a reality that discredits our wisdom, that shatters our knowledge. It is the mystery where we start from without presuppositions, without allegations, without doctrines, without dogmas.

Spencer and others "seem to be possessed with the idea that science has got the universe pretty well ciphered down to a fine point, while the Faradays and Newtons seem to themselves like children who have picked up a few pretty pebbles upon the ocean beach. But most of us find it difficult to recognize the greatness and wonder of things familiar to us. As the prophet is not without honor save [in his own country], so it is also with phenomena."[3]

The biblical man had not forfeited his sense of radical amazement. That "wonder is the feeling of a philosopher, and that philosophy begins in wonder" was stated by Plato[4] and maintained by Aristotle: "For it is owing to their wonder that men both now begin and at first began to philosophize."[5] To this day, wonder is appreciated as *semen scientiae*, the seed of knowledge, as something conducive to cognition, not indigenous to it. Wonder is the prelude to knowledge; it ceases, once the cause of a phenomenon is explained.[6]

But does the worth of wonder consist merely in its being a stimulant to the acquisition of knowledge? Is wonder the same as curiosity? To the prophets, wonder is a form of thinking; it never ceases. There is no answer in the world to ultimate amazement.*

Who is like Thee, O Lord, among the gods?
Who is like Thee, majestic in holiness,
Terrible in glorious deeds, doing wonders?

Exodus 15:11

Wonderful are Thy works,
And my soul knows it exceedingly.

Psalms 139:14

Many things has Thou done, O Lord my God,
Even Thy wondrous deeds and Thy thoughts toward us.
There is nothing to be compared unto Thee!
If I would declare and speak of them,
They are more than can be told.

Psalms 40:6

What is so wondrous about the world? What is there in reality that evokes supreme awe in the hearts of men? In his great vision Isaiah perceives the voice of the seraphim even before he hears the voice of the Lord. What is it that the seraphim reveal to Isaiah? "The whole earth is full of His glory" (6:3). It is proclaimed not as a messianic promise but as a present fact. Man may not sense it, but the seraphim announce it. It is not to Isaiah only that this fact is the essential part of his revelation. Ezekiel, too, when the heavens were opened by the river Chebar, hears the voice of a great rushing, while cherubim cry, "Blessed be the glory of the Lord from His place" (3:12).

Is the glory a secret of the angels? According to the psalmist, "The heavens declare the glory of God" (19:2). How do they declare it? "Day unto day utters *speech*, and night unto night reveals *knowledge*." Speech? Knowledge? What is the language, what are the words in which the heavens express the glory? "There is no speech, there are no words, neither is their voice heard . . ." And yet: "Their line goes out through all the earth, and their words to the end of the world." The song of the heavens is *ineffable*.

Is the glory something that is seen, heard, or clearly apprehended? In

---

* "The facts of the case from first to last are so wonderful that we venture to say that no general impression of Nature reached along scientific or any other lines can be even in the direction of being true that does not sound the note of joyous appreciation and of reverent wonder."—J. A. Thompson at the end of his Gifford Lectures on *The System of Animate Nature* (New York, 1920), p. 650.

the same vision in which the ubiquity of the glory is proclaimed, there is an intimation of man's suspended sensibility.

> *Go, and say to the people:*
> *"Hear and hear, but do not understand;*
> *See and see, but do not perceive."*
> *Make the heart of this people fat,*
>   *and their ears heavy*
>   *and shut their eyes;*
> *Lest they see with their eyes,*
>   *and hear with their ears,*
> *And understand with their hearts,*
>   *and turn and be healed.*

Isaiah 6:9–10

The glory is visible, but we do not perceive it; it is within our reach, beyond our grasp.

> *Lo, He passes by me, and I see Him not;*
> *He moves on, but I do not perceive Him.*

—*Job* 9:11

And still, the glory is not entirely unknown to us. That not only the heavens are able to declare it may be seen from the fact that the people are called upon to:

> *Declare His glory among the nations,*
> *His marvels among all the peoples.*
> —*I Chronicles* 16:24 (*See also Psalms* 145:5)

When "the voice of the Lord breaks the cedars . . . flashes forth flames of fire . . . shakes the wilderness . . ." then "in His temple all cry 'Glory' " (Psalms 29:9). It is, again, not an utterance in words. "The glory of God is to conceal words" ("a word," Proverbs 25:2).

What should be worshipped, what should be adored? Is there anything more than the world, more than what we see? Is not the world the end of perception and hence the only and ultimate object of adoration? It is hard to live under a sky full of stars and not be struck by its mystery. The sun is equipped with power and beauty for all eyes to see. Yet who could refrain from extolling its grandeur? Who could go beyond the realization that nature is the ultimate mystery? And is mystery the end?

It is natural for man to adore the great facts of nature, despite the injunction "Beware lest you lift up your eyes to heaven, and when you see the sun and the moon and the stars, all the host of heaven, you be drawn away and worship them" (Deuteronomy 4:19). There were even in the times of the Babylonian Exile those who turned their faces to the east and worshipped the sun (Ezekiel 8:16; compare II Kings 17:16, 21:3).

Indeed, the beauty of nature is a menace to our spiritual understanding; there is a deadly risk of being enchanted by its power.

> *If I have looked at the sun when it shone,*
> *Or the moon moving in splendor,*
> *And my heart has been secretly enticed,*
> *And my mouth has kissed my hand;*
> *This also would be an iniquity to be punished by the judges,*
> *For I should have been false to God above.*

—*Job* 31:26–28

To commune with the heart of Nature—this has been the accredited mode since the days of Wordsworth. Nature, Coleridge assures us, has ministrations by which she heals her erring and distempered child . . .

Well, she is a very lovely Nature . . . yet I confess a heinous doubt whether rustic stolidity may not be a secret effluence from her. You speak, and you think she answers you. It is the echo of your own voice. You think you hear the throbbing of her heart, and it is the throbbing of your own. I do not believe that Nature has a heart; and I suspect that, like many another beauty, she has been credited with a heart because of her face. You go to her, this great, beautiful, tranquil, self-satisfied Nature, and you look for—sympathy? Yes; the sympathy of a cat, sitting by the fire and blinking at you. What, indeed, does she want with a heart or brain? She knows that she is beautiful, and she is placidly content with the knowledge; she was made to be gazed on, and she fulfills the end of her creation. After a careful anatomization of Nature, I pronounce that she has nothing more than a lymphatic vesicle. She cannot give what she does not need; and if we were but similarly organized, we should be independent of sympathy. A man cannot go straight to his objects, because he has a heart; he cannot eat, drink, sleep, make money, and be satisfied, because he has a heart. It is a mischievous thing, and wise men accordingly take the earliest opportunity of giving it away.

Yet the thing is, after all, too deep for jest. What is this heart of Nature, if it exist at all? Is it, according to the conventional doctrine derived from Wordsworth and Shelley, a heart of love, according with the heart of man, and stealing out to him through a thousand avenues of mute sympathy? No; in this sense I repeat seriously what I said lightly: Nature has no heart.[7]

Is the cosmos an object worthy of our adoration? The Bible's answer is: No! The whole world utters adoration; the whole world worships Him. Join all things in their song to Him. The world's beauty and power are as naught compared to Him. The mystery is only the beginning.

Beyond the mystery is God.

The biblical man sees nature not in isolation but in relation to God. "At the beginning God created heaven and earth." These few words set forth the contingency and absolute dependence of all of reality. What, then, is reality? To the Western man, it is a *thing in itself*; to the biblical man, it is a *thing through God*. Looking at a thing his eyes see not so much form, color, force, and motion as an act of God. It is a way of seeing which has fortunately not vanished from the world.

I assert, for myself, that I do not behold the outward creation, and to me it is hindrance and not action. "What!" it will be questioned. "When the sun rises, do you not see a round disc of fire somewhat like a guinea?" Oh, no, no! I see an innumerable company of the heavenly host, crying, "Holy, holy, holy is the Lord God Almighty!" I question not my corporeal eye any more than I would question a window concerning a sight. I look through it, and now with it.[8]

Few are the songs in the Bible that celebrate the beauty of nature, and these songs are ample testimony to the fact that the biblical man was highly sensitive to form, color, force, and motion. And yet, because the link between the world and God was not broken in his mind, the beauty of the universe was not the supreme object of his adoration. To the biblical man, the beauty of the world issued from the grandeur of God; His majesty towered beyond the breathtaking mystery of the universe. Rather than being crushed by the mystery, man was inspired to praise the majesty. And rather than praise the world for its beauty, he called upon the world to praise its Creator.

What the psalmist felt in meeting the world is succinctly expressed in the exclamation:

Sing unto the Lord a new song;
Sing unto the Lord, all the earth.

—*Psalms* 96:1

Praise Him, sun and moon,
Praise Him, all you shining stars!
Praise Him, you highest heavens,
And you waters above the heavens . . .
Praise the Lord from the earth,
You sea-monsters and all deeps,
Fire and hail, snow and frost,
Stormy wind fulfilling His command!
Mountains and all hills,
Fruit trees and all cedars!
Beasts and all cattle,
Creeping things and flying birds!

—*Psalms* 148:3–9

The Egyptian priest could not call upon the stars to praise the gods. He believed that the soul of Isis sparkled in Sirius, the soul of Horus in Orion, and the soul of Typhon in the Great Bear; it was beyond his scope to conceive that all beings stand in awe and worship God. To the biblical mind the soul of everything that lives blesses His name. "All Thy works praise Thee" (Psalms 145:10). Whose ear has ever heard how all trees sing to God? Has our reason ever thought of calling upon the sun to praise the Lord? And yet what the ear fails to perceive, what reason fails to conceive, the Bible makes clear to our souls. It is a higher truth, to be grasped by the spirit.

Greek philosophy began in a world without God. It could not accept the gods or the example of their conduct. Plato had to break with the gods and ask: What is good? And the problem of values was born. And it was the idea of values that took the place of God. Plato lets Socrates ask: What is good? Yet Moses' question was: What does God require of thee?

The argument from design, expounded in Cicero's *De Natura Deorum*, infers the existence of a divine power from the purposeful structure of nature. Order implies intelligence. That intelligence is God. A classic formulation is found in a familiar passage in Paley's *Natural Theology* (1803), Chapter 1: "Suppose I had found a watch upon the ground . . . The mechanism being observed . . . The inference we think is inevitable that the watch must have a maker; that there must have existed, at some time, and at some place or other, an artificer or artificers, who formed it for the purpose which we find it actually to answer; who comprehended its construction, and designed its use."

The universe stands to God in the relation in which a watch is related to the mechanic who constructed it. The heavens are the works of His hands, just as the watch is the work of the watchmaker.

This comparison regards the universe as it does the watch, as a separate, independent, and absolute entity. Nature is a thing in itself, complete and self-sufficient at this present moment. The only problem we face concerns not the existence but the cause of nature; not the present, but the past. Since in the eighteenth century the ultimate structure and order of nature were thought of in mechanical terms, its origin or creation was also conceived of as a mechanical process, comparable to the process of constructing a watch.

The shortcomings of this view lie in its taking both the watch and all of reality for granted. To our *radical amazement*[9] the ultimate problem is not only how it came into being but also how is it that it is. The problem extends, furthermore, not only to the substance of the question but to the act of asking the question as well. We are amazed at our ability to ask that question. We cannot take the existence of the watch as a safe starting point whose existence is given and which merely arouses the question of who brought it into being. *The watch itself is a mystery.*

There is no word in biblical Hebrew for doubt; there are many words for wonder. Just as in dealing with judgments our starting point is doubt, so in dealing with reality our starting point is wonder. The biblical man never questions the reality of the world around him. He never asks whether the rivers, mountains, and stars are only apparitions. His sense of the mind-surpassing grandeur of reality prevented the power of doubt from setting up its own independent dynasty. Doubt is an act in which the mind confronts its own ideas; wonder is an act in which the mind confronts the mystery of the universe. Radical skepticism is the outgrowth of conceit and subtle arrogance. Yet there was no conceit in the prophets and no arrogance in the psalmist.

And so the biblical man never asks, Is there a God? To ask such a question, in which doubt is expressed as to which of two possible attitudes is true, means to accept the power and validity of a third attitude; namely, the attitude of doubt. The Bible does not know doubt as an absolute attitude. For there is no doubt in which faith is not involved. The questions advanced in the Bible are of a different kind.

> *Who has measured the waters in the hollow of his hand,*
> *And marked off the heavens with a span,*
> *Enclosed the dust of the earth in a measure,*
> *And weighed the mountains in scales,*
> *And the hills in a balance?*
>
> —Isaiah 40:12

This does not reflect a process of thinking that is neatly arranged in the order first of doubt, then faith; first the question, then the answer. It reflects a situation in which the mind stands *face to face* with the world rather than with its own ideas.

> *Lift up your eyes and see!*
> *Who created these?*
>
> —Isaiah 40:26

A question is an interrogative sentence calling for either a positive or a negative answer. But the sentence *Who created these?* is a question that contains the impossibility of one's giving a negative answer; it is an answer in disguise; a *question of amazement*, not of curiosity. This, then, is the prophet's thesis: There is a way of asking the great question which can only elicit an affirmative answer. What is the way?

At the end of the days I, Nebuchadnezzar, lifted my eyes to heaven and my power of knowledge returned to me.

This confession, reported in the Book of Daniel (4:31), gives us an inkling of how one can recover one's power of knowledge: *to lift the eyes to heaven.*

It is the same expression that Isaiah used: "Lift up your eyes on high and see: who created these?"

"What gives birth to religion is not intellectual curiosity, but the fact and experience of our being asked . . . Faith is not the product of search and endeavor, but the answer to a challenge which no one can forever ignore."[10] The heavens are a challenge. When you lift up your eyes, you are faced with the question.

Lift up your eyes on high. There is a higher form of seeing. We must learn how to lift up our eyes on high in order to see that the world is more of a question than an answer.

In the spirit of biblical tradition we must speak not of the foolishness of faith but rather of the *foolishness of unbelief,* of the *scandal of indifference to God.* What is called in the English language an atheist, the language of the Bible calls a *fool.*[11] "The fool says in his heart, There is no God" (Psalms 14:1). The wicked is indifferent. In his pride *"he will not seek [after God]:* There is no God is the sum of his thoughts" (Psalms 10:4).

This attitude does not imply any easygoing rationalism, the assumption, namely, that the belief in the God of Abraham, Isaac, and Jacob is in complete agreement with the common habits and notions of the human mind. What it does mean is that the denial of Him is a scandal to the soul, to a soul in which the likeness of God is not distorted or misguided by false certainties. How it is possible not to believe? How is it possible not to sense the presence of God in the world? *"The lion has roared, who will not fear?"* (Amos 3:8).

There is a plane of living where no one can remain both callous and calm, unstunned and unabashed; where His presence may be defied but not denied, and where, at the end, faith in Him is the only way.[12]

The following parable was told by Rabbi Nahman of Bratslav:

There was a prince who lived far away from his father, the king, and he was very, very homesick for his father. Once he received a letter from his father, and he was overjoyed and treasured it. Yet, the joy and the delight that the letter gave him increased his longing even more. He would sit and complain: "Oh, oh, if I could only touch his hand! If he would extend his hand to me, how I would embrace it. I would kiss every finger in my great longing for my father, my teacher, my light. Merciful father, how I would love to touch at least your little finger!" And while he was complaining, feeling and longing for a touch of his father, a thought flashed in his mind: Don't I have my father's letter, written in his own hand! Is not the handwriting of the king comparable to his hand? And a great joy burst forth in him.

When I look at the heavens, the work of Thy fingers (Psalms 8:4).

Death as Homecoming

OUR FIRST QUESTION is to what end and upon what right do we think about the strange and totally inaccessible subject of death? The answer is because of the supreme certainty we have about the existence of man: that it cannot endure without a sense of meaning. But existence embraces both life and death, and in a way death is the test of the meaning of life. If death is devoid of meaning, then life is absurd. Life's ultimate meaning remains obscure unless it is reflected upon in the face of death.

The fact of dying must be a major factor in our understanding of living. Yet only a few of us have come face to face with death as a problem or a challenge. There is a slowness, a delay, a neglect on our part to think about it. For the subject is not exciting but, rather, strange and shocking.

What characterizes modern man's attitude toward death is escapism, disregard of its harsh reality, even a tendency to obliterate grief. He is entering, however, a new age of search for the meaning of existence, and all cardinal issues will have to be faced.

Death is grim, harsh, cruel, a source of infinite grief. Our first reaction is consternation. We are stunned and distraught. Slowly, our sense of dismay is followed by a sense of mystery. Suddenly a whole life has veiled itself in secrecy. Our speech stops, our understanding fails. In the presence of death there is only silence, and a sense of awe.

Is death nothing but an obliteration, an absolute negation? The view of death is affected by our understanding of life. If life is sensed as a surprise, as a gift, defying explanation, then death ceases to be a radical, absolute negation of what life stands for. For both life and death are aspects of a greater mystery, the mystery of being, the mystery of creation. Over and above the preciousness of particular existence stands the marvel of its being related to the infinite mystery of being or creation.

Death, then, is not simply man's coming to an end. It is also entering a beginning.

There is, furthermore, the mystery of my personal existence. The problem of how and whether I am going to be after I die is profoundly related to the problem of who and how I was before I was born. The mystery of an afterlife is related to the mystery of preexistence. A soul does not grow out of nothing. Does it, then, perish and dissolve in nothing?

Human life is on its way from a great distance; it has gone through ages of experience, of growing, suffering, insight, action. We are what we are by what we come from. There is a vast continuum preceding individual existence, and it is a legitimate surmise to assume that there is a continuum following individual existence. Human living is always being under way, and death is not the final destination.

In the language of the Bible, to die, to be buried, is to be "gathered to his people" (Genesis 25:8). They "were gathered to their fathers" (Judges 2:10). "When your days are fulfilled to go to be with your fathers" (I Chronicles 17:11).

Do souls become dust? Does spirit turn to ashes? How can souls, capable of creating immortal words, immortal works of thought and art, be completely dissolved, vanish forever?

Others may counter: The belief that man may have a share in eternal life is not only beyond proof; it is even presumptuous. Who could seriously maintain that members of the human species, a class of mammals, will attain eternity? What image of humanity is presupposed by the belief in immortality?

Indeed, man's hope for eternal life presupposes that there is something about man that is worthy of eternity, that has some affinity to what is divine, that is made in the likeness of the divine.

The biblical account of creation is couched in the language of mystery. Nothing is said about the intention or the plan that preceded the creation of heaven and earth. The Bible does not begin: "And God said: Let us create heaven and earth." All we hear about is the mystery of God's creative act and not a word about intention or meaning. The same applies to the creation of all other beings. We hear only what He does, not what He thinks. "And God said: Let there be." The creation of man, however, is preceded by a forecast. "And God said: Let us make man in our image, after our likeness." The act of man's creation is preceded by an utterance of His intention; God's knowledge of man precedes man's coming into being. God knows him before He creates him. Man's being is rooted in his being known about. It is the creation of man that opens a glimpse into the thought of God, into the meaning beyond the mystery.

"And God said: Let us make man in our image [*tzelem*], after our likeness [*demut*] . . . And God created man in His image, in the image of God created He him" (Genesis 1:26ff.).

These words, which are repeated in the opening words of the fifth chapter of Genesis—"This is the book of the generations of man. When God created man, He made him in the likeness [*demut*] of God"— contain, according to Jewish tradition, the fundamental statement about the nature and meaning of man.

In many religions, man is regarded as an image of a god. Yet the meaning of such regard depends on the meaning of the god whom man resembles. If the god is regarded as a man magnified, if the gods are conceived of in the image of man, then such regard tells us little about the nature and destiny of man. Where God is one among many gods, where the word "divine" is used as mere hyperbolic expression, where the difference between God and man is but a difference in degree, then an expression such as "the divine image of man" is equal in meaning to the idea of the supreme in man. It is only in the light of what the biblical man thinks of God—namely, a Being who created heaven and earth, the God of justice and compassion, the master of nature and history who transcends nature and history—that the idea of man having been created in the image of God refers to the supreme mystery of man, of his nature and existence.

Image and likeness of God. What these momentous words are trying to convey has never ceased to baffle the biblical reader. In the Bible, *tzelem*, the word for "image," is nearly always used in a derogatory sense, denoting idolatrous images. (Numbers 33:52; I Samuel 6:5, 6, 11; II Kings 11:18; Ezekiel 7:20, 16:17, 23:14; II Chronicles 23:17). It is a cardinal sin to fashion an image of God. The same applies to *demut*, the word for "likeness."

"To whom will ye liken God? Or what likeness [*demut*] will ye compare to Him?" (Isaiah 40:18). "To whom will ye liken me, and make me equal, and compare me, that we may be like?" (Isaiah 46:5). "For who in the skies can be compared unto the Lord, who among the sons of might can be likened unto the Lord?" (Psalms 89:7).

God is divine, and man is human. This contrast underlies all biblical thinking. God is never human, and man is never divine. "I will not execute the fierceness of mine anger, I will not return to destroy Ephraim; for I am God and not man" (Hosea 11:9). "God is not a man, that he should lie; neither the son of man, that He should repent" (Numbers 23:19).

Thus the likeness of God means the likeness of Him who is unlike man. The likeness of God means the likeness of Him compared with whom all else is like nothing.

Indeed, the words "image and likeness of God" conceal more than they reveal. They signify something which we can neither comprehend nor verify. For what is our image? What is our likeness? Is there anything about man that may be compared with God? Our eyes do not see it; our minds cannot grasp it. Taken literally, these words are absurd, if not blasphemous. And still they hold the most important truth about the meaning of man.

Obscure as the meaning of these terms is, they undoubtedly denote something *unearthly*, something that belongs to the sphere of God. *Demut* and *tzelem* are of a higher sort of being than the things created in the six days. This, it seems, is what the verse intends to convey: Man partakes of an unearthly divine sort of being.

An idea is relevant if it serves as an answer to a question. To understand the relevance of "the divine image and likeness," we must try to ascertain the question which it comes to answer.

Paradoxically, the problem of man arises more frequently as the problem of death than as the problem of life. It is an important fact, however, that unlike other Oriental religions, where the preoccupation with death was the central issue of religious thinking, the Bible rarely deals with death as a problem.

There is no rebellion against death, no bitterness over its sting, no preoccupation with the afterlife. In striking contrast to its two great neighboring civilizations, Egypt with its intense preoccupation with the afterlife and Babylonia with the epic of Gilgamesh, who wanders in search of immortal life, the story of the descent of Ishtar, and the legend of Nergal and Ereshkigal, the Bible is reticent in speaking about these issues. The Hebrew Bible calls for concern for the problem of living rather than the problem of dying.

Its central concern is not, as in the Gilgamesh epic, how to escape death but, rather, how to sanctify life.

Man is man not because of what he has in common with the earth but *because of what he has in common with God*. The Greek thinkers sought to understand man as a *part of the universe*: the prophets sought to understand man as a *partner* of God.

It is a concern and a task that man has in common with God.

The intention is not to identify "the image and likeness" with a particular quality or attribute of man, such as reason, speech, power, or skill. It does not refer to something which in later systems was called "the best in man," "the divine spark," "the eternal spirit," or "the immortal element" in man. It is the whole man and every man who was made in the image and likeness of God. It is both body and soul, sage and fool, saint and sinner, man in his joy and in his grief, in his righteousness and wickedness. The image is not in man; it is man.

The basic dignity of man is not made up of his achievements, virtues, or special talents. It is inherent in his very being. The commandment "Love thy neighbor as thyself" (Leviticus 19:18) calls upon us to love not only the virtuous and the wise but also the vicious and the stupid man. The rabbis have, indeed, interpreted the commandment to imply that even a criminal remains our neighbor (Pesahim 75a).

The belief in the immortality of the soul seems to be derived from the belief that man is created in God's image. In Solomon's Wisdom (2:23 ff.) we read: "For God created man for immortality, and made him the image of his own peculiar nature; but by the envy of the devil death entered into the world."

According to the psalmist, however, it seems that not all people are saved from dying. It requires an act of God's ransoming the soul from the power of Sheol for the soul to be saved.

While there is no assurance that all souls are saved from Sheol, the psalmist does express the belief that some souls are saved.

Like sheep they are appointed for Sheol;
Death shall be their shepherd;
Straight to the grave they descend,
And their form shall waste away . . .
But God will ransom my soul from
  the power of Sheol,
For He will receive me.

—Psalms 49:14–15

Thou dost guide me with Thy counsel
And afterward Thou wilt receive me
  to glory.

—Psalms 73:24

While the theme of image and likeness of God implies no dichotomy of spirit and body, another theme describing man's coming into being implies such a dichotomy.

"The Lord God formed man of the dust from the ground and breathed into his nostrils the breath of life" (Genesis 2:7). Here the distinction is sharply drawn between the aspect of man that is derived from dust and the aspect of man that goes back to God. In the spirit of these words Ecclesiastes (12:7) speaks of the eternity of the soul: "The dust returns to earth as it was, and the spirit returns to God who gave it."

"It is the spirit in a man, the breath of the Almighty, that makes him understand" (Job 32:8).

The song of Moses calls upon man: "O that . . . they would consider their latter end" (Deuteronomy 32:29). Man is made of the dust of the earth, and dying is "going the way of all the earth" (Joshua 23:14; I Kings 2:1–2). Death is "a return to the ground, for from it you were taken: For dust you are, and to dust you shall return" (Genesis 3:19). Yet the general conception is not of death as a return to dust, a dissolving into nothing.

There is a certainty of faith that the human soul will not be lost but rather be "bound in the bundle of living in the care of the Lord your God" (I Samuel 25:29).

We are told:

Our existence carries eternity within itself. "He planted life eternal within us." Because we can do the eternal at any moment, the will of God, dying too is doing the will of God. Just as being is obedience to the Creator, so dying is returning to the Source.

Death may be a supreme spiritual act, turning oneself over to eternity: The moment of death, a moment of ecstasy. A moment of no return to vanity.

Thus afterlife is felt to be a reunion and all of life a preparation for it. The Talmud compares this world to a wedding. Said Rabbi Bunam, "If a man makes every preparation for the wedding feast but forgets to purchase a wedding ring, the marriage cannot take place." Similarly, a man may labor all his life, but if he forgets to acquire the means—to acquire the ring—the instrument of sanctifying himself to God, he will not be able to enter the life eternal.

Death may be the beginning of exaltation, an ultimate celebration, a reunion of the divine image with the divine source of being.

Dust returns to dust, while the image, the divine stake in man, is restored to the bundle of life.

Death is not sensed as a defeat but as a summation, an arrival, a conclusion.

"O God, the soul whom Thou hast placed within me is pure. Thou hast created it; Thou hast formed it; Thou hast breathed it into me. Thou preservest it within me; Thou wilt take it from me and restore it to me in the hereafter. So long as the soul is within me, I offer thanks before Thee . . . Lord of all souls. Blessed art Thou, O Lord, who restorest the souls to the dead."

The meaning of death is in return, regardless of whether it results in a continuation of individual consciousness or in merging into a greater whole.

We are what we are by what we come from. We achieve what we do by what we hope for.

Our ultimate hope has no specific content. Our hope is God. We trust that He will not desert those who trust in Him.

O Lord, Thou hast searched me and known me!
Thou knowest when I sit down and when I rise up;
Thou discernest my thoughts from afar.
Thou searchest out my path and my lying down
and art acquainted with all my ways.
Even before a word is on my tongue,
lo, O Lord, Thou knowest it altogether.
Thou dost beset me behind and before,
and layest Thy hand upon me.
Such knowledge is too wonderful for me;
it is high, I cannot attain it.
Whither shall I go from Thy Spirit?
Or whither shall I flee from Thy presence?
If I ascend to heaven, Thou art there!
If I make my bed in Sheol, Thou art there!
If I take the wings of the morning
and dwell in the uttermost parts of the sea,
even there Thy hand shall lead me,
and Thy right hand shall hold me.
If I say, "Let only darkness cover me,
and the light about me be night,"
even the darkness is not dark to Thee,
the night is bright as the day;
for darkness is as light with Thee.

—Psalms 139:1–12

The ultimate hope for a life beyond the grave was not born in reflection about the soul but rather in reflection about God and what He does and means to the soul. God's being a shelter and a refuge forever held meaning to life here and now as well as to life beyond.

The meaning as well as the mode of being which man hopes to attain beyond the threshold of dying remains an impenetrable mystery. Yet it is the thought of being in God's knowing that may be both the root and the symbol of the ultimate hope.

As said above, man's being in the world is, according to the Bible, preceded by man's being known to God. Human existence follows divine anticipation. "Before I formed you in the womb I knew you" (Jeremiah 1:5). We live in the universe of His knowing.

What guides and sustains our thinking about afterlife is relatedness to God. Apart from such relatedness and trust, there is no ground for such a hope.

The real issue is whether my existence here and now is exclusively being-in-the-world or whether it is also being-in-God's-knowledge, whether being in the world is not also living in the presence of God, transcended by His knowing, escorted by His radiance.

Righteous men are regarded as living even after they die (Berakhot 18a). Just as there is a life that is really death—"The wicked are dead while they are alive" (Berakhot 18b)—so there is death that is really life.

It is the experience that those who trust in Him are not abandoned while being in the world that gives strength to the hope of not being abandoned after passing the threshold of death and leaving the world.

Daily we pray: "In Thy hand are the souls of the living and the dead as it is written 'In His hand is the soul of every living thing, and the spirit of every human being' " (Job 12:10). "Into Thy hand I commit my spirit, O Lord, faithful God Thou savest me" (Psalms 31:6).

Life after death seems to be a transposition to a unique mode of being, presumably to being in the universe of divine knowing.

The primary topic of biblical thinking is not man's knowledge of God but man's being known by God. Man's awareness of God is awareness of God not as an object of thinking but as a subject. Awareness of God is awareness of being thought of by God, of being an object of His concern, of His expectation.

Surviving after death, we hope, is surviving as a thought of God.

The question that looms in relation to my own self is: Am I worthy of surviving, of being a thought of God? What is it about myself or my existence that has affinity to eternity?

Survival beyond death carries, according to Judaism, demands and obligations during life here and now. Conditions are attached to the hope of survival.

Eternity is not an automatic consequence of sheer being, and survival is not an unconditional epilogue of living. It must be achieved, earned.

Eternal is a moment of simultaneity of the human and the divine, a moment in which God and man meet.

The religious quest is a quest of the contemporaneity of God.

Simultaneity with God is the only element of permanence in the world.

In speaking of God we have faith and a sense of presence, but no image. In speaking of life after death we have hope and a sense of trust, but no image.

Death, what follows death, is a mystery defying imagination. Facing it, our language is silence. Yet while the body descends into the grave, trust remains, hope persists and enters a simile.

Marvelous and beautiful is life in the body, but more marvelous and more beautiful is life in a word. The word is greater than world; by the word of God all was created. The Book, Scripture, is an everlasting constellation of holy words. When a good man dies, his soul becomes a word and lives in God's book.

"And many of those who sleep in the dust of the earth shall awake, some to everlasting life and some to shame and everlasting contempt" (Daniel 12:2).

The decisive message of this passage is that death is not the final act, that there will be an awakening of those who sleep in the dust.

This is the hope that in dying I become a seed and that after I decay I am born again. Must the self remain the same rather than become the seed of a new self, a new being?

We trust Him who made us what we are and will make of us what He pleases.

In spite of the excellence which the afterlife holds in store for the righteous, there is no craving for death in the history of Jewish piety. While it is true that the condition of the life beyond is eternity, it was maintained that the quality of living here and now has an excellence not given in the afterlife: freedom, serving Him in freedom. It is greater to struggle on earth than to be an angel in heaven. Earthly life, mortal life, is precisely the arena where the covenant between God and man must be fulfilled.

The love of life calls for resistance to death, resistance to the last, unconditionally.

Life here is where partnership abides between God and man. With death, man surrenders his freedom, and only God's will is done. The soul is receptive, there is no room for freedom.

Life here and now is the task. Every moment can be an achievement.

The body is not a prison but an opportunity. Still, for all its glory, life here and now is regarded as a vestibule, as preparation. Yet no one looked forward with pleasure to life after death.

Just because the afterlife is a completion, life here and now is an opportunity, and it was considered a loss to leave the realm of here and now, because once the threshold is crossed, the opportunity is gone.

Life is revealing of the divine, while death is concealing. To be alive is to be in the midst of the people, and we must resist being taken away from the midst of the people. But once the moment of parting comes, a benediction is uttered: Blessed be Thou, our God, King of the Universe, the true Judge. Amen.

We must distinguish between being human and human being. We are born human beings. What we must acquire is being human. Being human is the essential—the decisive—achievement of a human being.

Human being finds its end in organic dissolution. But being human is not an organic substance; it is an action and a radiance of the personhood of man. The unity, the sum total of moments of personhood, is a presence that goes on in terms surpassing mere existence.

The organic process is of ambiguous significance in regard to the formation of being human. On the one hand, the organic process may compel the person to struggle for realization, but it is not always promoting it. Organic living is certainly not the total form of living.

The meaning of existence is in the sanctification of time, in lending eternity to the moments. Being human is a quest for the lasting.

Craving for God, longing for immediate perception of the divine, for emancipation from selfish desires and inclinations—such freedom can be achieved only beyond death.

It is a distortion to characterize the life of man as moving toward death. Death is the end of the road, and while moving along the long road of days and nights, we are really moving toward living, acting, achieving. Death is the end of the road, but not its meaning, not a refutation of living. That every moment of life is a step toward death is a mechanical view. Every moment of life is a new arrival, a new beginning. Those who say that we die every day, that every moment deprives us of a portion of life, look at moments as time past. Looking at moments as time present, every moment is a new arrival, a new beginning.

A man's kind deeds are used by the Lord as seeds for the planting of trees in the Garden of Eden. Each man brings about his own trees; each man creates his own Garden of Eden. In Judaism the primary dimension of existence in which meaning is both sensed and created is the dimension of deeds. Sacred acts, deeds of kindness, not only imitate the divine, they represent the divine.

Rabbi Simon ben Yohai states: "Honor the *mitzvot*, for the *mitzvot* are my deputies, and a deputy in endowed with the authority of his principal. If you honor the *mitzvot*, it is as if you honored me; if you dishonor them, it is as if you dishonored me."

And the secret of spiritual living is in the sense for the ultimacy of each moment, for its sacred uniqueness, for its once-and-for-allness. It is this sense that enables us to put all our strength into sanctifying an instant by doing the holy.

Every moment is a kingdom wherein every one of us is a king by the grace of God. Does the king know what to do with his might? Our task is to design a deed, a pyramid of deeds.

There are two separate themes: death and after-death. Death we must seek to understand in relation to life. After-death transcends that relation and must be thought of in different terms.

Death is not understood as the end of being but rather as the end of doing. As such it is a dramatic break, a radical event: cessation of doing.

We do not dwell on death. We dwell on the preciousness of every moment. Things of space vanish. Moments of time never pass away. Time is the clue to the meaning of life and death. Time lived with meaning thus is a disclosure of the eternal.

The problem is not how to mitigate the fear of death but how to conceive the meaning of death to which the meaning of life is related.

From the perspective of love, the death of an individual is absurd and without consolation. No argument can be advanced that would offer comfort to those who mourn. The words we offer to those in mourning —"May the Lord comfort you among those who mourn for Zion and Jerusalem"—carry the hope that there is comfort for those who mourn just as there is comfort for Jerusalem when in ruin.

The thought of death is a necessary component for human existence. It enables us to be open to ultimate demands regardless of personal needs.

Anxiety about death is really an anxiety about the ultimate confrontation that follows death. In other words, it is an anxiety about the afterlife rather than about dying itself.

Life with its conflicts and contradictions, absurdities and perplexities, hurts us with a puzzlement that may lead to despair. Afterlife, or the hope for the afterlife, is the hope for clarification, a hope for a participation in understanding the enigma of life on earth.

One motif that is continually coming to the fore in the research dealing with attitudes toward death in terminally ill patients is "that the crisis is often not the fact of oncoming death per se, of man's insurmountable finiteness, but rather the waste of limited years, the unassayed tasks, the lacked opportunities, the talents withering in disuse, the avoidable evils which have been done. The tragedy which is underlined is that man dies prematurely and without dignity, that death has not become really his 'own'."[1]

There is a paradox in relation to life. To be alive is cherished as the highest value. Yet when faced with the choice of either living or committing murder, for example, we are told, Be killed rather than kill. In the course of the ages, we have been admonished to cultivate readiness to die for the sake of sanctifying the name of God.

Death is the radical refutation of man's power and a stark reminder of the necessity to relate to a meaning which lies beyond the dimension of human time. Humanity without death would be arrogance without end. Nobility has its root in humanity, and humanity derived much of its power from the thought of death.

Death refutes the deification and distorts the arrogance of man.

He is God; what He does is right, for all His ways are just; God of faithfulness and without wrong, just and right is He.

Just art Thou, O Lord, in causing death and life; Thou in whose hand all living beings are kept, far be it from Thee to blot out our remembrance; let Thy eyes be open to us in mercy; for Thine, O Lord, is mercy and forgiveness.

We know, O Lord, that Thy judgment is just; Thou art right when Thou speakest, and justified when Thou givest sentence; one must not find fault with Thy manner of judging. Thou art righteous, O Lord, and Thy judgment is right.

True and righteous Judge, blessed art Thou, all whose judgments are righteous and true.

The Lord gave and the Lord has taken away; blessed be the name of the Lord.

Daily Prayer Book, from the Burial Service

In a broken world, cessation of living is a necessity. But someday "He will swallow up death forever and the Lord God will wipe away tears from all faces" (Isaiah 25:8).

When Rabbi Bunam was lying on his deathbed, his wife wept bitterly. When he noticed it he said to her, "Why do you cry? All my life has been given me merely that I might learn how to die."

The afterlife is thought of entirely in terms of one's trust in God.

Even though I walk through the valley of the
shadow of death,
I fear no evil;
for Thou art with me;
Thy rod and Thy staff,
they comfort me.

—*Psalms* 23:4

We do not know how to die in grace, because we do not know how to grow old gracefully. Growing old must be a process of cleansing the self, a way of getting ready for ultimate confrontation.

If life is a pilgrimage, death is an arrival, a celebration. The last word should be neither craving nor bitterness, but peace, gratitude.

We have been given so much. Why is the outcome of our lives, the sum of our achievements, so little?

Our embarrassment is like an abyss. Whatever we give away is so much less than what we receive. Perhaps this is the meaning of dying: to give one's whole self away.

Death is not seen as mere ruin and disaster. It is felt to be a loss of further possibilities to experience and to enhance the glory and goodness of God here and now. It is not a liquidation but a summation, the end of a prelude to a symphony of which we only have a vague inkling of hope. The prelude is infinitely rich in possibilities of either enhancing or frustrating God's patient, ongoing efforts to redeem the world.

Death is the end of what we can do in being partners to redemption.

The life that follows must be earned while we are here. It does not come out of nothing; it is an ingathering, the harvest of eternal moments achieved while on earth.

Unless we cultivate sensitivity to the glory while here, unless we learn how to experience a foretaste of heaven while on earth, what can there be in store for us in life to come? The seed of life eternal is planted within us here and now. But a seed is wasted when placed on stone, into souls that die while the body is still alive.

The greatest problem is not how to continue but how to exalt our existence. The cry for a life beyond the grave is presumptuous, if there is no cry for eternal life prior to our descending to the grave. Eternity is not perpetual future but perpetual presence. He has planted in us the seed of eternal life. The world to come is not only a hereafter but also a here-now.

Our greatest problem is not how to continue but how to return. "How can I repay unto the Lord all His bountiful dealings with me?" (Psalms 116:12). When life is an answer, death is a homecoming. "Precious in the sight of the Lord is the death of his saints" (Psalms 116:14). For our greatest problem is but a resonance of God's concern: How can I repay unto man all his bountiful dealings with me? "For the mercy of God endureth forever."

This is the meaning of existence: to reconcile liberty with service, the passing with the lasting, to weave the threads of temporality into the fabric of eternity.

The deepest wisdom man can attain is to know that his destiny is to aid, to serve. We have to conquer in order to succumb; we have to acquire in order to give away; we have to triumph in order to be overwhelmed. Man has to understand in order to believe, to know in order to accept. The aspiration is to obtain; the perfection is to dispense. This is the meaning of death: the ultimate self-dedication to the divine. Death so understood will not be distorted by the craving for immortality, for this act of giving away is reciprocity on man's part for God's gift of life. For the pious man it is a privilege to die.

APPENDICES

Interview at Notre Dame

INTERVIEWER: *What was your impression of Father Bernard Häring's talk on holiness in the Church and religious life?*

RABBI HESCHEL: Worship is the primary form of religious living. He who doesn't know how to worship doesn't know how to believe and what it means to be alive. In that sense, I would say that worship precedes faith. Father Häring's entire emphasis on the life of worship and prayer is one that I consider valid and indispensable.

Was there anything in his address that you would question?

Yes, I have one basic question. In his interpretation of worship and the role of the Holy Spirit, he was exceedingly Christ-centered. This raises some serious theological problems. Is it really necessary for a Christian to believe that the Creator of heaven and earth has resigned His power to Jesus and that God Himself, Omnipotent Father, is unable to reach men directly? What of the psalmist? Would you be willing to say that the psalmist didn't know how to pray? And what of those who do not accept the claim of the Church? Are the Jews and Mohammedans unable to pray or address themselves to God? Father Häring, by saying that the act of worship is an act in Christ, indicated that there is only *one* acceptable form of prayer. As a Jew, I must reject that, and I also consider it dangerous to Christians.

Don't you think that Father Häring would agree that one can pray directly to God? He would probably point to the Divine Office, the official prayer of the Church, which draws heavily from the Old Testament.

It is true that the "Hebrew Bible"—a term that should replace the condescending term "Old Testament"—stresses the relationship of immediacy between man and God. But I feel that within the new thinking that is taking place in the Church, there is need of a further clarification on this question. I know that the Church stresses the centrality of Jesus in the process of salvation. I do not think, however, it has had to stress the centrality of Jesus in the process of inspiration and worship.

Is the question "salvation through the synagogue" important in contemporary Judaism?

No. That's not our problem. One of the greatest sources of mutual understanding is that Christians and Jews have different problems. In Christianity, the problem of salvation is paramount. In Judaism, other issues are central. I can best illustrate this by a little story. One of my ancestors was Rabbi Levi Itzhak, a Hasidic rabbi, one of the great saints in Jewish history. He once said: "I know very well that I am unworthy of eternal life, because I am a sinner and have always failed to do the will of God. What will happen to me when I come before the heavenly court? The decree will certainly be that I enter hell, and that will be the will of God. What greater joy is there than to do the will of God? I will utter a benediction and run to hell in order to suffer, because such is the will of God." We believe in an afterlife. We believe that every one of us individually will be called upon to give account of the life we lived. We are *not* saved by the synagogue; our destiny will be determined by what we do or fail to do. The commandment, the *mitzvah*, to serve God, is a term more central than the term "salvation." Shall I give you another example?

Yes, please do.

This is a story of another of my ancestors. His name was Rabbi Dov Baer, the "Great Preacher" of Mezhiritch. He was the successor to the Baal Shem, the founder of Hasidism. He was a poor man who made his living teaching little children. But it happened that there were exceedingly few children in the community and the income he received was not sufficient. On the eve of the Passover, his wife told him that they had no money to buy the matzo, wine, and candles for the feast. He assured his wife that God would take care of them, and he went to the synagogue to pray. When he returned, he saw candles in the window, and as he went inside, he saw the table set for the feast. He also found a stranger in the house whom he greeted briefly. Then the family celebrated the ancient rite. Afterward, his wife told him that this man had come to their house and asked if he could celebrate the Passover with them. He had with him all the necessary supplies. The rabbi was overcome with gratitude and asked the man what he could do for him to repay his kindness. The man said, "Rabbi, I am a happy man, successful and well-to-do, but my wife never gave me a child. I have uttered many prayers, but God never answered my petition. Would you pray for me?" The rabbi said, "A year from now (using the scriptural way of talking), your wife will be a mother." Suddenly the rabbi heard a voice from heaven saying, "Since you have made the promise, you shall not share in the life to come." There was a decree in heaven that this man should not be a father and the rabbi should have been aware of this. Since he was a man of spiritual powers, he must have known this. But still he defied it. When the rabbi heard that he would never enter heaven, he was overwhelmed with great joy and started to dance in ecstasy. People asked him why he was so happy, and he said to them, "All my life I have had one great fear: that I serve God only to have a share in the life to come. I was never sure if my service was really genuine and pure. Now I know. Now I can serve God out of love, and I will receive no reward. How happy and wonderful will be my life knowing that I am really doing the will of God."

What is the Jewish conception of the afterlife?

We have no information about it. The only thing we know is what is given to us in the Talmud in the name of one of the sages of the third century. We are told that the world to come is a sphere, a realm where the good people sit with crowns on their heads receiving joy of *visio Dei*—the joy of inhaling the glory of God's presence. That's all we know. We don't know what the *visio Dei* means, or the significance of the "crowns." So we must allegorize, and we say that a crown is made up of the good and sacred moments in our life here on earth and the good deeds that we do in this life.

What happens to the evil man who rejects God?

From the Torah we know only so much about the will of God. The afterlife remains a mystery. But we can say that Jewish tradition certainly teaches that there is a way of survival for the wicked that we call Sheol.

Death is not seen as mere ruin and disaster. It is felt to be a loss of further possibilities to experience and to enhance the glory and goodness of God here and now. It is not a liquidation but a summation, the end of a prelude to a symphony of which we have only a vague inkling of hope. The prelude is infinitely rich in possibilities of either enhancing or frustrating God's patient, ongoing efforts to redeem the world.

Death is the end of what we can do in being partners to redemption. The life that follows must be earned while we are here. It does not come out of nothing; it is an ingathering, the harvest of eternal moments achieved while on earth.

Unless we cultivate sensitivity to the glory while here, unless we learn how to experience a foretaste of heaven while on earth, what can there be in store for us in the life to come? The seed of life eternal is planted within us here and now. But a seed is wasted when placed on iron, into souls that die while the body is still alive.

You mentioned that your ancestors were rabbis.

Yes, I can trace my family back to the late fifteenth century. They were all rabbis. For seven generations, all my ancestors have been Hasidic rabbis.

You once wrote that "the dignity of human existence is in the power of reciprocity." When I first read that, I immediately thought of Martin Buber. Was I correct?

I will tell you how I understand that statement. Reciprocity has two meanings: in relation to man and in relation to God. I am not sure that Buber used reciprocity in this second sense. In fact, I doubt it. I have found great inspiration in Psalms 116:12: "What can I render to the Lord for all His bounties toward me?" This is the basic notion of reciprocity. One of the prerequisites for faith is gratitude. It is the essential attitude that makes a person human. It is out of gratitude that we learn how to praise, how to pray. In the Jewish liturgy, praise is the outstanding form of prayer. We must learn how to praise in order to know how to implore. First we sing, then we believe. Praise precedes faith. If we look at the Psalms, we see that above all the psalmist is overwhelmed by sensing the Creator in His creation. He is grateful for every perception—for the moment of being alive.

Have you been greatly influenced by Martin Buber?

I would not say so. I consider the important insights in Buber to be derived from Hasidic tradition, and these I knew before I met him. I served as his successor in Frankfurt am Main when the Gestapo would not allow him to teach anymore. He asked me to take over his work. I knew him intimately for many years.

What are the significant contributions Buber made to Judaism and to the philosophy of religion?

Permit me to enumerate a few major contributions. First of all, he discovered Hasidism for the West, for the non-Jewish world. And through this he also brought Hasidism to many Jews who were alienated from it and didn't know what it was. Second, he wrote widely on Zionism. Third, he was very successful in interpreting Hasidism in modern philosophical terms. Fourth, he translated the Hebrew Bible into German in a creative way. He was, above all, a profound thinker, a major surprise in the intellectual climate of the twentieth century.

How did Buber feel about organized religion?

Let me explain. Jewish thinking and living can be adequately understood only in terms of a dialectic pattern, containing opposite or contrasted properties. As in a magnet, the ends of which have opposite magnetic qualities, these terms are opposite to one another and exemplify a polarity that lies at the very heart of Judaism, the polarity of ideas and events, of *mitzvah* and sin, of *kavanah* and deed, of regularity and spontaneity, of uniformity and individuality, of *halacha* and *agada*, of law and inwardness, of love and fear, of understanding and obedience, of joy and discipline, of the good and the evil drive, of time and eternity, of this world and the world to come, of revelation and response, of insight and information, of empathy and self-expression, of creed and faith, of the word and that which is beyond words, of man's quest for God and God in search of man. Even God's relation to the world is characterized by the polarity of justice and mercy, providence and concealment, the promise of reward and the demand to serve Him for His sake. Taken abstractedly, all these terms seem to be mutually exclusive, yet in actual living they involve each other; the separation of the two is fatal to both. There is no *halacha* without *agada,* and no *agada* without *halacha.* We must neither disparage the body nor sacrifice the spirit. The body is the discipline, the pattern, the law; the spirit is inner devotion, spontaneity, freedom. The body without the spirit is a corpse; the spirit without the body is a ghost. Thus, a *mitzvah* is both a discipline and an inspiration, an act of obedience and an experience of joy, a yoke and a prerogative. Our task is to learn how to maintain a harmony between the demands of *halacha* and the spirit of *agada.*

The weakness of Buber's conception is in his stressing one aspect to the exclusion of the other.

Did he hold that revelation was a kind of vague exchange?

No, not an exchange. Rather, he believed it is a vague encounter. That is untenable. A Jew cannot live by such a conception of revelation. Buber does not do justice to the claims of the prophets. So I have to choose between him and the Bible itself. The Bible says that God spoke to men—a challenging, embarrassing, and overwhelming claim. I have trouble with many of the things He said, but I have to accept them. If I don't accept the claim that God spoke to the prophets, then I detach myself from the biblical roots. Buber was a person of depth and greatness, but on many points he was not able to reach the Jewish people. One of the weaknesses in Buber, who was an exceedingly learned man, was that he was not at home in rabbinic literature. That covers many years. A lot has happened between the Bible and Hasidism that Buber did not pay attention to.

Would you go so far as to say that he had a greater influence on the non-Jewish world than on the Jewish world?

Many people say so.

Do you agree?

It is hard to know exactly how to measure influence. I must know my limitations. There are certain things I know and other things I do not.

What can Christianity learn from Judaism?

To be a witness to the God of Abraham, of Sinai, openness to God's stake in the ongoing history of the Jewish people. There are many things that Judaism teaches: the importance of simple common deeds, sanctification of time, and a sense of wonder and radical amazement. But all these things flow from the primary witness to the God of Abraham. The idea of witness, that is, sensitivity to God's presence, is, above all, the primary, existential aspect of Judaism. Other things, such as the mysterious immediacy in relation to God, radical monotheism, and the concept of man, are aspects of witness.

Would you please explain the Judaic concept of man.

We start with the certainty that God is involved in human life. This means that the primary task of man is to realize that God has a stake in his life. We also believe that the Jewish people are not the same since Sinai. They are called upon to carry out the commandments of the Torah, the Law. Man is by his very being a man in travail with God's dreams and designs. In the Bible, we read about the creation of all *other things*: "And then God said. And so it was." But when God came to create man, He first had a vision of man. He said: "Let us make man in our vision." In other words, the vision of man preceded the creation of man. We may say that God has a vision or expectation of man. It is our task to recover it. That's why man is a messenger for God—*the* messenger. God is in our midst. Our most important problem is the problem of responsiveness, obedience to the Law, openness, listening to Moses, Amos, Rabbi Akiba; our privilege is being a part of the Jewish community, past and present.

I think that a Christian would agree with all you have said.

If he agrees with all that, then he is a Jew.

Perhaps this is what Pope Pius XI meant when he said, "Spiritually, we are Semites."

But Christians leave out the possibility and the greatness of Mosaic Law. A Christian theologian would say that the Law is an imposition. We feel the blessing and the love of the Law; we sense God's will. A Jew is committed to the idea that he is able to be attached to God directly. We have the certainty of being able to live a life that is compatible with His presence. In other words, the will of God is within the scope of human understanding. The Torah has not been abolished. We have the gift of the word. What is the Bible? The presence of God is found in many ways, but above all God is found in the words of the Bible. We believe that we are living in the ancient Covenant of Sinai. This is not a matter of feeling or even a matter of faith. It's a reality. God is waiting for the sinner. Up to the last day, God is waiting for his return. Man has to respond. The question of original sin is not of primary importance for the Jew. The problem is not how shall I be saved. The problem is how shall I serve God at this very moment. My challenge is how can I be honest and helpful toward my neighbor in the presence of the Father.

Surely the Hebrew Bible is an essential element of the total Christian view.

But what did you do to the Hebrew Bible? You made it an "old" book of Law that very few people read. I have encountered many wonderful priests whose spirituality I greatly admire who haven't read the Hebrew Bible. Recently, a very fine, inspired priest, a man advanced in years, told me: "I am now reading for the first time the Hebrew Bible. What a great work it is." The fact is that Catholics read only the Psalms from the Hebrew Bible. They read papal encyclicals, Christian authors, and, of course, the New Testament. But they forget the Hebrew Bible.

What else does a Jew expect from Christianity?

We are a small group always in danger. History has shown that our situation has always been precarious—on the brink of disaster. For almost two thousand years, the Church has tried to understand itself as an antithesis to Judaism. I am not speaking about the results of such hostility. I am speaking about the scandal of rejecting the genuine roots of Christian belief. Jesus was a Jew. His disciples were Jews. Jesus prepared for the Sabbath, sanctified the Seventh Day, read the traditional prayers, and recited and interpreted the Bible.

To answer your question, I would say that the most that Christianity can do is to be faithful to its ultimate roots. Christians must abandon the idea that the Jews must be converted. This is one of the greatest scandals in history. It reminds me of a spiritual Oedipus complex. "Honor your father and your mother." Your mother and father were both Jews. The first thing you could do for us is to be genuine in your Christian faith and to be a witness to the God of Abraham. I recognize in Christianity the presence of holiness. I see it; I sense it; I feel it. You are not an embarrassment to us, and we shouldn't be an embarrassment to you. We can help each other on many levels. The Jews have a good memory of what the Bible means. The Christians have had great experience in proclaiming the message of the God of Abraham to the Gentiles and have been able to preserve many ancient insights and loyalties in their spirituality. A Christian should realize that a world that does not have Israel will be a world without the God of Israel. A Jew, in his own way, should acknowledge the role of Christianity in God's plan for the redemption of all men.

What is the goal of Christian-Jewish cooperation?

The purpose of such interreligious cooperation is not mutual refutation. It is to help one another share insight and learning. We must also search for the sources of devotion and for the power of love and care for man. More than ever before we need each other's help, and we need the courage to believe that the word of the Lord endures forever. We must keep ourselves sensitive to God around us and listen to His word in the Bible.

Religion is a means, not an end. Over all stands the Creator and Lord of history, He who transcends all.

Recently a New York minister suggested that Christians join Jews in observing Saturday instead of Sunday as the Sabbath. What do you think of this?

It should not be done just for ecumenical reasons. One should serve God not for the sake of the ecumenical movement but for His own sake. There is much involved here. What is the nature of Christian faith? If it is a biblical faith, then you take the Ten Commandments seriously. So why did the Christians change the Holy Day? I cannot understand it. Historically, it was not necessarily done for spiritual reasons. My task is not to tell the Christian what to do. My task is to help him, not to debate with him.

Your life has been dedicated to theology, the study of the word of God. What are the main characteristics of Jewish theology?

Jewish theology must never be detached from the human situation. The standard of Jewish theology is the degree to which it may affect the life of the Jew, his thoughts as well as his concrete action. A person goes astray if his theory far outstrips his actions. It was a major principle in early Hasidism: Beware, lest your wisdom transcend your fulfillment or concrete service. With every new insight that comes to you, seek to carry out a new act of serving Him . . . As to the term itself, "theology" is not quite accurate to a Jewish thinker. I once said in my book *Man Is Not Alone* that the Bible is not man's book about God but rather God's book about man. In this sense, the real concern is to discover what God requires of man—what is God's expectation for man. Anthropology is central to theology. I often use the term "philosophy of religion," but then I have to define it.

What do you mean by philosophy of religion?

The term "religion" in the phrase "philosophy of religion" may be used either as an object or as a subject. In the first sense, philosophy of religion is a critique of religion; religion as a theme or object of examination. In this sense, we employ, e.g., the term "philosophy of science." In the second sense, philosophy has a meaning comparable to the meaning of a phrase such as the "philosophy of Kant" or the "philosophy of Plato."

Now, Judaism is a source of ideas, basic insights, perspectives, and teachings. The task of the philosophy of Judaism is twofold: radical self-understanding in terms of its own spirit, as well as critical reassessment of Judaism from the point of view of both our total knowledge and our immediate situation.

With this distinction in mind, how would you relate it to the contemporary theological quest?

We are challenged from two directions, by the insecurity of faith and by the earnestness of our commitment to the Bible. It is necessary to look at the Bible from the perspective of our situation and to look at our situation from the perspective of the Bible.

Modern theology must seek to recover the uniqueness of biblical thinking, of categories with which to face ultimate problems. The perspective from which we look at reality determines our way of formulating our problems. We have long been accustomed to search in the Bible for answers to non-biblical problems. The result is confusion. The Bible is the *ancilla theologiae*. What I plead for is a search for the intellectual relevance of the Bible.

Do you have any observations about the direction this search should take?

Let us take, for example, the problem of being, which is the central metaphysical problem today. For the biblical mind, being is not the primary question. The Bible is concerned with creation, God's care for creatures. To be or not to be is *not* the question. We have being. The problem is living. The whole conception of the person and of man has been distorted because we have overemphasized ontology. Biblical theology approaches man in a different way. The right question is not "How do I know God?" but "Am I known by God?" This is the basic issue. We have pagan questions, and we seek biblical answers. To understand the Bible, we must know that the Bible has answers to ultimate questions. But first of all, we must know what the ultimate questions are.

Do you think that insensitivity to God is a major problem today?

Yes, it is. But to deal with sensitivity to God is already an advanced problem. We cannot begin with God until we have first dealt adequately with certain pre-theological presuppositions. The way I relate myself to this chair will determine the way I relate myself to God. We must analyze some basic pre-theological directions or attitudes, such as the sense of wonder, reverence, and gratitude. These prerequisites are not cultivated in our society. Thus, the problem today is not sensitivity to God. We are not even sensitive to God's creation. Unless we know how to be sensitive to God's glory and know something of His presence in the world, we will never know anything about His essence.

You spoke of the insecurity of faith. How should theology face this challenge?

First by saying *mea culpa*. Religion has been reduced to institution, symbol, theology. It does not affect the *pre-theological* situation, the pre-symbolic depth of existence. To redirect the trend, we must lay bare what is involved in religious existence: we must recover the situations that both precede and correspond to the theological formulations; we must recall the questions that religious doctrines are trying to answer, the *antecedents of religious commitment*, the presuppositions of faith. A major task of philosophy of religion is, as said before, to rediscover the questions to which religion is an answer. The inquiry must proceed both by delving into the consciousness of man and by delving into the teachings and the attitudes of the religious tradition.

The urgent problem is not only the truth of religion but man's capacity to sense the truth of religion and the authenticity of religious concern. Religious truth does not shine in a vacuum. It is certainly not comprehensible when the antecedents of religious insight and commitment are wasted away; when the mind is dazzled by ideologies that either obscure or misrepresent man's ultimate questions; when life is lived in a way that tends to abuse and to squander the gold mines, the challenging resources of human existence. The primary issue of theology is *pre-theological*; it is the total situation of man and his attitudes toward life and the world. I discussed this in my book *The Insecurity of Freedom*.

Your recent writings reflect your concern with man's deepening alienation from God and the world's drift toward destruction.

I am really a person who is in anguish. I cannot forget what I have seen and been through. Auschwitz and Hiroshima never leave my mind. Nothing can be the same after that. After all, we are convinced that we must take history seriously and that in history signs of the future are given to us. I see signs of a deterioration that has already begun. The war in Vietnam is a sign that we don't know how to live or how to respond. God is trying us very seriously. I wonder if we will pass the test. I am not a pessimist, because I believe that God loves us. But I also believe that we should not rely on God alone; *we* have to respond. It is so important that all of us, regardless of our religious affiliation, remember that we all stand under the hand of God and must *act* with this in mind. As important as it is to discuss theological subtleties, it is much more important to know how to save men from being liquidated.

Have you any suggestions how the churches may work to save man from destruction?

Responsible religious people should discover the real moral problems. The churches should be more concerned with how to save the humanity of man, God's image within man. The prophetic dimension is indispensable. Looking at the past, we may think that the prophet was the most superfluous man that ever lived. The Law was given, the message was there. With the temple and the priests, why was there need for prophets? Apparently it was within the Divine Plan that besides the Law there also be some men who with prophetic vision could remind others of God's message.

What advice would you give those religious people who tend to become discouraged when they see so much evil in the world?

For man to be frustrated is a cardinal sin. Man is not alone in his concern for justice; God is with him. Therefore, we must continue to fight to the last breath. As a criticism, I must say that religious people are often too concerned with trifles and lose sight of greater issues. How can a religious community tolerate violence? This is one of the things I do not understand. I believe that church members can do much to overcome evil if they unite. Why don't all those affiliated with churches—and synagogues—gather together some afternoon and fill the streets with one voice of protest against the killing of innocent civilians. The protest of these many millions of believers would have a great effect, and President Johnson could not ignore it. They should not cease to utter their disgust that America permits civilians to be killed. This is one practical way to carry out the will of God.

I once read that for the Jews a basic difficulty with Christianity is that the "God of Christians is humble, and we Jews cannot accept such humility." Do you agree with this?

No. There is a passage in the Talmud that says just the opposite: "Wherever you find God's grandeur, you find His humility." The divine pathos is a basic category in our understanding of God. I have written about this in my books *The Prophets* and *Theology of Ancient Judaism*, Vol. 1. The issues between Jews and Christians are quite different. We reject the Incarnation; we insist on God's transcendence, and we make absolute the difference between God and man. We don't acknowledge the messiahship of Jesus, because we expected and continue to expect that the Messiah will bring about a radical change in concrete history. We cannot accept the Christian claim that Jesus abolished the Law. To us the Law continues to be valid.

What of Buber's observation that the Church is oriented toward the individual, while Judaism is concerned with the community?

This is an oversimplification that is partly true and partly not true. One of the characteristics of Judaism is the complete identity of the people, or community, and the faith. For example, it is impossible for us to write a history of a Jewish church as a church. We have only a community. Christianity is a universal religion; there are many communities in Christianity, but there is no strict identity between community and faith. In other words, in Judaism there is a greater emphasis upon *qahal*, the holy community, in a total way than in Christianity. This can be illustrated by the saying of a rabbi in the first century: "I am willing to be a sacrifice for my people." This can be understood in the sense that "I am ready to give myself up completely, as long as the community remains intact."

The Catholic Church certainly looks upon herself as the ecclesia, the sacred, worshipping community. The communitarian aspect is as strong in Christianity as in Judaism.

I wish it were, but it isn't.

Do you mean theologically or historically?

I am not competent to judge theologically, but historically, Christianity has not stressed the idea of community. Let me give you an example. In my childhood I could not understand how German and French soldiers, both claiming Christianity as their religion, could kill each other. You call this a community? Maybe you can give me a theological answer for this, but for me it is inconceivable that such a thing should happen in a community. It is fratricide. You are not one people if you kill each other. This is your challenge, and I pray that you can meet it. So far you have not.

Do you have any observations concerning the role of the Jews in the present ecumenical dialogue?

We are now at the beginning of a new period in the history of religious cooperation between Christians and Jews. The fact that last year I was appointed the Harry Emerson Fosdick Visiting Professor at Union Theological Seminary is a sign of the change. I have had hundreds of conversations and meetings with Christians, and if I discovered that we have many disagreements, I also discovered that there is much upon which we can agree. It is true that our dogmas and ways of worship are different. But we both worship the God of Israel. We are both committed to the Hebrew Bible as the word of God, to some of the commandments as the will of God, to the sense of contrition, and to the conviction that without the holy, the good will be defeated. Our prayer is for Christians to continue to serve and to worship God.

However, I have one complaint. Give up the idea of the mission to the Jews, the idea of converting the Jews. It is arrogant to play God. Once the Christians give this up, much of the tension will be relieved. Christianity, as an expression of Providence, is no problem for us. It is true that you have a number of ideas that I wish you would modify, and in fact you are modifying many of them.

Some Jews are suspicious of the ecumenical movement and fear that if all Christians unite, then the Jews will again be persecuted.

You can't blame the Jews for such fear. I have been stoned and beaten up many times in Warsaw by young boys who had just come out of church. What do you expect the Jews to feel? Do you think I can forget the long history of my people and the horrible things that have happened to us in the last thirty years? The Jew is afflicted with anxiety. The psalmist frequently reminds us that there is no security in this world. But I believe that God will purify the heart and will give wisdom and grace to His sons. I take consolation in the words of Rabbi Johanan Ha-Sandelar, a disciple of Rabbi Akiba, who said: "Every community which is established for the sake of heaven will in the end endure; but one which is not for the sake of heaven will not endure in the end."

Carl Stern's Interview

with Dr. Heschel

CARL STERN: *I brought these books from home. They're only a small portion of the books you've written. What was there in your life, especially your early life, that would give you the thoughts to fill so many books?*

DR. HESCHEL: Hard work, training, and a good environment. I was very fortunate in having lived as a child and as a young boy in an environment where there were many people I could revere, people concerned with problems of the inner life, of spirituality and integrity. People who have shown great compassion and understanding for other people.

But your life itself has not been an easy life. You escaped from Poland just before the Nazis came in. What experiences of life have found their way into these books?

I would say again, my background, my early upbringing. I would criticize my early upbringing as deficient in one respect and very rich in another respect. Deficient in what may be called the art of relaxation, sports. I'm not the sporting type, unfortunately. But very rich in moments of exultation. This enabled me to stand a little bit above the circumstances of life and to take a perspective from which I could see the world, so to speak, from a higher point of view. In other words, I was trained as a child to live a life, or to strive to live a life, which is compatible with the mystery and marvel of human existence.

And learning about it.

And learning about it.

What is the role of learning?

The role of learning is decisive. First of all, the supreme value ascribed to learning and learning being a source of inspiration, learning being the greatest adventure, learning being a source of joy, and, in fact, learning for the purpose of discovering, of the importance of self-discipline; the realization, namely, that a life without discipline was not worth living.

Perhaps a life without surprise is not worth living either. You recently told an interviewer that "what keeps me alive is my ability to be surprised." What has surprised you lately?

Everything. This may be my weakness. You know, you once quoted a statement from the Book of Ecclesiastes: "There is nothing new under the sun." And I disagreed with that statement. I would say there is nothing stale under the sun except human beings, who become stale. I try not to be stale. And everything is new. No two moments are alike. And a person who thinks that two moments are alike has never lived. The secret of it is a very profound principle of philosophy. And that I would call the sense of the unique. Do you know that among a billion faces in this world, no two faces are alike? The other day a person complained to me that he went to the Metropolitan Museum of Art and he was bewildered because no two paintings looked alike.

One of the most arresting titles of your many books would be this one: God in Search of Man. *Is God in search of man?*

That's a paradox. In fact, if God consulted me, I would tell Him . . .

Does He?

He doesn't. He's too wise to consult me. I would say, "Why do you care about man?" The biggest message of the Bible of the prophets of Israel is that God takes man seriously. You remember He created Adam and Eve and they immediately failed. He was disappointed, but He kept them alive. Then they gave birth to two boys, very nice boys. I'm sure they got some very excellent education, certainly in a good environment. They didn't live in the slums, you know. And you know what one brother did to the other. God should have been disgusted. He said, "No, I will keep the human species alive. I'm waiting. Maybe someday there'll be a righteous generation." And throughout history, as seen by the Bible, there is one disappointment for God after another. But He's still waiting, waiting, waiting for a mankind that will live by justice and compassion. He's in search of man.

Now let me say to you, there are essentially three points. One, *God in Search of Man*, to me, is a homily of all the Hebrew Bible. Two, it expresses the idea of Judaism about the position of man in the universe. Man is terribly important. If God is so concerned about man, which surprises me again, why shouldn't God be concerned more about, let us say, cosmic energy or the astronaut techniques? He's interested in widows and orphans in Jerusalem. My Lord, if He were to ask me, I would say, "It's beneath your dignity. You, God of the Universe, should be concerned about the poor, about the disadvantaged." Yes, He is. Man is very important to God.

And the third point?

The third point would be the nature of religion. The nature of religion is not just a long-range feeling of man searching for God. I think that God is more in search of man than man is in search of God. He gives us no rest. We have for generations, for decades, for centuries, tried to refute the existence of God, as if He didn't exist. But in spite of everything, man is still searching. Man is still waiting. Man is still longing. Man has discovered a new discovery. That a man without God is like a torso, a body without a head.

But man is searching also, because, if you'll forgive me, there's a certain absurdity, a certain purposelessness, or perhaps an undiscoverable purpose. Let me cite an example. Ten days before Martin Luther King was killed, you, as a good friend of his, addressed a convention of the Rabbinical Assembly. And you said, "Martin Luther King is a sign that God has not forsaken the United States of America." And yet ten days later he was dead in the most cruel and purposeless fashion. It's that sort of question that challenges faith. How do you explain that?

If we understand the Bible properly, and very few people these days study the Bible properly—we itemize the Bible and tear it to pieces instead of immersing ourselves in the thoughts of the Bible—we discover that God shares life with man and He has given man freedom. A very questionable gift, and the most outstanding gift man has. Man can do anything. When the first son of the first couple decided to murder his brother, he did what he pleased. And God did not interfere.

But that raises the question, though—if you're saying that if God were to control every aspect of man's life, it would not be living—that raises the question: Why pray to God, then? If God is not going to interfere, if God is not going to intervene, if God is not going to help, what is the role of prayer?

First of all, let us not misunderstand the nature of prayer, particularly in Jewish tradition. The primary purpose of prayer is not to make requests. The primary purpose is to praise, to sing, to chant. Because the essence of prayer is a song, and man cannot live without a song.

Prayer may not save us. But prayer may make us worthy of being saved. Prayer is not requesting. There is a partnership of God and man. God needs our help. I would define man as a divine need. God is in need of man.

In history, He cannot do the job alone, because He gave us freedom. And the whole hope of messianic redemption depends on God and on man. We must help Him. And by each deed we carry out, we either retard or accelerate the coming of redemption. Our role in history is tremendous. I mean, our human role.

Absurdity, yes, plays a major role. In fact, it's the greatest challenge to existence, not only to religion. The greatest challenge to all activities— to political activities, economic activities, to all ideas of progress are encountered with absurdity. And if I were to be asked what is the meaning of God—a difficult question to answer in one sentence.

Well, I'll ask you. What is the meaning of God?

I would have to use a number of sentences. One is the certainty that there is a meaning beyond mystery. That holiness conquers absurdity. And without holiness, we will sink in absurdity.

Where is holiness? Is it what's in the Bible? Is that where one finds holiness?

I don't believe in a monopoly. I think God loves all men. He has given many nations, He has given all men an awareness of His greatness and of His love. And God is to be found in many hearts all over the world. Not limited to one nation or to one people, to one religion.

But you have to understand, again, to come back to the problem of uniqueness. What has the Hebrew Bible given us in particular that is not to be found anywhere else? I would say the particular appreciation of the greatness of man, of man's tremendous potentiality as a partner of God. This idea, to me, is not to be found anywhere else.

But is that the potential of being fulfilled—we talked a moment ago about Martin Luther King. You've been active in the civil rights movement since, I guess, the early sixties; you marched at Selma with Dr. King. I think it's fair to say, though, that you've written about the "monstrosity of inequality." I think that's the expression you used. I think it's fair to say that in the past few years the American community has hardened its attitude toward equality in jobs, housing, schools, and so on. How is that carrying out a potential?

You know, do I have to tell you that life is a drama? Do I have to tell you that we are not in the midst of an automatic progressive development of humanity? There are ups and downs. At this very moment, there is a down. There's a depression. There is a renewal of prejudice, which is a poison. As a person committed to biblical faith, I would say what keeps humanity alive is the certainty that we have a Father. But then I also have to remember that God is either the father of all men or of no man.

And the idea of judging a person in terms of black or brown or white is an eye disease.

You've also said you're an optimist against your better judgment.

Yes.

But you're still an optimist.

I'm still an optimist.

You first gained prominence as a scholar writing about the prophets. Is it possible for a modern prophet to come to us? Or is that just pre-biblical?

Again, Mr. Stern, your questions are very rich, and very complex, and very meaningful, and since time is so limited and precious, I will have to give you short answers and only partial answers.

The idea of a prophet is complex and consists above all of two things. Of the message or the substance of what the prophet has to say from some extraordinary claim to an experience which is not given to other men. Let us ignore the second, let us take the first.

What's so great about the message of the prophet, about the prophet as a character? I would say the prophet is a man who is able to hold God and man in one thought, at one time, at all times. This is so great and this is so marvelous. Which means that whatever I do to man, I do to God. When I hurt a human being, I injure God.

Now, their thoughts—their message—continue to be so relevant today that I venture to say, and I've had this experience with many distinguished philosophers when we get together to discuss contemporary social problems, that the ultimate source of hope for all of us, whether it be Protestant or Catholic or secular philosopher, was suddenly our reliance on a hope uttered by the prophets of Israel. Therefore, I would say the spirit of the prophet, the message of the prophet, is very much alive. The kind of men who combine a very deep love, a very powerful dissent, a painful rebuke, with unwavering hope. The prophet as a witness to the great mystery— or to what I would call meaning beyond mystery—in that regard could still be alive and should serve as an example.

Are you talking about a rebirth of their knowledge in the mouths of others, or is that not to be?

No, I mean an identification. May I make a personal statement here. I've written a book on the prophets. A rather large book. I spent many years. And, really, this book changed my life. Because early in my life, my great love was for learning, studying. And the place where I preferred to live was my study and books and writing and thinking.

I've learned from the prophets that I have to be involved in the affairs of man, in the affairs of suffering man. And I would like to say that one of the saddest things about contemporary life in America is that the prophets are unknown. There's a complete decline of the Bible in American education. No one knows the prophets. There are countless intellectuals, who may be great authorities on literature, who have never read the prophets, really, have never been touched by them. And this, I'm sorry to say, is a little bit of a disaster. The great examples we need today are the ancient prophets of Israel.

I say that this book on the prophets which I wrote changed my life. And I think that anyone who reads the prophets will discover, number one, that the prophets really were the most disturbing people who ever lived. It's not easy to be a . . .

Oh, you mean they were abrasive, when you say "disturbing"?

Abrasive, disturbing, giving me a bad conscience.

Well, are you a prophet? You've been abrasive at times, particularly concerning the Vietnam War. You've said a great deal about that.

I won't accept this praise, because it's not for me to say that I am a descendant of the prophets, which is an old Jewish statement. It is a claim almost arrogant enough to say that I'm a descendant of the prophets, what is called *B'nai Nevi'im.* So let us hope and pray that I am worthy of being a descendant of the prophets.

You've said during the height of the agitation over the Vietnam War that it was the greatest religious issue. What made the Vietnam War a religious issue?

Of course it's a religious issue, for what does God demand of us primarily? Justice and compassion. What does He condemn above all? Murder, killing innocent people. How can I pray when I have on my conscience the awareness that I am co-responsible for the death of innocent people in Vietnam? In a free society, some are guilty, all are responsible.

At this time, one year ago, I was covering a trial of priests and nuns— the Berrigan trial in Harrisburg, Pennsylvania. Prospective jurors, one after another, when being questioned by the judge and lawyers, said they thought it was wrong for clergymen to be involved in politics, that their job is to administer to spiritual needs. Why don't you stick to spiritual needs?

That's a very good statement. In fact, it's such a good statement that if the prophets were alive, they would already be sent to jail by these jurors. Because the prophets mixed into social-political issues. And, frankly, I would say that God seems to be a non-religious person, because, if you read the words of God in the Bible, He always mixes in politics and in social issues.

My Lord, you, God, should worry about spirituality and not about politics and social injustice. Do you hear me? Pardon me.

This is precisely what I said before. The prophets are forgotten. No one reads the prophets. They have not touched the mind of America. And this is why such statements come out. What is the greatest concern in the Bible? Injustice to one's fellow men, bloodshed. What is the greatest dream of the prophets and of the Bible? Peace.

The only men in antiquity—no philosopher in Greece, no philosopher anywhere in the world, in India or in China, was capable of dreaming even that there would be a time when war would be abolished and there would be peace. This is the message of the prophets.

In one of your earlier writings you said: "No philosophy can be the same after Auschwitz and Hiroshima." Is that what you meant? What change did they make in your philosophy?

I think I indicated to you completely the unreliability of our cultural securities, of our cultural foundations. If Germany, which developed such a high culture, such marvelous music, so many beautiful cathedrals, so many scientists—if the German people were capable of doing what they did, how can I rely on humanity?

There is a drive for cruel deeds in all men, as there is a drive for goodness in all men. But you need more than a drive for goodness to overcome the drive for evil. You need some greater help. And that greater help, I believe, is a little fear and trembling and love of God.

Yet you are convinced of man's nobility. You write: "Man is concerned with ends, not only with needs." So you suggest that's what makes man superior to all other things?

Yes, I am. I must say that in the tradition of Judaism, I have a very high estimation of the nature of man. And frankly, I do it in defiance of many theories current in the academic life of America, in the contemporary literature of America, and in other countries. Yes, if I were to say what challenges me most in the Hebrew tradition, it is the high view Jewish tradition takes of the nature of man.

You say there is a uniquely Jewish view of man?

Yes. Let me first stress one point. The point is what is mentioned in the beginning of the Book of Genesis, that God created man in His own image. Frankly, if Moses had consulted me, I would have told him, "Don't say it." It's an impossible statement. First of all, it is absurd to say that man is created in the image of God. And second, it contradicts a major principle of the Ten Commandments. It says, "Thou shalt not make an image of God." So God made an image of God Himself, against His own law.

It is a scandalous statement. Upon thinking about it further, I realized that I have to understand its meaning. And this I believe is its meaning. You see, God is invisible, totally invisible. Any thought of Him is so inadequate, He's almost unthinkable. Any time, any moment I think, I know, I assume that my thought of God is adequate, then I know that I fail. He's so mysterious and so surpassing the power of the human mind that I always have to live in the paradox around Him, pray often. And realize that I am capable of being, of experiencing being thought of by Him rather than thinking of Him.

Now, God is invisible. But you can't live without God. So God created a reminder, an image. What is the meaning of man? To be a reminder of God. God is invisible. And since He couldn't be everywhere, He created man. You look at man and you are reminded of God.

But there are men who live without God.

Let me first conclude my essential idea. What is the mission of man, according to the Jewish view? To be a reminder of God. As God is compassionate, let man be compassionate. As God strives for meaning and justice, let man strive for meaning and justice.

If there are people who don't believe in God, I would say God's mercy is so great that He helps even those who don't believe in Him.

But, philosophically speaking, they have very little foundation. Because I say again to you what I indicated to you before in our conversation: the whole basis for moral behavior, for moral acts, is very precarious. Why should I sacrifice my interests in order to help another human being, at a high cost to myself?

There was an old idea in America that virtue pays. And the idea was very helpful to many people, until some of us discovered that crime pays even more. And it does. So why not commit a crime?

I say again, the situation is too serious, too precarious, to be left alone—for man to be left alone. I say that this world in itself is so fantastically mysterious, so challengingly marvelous, that not to realize that there is more than I see, that there's endlessly more than I can express or even conceive, is just being underdeveloped intellectually.

But that is the wonder of it, the torment that man has. The problem-solving machine that he is. That, you think, is, I detect, the essence of being—of living a human life.

Yes, you see, that is true. But one of the greatest sins of contemporary education is to give the impression that you can solve all problems, or that there are no problems. Actually, the greatness of man is that he faces problems. I would judge a person by how many deep problems he's concerned with.

But is not the quest of religion, though, to give one a sense of inner peace?

You have to understand the meaning of inner peace. Let me give you first an example of a person who has no problems. Let me give you a dramatic, fictitious picture. Here stands a man—and I'll tell you this is a man who has no problems. Do you know why? He's an idiot.

Because a man has problems. And the more complicated, the richer he is, the deeper are his problems. This is our distinction, to have problems, to face problems. Life is a challenge, not just a satisfaction. And the calamity of our time, to a Jew's life, is to experience pleasure only. I'm not against pleasure. But the greatness of life is the experience of facing a challenge rather than just having satisfaction.

I would be frightened if I were to be ruled by a person who is satisfied, someone who has the answers to everything.

In a very deep sense, religion is two things. First of all, it's an answer to the ultimate problems of human existence. And it also has another side. It is a challenge to all answers. It is living in this polarity of these two points.

But there are so many religions that say come to us and you will have no problems, we will solve your problems. Here's the word of God, He will solve your problems. You don't accept that.

I don't accept it, because it contradicts everything I have learned from life, from experience, from philosophy, from history, and from the Bible. If I look in the Bible, God is full of problems. He made and created man. He created man with his own will, with his own freedom. And man is a problem to Him. Look at the Bible. God is always wrestling with the problem of man. Even God has problems.

This is a deep ingredient of existence—problems. And the tragedy of our education today is that we are giving some easy solutions: Be complacent, have peace of mind, everything is fine. No! Wrestling is the issue; facing the challenge is the issue.

You've said other things about education. I'm going to pull out a quote of yours that I had written down some time ago. You said: "Our system of education stresses the importance of enabling the student to exploit the power aspect of reality. We fail to teach them how to revere." You were most concerned about the problem of reverence, the absence of reverence. What is so important about reverence?

You see, the nature of reverence is perception of a value which is precious. Whom do I revere? I revere a man who has succeeded in helping many poor people.

You're saying, "Who is worthy of being revered?"

Worthy of being revered. When I look at the statue of Moses of Michelangelo, I revere the name of Michelangelo because he lifts me up to a level which I myself couldn't reach.

One of these books—I couldn't reach into it quickly enough—contains your belief that one of the most important of the Ten Commandments is "Honor thy father and mother," because it contains this element of reverence. But wouldn't young people today tell you that perhaps their parents, some of them, are not worthy of revering?

First of all, this I believe is a central issue. About eleven years ago I gave a speech at the White House Conference on Children and Youth. And I suggested the problems are not children and youth, the problems are the parents.

I am a father, I have a daughter. I love her dearly. And I would like her to obey the commandments of the Torah. I would like her to revere me as her father. And I asked myself the question again and again, "What is there about me that would be worth her reverence?"

Unless I live a life that would deserve her reverence, I would make it impossible for her to live a life of Judaism. Consequently I go back to this problem that you are raising. If the children complain about the father, there are two aspects to it. Maybe they are right, and maybe they are wrong. Maybe they are right. If I grew up and hear my father speak in a way that could evoke my contempt and my distrust, I would have a tough time revering him. Fortunately, I had a very noble father.

Do you have a message for young people?

For young people I still have a message. I would say that in spite of the negative qualities they may discover in their fathers, they should remember one thing, and the most important thing—the most important thing is to ponder the mystery of their own existence.

The people who represent the mystery of my existence: father and mother. And the less I have reverence for the mystery of my existence, regardless of the special faults of my parents, I'm simply not human. Because to be human consists of a number of qualities or sensibilities. One of the central sensibilities is a sense of mystery of my own existence. Without it, I cease to be human. I may be a human being, but I'm not being human. And this is really, as you know, the topic of my book *Who Is Man?*

Now I would say it is the most indispensable commandment to live by: Honor or revere your father and mother.

Jewish young people . . .

Forgive me if I add just one other thing.

Yes.

Shouldn't a child realize how much his parents have done for him, for their children, in bringing them up? How much sacrifice, how many efforts, how many sleepless nights, how much love. Isn't it scandalous not to appreciate the sacrifice of parents? After all, it takes two things to sense what is evil in a person.

There's an old tradition in Judaism saying that if I see evil in another human being, it's an indication that there must be something of that evil in myself; and vice versa—if I see something good in a person, it is a sign there is something of that good in me.

So I would say it requires a little character training on the part of young people.

You write frequently of insight and compassion. I think that is the essence to your mind of a religious person, isn't it?

I would say so.

I started to ask you a question before. Young Jewish people are today encountering large numbers of Christian evangelist groups, some of them well organized, seeking to convert them. Do you have a view on proselytizing?

As you may know, I've been very much involved with the Ecumenical Council in Rome. I was the major Jewish consultant to Cardinal Bea.

That's why I had a hunch you have quite a view on proselytizing.

And I had conversations with the present Pope, Pope Paul. It's no secret anymore; it was a secret that one of the issues I fought for in the preparation of the schema about the Jews was to eliminate once and for all the idea of mission to the Jews.

One of the biggest scandals in the history of the Church was to try to make Christians out of Jews. Now, Christianity is a religion for which I have very great respect. I have great reverence for many Christians. But I also have to remind them that my being Jewish is so sacred to me that I am ready to die for it. And when a statement came out of the Ecumenical Council expressing the hope that the Jews would eventually join the Church, I came out with a very strong rebuke. I said, "I'd rather go to Auschwitz than give up my religion."

And I succeeded in persuading even the Pope, the head of the Church, you realize; he personally crossed out a paragraph in which there was a reference to conversion or mission to the Jews. The Pope himself. And the declaration published by the Ecumenical Council—if you study it carefully, you will notice the impact of my effort. There isn't the slightest reference to mission to the Jews.

This great, old, wise Church in Rome realizes that the existence of the Jews as Jews is so holy and so precious that the Church would collapse if the Jewish people ceased to exist. If there are some Protestant sects who still cling to this silly hope of proselytizing, I would say they are blind and deaf and dumb.

Would it be a better world if we were all of one religion?

No.

Would there be less strife?

No. As far as I can judge, and I try to judge God's will from history, it seems to be the will of God that there be more than one religion.

I think it's a very marvelous thing to realize. You know, if I were to ask the question whether the example I think you gave before—whether the Metropolitan Museum should try to introduce that all paintings should look alike, or I should like to suggest that all human faces should look alike—how would you respond to my proposal?

I would be against it.

I'm glad. We agree.

I think also, though, in your writings you've indicated that even where one religion has been adopted in the state, there's no evidence that that has brought any happiness or any new high points of religious feeling. Isn't that correct?

Yes, I think it is the will of God that there should be religious pluralism.

Your esteem for religious colleagues is greater than your esteem for politicians. I think you once said that the most depressing word in the English language is "politician." Politicians are necessary, aren't they? Why disparage them?

No, I'm not against politicians in their vocation. I'm against politicians in their tactics. Against the very meaning, the semantic meaning of the word "politician."

Now let me elaborate. It may take me two minutes to explain it to you. I consider the heart of the problem of human existence is to fight against mendacity, against lying. I would like to use a word which may be too often used, but it's still the most important word—and that is "honesty," or "sincerity," or "trust."

The tragedy of our time is, we don't trust each other. The Golden Rule today is not "Love thy neighbor as thyself" but "Suspect thy neighbor as thyself." We suspect all politicians because we know in advance they don't mean what they say and they don't say what they mean.

Is that justified? That suspicion?

Ask the people in the country. You're asking me? I'm only one citizen. I have only one vote.

If you go to the country and ask them, "What do you think of politicians?," they'll say a politician is a synonym for a person who is not necessarily truthful. Right? Do you mind my elegant way of speaking?

We have a type of politician today—I suppose we've always had, and I don't want to identify anyone—who tells us that he is doing what the people want. And, in fact, that may be so. Of course, that doesn't reach to the question of leadership. Should our leaders give us what we want, or is there some other role?

I think there is another role. By the way, I am against the word "politician." I have great respect for the word "statesman." It's very interesting, the word "statesman" is not used. "Politician" is used. "Statesman" is a great word.

Now, about doing what the people want—I'll tell you what the people want. One of the major inclinations in every human being is a desire to be deceived. Self-deception is a major disease.

To be told what one wants to hear?

Yes. You want to be deceived.

The task of a statesman is to be a leader, to be an educator, and not to cater to what people desire almost against their own interests. To be a leader.

The great question of today is mendacity. We live in a world full of lies. And the tragedy that our young people—or maybe it's good—the young people have discovered how many lies are uttered daily and every moment. They can't stand it. If there's anything they despise, it's someone who is phony, false rhetoric. We call it "credibility gap"—what we mean really is lying.

Some politicians have told us they're going to do something about solving the problem of the difficult finances that church-related or religiously oriented schools are in now. Would that be good? Is it wise for the government to help out those religiously oriented schools that are in difficulty?

This is a complex issue constitutionally.

I won't ask you to go to the constitutional question.

Yes, but I can give you an answer only from my point of view. The secular schools have failed. They have failed on a variety of levels. Let me give you an example. I don't want to pigeonhole the human soul, but quite obviously the human soul has several capacities. Let's say mind, will, emotion. It's true, the schools give plenty of information, food for the mind, but do nothing about training of emotions, do nothing about the training of the will.

For example, one of the most important things in life a human being faces is not only to know how to build a machine but also how to overcome envy. It's an irrational destructive power in every man. What does the school do about it? The secular school? Nothing. So I'm disappointed. The American educational system on all levels has proved to be a terrible disappointment.

Religious schools? That's a new problem. I only wish I could tell you the religious schools are doing a perfect job. I would say the religious schools deserve support because they are doing partly a good job. They at least teach people some of the great classical ideas of the religious tradition. And we cannot live without religious tradition. Because take away the religious tradition, what is left? You know what is left. Read contemporary literature. And give contemporary literature—the novels— as a source of inspiration for our young people. What will they get?

The Psalms no one reads. You're not allowed to read the Psalms in school. How can you be human without being able to pray? We need religious education.

The problem is whether religious education is in such a splendid state—it isn't, but that's a separate problem. I think that aid to religious schools in some form that would not contradict the constitutional regulations would in the long run prove a blessing. The original fear of supporting religious schools was because religion was a tremendous power at that time, a power we were afraid of. They would compete with the state, with the idea of equality. By now religions are so weak in America, there's little to be afraid of in religious power. Therefore, I would definitely say aid for religious schools in some form would be a great contribution.

You believe that organized religion is in a weakened condition?

I think so, but we have to put the blame not only on the religious people, on the religious establishments, but also on the people who belong to those establishments, on the members, on the plain people.

You see, actually the role of religion has declined as the result of countless assaults from all directions. So what is the outcome? In the past, a hundred years ago, two hundred years ago, a parent who had a gifted boy had a great dream—his son should be a rabbi, a minister, a priest. Today a man who has a gifted boy would like him to be a doctor of medicine, a banker, a lawyer. So the gifted boys are being kept away by many people. Blame the people.

But the religious leaders are also to blame. There is a decline in religious thinking, in religious passion, a detachment from the real problems.

Let me say to you the following: The central problem in the Bible is not God, but man. The Bible is a book about man, rather than man's book about God. And the great problem is how to answer, to respond to the human situation. And somehow religious leaders very often become petrified in their own traditions and understanding and can't relate to the burning issues of the day.

How is it responding today?

How is it responding today? Not too well. A great many religious leaders have given up faith altogether. They are deluding themselves. What I told you before—self-deception is a major passion in human life.

There are a great many people who read the word of God and don't believe in Him. Let me give you an example. One of the most popular definitions of God common in America today was developed by a great Protestant theologian: God is the ground of being. So everybody is ready to accept it. Why not? Ground of being causes me no harm. Let there be a ground of being, doesn't cause me any harm, and I'm ready to accept it. It's meaningless.

Isn't there a God who is above the ground? Maybe God is the source of qualms and of disturbing my conscience. Maybe God is a God of demands. Yes, this is God, not the ground of being. The result is, we have religious institutions without religious belief. We have a wave of non-belief.

I have suddenly discovered that William James was not right when he spoke about—he was right, by the way, I'm saying it rhetorically—there is a will to believe, but there is today a will to disbelieve. And that will is very powerful.

To this very day our young people are craving some deeper meaning. Our young people are craving a religious outlook. And what they get is stone and not bread.

What you've said, though, is that there's something more than relevance needed. That that's an overused expression. You use the term in your writings, "validity." Religion must have validity. What makes a religion valid?

If it is true, if it corresponds to real urgencies and questions and problems. Let me give you an example of what I mentioned to you before.

Our entire civilization today—we've all gone under one idea: interest or need. And we are taught the greatest thing alive is to satisfy one's needs and interests. Actually, our way of living revolved around one principle: self-interest. Self-interest. There is nothing else but self-interest.

This is a fallacy according to religion. And religion is right, valid. Because if everything is self-interest, then there is no love. Can you imagine humanity without love? If love is only self-interest, then love is a fake, a pretense.

You're telling me of the nature of man, not the nature of God, aren't you?

Yes. The nature of God is that man should have ends, not only needs. The difference between an animal and man is not in needs. An animal has needs. Man has needs, too. But man, in addition to needs, has to have ends, goals to strive for. The great task of religion is to teach man how to convert ends into needs. But what we do instead is to convert needs into ends. And needs are unreliable as a standard, because some needs are authentic, some needs are false.

Look at advertisements. Advertisement is trying to evoke in us needs which we are not in need of. Can you imagine, a day will come when I will feel all of a sudden that I can't live without color television. Television is not enough, it has to be a color television. I will give away the last penny I have because advertisement has convinced me that without color television I can't survive. Right? And a million other things. I have to have at least a summer home and a winter home, because without a winter home and a summer home, I'm not a respectable citizen. I read it in an advertisement, so it becomes a need.

Religion says no. Man's distinction is to live by ends and for ends and goals and not only satisfy needs. I am not against the satisfaction of needs. It's a necessary function of man. We have to satisfy our authentic needs. It's very important. We are against asceticism. We love life. But there are also ends and goals to be served. And this is the difference between animal and man.

But ask an average man, What are your goals in life? He'll tell you: Life insurance, a Cadillac, and a color television.

You wrote a book entitled Who is Man? *And you dealt with some of these questions. Is there anything else you want to add to your definition?*

Oh, out of pain and anguish I wrote that book. Because I consider man to be left without friends in the world. Wherever I look, books I read, it's full of contempt for the nature of man. *The Naked Ape*—man is all violent, man is essentially an animal. America spends hundreds of millions of dollars to study the behavior of animals in order to understand man. Because, essentially, man is an animal.

Now, I'm asking you, what bigger insult is it to man to say that man is essentially a beast, except that he has the ability to make tools or to speak?

My definition of an ape is: An ape is a human being without the ability to speak. Just as valid as to say that man is an animal with an ability to speak.

Now what I tried to do in this book is to counter, to fight the ongoing dehumanization of man, which I see in every step, everywhere. May I give you an example?

A few years ago—it was in 1965 in Los Angeles, California, the National Conference on Vietnam. I was one of the speakers against the war in Vietnam. Other speakers were in favor of Vietnam. Mr. Bundy, Under Secretary of State of the State Department, spoke. Of course, the major tone of the speakers who defended the war in Vietnam thought we had already won the war in Vietnam. Only who destroys our peace, our victory in Vietnam? The American reporters, because you know we have won the war in Vietnam.

You're saying this is what Mr. Bundy was saying?

Mr. Bundy and his friend, the professor of political science at the University of Berkeley.

But then there was a luncheon. The luncheon was served in the Ambassador Hotel, where the tragic assassination of Robert Kennedy took place. A beautiful luncheon; you had to pay fifteen dollars to eat that lunch. It was served on marvelous china, as befitting a time when we kill people in Vietnam. And the people had the privilege of addressing questions to the speakers.

So the speaker who defended the war in Vietnam suddenly was challenged by a question by a poor lady who stood up and said, "How can you defend the war in Vietnam if you realize that so many innocent people are being killed in the process?" So this great professor, chairman of the political science department at the University of California in Berkeley, stood up and said, "My lady, you don't seem to realize that the natural population increase in Vietnam is larger than the number of people killed."

What greater example of dehumanization do you need?

I see it every day. I see it every day. May I tell you a story that actually happened?

I know a father who was professionally busy when his wife gave birth to a baby. And the first chance he had to see his baby was when the mother and the baby came home. So finally he arrived, went over to the baby. The baby was in the crib. And he looked startled, amazed. His friend asked him, "Why do you look so startled?" His answer: "I cannot understand, how can they make such a crib for only $29.50."

Lots of people have compassion and are a great deal more human than the gentleman that you've just suggested and yet do not subscribe to organized religion and have no understanding or belief in God as an entity. What is missing from their lives? Why would that sadden you?

Oh, many things. Unless I feel that my life is accountable to Him, who's much greater than I am, I could not always control my mean leanings. I would not always be ready for self-sacrifice.

Number two, my life would be poor. The deepest passion in any real human person is a craving for meaning of existence. What kind of meaning of existence can I find in the fact that I can make a few dollars? That I have a little success? Here I am and tomorrow I'm gone. What's the meaning of everything? What's the meaning of our society? What's the meaning of our world?

God is the meaning beyond absurdity. Wherever I go, I encounter absurdity.

Consistent with the Jewish faith, you never write much—in fact, I don't recall you writing at all—about a life hereafter. Lots of religions are predicated on the idea of salvation rather than this earthly existence. You don't talk about that sort of thing. Why is that?

Actually, I did write an essay on this problem, which I read at the International Conference on Death, in Florence about three years ago. But frankly, I'll give you the real answer. We believe in an afterlife. But we have no information about it.

And therefore you can't write about it?

I could write about it in terms of belief.

Or expectation or hope?

I did. I did.

But you think that's less important than life on earth?

I think that's God's business—what to do with me after life. Here it's my business what to do with my life. So I leave it to Him. I am so busy trying to live a good life, and don't always succeed, that I have no time to worry about what God's going to do with me once I'm in the grave. Who knows what He expects of me in the grave?

And through all this, I find this uniqueness in your feelings of a collaborative effort between God and man.

Yes.

It's a sharing.

Yes.

It's a powerful concept. I'm not sure I know how we can help God.

You see, there is an old idea in Judaism found in the Bible, strongly developed by the rabbis, and very little known. And that is that God suffers when man suffers.

There's a very famous text that says: Even when a criminal is hanged on the gallows, God cries. He says, "Woe unto me." He is very unhappy when man is unhappy. There is this great sympathy of God on the part of man. God identifies Himself with the misery of man. I can help Him by reducing human suffering, human anguish, and human misery.

We have just about a minute or so left. I should have said at the start of this hour, before we began this hour, that Dr. Heschel indicated an interest in directing a message to young people. And I don't know that I ever in the past hour gave you the chance I promised that I would give you.

I would say to young people a number of things. And we only have one minute.

I would say, let them remember that there is a meaning beyond absurdity. Let them be sure that every little deed counts, that every word has power, and that we can, everyone, do our share to redeem the world in spite of all absurdities and all the frustrations and all disappointments. And above all, remember that the meaning of life is to build a life as if it were a work of art. You're not a machine. And you are young. Start working on this great work of art called your own existence.

One of the ways of doing it—two ways of doing it—is, one, remember the importance of self-discipline; second, study the great sources of wisdom. Don't read the bestsellers. And, third, remember that life is a celebration or can be a celebration. There's much entertainment in our life. And entertainment is destroying much of our initiative and weakens our imagination. What's really important is life as a celebration.

In a very deep sense I would say that the addiction, the drug addiction from which so many people suffer, is due to the fact that man cannot live such a shallow life, stale. He needs exultation. He needs moments of celebration. One of the most important things is to teach man how to celebrate.

You talked earlier of slanders. May I give you an example of something which is not a slander. Perhaps the most astute comment on your work was made by Professor Marty of the University of Chicago. He said, "Rabbi Heschel's work, unlike other philosophers', is directed not only at the mind but at the heart and the will." I couldn't have said it so perceptively. Thank you very much for being with us.

NOTES

Introduction

[1] *The Earth Is the Lord's* (London, New York, 1964), p. 21.

[2] Carl Stern interview; reprinted in this volume.

[3] Individual poems occasionally were published in journals; "Lied" appeared in the 1926–27 issue of *Warsaw Writings*, published by the Union of Yiddish Writers and Journals in Warsaw. Another appeared, translated into German by Leo Hirsch, "Ich und Du," in *Der Morgen* (Berlin), XI Jahrgang 1935–36 (June 1935), p. 127.

[4] Universitätsarchiv, Humboldt Universität, Berlin.

[5] See Henryk Halkowski, "A Brand Plucked from the Fire: Polish Traces of Abraham Joshua Heschel," unpublished manuscript. Halkowski cites the archives containing the correspondence of the Polish Academy of Science and Letters in Cracow for arrangements concerning publication of *Die Prophetie*.

[6] Halkowski writes, "Since the author was a Jew and a Polish citizen, the German office (Reichsschrifttumskammer) demanded that he should present a note from the Polish General Consulate in Berlin stating that 'the sale of this work was desirable and would contribute to the [betterment] of relations between Polish and German science.'"

[7] Otto Eissfeldt, *Theologische Studien und Kritiken* (1936), p. 214.

[8] Sven Nilson, *The Philosophical Review*, Vol. 46, September 1937, p. 556.

[9] "No Religion Is an Island."

[10] Letter from Clarence Pickett, American Friends Service Committee, dated June 12, 1939, to American consul in Warsaw.

[11] *Maimonides*, trans. Joachim Neugroschel, p. 131.

[12] Did Maimonides Strive for Prophetic Inspiration?" *Louis Ginzberg Jubilee Volume* (New York, 1945), pp. 159–88.

[13] His book on Abravanel was published in Polish translation in Lwow in 1938.

[14] Abraham Heschel, *Don Jizchak Abravanel* (Berlin, 1937), p. 30.

[15] Rachel Wischnitzer, *Jüdisches Gemeindeblatt* (Hamburg), No. 7, July 16, 1937.

[16] "Marranos von Heute," *Gemeindeblatt der jüdischen Gemeinde zu Berlin*, September 16, 1936.

[17] Letter dated September 24, 1938. Feuchtwanger was editor of the *Bayerische Israelitische Gemeindezeitung*.

[18] "Religion and Race," in *The Insecurity of Freedom* (New York, 1966), p. 86.

[19] Letter from the Oberster Rat der Jüdischen Kultusgemeinden-Verbände in Boehmen, Mähren, und Schlesien, dated February 16, 1938.

[20] Gustav Fleischmann, "The Religious Congregation, 1918–1938," in *The Jews of Czechoslovakia*, Vol. 1 (Philadelphia, 1968), pp. 313, 316–18; Hugo Stransky, "The Religious Life in the Historic Lands," in ibid., pp. 345–47.

[21] See Michael Meyer, "The Refugee Scholars Project of the Hebrew Union College," in Bertram Wallace Korn, ed., *A Bicentennial Festschrift for Jacob Rader Marcus* (New York, 1976), pp. 359–75.

[22] *Israel: An Echo of Eternity* (New York, 1969), p. 113.

[23] Angela Grayboys, *Ratio and Pathos: Abraham Joshua Heschel and Some of His Critics.* Hebrew Union College Rabbinic Thesis, 1989, p. 143.

[24] The essays on Hasidism have been translated into English and published as *The Circle of the Baal Shem Tov*, edited by Samuel H. Dresner (University of Chicago Press, 1985). Although Heschel received the Guggenheim, the biography on the Baal Shem Tov was never completed.

[25] *The Earth Is the Lord's*, p. 98.

[26] "Toward an Understanding of Halacha," p. 133.

[27] *Man Is Not Alone*, p. 170.

[28] "An Analysis of Piety," p. 310.

[29] Ibid., p. 312.

[30] Ibid., p. 317.

[31] Ibid.

[32] "The Holy Dimension," p. 320.

[33] Ibid., p. 322.

[34] "Prayer," p. 341.

[35] The name was changed some years after my father's death to Clergy and Laity Concerned

[36] "The Holy Dimension," p. 321.

[37] "Prayer," p. 353.

[38] *The Sabbath*, pp. 48, 6.

[39] Reinhold Niebuhr, "Masterly Analysis of Faith," *New York Herald Tribune Book Review*, April 1, 1951.

[40] Ibid.

Existence and Celebration

[1] Harry L. Lurie, *A Heritage Affirmed* (Philadelphia, 1961), p. 9.

[2] *The Sayings of the Fathers* I, 2.

Israel as Memory

[1] *Berachoth* 3b; *Midrash Tehillim* 22.8; see Yerushalmi, *Berachoth* 3d.

[2] See S. Schechter, *Studies in Judaism* (Philadelphia, 1908), second series, pp. 205 ff.

Symbolism and Jewish Faith

[1] Jacob Burckhardt, *Force and Freedom* (New York, 1943), pp. 191, 318.

[2] Hugo Winckler, *The Tell-el-Amarna Letters* (Berlin, 1896), pp. 48 ff. J. A. Knudtzon, *Die El-Amarna-Tafeln*, (Leipzig, Vorderasiatische Bibliothek 1915), pp. 178 ff. (no. 23), 1050 ff.

[3] *Cf.*, for example, Deuteronomy 27:15; Leviticus 4:15.

[4] Deuteronomy 4:16; Ezekiel 8:3, 5; 2 Chronicles 33:7, 15. However, by means of a metathesis, Ibn Ezra finds the word *selem* in *sulam* (ladder); *cf.* his interpretation of Jacob's ladder in his *Commentary* on Genesis 28:11.

[5] See A. T. Glassberg, *Zikron Berith la-Rishonim* (Berlin, 1892), pp. 176 ff., 231 ff.

[6] Thomas Carlyle, *Sartor Resartus* (New York, 1937), Book III, Chapter 7, pp. 253–54.

[7] Ibid., Book I, Chapter 11, p. 72.

[8] H. F. Dunbar, *Symbolism in Medieval Thought and Its Consummation in the Divine Comedy*, Yale University Press, New Haven, 1929, pp. 15 f.

[9] See my *The Sabbath, Its Meaning to Modern Man* (New York, 1951), pp. 4 ff.; "Space, Time, and Reality," *"Judaism,"* I, 3, July 1952, pp. 268 ff.

[10] William Edward Addis and T. Arnold, "Latria," *Catholic Dictionary*, Catholic Publication Society Company (London, 1884), p. 505.

[11] Charles R. Morey, *Medieval Art* (New York, 1942), pp. 104 ff.

[12] Rabbi Yeheskel Landau, *Noda be-Yehudah*, Second Series, *Orah Hayim*, responsum 19.

[13] *Rosh Hashanah* 24a; *Avodah Zarah* 43a.

[14] *Mekilta* to Exodus 20:16.

[15] *Tselem elohim* in Genesis 1:27 is translated in the Septuagint *kat' eikona theou*.

[16] *Leviticus Rabba* 34, 3; see also *Midrash Tehillim*, 103. Significant are the statements in *Jer. Berachoth* III, 8a, and *Moed Katan* 83a.

[17] *Genesis Rabba* 24, 8.

[18] *Genesis Rabba* 8, 12.

[19] *Avodah Zarah* 43b.

[20] *Deuteronomy Rabba* 1, 10.

[21] See *Deuteronomy Rabba* 5, 9.

[22] *Moed Kattan* 15b.

[23] *Deuteronomy Rabba* 1, 10.

[24] See H. Vaihinger, *The Philosophy of "As if"* (London, 1935), pp. 29 ff.

[25] *Kiddushin* 31a; *Baba Kamma* 38a, 87a.

[26] Job 13:15.

[27] *Yebamoth* 13b; *Niddah* 16a; *Taanith* 26b.

[28] *Leviticus Rabba* 30.

[29] See my *Man Is Not Alone* (Philadelphia, 1951), pp. 3 ff.

[30] Everett W. Hall, *What Is Value? An Essay in Philosophical Analysis* (New York, 1952), pp. 247–48.

[31] Thomas Carlyle, *On Heroes, Hero-Worship, and the Heroic in History* (New York, 1841).

The Spirit of Jewish Prayer

[1] Ovid, *Tristia*, III, 8.11.

[2] J. Royce, *The Problem of Christianity* (1913, 1), pp. 172, 408 ff.

[3] E. S. Ames, *Religion* (New York, 1929), p. 132.

[4] E. W. Lyman, *The Meaning of Truth in Religion*, p. 33.

[5] Midrash Tehillim 5:6.

[6] A discussion of this view, which is so popular today, is found in I. Segond, *La prière, étude de psychologie religieuse*, Paris, 1911, p. 52.

[7] Cf. A. J. Heschel, "Prayer" in *Review of Religion*, 1945, p. 156.

[8] Midrash Tehillim 5:7; Exodus Rabbah 21:5.

[9] Yerushalmi Berachot 4:4.

[10] *Man Is Not Alone*, p. 88.

[11] Ibid., Chapter 8.

[12] E. S. Ames, *Religion*, p. 217.

[13] *Man Is Not Alone*, Chapter 23.

[14] Mishneh Torah, Laws of Prayer, Chapter 4:6.

[15] Isaiah 29:13.

[16] Berachot 32a.

[17] Bahya, Commentary to the Torah, Parshat Ekev.

[18] Berachot 6b.

[19] Maharal, *Netivot Olam*, "HaAvodah," Chapter 2.

Toward an Understanding of Halacha

[1] Sukkah 52b.

[2] Morton M. Berman, "The Survey of Current Reform Practice by Laymen," delivered at the forty-second general assembly of the Union of American Hebrew Congregations, April 22, 1953.

Jewish Theology

[1] *Isaiah* 43:12.

[2] *Sifre Deuteronomy* 33:5.

The Mystical Element in Judaism

[1] *Zohar* (to which all unspecified references in the following notes relate. The translation used is that mentioned in the Bibliography) II, 23a.

[2] I 241a.

[3] II 15b.

[4] II 20a.

[5] I 156b.

[6] II 2a.

[7] II 15b.

[8] III 128a.

[9] Cf. *Midrash Rabbah* (London, 1939), Gen. XVII; Mid. Hag. Gn. 2, 7.

[10] *Pesik*, ed. Buber, XXVI, 166b.

[11] III 65b.

[12] Gen. R., *op. cit.*, LXIX. 3; Cf. Louis Ginzberg, *Kabbalah*, JE, v. 3.

[13] Gen. R., *op. cit.*, XLVII. 6; LXXXII, 6.

[14] II 75a.

[15] II 76a.

[16] II 23b.

[17] II 12a.

[18] II 144a.

[19] I 164a.

[20] III 92a–92b.

[21] III 64b.

[22] II 143a.

[23] III 64a.

[24] II 220b.

[25] III 109b.

[26] II 42b.

[27] I 21a.

[28] III 288a.

[29] II 146b.

[30] *Tikkune Zohar*, 1.

[31] II 23a; cf. I, 27a; II 158a.

[32] On the concept of *Shekinah* in rabbinic literature, cf. J. Abelson, *The Immanence of God in Rabbinical Literature* (London, 1912).

[33] II 21a–21b.

[34] II 26b.

[35] I 22b.

[36] I 76a.

[37] I 230a.

[38] II 120b.

[39] I 61a.

[40] II 118b.

[41] II 9b.

[42] III 77b.

[43] II 161b.

[44] I 23b.

[45] II 216a–b.

[46] II 213b.

[47] III 67a.

[48] III 61a.

[49] III 78b.

[50] II 144b.

[51] II 154a.

[52] II 136b.

[53] I 125b; cf. I 99b.

[54] *Sefer Hassidin*, ed. Wistinetzki (Frankfurt, 1924). Cf. *Zohar* I 105b.

[55] III 58a; III 23a.

[56] II 99a.

[57] III 73a.

[58] Cf. Robert Gordis, "The Bible as a Cultural Monument," see also Louis Finkelstein, "The Jewish Religion: Its Beliefs and Practices," Chapter 42.

[59] III 53b.

[60] I 134b–135a.

[61] III 75b.

[62] II 95a.

[63] III 52a.

[64] III 152a.

[65] III 55b–56a.

[66] II 100b.

[67] III 59a.

[68] II 218b.

[69] I 70b.

[70] II 145b.

[71] III 55a.

[72] III 40b.

[73] II 55b.

[74] II 57a.

[75] III 63a.

[76] Cf. Abraham Heschel, *Die Prophetie* (Cracow, 1936), pp. 56–87, 127–80.

[77] For the influence of kabbalah on the philosophic thought of the Renaissance, see Alexander Altmann, *Judaism and World Philosophy*, pp. 980–81.

BIBLIOGRAPHY

Only an inkling of the vast literature of Jewish mysticism can be offered here. It was considered proper to dwell primarily upon one phase of the kabbalah, the history of which abounds in thoughts and events. The *Zohar*, the authoritative book of the movement, was chosen as the basis of our chapter.

GINZBERG, LOUIS, "Kabbalah," in *The Jewish Encyclopedia*, III, 456–79. New York and London, 1902.

SCHOLEM, GERHARD G., *Major Trends in Jewish Mysticism*. Jerusalem, 1941.

WAITE, ARTHUR E., *The Holy Kabbalah*. London, 1929.

The Zohar. Translated by Harry Sperling and Maurice Simon. 4 vols. London, 1931–1934.

A Preface to an Understanding of Revelation

[1] *Man Is Not Alone*, Vol. 1, pp. 68 ff.

[2] *Genesis Rabba*, ch. 39.

God, Torah, and Israel

[1] See Abraham J. Heschel, *Torah Min Ha-Shamayim b'Espaklaria shel Ha-Dorot* (*Theology of Ancient Judaism*, Vol. II) (London and New York, 1965), pp. 3 ff.

[2] About another term for revelation, "Torah from Sinai," see Heschel, *op. cit.*, Vol. II, pp. 1 ff.

[3] See a discussion of this problem in Heschel, *op. cit.*, Vol. II, pp. 8 ff.

[4] This story is mentioned in an essay by Deissman which regretfully I cannot locate now.

[5] *Yerushalmi*, Peah 1:1 (15d).

[6] *Genesis Rabba* 1:2.

[7] *Tankuma*, Tavo 3.

[8] *Genesis Rabba* 10:1.

[9] *Avodah Zarah* 3b; *Sanhedrin* 99b.

[10] *Exodus Rabba* 33:6; see also *Tanhuma, Tarumah* 3.

[11] *Exodus Rabba* 33:1; see *Leviticus Rabba* 30:13.

[12] *Tanhuma*, Pekuday 4.

[13] *Pesiktha de Rab Kahana* 1:4; see Abraham J. Heschel, *op. cit.*, Vol. I, pp. 66 ff.

[14] *Aboth*, ch. 5, end.

[15] *Shabbath* 31a.

[16] *Response of the Marharit* (Joseph of Trani), Part I, 100.

[17] *Berakoth* 8a.

[18] *Shabbath* 31b.

[19] *Berakoth* 33b.

[20] *Yalkut Shimoni, V'ethanan*, 837.

[21] *Yebamoth*, p. 79a.

[22] *Leviticus Rabba* 22:6; *Midrash Tehillim* 27:2.

[23] *Peah* 1:1.

[24] Rashi to *Taanith* 7a.

[25] *Taanith* 7a; *Sifre Deuteronomy*, Piska 306.

[26] *Aboth* 1:17.

[27] *Aboth* 2:12.

[28] *Menachoth* 110a.

[29] *Betzah* 16a.

[30] *Berakoth* 17a.

[31] *Pesachim* 50b; *Yerushalmi*, Hagiga 1:7 (76c).

[32] *Shnei Luhoth HaBrit*, p. 371b; see also Yehiel Halperin's *Arche He Kinuyim*, "Avodah Zarah," "All worship not performed for the sake of heaven is to be termed idolatry."

[33] *Yerushalmi*, Berakoth 9:5.

[34] *Kiddushin* 57a.

[35] *Yebamoth* 6a–b; *Sifre*, Kedoshim 90d.

[36] Rabbi ben David, *Commentary on Sifre*, ibid.

[37] Rashi to *Berakoth* 54a.

[38] *Berakoth* 2:2.

[39] *Avodah Zarah* 17b.

[40] *Yebamoth* 109b.

[41] *Yebamoth* 49b, Rashi *ad locum*.

[42] Rabbi Moses Cordevero, *Shiur Koma*, ch. 121, Rabbi Moses Alshech, *Torath Moshe*, "Shmini," 9b.

[43] *Rosh Ha Shanah* 21b.

[44] *Genesis Rabba* 17:5.

[45] *Pesiktha de Rab Kahana*, ch. 38 (ed. S. Buber), p. 158b; see Solomon Schecter, *Aspects of Rabbinic Theology* (New York, 1909), for a note on textual recensions and variants of this source, pp. 293 ff., 294, n. 1.

[46] *Leviticus Rabba* 32:8; see *Ecclesiastes Rabba* 4:1, and *Zohar*, Mishpatim, p. 113b.

[47] Commentary on the Torah, "Kedoshim," beginning.

[48] *Tanhuma*, "Tisah" 21.

[49] *Sanhedrin* 99b.

[50] *Berakoth* 17a.

[51] *Aboth* 6:10.

[52] *Kiddushin* 32a.

[53] Rabbi Menachem Recanati, *Taamei Ha-Mitzvoth*, "Introduction." See Gershom G. Scholem, *On the Kabbalah and Its Symbolism* (New York, 1955), p. 44.

[54] *Zohar*, Beshalach 60a.

[55] *Zohar*, Yithro 90b.

[56] *Tikunai Zohar* 421, 60b.

[57] *Zohar*, Emor 93b.

[58] *Zohar*, Va Yikra 21a.

[59] Rabbi Moses Hayyim Luzzatto, *Adir Ba-Marom*, p. 61; Rabbi Hayyim of Velozhin, *Nefesh Ha Hayyim*, pp. 4, 11.

[60] *Yerushalmi*, Hagigah 1:7 (76c); *Ekah Rabbathi*, Pesiktha 2; see also Rav in Nedarim 81a and Rabbi Jonah Gerondi quoted in the "Ran" *ad locum*.

[61] *Pesachim* 50b; see *Taanith* 7a.

[62] *Yoma* 72b, Rashi *ad locum*.

[63] *Shabbath* 31a.

[64] *Pesiktha Rabbathi*, ch. 34 (ed. Buber), 139a.

[65] Rabbi Solomon Alami; *Iggereth Ha Musar*, ed. by A. M. Habermann, pp. 40 ff.

[66] *Tifereth Yisrael*, Introduction.

[67] *Mei Ha Shiloack*, Va Yeshev.

[68] *Genesis Rabbathi*, p. 144; *Seder Elijah Rabbah*, ch. 15, p. 71; see Rabbi Samuel bar Rabbi Isaac at *Genesis Rabba* 1:4; also *Sifre Deuteronomy*, Re'eh 69, 74, 138, 141—"The last is most precious," compare *Mekilta of Rabbi Simeon Bar Yohai*, p. 31, and *Genesis Rabba* 78:8.

[69] *Tanhuma* (ed. Buber), Noah 19.

[70] *Menachoth* 53b. Maimonides, who lived in an age of severe persecutions of the Jewish people, went beyond these utterances in saying: "As it is impossible for God to cease to exist, so it is impossible for Israel to be destroyed and to disappear from the world." *Iggereth Teman*, ed. by A. Halkin (New York, 1952), p. 25. See Karl Barth, *Church Dogmatics*, Vol. III, Part 3, ed. by G. W. Bromiley and T. P. Torrance (Edinburgh, 1958), p. 218: "The Jews can be despised and hated and oppressed and persecuted and even assimilated, but they cannot really be touched; they cannot be exterminated; they cannot be destroyed. They are the only people that necessarily continue to exist, with the same certainty as that God is God."

[71] *Ecclesiastes Rabba* 1:4,9; compare *Sifre Deuteronomy*, "Ekev," Piska 47.

[72] *Mekilta*, Ki Tissa; compare Mark 2:27.

[73] *Yalkut Shimoni*, Esther 1056.

[74] *The Book of Beliefs and Opinions*, Treatise III, ch. 7, tr. by Samuel Rosenblatt (New Haven, 1948), p. 158.

[75] *Kuzari*, II, 56; see *Seder Elijah Rabba*, p. 112. Compare John 4:22: "Salvation is from the Jews." See Raymond E. Brown (ed.), The Anchor Bible, *The Gospel According to John, ad locum*. In the Gospels, Israel carries the special sense that the people thus named is the people of God.

[76] *Sifre Deuteronomy* 346.

[77] *Seder Elijah Rabba*, ch. 21.

[78] *Midrash Tehillim*, ch. 83:2.

[79] *Midrash Tehillim* (ed. Buber), pp. 240 ff.

[80] *Numbers Rabba* 13:6; compare *Genesis Rabba* 3:9.

[81] *Genesis Rabba* ch. 30; unlike *Theodor*, p. 277.

[82] *Pesiktha de Rab Kahana* (ed. Buber), XXVI, p. 166b; compare the two versions.

[83] *Genesis Rabba* 69:3.

[84] *Genesis Rabba* 47:6; 82:6.

No Religion Is an Island

[1] Reinhold Niebuhr, *Pious and Secular America* (New York, 1958), p. 108.

[2] Paul Tillich, *Christianity and the Encounter of the World Religions* (New York, 1963), p. 95.

[3] *Ecumenical Review*, XVI, No. 1, October 1963, p. 108.

The God of Israel and Christian Renewal

[1] Leslie Dewart, *The Future of Belief* (New York, 1966), p. 183.

[2] See *Dialogue on the Way*, edited by George A. Lindbeck (Minneapolis, 1965), pp. 137, 222.

[3] "We do without God and hold to Jesus Christ." Thomas Altizer and William Hamilton, *Radical Theology and the Death of God* (New York, 1966), p. 33.

[4] Emil Brunner, *The Divine Imperative* (Philadelphia, 1947), p. 586.

[5] Maxim Gorki, *A Night's Lodging* (or *Submerged*), Act III.

[6] *Mechilta*, to Exodus 16, 32.

[7] *Sanhedrin* 99a.

[8] F. J. Foakes Jackson and Kirsopp Lake, *The Beginnings of Christianity*, Part I, *The Acts of the Apostles*, Vol. IV, p. 8.

[9] G. T. Stokes, *The Acts of the Apostles* (New York, 1903), p. 29.

[10] R. B. Rackham, *The Acts of the Apostles* (London, 1901), p. 7; A. W. F. Blunt, *The Acts of the Apostles* (Oxford, 1922), p. 132.

[11] F. F. Bruce, *Commentary on the Book of the Acts* (Grand Rapids, MI, 1954), p. 38.

[12] William F. Howard, *St. Luke* (*The Interpreters Bible*), p. 308; E. Earle Ellis, *The Gospel of Luke* (London, 1966), p. 245. Alfred Plummer, *Commentary on . . . St. Luke*, The International Critical Commentary (New York, 1896), p. 483, lists six possible meanings.

The Holy Dimension

[1] Cf. the author's "Analysis of Piety," *Review of Religion*, VI, 1942, pp. 293–307.

Faith

[1] See the author's *The Holy Dimension, The Journal of Religion*, XXIII, 1943, pp. 117, 124.

The Biblical View of Reality

[1] A. J. Heschel, *Man Is Not Alone* (New York, 1951), p. 55.

[2] Compare the references in Brown-Driver-Briggs, *A Hebrew and English Lexicon of the Old Testament* (Oxford, 1906), p. 761.

[3] *Collected Papers of Charles S. Peirce*, edited by Charles Hartshorn and Paul Weiss (Cambridge, 1934), V, 45.

[4] *Theaetetus*, 155d.

[5] *Metaphysics*, Is, 182b12.

[6] *Mechanics*, 847a11.

[7] *The Works of Francis Thompson*, III, pp. 80–81.

[8] William Blake, *A Vision of the Last Judgment*.

[9] Heschel, pp. 11 ff.
[10] *Ibid.*, p. 76.
[11] *Nabhal.* See Brown-Driver-Briggs, p. 614.
[12] Heschel, p. 68.

Death as Homecoming

[1] Herman Feifel, *The Meaning of Death* (New York, 1959), p. 127.

SOURCES

I. Existence and Celebration

"To Be a Jew: What Is It?," *Zionist Quarterly*, vol. 1, no. 1 (Summer, 1951), pp. 78–84.

"The Moment at Sinai," *American Zionist*, vol. 43, no. 7 (February 5, 1953), pp. 18–20.

"Existence and Celebration," lecture delivered in Montreal to Jewish Federation (New York: Council of Jewish Federations and Welfare Funds, 1965).

"Hasidism as a New Approach to Torah," *Jewish Heritage*, vol. 14, no. 3 (Fall–Winter, 1972), pp. 4–21.

"Israel as Memory" (excerpted from *Israel: An Echo of Eternity*), *Jewish Heritage*, vol. 14, no. 4 (Spring, 1973), pp. 41–45.

"We Cannot Force People to Believe," *Who Is a Jew: A Reader*, ed. Solomon S. Bernards (New York: Anti-Defamation League of B'nai B'rith, 1959), pp. 38–39.

"A Time for Renewal," address delivered at the 28th World Zionist Congress in Jerusalem on January 19, 1972, in *Midstream*, vol. 18, no. 5 (May 1972), pp. 46–51.

"*Pikuach Neshama*: To Save Our Soul," translated from Hebrew (New York: Baronial Press, 1949).

"The Meaning of Repentance," *Gemeindeblatt der jüdischen Gemeinde zu Berlin* (September 16, 1936), p. 2.

"On the Day of Hate," translated from the Yiddish "In tog fun has," printed under the pseudonym "Itzig" in *Haynt*, Warsaw, May 10, 1933. (Reprinted in 25 *Yor Yung Vilne* [1929–54], ed. Leizer Ran [New York: Nusakh Vilne, 1955], pp. 43–44).

II. No Time for Neutrality

"No Time for Neutrality" is an unpublished manuscript.

"Symbolism and Jewish Faith," *Religious Symbolism* (Religion and Civilization Series), ed. by F. Ernest Johnson (New York: The Institute for Religious and Social Studies: Harper & Brothers, 1954), pp. 53–79.

"The Spirit of Jewish Prayer," *Proceedings of the Rabbinical Assembly of America*, vol. 17 (1953), pp. 151–215.

"Toward an Understanding of Halacha," *Yearbook of the Central Conference of American Rabbis*, vol. 63 (1953), pp. 386–409.

"Yom Kippur" ["Remarks on Yom Kippur"] *Mas'at Rav* (A Professional Supplement to *Conservative Judaism*), August 1965, pp. 13–14.

"Teaching Religion to American Jews," *Adult Jewish Education* (Fall, 1956), pp. 3–6.

"Jewish Theology," *The Synagogue School*, vol. 28, no. 1 (Fall, 1969), pp. 4–18.

"The Mystical Element in Judaism," *The Jews: Their History, Culture, and Religion*, ed. by Louis Finkelstein (New York: Harper & Brothers, and Philadelphia: The Jewish Publication Society of America, 1949), pp. 602–23 (in vol. 2 of the 2-volume edition and in vol. 2 of the 4-volume paperback edition).

"A Preface to an Understanding of Revelation," *Essays Presented to Leo Baeck on the Occasion of His Eightieth Birthday* (London: East and West Library, 1954), pp. 28–35.

"God, Torah, and Israel," translated from the Hebrew *Torah min ha-Shamayim*, vol. 3, by Byron Sherwin, in *Theology and Church in Times of Change: Essays in Honor of John Coleman Bennett*, ed. by Westminster Press, 1970), pp. 71–90.

III. Toward a Just Society

"The Meaning of This War (World War II)," *Liberal Judaism*, vol. 11, no. 10 (February 1944), pp. 18–21.

"The Plight of Russian Jews," *United Synagogue Review* (Winter, 1964), pp. 14–15, 26–27.

"The Moral Dilemma of the Space Age," *Space: Its Impact on Man and Society*, ed. by Lilian Levy (New York: Norton, 1964), pp. 176–79.

"Required: A Moral Ombudsman," *United Synagogue Review*, vol. 24, no. 3 (Fall, 1971), pp. 4, 5, 28.

"The Reasons for My Involvement in the Peace Movement," *Journal of Social Philosophy*, vol. 4 (January 1973), pp. 7–8.

"In Search of Exaltation," *Jewish Heritage*, vol. 13, no. 3 (Fall, 1971), pp. 29, 30, 35.

"A Prayer for Peace," *Jewish Heritage*, vol. 13, no. 2 (Spring–Summer, 1971), pp. 7–11.

IV. No Religion Is an Island

"No Religion Is an Island" (Inaugural lecture as Harry Emerson Fosdick Visiting Professor at Union Theological Seminary, New York), *Union Seminary Quarterly Review*, vol. 21, no. 2, part 1 (January 1966), pp. 117–34.

"Choose Life!," *Jubilee*, vol. 13, no. 9 (January 1966), pp. 37–39.

"On Prayer," *Conservative Judaism*, vol. 25, no. 1 (Fall, 1970), pp. 1–12.

"The God of Israel and Christian Renewal," *Renewal of Religious Thought: Proceedings of the Congress on the Theology of the Church Centenary of Canada, 1867–1967*, ed. L. K. Shook, C.S.B. (Montreal: Palm Publishers, 1968), pp. 105–29.

"What Ecumenism Is," *Face to Face: A Primer in Dialogue*, ed. by Lily Edelman (Washington: B'nai B'rith Adult Jewish Education), reprinted in *Jewish Heritage*, vol. 9, no. 4 (Spring, 1967), pp. 1–4.

"What We Might Do Together," *Religious Education* (March–April 1967), pp. 133–40.

"Reinhold Niebuhr: A Last Farewell," *Conservative Judaism*, vol. 25, no. 4 (Summer, 1971), pp. 62–63.

V. The Holy Dimension

"An Analysis of Piety," *The Review of Religion*, vol. 6, no. 3 (March 1942), pp. 293–307.

"The Holy Dimension," *The Journal of Religion*, vol. 23, no. 2 (April 1943), pp. 117–24.

"Faith," *The Reconstructionist*, vol. 10, no. 13 (November 3, 1944), pp. 10–14; no. 14 (November 17, 1944), pp. 12–16.

"Prayer," *Review of Religion*, vol. 9, no. 2 (January 1945), pp. 153–68.

"The Biblical View of Reality," *Contemporary Problems in Religion*, ed. Harold A. Basilius (Detroit: Wayne University Press, 1956), pp. 57–76.

"Death as Homecoming," *Genesis of Sudden Death and Reanimation, Clinical and Moral Problems Connected* (*Genesi della Morte Improvvisa e Rianimazione*), Florence, Palazzo Pitti,

January 10–14, 1969, Proceedings of the 1st International Congress, ed. Vincenzo Lapiccirella (Firenze: Marchi & Bertolli, 1970), pp. 533–42 [English text], pp. 523–33 [Italian translation].

Appendices

Interview at Notre Dame, from *Theologians at Work*, ed. Patrick Granfield (New York: Macmillan, 1967).

Carl Stern's Interview with Dr. Heschel. Originally broadcast on NBC–TV on Sunday, February 4, 1973, under the auspices of *The Eternal Light* (produced by the Jewish Theological Seminary of America).

ACKNOWLEDGMENTS

The editor gratefully acknowledges permission to reprint the following:

"The Moment at Sinai," *American Zionist* (February 5, 1953), pp. 18–20. By permission of *American Zionist*.

"We Cannot Force People to Believe," *Who Is a Jew?: A Reader*, ed. Solomon S. Bernards (New York: Anti-Defamation League of B'nai B'rith, 1959), pp. 38–39. By permission of the Anti-Defamation League of B'nai B'rith.

"A Time for Renewal," *Midstream* (May 1972), pp. 46–51. By permission of *Midstream*.

"On the Day of Hate," English translation by Leonard Wolf. By permission of Leonard Wolf.

"Symbolism and Jewish Faith," *Religious Symbolism*, ed. F. Ernest Johnson (New York: The Institute for Religious and Social Studies, 1955), pp. 53–79. By permission of the Louis Finkelstein Institute.

"The Spirit of Jewish Prayer," *Proceedings of the Rabbinical Assembly of America*, ed. Rabbi Max Weine, vol. 17 (1953), pp. 151–215. Copyright 1953 by the Rabbinical Assembly. By permission of the Rabbinical Assembly.

"Toward an Understanding of the Halacha," *Yearbook of the Central Conference of American Rabbis*, vol. 63 (1953), pp. 386–409. By permission of the *Yearbook of the Central Conference of American Rabbis*.

"Yom Kippur," *Mas'at Rav*, Professional Supplement to *Conservative Judaism* (August 1965), pp. 13–14. Copyright 1965 by the Rabbinical Assembly. By permission of the Rabbinical Assembly.

"Anniversary of the Emancipation Proclamation," *The United Synagogue Review* (Winter 1964), pp. 14, 26–27. By permission of the *United Synagogue Review*. Reprinted here as "The Plight of Russian Jews."

"The Mystical Element in Judaism," *The Jews: Their History, Culture, and Religion*, ed. Louis Finkelstein (New York: Harper & Brothers, 1949), pp. 602–23. By permission of HarperCollins Publishers.

"God, Torah, and Israel," trans. Byron Sherwin, *Theology and Church in Times of Change: Essays in Honor of John Coleman Bennett*, eds. Edward LeRoy Long, Jr., and Robert Handy (Philadelphia: Westminster Press, 1970), pp. 71–90. By permission of Westminster John Knox Press.

"The Moral Dilemma of the Space Age," *Space: Its Impact on Man and Society*, ed. Lilian Levy (New York: Norton, 1964), pp. 176–79. By permission of Maxwell Aley Associates Literary Agency for Lilian Levy.

"Required: A Moral Ombudsman," *United Synagogue Review* (Fall, 1971), pp. 4, 5, 28. By permission of the *United Synagogue Review*.

"The Reasons for My Involvement in the Peace Movement," *Journal of Social Philosophy*, vol. 4, no. 1 (January 1973), pp. 7–8. By permission of the *Journal of Social Philosophy*.

"No Religion Is an Island," *Union Seminary Quarterly Review* (January 1966), pp. 117–34. By permission of the *Union Seminary Quarterly Review*.

"On Prayer," *Conservative Judaism* (Fall 1970), pp. 1–12. Copyright 1970 by the Rabbinical Assembly. By permission of the Rabbinical Assembly.

"What Ecumenism Is," *Face to Face: A Primer in Dialogue*, ed. Lily Edelman (Washington, D.C.: B'nai B'rith, Adult Jewish Education, 1967), pp. 1–4. By permission of the Commission on Jewish Education/B'nai B'rith Books.

"The People of the Covenant," *Theologians at Work*, ed. Patrick Granfield (New York: Macmillan, 1967), pp. 69–85. Copyright 1967 by Patrick Granfield. By permission of Simon & Schuster Inc. Reprinted here as "Interview at Notre Dame."

"What We Might Do Together," *Religious Education*, vol. 62, no. 2 (March–April 1967), pp. 133–40. By permission of *Religious Education*.

"Reinhold Niebuhr: A Last Farewell," *Conservative Judaism* (Summer 1971), pp. 1–12. Copyright 1971 by the Rabbinical Assembly. By permission of the Rabbinical Assembly.

"The Holy Dimension," *The Journal of Religion* (April 1943), pp. 117–24. Copyright 1943 by the University of Chicago. All rights reserved. By permission of the University of Chicago.

"Faith," *The Reconstructionist* (November 3, 1944), pp. 12–16. By permission of *The Reconstructionist/Reconstructionism Today*.

"Carl Stern's Interview with Dr. Heschel." Copyright 1973 by the National Broadcasting Company, Inc. All rights reserved. By permission of the National Broadcasting Company.